Father James Page

FATHER JAMES PAGE

An Enslaved Preacher's Climb to Freedom

Larry Eugene Rivers

Johns Hopkins University Press

Baltimore

Johns Hopkins University Press
2715 North Charles Street
Baltimore, Maryland 21218-4363
www.press.jhu.edu

Library of Congress Cataloging-in-Publication Data

Names: Rivers, Larry E., 1950– author.
Title: Father James Page : an enslaved preacher's climb to freedom /
Larry Eugene Rivers.
Description: Baltimore : Johns Hopkins University Press, 2021. |
Includes bibliographical references and index.
Identifiers: LCCN 2020018814 | ISBN 9781421440309 (hardcover) |
ISBN 9781421440316 (ebook)
Subjects: LCSH: Page, James, 1808–1883. | Baptists—United States—Clergy—
Biography. | African American clergy—Biography. | African American
Baptists—Biography. | Slaves—United States—Biography. | Freedman—
United States—Biography.
Classification: LCC BX6455.P34 R58 2021 | DDC 286/.1092 [B]—dc23
LC record available at https://lccn.loc.gov/2020018814

A catalog record for this book is available from the British Library.

*Special discounts are available for bulk purchases of this book. For more
information, please contact Special Sales at specialsales@jh.edu.*

Johns Hopkins University Press uses environmentally friendly book
materials, including recycled text paper that is composed of at least
30 percent post-consumer waste, whenever possible.

To Betty Jean

CONTENTS

Given the demands of teaching four classes per semester and—for seven years—a college presidency, it has taken me nearly a quarter century to complete this study of Father James Page. Many people helped me to complete the journey. Some offered frank yet helpful suggestions that made this biography a better one. They came from various economic, social, and political backgrounds. Many are outstanding scholars with whom I have had the pleasure of working over many years. For their invaluable advice and assistance, I thank Jane Landers, Daniel Schafer, Kathleen Deagan, James M. Denham, Edward Baptist, John David Smith, Christopher Meyers, John Dunn, David Williams, Michael Gomez, Darlene Clark Hine, William Hine, Stanley Harrold, Patricia Griffin, Dennis Dickerson, Julius Scipio, Lisa Scipio, Nancy Hewitt, Chanta Haywood, Wilma King, Orville Vernon Burton, Ben Crump, David J. Coles, Jerome Clayton, Jody Norman, Mary Ann Cleveland, Joe Knetsch, Nathan Woolsey, Freddie L. Parker, Mark I. Greenberg, Susan Parker, Susan Grace Lee, Betty Dinkins, Carol M. Johnson, Otha Leon Kincy, Rosemonde W. Lowe, Anthony Dixon, Ronald and Lenita Joe, Linda Fortenberry, William Chamberlain, Karl Brockenbrough, and the late William James "Billy Bags" Taylor Jr. Further, I deeply appreciate the sustained support over the years of Rev. RB Holmes Jr., pastor of Tallahassee's historic Bethel Missionary Baptist Church, and his wife, Dr. Gloria Price Holmes. Samuel Dixie Jr. afforded me critical perspectives, while Judy Davis indexed the book. Bob Holladay, Fred R. van Hartesveldt, Paul Ortiz, and Lewis Baldwin read drafts and offered their useful comments. I owe a debt of gratitude to Fort Valley State University (FVSU) artist Ricky Callaway for his illustrations. I give special thanks to Lucille Alexander, the late Aquilina Howell, and the late Eva Manning because they gave me remarkable long-forgotten material on Father James Page. Without access to these illuminating—not to say critical—documents, this project would have been much harder to complete.

I cannot stop there. Additionally, I am grateful to the Florida A&M University (FAMU) community for its support. Specifically, I thank President Larry Robinson and his staff for their overall support of this project. I appreciate my longtime colleague Dr. Valencia Matthews, dean of the College of Social Sciences, Arts, and Humanities, for her support and friendship. Rodner Wright, dean of the School of Architecture and Engineering Technology, also offered his support. Aubrey M. Perry and Clarice Perry over the years nurtured my professional life and scholarly understandings as well. I have appreciated the encouragement from many colleagues in the FAMU Department of History, Political Science, Geography, and African American Studies, especially David H. Jackson Jr., Kyle Eidahl, Reginald Ellis, Ufot Inamete, Darius Young, and Kyle Harris. For their great illustrations, I thank Harris Wiltsher and Erika Willis. FAMU librarians deserve thanks as well for putting up with over me many years, many months, and many weeks as I compiled the research to complete this study. Specifically, I acknowledge the kindness of Faye Watkins, Anatole E. McCloud, Gloria Woody, Pamela Monroe, Alvin Lee, Priscilla B. Henry, Fay Williams, George Bruton, Jasmine Wilkes, and Carla Thomas. Nashid Madyun at the Meek-Eaton Southeastern Regional Black Archives Research and Museum at FAMU meanwhile provided yeoman service to the cause. I extend gratitude to my many graduate students over the years for their assistance, especially Sabrina Romain, who assisted me with much of the research and the reading of numerous drafts.

I owe a great deal to my friend of more than thirty years, Canter Brown Jr., and his wife, Barbara Gray Brown, for their generosity and encouragement. It has been a pleasure working with Canter on a range of projects too numerous to list here. As an outstanding nineteenth-century scholar, his generosity, sage advice, and overall assistance have proven helpful to me time and time again. My friend, I hope that the years ahead will allow us to write more about the unsung heroes and heroines who helped to create our great nation!

I benefited enormously from those who taught me how to think about race, gender, education, politics, and social justice in nineteenth-century society. I owe much to the instruction of my former teacher, retired Regents professor of history at FVSU, Dr. Donnie D. Bellamy. Mrs. Juanita Bellamy, I must add, fed me when I had no money to feed myself. I also thank fellow

FVSU alumnus the late John Wesley Blassingame for an inspiring 1970 seminar that put me on the path to researching and writing about the antebellum period in America. My first doctoral advisor, Roland M. Smith, at Carnegie Mellon University provided me with invaluable advice and pushed me to complete my degree. Additionally, I thank my doctoral advisors at Goldsmiths, University of London, Peter D. Fraser and David Killingray, for their guidance.

Johns Hopkins University Press furnished me with two very meticulous anonymous readers who reviewed the manuscript. They offered voluminous suggestions for improvement and made the final draft a better one. I am fortunate to have had the opportunity to work with Laura Davulis, acquisitions editor. She guided me through this tedious process, along with Carrie Watterson, who copyedited the manuscript. I thank Esther P. Rodriguez and Juliana McCarthy for their assistance in bringing this manuscript to publication.

My nuclear and extended families mean so much to me. I appreciate them for their support over almost forty years of researching and writing about the African American experience. To my late parents, Felix and Lavonia Rivers, thank you for instilling in me the values of respect for humankind. My seven siblings have been there for me through thick and thin! Thank you sisters Phyllis, Harriet, and Trish as well as brothers Raymond Sr., Allen Sr., Felix III, and Donald. My mother-in-law and father-in-law, the late Annie Mae and Willie James Hubbard, treated me always as their own, as have sisters-in-law Willie Mae, Delores, Bernice, Regina, Nell, Cynthia, and Cindy, and my brothers-in-law, Charles, Charlie, Robert, and Roy. Last, but by no means least, I thank our sons, Larry Omar, now a tenured associate professor of history, and Linje Eugene, an attorney and real estate entrepreneur, for their love and support over the years. And now to my bride of forty-two years, thanks Betty Jean Hubbard Rivers from Dry Branch, Georgia, for your love and unconditional support. This book is dedicated to you! Enough said!

Of course, responsibility for errors is all mine.

Father James Page

Introduction

On Sunday, March 18, 1883, a multitude of mourners overwhelmed Florida's capital city and its Bethel Baptist Church to honor the life and service of a onetime enslaved preacher named James Page. At the time boasting a population of only about 2,500 persons, Tallahassee rarely had witnessed such an outpouring of grief or sentiment. The *Weekly Floridian* noted that "a large concourse of colored and white citizens, aggregating about three thousand persons," paid their last respects to Father James Page. The racially mixed assemblage included elements of the Odd Fellows, the Good Templars, and Good Samaritans, all determined to show support and express condolences for a man whom they considered a remarkable individual and a true man of God. Even the *Weekly Floridian*, a white conservative newspaper, felt compelled to note the deceased, the event, and its magnitude: "He had been a faithful laborer in the master's vineyard, was a man who had great influence with his race, which was always exerted for their well-being, and was respected alike by whites and black people."[1]

Since that late winter day 136 years ago, Page's claim on the community that he touched has remained strong and vibrant. Annually, people have gathered to celebrate Father James Page's memory at the Baptist church that he established. On these well-attended occasions, speakers have competed to praise Page's achievements as an enslaved preacher and, later, free black religious leader who pressed for the political, social, and economic advancement of his race. As the celebrations have illustrated, this long-deceased figure

of the past has retained a noted presence in the memory of slavery and freedom, not only in Florida but also beyond the state's borders. During the present era when people have found themselves questioning the integrity and
unusual behavior of many leaders, the high regard in which Page's contemporaries held his life and leadership stands out in even higher relief.[2]

These facts alone call out for a careful and close examination of the man
who inspired others through his civic and religious leadership. The remarkable range of Page's story, a life that played out over a seventy-five-year span,
took him from the vital center of early nineteenth-century slavery—through
heartbreak, loss, and forced relocation—to a raw frontier where his keen intelligence and heightened sense of human dignity permitted him first to
survive and then to thrive. Along the way he demonstrated qualities of loyalty, concern, diligence, and consideration that drew others to him and allowed his message to overcome daunting racial and political barriers. Through
it all, Page avoided compromising himself, his values, or his faith. He thus
left a role model of enduring value for the benefit of subsequent generations.

Page first attained prominence as an enslaved preacher and counselor
over a thirty-eight-year period that commenced upon his forced relocation
to Florida during the late 1820s and continued through the Civil War. Seven
of the ten chapters that follow accordingly detail his slave-era ministry and
life surrounding it. During this period Page labored on his enslaver's behalf
in capacities that eventually saw him administering day-to-day plantation
operations and serving as a trusted confidant to the master and his family.
Yet, the pastor managed to commence his ministry as a "church without
walls" within several months of arriving at his new home in Middle Florida's
emerging plantation belt. In the years that followed, he may well have become one of the most traveled enslaved preachers of the antebellum era,
preaching the word of God to enslaved people in states such as Georgia, Alabama, Mississippi, North Carolina, and South Carolina. He even established
connections with West Africa.[3]

⁓

This study thus lays emphasis on this period to find in the complexities of his
ministry insights previously not addressed or else considered only sparingly
by historians of the antebellum South. Most scholars who have touched
upon enslaved preachers at all unfortunately have dismissed them as relatively minor players during the antebellum period. Thus far, no scholarly,
full-length biography of any nineteenth-century enslaved preacher from slavery to freedom has been published. This remains the case with James Page

even though his achievements in life were substantial, impressive, and enduring. A few memoirs and short autobiographies of other such men have come to public attention, although their impact understandably has been limited.[4]

Many extant biographies of slave preachers concern the eighteenth century and largely amount to uncritical accounts written either by friends or white contemporaries. They tend to emphasize the influence of white and mostly European religious practices upon the development of various Afro-Christian religious customs, giving little or no attention to the enslaved preacher's original and creative thoughts. In the pages of most such biographies, we hear only small whispers, if anything, in the enslaved preacher's voice. Moreover, as those volumes underscore, studies on slave religion have been colored with prejudice. An important exception should be noted. Nancy Bullock Woolridge's ten-page essay entitled "The Slave Preacher: Portrait of a Leader" appeared in the *Journal of Negro Education* in 1945. She focused on bondservant perceptions of the enslaved preacher, the treatment preachers received from both blacks and whites, and the religious and temporal influences preachers wielded within the slave community. Given the essay's brevity, Woolridge provided only a quick look at her subject. Still, she included references to a few nineteenth-century preachers who transitioned from slavery to freedom as did James Page.[5]

Of course, biographies of individual black clergymen of Page's times do exist. Henry McNeal Turner, Daniel Payne, and James Walker Hood—to name several—deservedly have received serious study. Quite differently from Page, though, they exerted ministerial influence primarily during postbellum times rather than during the perilous era of plantation slavery. This biography fills that gap by critically examining how a nineteenth-century enslaved preacher overcame seemingly insurmountable odds to emerge as a leader of his people during slavery and after emancipation.[6]

During the mid-twentieth century, with the advent of the civil rights movement, historians began to address slavery—at least partially—from the perspective of the enslaved. Kenneth M. Stampp's *The Peculiar Institution* helped launch the revisionist trend in 1956, the year of the Montgomery bus boycott. Scholars John Blassingame, Charles V. Hamilton, Donnie D. Bellamy, David Dennard, Peter Wood, Charles Joyner, Eugene D. Genovese, and others followed suit, adding new works that revealed more about slave life through the eyes of the enslaved and, in more than a few cases, even touched upon enslaved preachers. In later decades scholars such as Michael

Gomez, Edward Baptist, David Blight, Paul Ortiz, Orville Vernon Burton, Walter Johnson, Lewis V. Baldwin, Richard J. M. Blackett, Steven Hahn, Damian A. Pargas, Annette Gordon-Reed, Wilma King, Darlene Clark-Hine, Loren Schweninger, James Oakes, Drew Gilpin Faust, Henry Louis Gates Jr., Peter Kolchin, Linda Schwartz, Philip Morgan, P. Sterling Stuckey, Eric Foner, Sven Beckert, Jeff Forret, John David Smith, Jane Landers, Daina Ramey Berry, Manisha Sinha, and others further expanded the body of literature considering how enslaved people perceived slavery and developed their own sense of identity. These important studies notwithstanding, the fact remains that, within the rubric of slave religious practices, we know only small pieces of information concerning how the enslaved preacher functioned as a member and leader in the slave quarters.[7]

This state of affairs persists despite numerous clarion calls for more scholarly research and writing on this topic. Historian David Dennard, for instance, aptly made this case in his 1987 doctoral dissertation "A Study of Slave Preachers." As he bluntly noted, "Slave preachers . . . have not received much attention in scholarly publications on American slavery." This situation constituted an unacceptable omission because, as Dennard added, "[These men and women] were the spiritual architects of the black church and helped to establish many of the traditions and practices that are still salient in the religious life [of African Americans today]." He concluded, "One still looks in vain for detailed studies of slave preachers and their varied contributions." An estimated ten thousand enslaved preachers, men and women, ministered in the South from 1800 to 1860. Mostly, their stories still await detailed scholarly attention two centuries later.[8]

The handful of exceptions offers little by way of compensation. Autobiographies and biographies that touch upon the enslaved preacher's experience, such as those of Lucius H. Holsey and John Jasper, lack deep analysis and critical evaluation. They focus on the daily lives of these individual men while declining to explore how their subjects' theologies, leadership styles, attitudes, and beliefs affected the overall slave community. In such books, enslaved preachers often appear merely as agents of social control who responded to the slaveholders' bidding with unquestioning obedience.[9]

Any number of prominent historians have adopted social control and paternalism as a theoretical model to explain the character and behavior of enslaved preachers. They have argued, at the base level, that the enslaved preacher generally served as a pawn of the slaveholding class. Stanley Elkins and Eugene Genovese, among others, declared many enslaved preachers to be "sambos" or, in other words, bondservants who internalized behaviors that benefited the slaveholder as opposed to the enslaved. Genovese's classic *Roll, Jordan, Roll* utilized twenty-five or so pages to portray the enslaved preacher as, among other things, an accommodationist leader who, more often than not, submitted to the power and authority of the slaveholder. Genovese viewed the master-slave relationship through the paternalistic theoretical framework, with the bondservant losing a great deal of agency in this alleged compromise. The paternalist model as employed by Genovese falls short when analyzing the relationship between John Parkhill, the enslaver, and James Page, the enslaved. As will be seen in the following chapters, Parkhill acted as an obsessed racial capitalist more interested in maximizing profits than in treating Page or any of his other enslaved blacks with genuine kindness and care.[10]

Genovese saw the master-slave relationship as favoring the former with the latter having little power. However much the uneven power relationship between master and slave constrained James Page's life, this simplistic construct is inadequate. The assumption that enslaved preachers generally possessed no real sense of agency and simply served as instruments of slave owners cries out for the full examination of individual lives. James Page defied such stereotypes, as did countless other men and women of faith; however, he was not a man bent on self-destruction. Given that most, if not all, material blessings were bestowed upon the enslaved by the enslaver, Page still tried to live nonetheless as a man of his own mind and will.

Helpfully, in 1978 Albert J. Raboteau broke new ground by focusing specifically on the religious life of bondservants and the significant role played by enslaved preachers. His *Slave Religion: The "Invisible Institution" in the Antebellum South* analyzed the importance of these leaders in the evolutionary convergence of European Christianity with African American religious traditions that produced Afro-Christian religion. Raboteau portrayed enslaved preachers not as one-dimensional figures but rather as multilayered human beings with emotions, original thoughts, and aspirations. He dedicated much of his discussion to their leadership skills and ability to mediate between blacks and whites. Raboteau noted how significant their actions proved in developing secret meeting places for black worship, as well as their role in spurring the independent black church movement when Emancipation Day arrived. Still, even in this fine work, the author presented his analysis of the enslaved preacher on only a few pages of the more than four-hundred-page book.[11]

Raboteau fortunately and creditably proved the importance of the slave preacher in the quarters community. However, he concluded—much as did Genovese—that slave ministers were "usually illiterate" though possessing "a native wit." Following upon similar lines of interpretation, Peter Kolchin characterized enslaved preachers as "often illiterate and almost always ignorant of the finer points of theology." This general perception may well contain some elements of truth, but it does not mean they were less intelligent than their literate colleagues. Page was literate and thus perhaps not representative of enslaved clerics. His individual story is exceptional: he used his skills as a minister to teach others literacy while standing out for his success at engaging the white man's world as a highly skilled bondman. As his life proved, such talents and abilities impressed and inspired in contexts far beyond mere preaching. Page's story offers an unprecedented glimpse into life from the perspective of a literate enslaved preacher and later free religious leader.[12]

Nearly a generation passed before the scholarly literature on enslaved preachers took another substantial step forward. In 1999, Bettye Collier-Thomas's well-researched and sharply written *Daughters of Thunder: Black Women Preachers and Their Sermons, 1850–1979* focused on dozens of sermons offered by fourteen African American women ministers. As with Raboteau, though, Collier-Thomas did not engage in a deep inquiry into the enslaved preacher, as only two of the ministers she studied preached prior to emancipation. Chanta Haywood's subsequent *Prophesying Daughters: Black Women Preachers and the Word, 1823–1913* broke new ground through the examples of four women. Half labored only in the post-emancipation world. Just as with Collier-Thomas, Haywood had not intended for her efforts to represent a full-length biography of any single woman preacher.[13]

Beyond such book-length efforts, a modest number of smaller studies have become available. At least three have appeared over the past sixty years on the popular eighteenth-century enslaved preacher George Liele. As recently as 2012, David T. Shannon Sr., Julia Frazier White, and Deborah Van Broekhoven issued an edited anthology entitled *George Liele's Life and Legacy: An Unsung Hero*. The work underscored the importance of enslaved preachers by focusing, unlike previous studies, on Liele's development as a theologian and his Calvinist beliefs. To their credit, these scholars sought to reevaluate the contributions made by a prominent enslaved preacher. The fact remains that the work does not constitute a scholarly full-length biography.[14]

Suffice it to say that a study set in the context of Florida and its frontier heritage is even more difficult to find than a full-length study of an enslaved preacher generally. Patricia C. Griffin's 2009 *The Odyssey of an African Slave* highlighted the experience of Sitiki, later known as Jack Smith, who preached the Methodist creed in St. Augustine before and after slavery. Griffin's narrative, though, broached the subject of enslaved preachers—mostly Jack Smith—only briefly. Otherwise, James Page stands out as the individual who has commanded the largest portion of the limited attention that enslaved preachers have received from Florida's historians. Leslie Ashford's 1989 *Journal of African American History* essay on Page mainly provided a list of his accomplishments and praised him as a person whom whites trusted. But she did not offer an in-depth look at Page's family life, theology, acts of defiance during slavery, or political perspective developed after emancipation. My brief essay on Page came a few years later in *Florida's Heritage of Diversity: Essays in Honor of Samuel Proctor.* Its ten pages similarly clung to a single theme: Page's role as a race leader during and after slavery.[15]

◌

This biography of Father James Page examines the life and service of one particular enslaved preacher, detailing his journey from slavery to freedom. Although Page's life was unusual for an antebellum enslaved preacher, it still allows inferences as to the figure's overall significance and his deep-rooted impact on the making of Afro-Christian religion, black leadership, and the broader black freedom struggle in America. Most importantly, men and women enslaved preachers—whether literate or not—provided important support to the slave family and to religious faith in general. Ultimately, Page showed that an individual can live life well without exploiting fellow human beings in order to succeed. Through everyday contact with enslaved blacks and, later, freed men and women, Page learned that true dedication and caring for others without expecting anything in return is the distinction of black Christianity. A discussion of at least four interlocking themes affords context. Page, above all, was a survivor. In line with that fact, the first theme is the influence of his parents, owners, and childhood experiences upon the man he would become. Employing his written words and voice where available, the narrative details his traumatic separation from parents, forced migration, and journey from his youthful enslavement to his subsequent freedom.

Other guiding themes additionally propel his story. The second focuses on Page's early interest in religion and his subsequent desire to become a man of the cloth. Virtually everything that he undertook during and after slavery linked directly to his religious proclivities, thoughts, and worldview. Page endeavored to inspire enslaved parishioners by juxtaposing their lives to some of the old Hebrew stories, especially the one of Moses and the children of Israel's release from slavery in Egypt. Another theme explores the impact of Page's private life on his preaching, family life, and leadership before and after slavery. And a final theme focuses on what Page's life meant during the times in which he lived and what, if any, implications his life may carry for our times.

In a general sense, this biography also seeks to illuminate how religious leadership—in Page's case—evolved into political and educational leadership during the Reconstruction era. By shedding critical light on one enslaved preacher who became a free black leader, this biography seeks to present Page's story in its complexities and variations. Here again is a subject that historians have treated only lightly, whether in consideration of the broad range of black political leadership during the postbellum era or of the narrower question of a black minister who espoused conservative political ideas within the context of a radically revolutionized world. Howard Dodson in the foreword to Eric Foner's 1993 contribution *Freedom's Lawmakers: A Directory of Black Officeholders during Reconstruction* stated the case directly. "Until recently, little was known about black Reconstruction lawmakers," he asserted. "The collective biographies painted by ex-Confederate leaders during the 1860s and sustained in American history texts through the 1960s were neither flattering nor revealing." Dodson singled out insights from W. E. B. Du Bois, A. A. Taylor, Thomas Holt, Joel Williamson, John Hope Franklin, Leon Litwack, Ira Berlin, and Foner as contributing "immensely to the clarification of the complex roles of African Americans in this seminal moment in American political history." Numerous others have joined that elite company in the intervening years. Nonetheless, vast gaps remain in our understanding, especially of the role and actions of conservative leaders.[16]

Those who study Florida history notably have enjoyed the benefit of solid treatments of postbellum black leadership not available for many other places, even though no study of conservative leadership has emerged other than those of James Page mentioned earlier. Joe M. Richardson began the trend in 1973 with publication of *The Negro in the Reconstruction of Florida, 1865–1877*. His Florida State University student Canter Brown Jr. particularly has pressed the subject forward in a variety of works. They have included, most notably, *Florida's Black Public Officials, 1867–1924*, released in 1998. Professor Brown and I subsequently cowrote two studies of black religious leadership during the Reconstruction and Redemption periods: *Workers in the Vineyard of the Lord: The Beginnings of the AME Church in Florida,*

1865–1895 and *For a Great and Grand Purpose: The Beginnings of the AMEZ Church in Florida, 1864–1905.*[17]

In Florida, Father James Page lived the last quarter of his life as a free man preaching, witnessing, and participating in the successes and failures of Reconstruction and its aftermath. He lived to see the rise of the Republican Party (which he joined); to fight for the rights of blacks during the early part of Reconstruction; and to witness passage of the Thirteenth, Fourteenth, and Fifteenth Amendments to the US Constitution. Further, he watched as his party turned away from blacks with the 1876 election of Rutherford B. Hayes to the presidency, a turning point that in large part signaled the end of Reconstruction in the South, or at least Florida. Father Page, as he was known, also helped spark life in numerous churches in Florida and throughout the South. He endured the toll of racial violence. Through it all he maintained a calm, steady, and conservative voice that often met with rejection at the polls but that reinforced the esteem in which he was held, reflecting the importance of his willingness to stand contrary to prevailing thought and opinion.

This story exists in so much detail because of an enduring desire to lift this man's extraordinary life out of the shadows. It tells a larger tale of how one black man tried to lead his race to achieve political, educational, economic, and social justice goals in Florida and the South during turbulent times. The text focuses on Page's complexity in all its forms while ultimately assessing his character and contributions to his race and humankind. I found him to have been kind, likeable, mild, yet smart, with a strong sense of purpose. Never one to publicly espouse radical ideals, he nevertheless accomplished radical ends such as becoming a preacher willing to speak "inflammatory words." He believed in black self-determination and independence through land ownership, political participation, and operation of businesses and other commercial enterprises. However, he never pushed for the education of women or advocated women's rights in the pulpit or in the political arena. He likewise conducted his home life as a strong family patriarch. He kept his wife, Elizabeth, for example, close to their home when not working for the master's family. Despite being a schoolteacher, Page never taught his wife how to read or write. When he died in 1883, Elizabeth had to sign all legal documents with the mark of *X*, and she would continue to do so even days before her death two years later. Because he mastered reading and writing when few blacks possessed those skills, Page at times might have appeared arrogant and paternalistic to those under his charge. He could be overly sensitive to those who criticized him. He was a human being filled with potential and possessed of flaws. He lived the most human of lives, one filled with highs and lows, disappointments, failures, and successes.[18]

∽

A few words about the research behind this book. About thirty years ago while teaching an undergraduate class in African American history, I came across bits and pieces of historical data that offered an intriguing glimpse into the life of what appeared to me to be an extraordinarily interesting person. Slowly, I began—as all biographers do—to amass considerable, if disconnected, detail. As I dug deeper, though, I received a tremendous boost when I found in the Southern Historical Collection ten letters written by James Page covering various aspects of his life. Then, four years ago I experienced a similar revelation with discovery of an interview conducted with James Page three years before his death. Despite fading memory that probably robbed the account of some richness and depth, the interview furnished nuanced inferences of what life had been like for the onetime enslaved preacher, overseer, and postbellum leader of his race. The Page interview admittedly left more questions unanswered than answered, given that it derived from a man who routinely sought to mask his true self from perhaps everyone but his wife. Additionally, I came across contemporary reflections of the once enslaved preacher written in 1905 by one of the deacons of his church. With the clues thus afforded to me, I began my journey to complete a full-length biography of Father James Page.

CHAPTER ONE

Early Life in Virginia

I remember my father told me that he asked the Col. to [sell] us to him but the Col. would hear none of it. I really miss my father to this day. I played in the neighborhood with White boys and Black boys when I was young, and we had a lot of fun playing together.

—James Page

"I was born in the house, I think, of Col. John Parkhill, my master[,] around 1808 in Richmond, Virginia, and I like to call her Virginny," the elderly James Page mused one winter day seventy-two years later. A Parkhill daughter eagerly added detail, particularly that "John Parkhill . . . owned his mother. His father was free." Page's memory in 1880—he then resided in Tallahassee, Florida, nearly eight hundred miles south of his native home—was nurtured not by bitter impressions but by warm recollections of those earliest of times. "My father was Coyer Page and he was a dark skin[ned] man who came to see me and my mother and brother as often as he could," he detailed. "I don't remember much about his background or where he was born. And I always knew my father as a free man who loved us and his freedom very much. He would always tell me he was a free man. I remember him being a good swimmer too. He did wood work for people at the Port of Richmond I think. I loved the times when my father would visit[,] and he cared very much for my mother and us. Now I don't remember a whole lot about my mother. I remember her name was Susie and I remember that she was owned by a man call[ed] Mr. Page before he sold her to the Col. She had me and my little brother Thomas. I liked to call him Tom." Page continued, "I think my mother had Tom when I was seven or eight, and she helped to take care of me and my brother, and she loved us very much. She would also make clothes for us to wear while making clothes for other servants in Virginny to[o]. One thing I enjoyed was the time I spent with my mother and father as a little boy in Richmond." Described only in later life "as a man of large frame, courtly-looking [with a] robust constitution," young Page's formative years as an enslaved child started with a father and mother he knew and loved.[1]

Thus commenced the humble beginnings of a well-lived life, one that—given persistence, introspection, determination, and faith—brought comfort to thousands of James Page's fellow bondservants and afforded desperately appreciated leadership to members of his race in years of civil war, reconstruction, and redemption. While this future could not have been forecast at the time of his birth, the times at least boded auspiciously. Fundamental changes engulfed the nation in 1808, while the births of others quietly portended the arrival of a generation whose lives and careers altered the nation's fabric and the institution of slavery forever. A harbinger of things to come, the nation on January 1, 1808, outlawed the importation of slaves. As W. E. B. Du Bois later asserted, "The first great goal of anti-slavery effort in the United States had been, since the Revolution, the suppression of the slave-trade by national law."[2]

If the termination of the African trade set the stage in 1808 for the 1820s forced mass migration of enslaved people—including James Page—from the Chesapeake states to the Deep South, then President Thomas Jefferson's Embargo Act, implemented the same year, presaged the nation's economic transformation in the decades that followed. Although the law remained in force only until March 1, 1809, the attempt to extricate the United States from European entanglements failed, sparked resistance, encouraged sectional division, and undermined faith in the national government's ability to conduct its affairs. The measure did, however, serve well to invigorate home-grown efforts to foster industry and manufacture, touching Richmond, Virginia, profoundly. The replacement of wood by anthracite coal to fuel ship and railroad engines aided and abetted the transformation that ensued. Carbon, coupled with the chains of slavery, fueled the American Industrial Revolution.[3]

Additionally in 1808 and the weeks following occurred the births of two baby boys whose attitudes, actions, and conflicts decades later helped to blaze the nation's path toward civil war and the abolition of slavery and altered James Page's life acutely. The first was Jefferson Davis, who arrived in Fairview, Christian County, Kentucky, on June 3. Within three years the parents of the future US senator, secretary of war, and president of the Confederate States of America had turned south to Louisiana on a journey that ultimately took them by 1812 to Mississippi. Less than a hundred miles northeast of Fairview, Abraham Lincoln entered the world in Hodgenville, Kentucky, on February 12, 1809. His family, too, soon opted for the road. The Lincolns' travels led them north, however. This ensured that young Abe would mature not in the slaveholding South but in the free states of Indiana and Illinois. As would ring true in Page's case, a journey made all the difference in the world. While men of influence such as Davis and Lincoln had a profound impact on the lives of many people, so too did James Page and other literate and illiterate enslaved preachers affect the lives of millions of people. What Page and his cohorts did from a grassroots perspective manifested itself time and time again in the religious themes of slave resistance as well as the abolitionist movement. Their impact would be felt by many during and after Reconstruction as well.[4]

Men such as Lincoln and Davis would invariably affect Page's life in later years, but others naturally mattered far more to him during his formative years. His parents, Coyer and Susie Page, with brother Tom, stood foremost among them. Owner John Parkhill may not have equaled or exceeded their sway, but he came as close as reasonably was possible. While Parkhill's actions and behavior, as will be seen, sometimes brought Page intense pain, he typically treated the boy and young man as an intelligent human being deserving of at least a modicum of respect. "Me and the Col. had some good times together," Page confirmed. "He was always a very proud man. Mr. Parkhill was sure a good man. We did things for each other."[5] Yet the quid pro quo relationship suffered nonetheless from a deficit of reciprocity from Parkhill up until the time of his death in 1855. In doing "things" for Page, the enslaver allowed his "special servant" privileges only as long as they did not adversely affect him financially.

There were several John Parkhills, which is to say, the process of aging understandably brought changes in the man's outlook, attitudes, and conduct, as did economic strains and complications between him, his friends and relations, and the law. As a youth and a hot-blooded Irishman not disposed to religious convictions, he nonetheless was remembered by his third wife, Lucy Beverly Randolph Parkhill, as a "pious manly man." As Lucy explained, John came into the world on "old Christmas" day in 1786, in Londonderry. She insisted that the Parkhills at one time had been "highly respectable and influential in their [home] country . . . [, and] they had been wealthy—had been large pub owners—with many tenants, and the senior Parkhill also served as a minister of the peace." She conceded, however, that family members "lived in profusion and wastefulness, which finally brought

John Parkhill was James Page's master until Parkhill's death in 1855. State Archives of Florida, Florida Memory

them to poverty." John Parkhill came as the sixth of his parents' children. If family lore can be believed, Samuel wanted to protect his youngest son from the beggarly lifestyle that loomed for him in Ireland. So, in 1802 when John reached age sixteen, the elder Parkhill purchased for him a one-way ticket to New York. The youngster took with him a letter of introduction to friends and ended up doing odd jobs, from cabin boy to cook at various hotels. Three years or so after his arrival in the United States, Parkhill yearned for better opportunities. By chance while waiting on a table, he overheard a conversation in which Richmond, Virginia, was mentioned as a place where men could find jobs and make a good living. With few resources, the nineteen-year-old lad headed for what he hoped was the promised land.[6]

The move for Parkhill, to the future home of enslaved James Page, turned out to be a fortuitous one. He arrived in Richmond with ideas of becoming wealthy that were not entirely unrealistic. Virginia was the largest and wealthiest state in the Union, and—with profits generated from slave labor—its capital city reigned as a center for commerce and, increasingly, industry. Parkhill at first did what he knew best by working in hotels and performing odd jobs. Along the way he made important friends. According to Lucy Parkhill, her husband "passed one night by a large dwelling and[,] hearing singing[,] stopped to listen." She continued, "It was the home of a Mrs. Gamble, also Scotch-Irish and they were singing the old familiar hymns or psalms that were sung at family prayer at his Irish home. After that he went every night and stood outside of the fence to listen at the home of family prayer." Eventually, Parkhill introduced himself and was befriended by the families of prominent merchants John and Robert Gamble.[7]

After associating with the Gambles and like-minded people of Irish or Scots-Irish descent, Parkhill quit his odd jobs to pursue steady work cleaning and maintaining a merchant's store. The young man bided his time, saved his money, and in 1807 began operating a general store of his own. Historian Frank J. Byrne asserted that "a substantial majority of antebellum merchants were native-born Southerners," yet Parkhill, much as had the Gambles, managed to enjoy prosperity as an immigrant. One reason lay in the fact that by the summer of 1808, if not from the beginning, he benefited from a partnership with another Ulsterman. Known to history for his involvement with the Irish troubles of the late eighteenth century as a colonel in the military wing of the United Irishmen, Andrew Bryson Jr. managed eventually to elude British authorities. He made his way to New York not long before Parkhill's arrival there Whether the young immigrants encountered one another in New York or only in Richmond, they undertook business together as Bryson & Parkhill. The concern operated from a building "at the sign of the Golden Key, on Main Street, at the corner below the street leading to Mayo's bridge." This meant easy access to docks and the James River and Kanawha Canal. From that location they dispensed assorted dry goods, teas, hardware, paints, turpentine, sugar, molasses, rice, coffee, "Spanish segars," and—perhaps most importantly—"Old Jamaica, Antigua, W. India and N. England Rum."[8]

As the senior man in the partnership, if only by a few years, Bryson evidently exerted significant personal influence on Parkhill. In one area particularly, this dynamic appeared clear: he would have a great impact on how the future slaveholder treated James Page and other bondservants. Bryson's voyage to the New World had included a visit to the Caribbean. In Martinique, especially, the Irish revolutionary recoiled at the brutality of punishments and the institution generally. Of one incident, he recorded, "While the punishment is inflict[ed], the poor feeble old man Stands erect, braces every Nerve, & Casting his languid Eyes toward heaven Seems to call on the Judge of all the Earth to attest his innocence. Not a word, not a Sigh escapes his lips, though they Should Beat the Flesh in Slices of[f] his emaciated body. Poor miserable Creatures; what a lot is yours in this World, or rather, what will be the Fate of your present tormentors in the Next? Surely it will be more tolerable for Sodom & Gomorrah than for the Inhabitants of these Isles, in that Day when the world & the Inhabitants thereof will be Judged by him who is Able to make manifest the Secrets of all hearts; and not only for them, but for every person who has been concerned in that cruelest of all Trafficks." Little wonder that Bryson & Parkhill proved willing to employ at least one person of color in a responsible position and, from all accounts, treated him with a modicum of respect. Edmund Randolph, William Wirt, and Robert Gamble, among other prominent men, later attested to mulatto clerk Christopher McPherson's "talents and integrity."[9]

It happened that Parkhill purchased his first enslaved person at about the time in 1807 that the business opened. This was Susie Page. As noted earlier, Page recalled that his master obtained her from "a man call[ed] Mr. Page." Likely this was former Virginia governor John Page, who then resided in Richmond and would die the following year. Parkhill, a single man who lived above his store, brought Susie there. Although Page insisted that his mother worked in the household solely as a seamstress, at this early time it is probable that she performed general purpose duties as well. Pregnant by Coyer when she made the transition to her new home, Susie gave birth in due course, as Page put it, "in the house." By then, Bryson's influence about the treatment of enslaved people had begun to pervade whatever attitudes Parkhill previously had espoused.[10]

As a man of his time and place who yearned for prestige and wealth, Parkhill—in the face of his partner's antislavery outlook—sought nonetheless to accumulate more enslaved persons in order to grow his business and demonstrate his newfound prosperity. With time's passage he in fact became a sharp-eyed observer of those who possessed or did not possess enslaved human beings. Through keen insight honed by extensive travels, he assessed whether those whom he encountered had "negro servants" and, if so, how many. Put bluntly and as was true of many men of his kind, Parkhill measured the wealth and status of others by the bondservants they owned. The culture of slavery eventually subsumed his very being. A first-generation slaveholder, he ultimately learned by sometimes bitter experience how to be an efficient master. Increasingly distracted in his later years by his troubles, ironically Parkhill grew ever more dependent upon his second bondservant, Page, as his mainstay.[11]

Parkhill took his first substantial step toward growing his slaveholding when Page was two years old. On July 19, 1810, at age twenty-four he married Eleanor Williamson Quarles in Essex County on the Rappahannock River northeast of Richmond. She was the only daughter of planter and noted Revolutionary leader Capt. William Henry Quarles and his second wife, Mary Williamson. Nuptials may have quickly occurred anticipating Henry Quarles's death, which took place on October 17. The event dramatically changed Parkhill's fortunes and Page's home environment. Either at the time of the wedding or else upon the death of Eleanor's grandmother Susanna Williamson in early 1811, Parkhill came into possession of at least nine individuals. According to Susanna's will they were "Beck, Betty, and her daughter Becky, Sary, Lucy, Stephen, Ames, Reuben, and George."[12]

Page's father influenced his son's personal development, although rarely present in the home. Given that the lad spent the first eighteen years of his life with his mother, Susie, she not surprisingly had a more indelible impact on his attitudes, behavior, and worldview than did his father, Coyer. John Parkhill had, as well, a strong influence on Page's maturity. The slave master's demeanor as family head, husband, and father in turn shaped, in part, the development of young Page's attitudes and conduct as well. As a product of the late eighteenth and early nineteenth centuries, Parkhill seemingly adopted the era's patriarchal ideology that men stood supreme in their households as provider and protector and that "male dominance characterize[ed] southern society." For men such as Parkhill, a family in good part meant having sons and naming them after members of the family, sons who would perpetuate the estate, plantation, or business Women were viewed as perpetuators of the family. Accordingly, they assumed the role of wives and mothers. In some male-dominated homes where more extreme attitudes prevailed, white women might be treated as mere property to be owned in the same manner as enslaved blacks like James Page. This "white property" was to be restricted to the household as helpmates to their husbands. That is, women were to be seen and not heard. They were not to involve themselves with outside projects or ventures without the husband's express permission. Given his master's example and the nature of the world in which he matured, Page eventually adopted Parkhill's patriarchal philosophy. His future handling of gender, particularly with his wife, shows this philosophy clearly.[13]

To what extent Parkhill's patriarchal pose set the tone of his household immediately following his marriage to Eleanor Quarles remains a mystery. It is known that within a matter of days or a few weeks at best she became pregnant with their first child. The household naturally turned much of its attention to her needs as the pregnancy—apparently a troubled one—developed. Enslaved laborers whom the expectant mother had brought to the home attended her directly. Page's mother, Susie, now concentrated on seamstress duties. Tragically, Eleanor died from complications of childbirth on April 9, 1811. Her infant son, Samuel Henry Parkhill, passed two days later.[14]

While a child of Page's age would have little noticed the commotion of the pregnancy, the household gloom that ensued after the deaths doubtlessly touched all within its walls. John Parkhill, having loved his bride ardently, lapsed into depression. He left no account of his actions or feelings at the time, although John H. Rice, a Presbyterian minister who stayed with him one year later, briefly noted his disposition. "Mr. Parkhill was lonely in his dwelling, having lately been deprived of his young and lovely wife about a year after their marriage," Rice's biographer recorded. "Unwilling to alter his domestic arrangements, he cheerfully received the minister and his wife to his house, to make part of the family." That summer visit of Reverend and Mrs. Rice led in June 1812 to the organization of Richmond's first Presbyterian church. It resulted also in Parkhill's conversion to Presbyterianism in the wake of his grief. "Mr. Parkhill was an active and judicious helper in the congregation from the first," the Rice biographer detailed. "A polished, well-educated Irishman, he knew how to appreciate the family that lodged under his roof; and under the instructions of Mr. Rice became a devoted Christian."[15]

John Parkhill's conversion introduced serious attention to religion within the household and, specifically, the Bible and Bible reading. The master's intensity on the subject led him in May 1813 to join with Reverend Rice and others to establish the Virginia Bible Society. It and similar organizations aimed to ensure "a general and adequate supply" of copies of the Bible for all "who are disposed to use it." Within three years and as a manager of the state association, he helped to create the American Bible Society as well. By then Parkhill had begun to teach Page to read and write so that he could partake of the Good Book's wisdom and teachings, with dynamic consequences that the enslaved lad later explained. "I wanted to preach more than anything else I did since a little boy in Virginny," he expressed. "I always felt one of the best things I could do for my people was to help them become more Godly. I always wanted to learn to read and write so I could become a good preacher. As I told you before, as a boy around seven or eight, I think, I kept having these same dreams over and over again that God wanted me to preach when I went to church with the Col. [Parkhill]. We liked going to the big church meetings in the woods. I could read at the time a few verses in the Bible as a young boy. And as I said before, the Col. approved of my desire to preach. [A little later,] I felt really good when I was preaching and even asked the Col. what he thought about me preaching some. He thought it was a good thing for me to do, and as I said, I made sure to get permission to preach."[16]

During the era when Parkhill began teaching literacy skills to young Page, other black youths and adults, including Gabriel Prosser and Nat Turner, were also learning how to read and write or else already utilizing such skills. Interestingly, Parkhill's father-in-law Charles Copland had known Prosser and may well have passed on stories of his acquaintance to Page. Despite their shared literacy, Page, Prosser, and Turner were starkly different in significant ways. All three men became leaders in their own right during the antebellum period, but they traveled drastically different roads. While in Virginia, Page remained a Presbyterian while Gabriel connected with the more revolutionary Baptist denomination. Nat Turner became simply a nondenominational Christian enslaved preacher. Page was never radicalized like Gabriel and Nat but remained a devoted Christian minister who affected enslaved lives within the slave system, while Gabriel and Nat tried to ignite more far-reaching change outside the slave system through their rebellions.[17]

Parkhill's instruction of Page probably ebbed somewhat during the early months of 1813. Parkhill's conversion and early Bible Society work took more of his time. This was also a grief-stricken time for Page's master as well. For one thing Andrew Bryson, Parkhill's business partner, died October 6, 1813, of unrecorded causes. Whether Bryson's final illness meant his early withdrawal from Bryson & Parkhill or the partnership concluded at the time of his death is not known. In either case Parkhill continued retail operations. In spring 1814 he joined with several other men to initiate an industrial concern, the Richmond Union Air Furnace. The enterprise offered "castings in brass and wrought-iron work" of fine quality. Meanwhile, financial complications endured by his landlord must have unsettled Parkhill's household, including young Page. That summer the Circuit Court of the United States sitting at Richmond ordered the sale for debt of the "Lot & Tenement in the city of Richmond, now in the occupancy of John Parkhill, Esq."[18]

Looming over other concerns, war with Great Britain had flared in summer 1812. The Parkhill household including Page at first felt its impact primarily from the spectacles of volunteer troops drilling in public and their gala departures from the city. Norfolk, for example, welcomed Capt. Robert Gamble's cavalry in March 1813. "The order and cheerful submission to the most rigorous discipline does them great Honor," an onlooker recorded. "They were the first on the Grand Parade, and made a truly Martial appearance, the men are in high health and spirits, and their Horses in excellent condition." Celebration quickly turned to panic in early summer. "On Wednesday last [June 30], about noon, an express arrived here to the executive, giving information that the British were coming up the James River, with their shipping, and that a number of barges and transports were then as high up as Sandy Point, and were landing troops on this side of the river, with an intention, it was supposed, to come to Richmond," a local man detailed. "Alarm guns were immediately fired, and the whole city thrown into the greatest confusion, some supposing, from the suddenness of the alarm, that the enemy were near at hand. In less than half an hour all the volunteer companies and the city militia, as well as every other inhabitant able to shoulder a musket, assembled on the Capitol square, prepared to march to meet the foe."[19]

Fortunately, the military threat of summer 1813 soon subsided, but in April the next year a different sort of challenge appeared in the form of Admiral of the Fleet Sir George Cockburn's proclamation offering freedom and land to "all persons who may be disposed" to enter British lines to escape slavery. "Our negroes are flocking to the enemy from all quarters, which they convert into troops, vindictive and rapacious—with a most minute knowledge of every bye path," a military official reported from Westmoreland County in August. The master might not have shared word of these developments within the Parkhill household, but James Page had other sources of information. Most importantly his father, Coyer Page, a free man working at the Richmond docks, had full access to information about current events and often visited with his wife and others. Young Page recollected his master as sometimes angry with Coyer, and those memories seemed to have originated from encounters at this time. In any event, at age five Page was too young to understand the full meaning of the explosive situation. Still, children sense an atmosphere of apprehension, uncertainty, and insecurity. Seeds of his future conservative outlook could well have germinated out of such wartime experiences.[20]

Underscoring that possibility, the threat posed by Cockburn altered from theoretical to immediate during summer 1814 in a manner that touched the Parkhill household directly. On July 28, British troops commenced raiding on the Virginia side of the Potomac River. "From Richmond, Virginia, we learn that the enemy have engaged in their wonted depredations near Yeocomico," one report specified, "burning, plundering and stealing negroes." The feint masked a major landing in Maryland that by August 24 led to capture of the nation's capital. "To Arms! To Arms!" cried one Richmond editor. "At length a blow is struck, which must rouse the most listless and incredulous— a blow, which would near 'create a soul under the ribs of death.' *Prepare*, prepare; the Philistines be upon you. In what words shall we break the tidings to the ear? The blush of shame, and of rage, tinges the cheek, while we say that Washington has been in the hands of the enemy!—The Capitol and the President's house are in *ruins!*" Governor James Barbour hurriedly called for "the aid of Volunteers of every description." Barbour ordered, "Let all Volunteers bring with them knapsacks, clothes, & all arms and accoutrements in their possession; let them repair to the City of Richmond." John Parkhill joined those who came forward. Despite Barbour's fear of an attack on Virginia's capital, the enemy instead advanced on the upper Chesapeake's principal port. Immediate fears in Richmond soon subsided, especially after the British failed in mid-September to capture Baltimore. Corporal Parkhill served only twenty-three days. All of these forceful events had to confound young James and his mother.[21]

The devastating War of 1812 ended a few months later with the Treaty of Ghent, and the peace that ensued quickly brought fundamental change to the Parkhill household. On January 31, 1815, John Parkhill wed Elizabeth Copland (sometimes Copeland), daughter of highly regarded Richmond attorney Charles Copland. The union lifted Parkhill's spirits while repairing whatever damage Bryson's death and the War of 1812 had wrought to his personal fortune. The dowry's terms have remained secret, although Elizabeth is known to have brought with her an extended family of enslaved human beings. As James Page recalled, "Col. Parkhill got six more servants when he married Mrs. Elizabeth." Most of the Copland bondpeople came from the Virginia area. "Sally Ann, a girl and William, a very small boy[, were the] children of Mary" and came as a family unit. The other three bond-servants, two young boys and a young girl, possessed no apparent family ties with the others. The six individuals—along with Page, his mother, and brother—comprised most of the nine enslaved human beings that Parkhill was known to possess in 1820. This fact suggests that Parkhill had been forced to sell or return virtually the entirety of his first wife's enslaved property. Also, some of Elizabeth Copland's enslaved persons were sold and replaced by others before the Parkhills' migration to Florida in 1827.[22]

The marriage and Elizabeth's dowry brought to the Parkhill household more than enslaved laborers. About this time, for instance, Parkhill obtained an impressive family residence in Richmond's fashionable Libby Hill neighborhood. Parkhill also enjoyed the benefits of his father-in-law's extensive professional and personal connections. Charles Copland's strong Federalist views and his legacy of association with major figures in Virginia political circles meanwhile influenced the atmosphere in which James Page was maturing. No association for which the attorney was noted likely meant more to young James than did Copland's ties to Gabriel Prosser. Copland, as a House of Burgesses member, had served as defense counsel to the bondman in 1799 on a criminal charge heard in Richmond. Copland had saved the enslaved blacksmith from the gallows by virtue of a statute that afforded the accused "benefit of clergy." Historian Douglas R. Egerton explained, "If he could recite a verse from the Bible—as well he could, thanks to the religious faith of his Baptist parents—he had the option of being 'burnt in the left hand [by] the Jailor in Open Court.'" Gabriel's association with the Baptist faith, alongside his brother Martin Prosser, linked the church in the minds of many Richmond bondmen with slave resistance. During the summer of 1800, in an attempt to follow up on the Haitian slave revolts that occurred earlier in the decade—what historian Paul Ortiz characterized as "the world's only successful slave revolution,"—Gabriel endeavored unsuccessfully to seize the capital city as part of a general slave uprising. To an impressionable James Page, the denomination must have seemed daring, if not radical, in theology and social outlook. But Page also realized that neither the Baptist Church nor Charles Copland could save the literate enslaved blacksmith from the gallows.[23]

The immediate postwar years delivered to young Page a living environment that combined a more affluent and genteel atmosphere with an enhanced consciousness of the potential brutality of slavery, the willingness of some to resist its bonds coupled with the terrible punishments meted out to those who did, and awareness of a faith that seemed associated with race and antislavery advocacy. The affluence, to the extent that it constituted a factor, persisted for several years as Parkhill expanded his business interests either individually or in connection with partners or institutions. Of future significance, John's younger brother, Samuel, joined him in Richmond. In 1818 they transformed John Parkhill & Co. into John and Samuel Parkhill. In a lesson that both learned painfully in Florida, the brothers soon discovered to their chagrin that good economic times do not last forever. A severe economic downturn known as the Panic of 1819 caused much of the nation and Richmond, particularly, to suffer catastrophic losses. Real estate and slave prices plummeted, banks desperately called loans, commodity exports dropped precipitously, and bankruptcies soared. Richmond's mercantile community, including the Parkhills and their friends, reeled.[24]

Reverses born of the Panic of 1819 and its aftermath provided the context for a transformative event of Page's youth. Whether the Parkhills sometimes gave Page money or not, they gave him something more valuable and powerful—the gift of literacy. John and Elizabeth, as Page remembered, "taught me how to read and write along with some of the Parkhill children when I was a little boy." By the 1820s Parkhill had capitalized on studies intended to verse the enslaved child in the Bible to serve his own business needs. Page explained the evolution: "The Col had a store. And because I could read a little bit, I used to like it when he left me to take care of the store." Page added of his clerical duties, "I always did a good job for him."[25]

A second transformative event for Page also can be credited to the era. Its background concerned the region's steadily growing free-black population and fears of the impact this despised group would have on enslaved persons. Slaveholding Virginians such as Charles Fenton Mercer, James Monroe, and John Randolph joined with others to rid the state of this reviled class of people that included Coyer Page. At the port of Richmond, he and other free black men could usher enslaved blacks to stow away on ships that would take them to other Atlantic World free communities. In Marie Tyler McGraw's words, "The American Colonization Society [ACS] was founded in Washington, D.C., to encourage the emigration of American free blacks to Africa." This "benevolent colonization" from 1816 to 1840 "stemmed from," as historian David Blight noted, "a complicated set of motives on the part of some white Americans." Whether the benevolence of some whites toward the blacks to be relocated outside the continental United States was genuine or contrived, most free blacks, including the self-emancipated icon Frederick Douglass, came to abhor the ACS, believing that America was the country of their birth and that they had as much right to remain as others born in the country. Still, the repatriation of blacks to Africa appealed to some race members, especially given laws that closely monitored and circumscribed their daily life and activity.[26]

Coyer Page numbered among the hundred or more free blacks who departed Richmond for Liberia during the years from 1820 to 1830. Like the others, he was compelled to deal with constant discrimination and irritations derived from laws, regulations, and customs. Further, he faced increasing resistance from John Parkhill when he sought to see his wife and children. Their master, whose finances teetered precariously in the aftermath of the Panic of 1819, meanwhile surely feared attempts to alienate his property. Page recounted, "I think he [Coyer] left us because he and the Col. would talk[,] and Mr. Parkhill would get a little mad when my father came to visit us. My mother would go into the back of the house when they would talk. But, he sometimes would sneak and see us without the Col. knowing it." Much like in slave Harriet Jacobs's recollection, Page remembered his father trying to purchase his family from their enslaver to no avail: "I remember my father told me that he asked the Col. to [sell] us to him but the Col. would hear none of it. I really miss my father to this day." Sometime in the mid-1820s, Coyer Page left America forever for a new home in Africa. Richmond's First Baptist Church had become the epicenter for coordinating ACS activities, and its representatives assisted him. Understandably, most free blacks possessed little if any money and required total or partial sponsorship by the ACS. Page's father was one of those whose travel expenses were defrayed at least partially. Page did not record exactly when his father departed. He simply noted that "my father stop[ped] coming by to see us." Upon Coyer Page's arrival in Liberia, though, his adventure abruptly ended. While debarking he reportedly fell overboard and drowned. James insisted that his father had been a good swimmer. The actual circumstances of the death accordingly remain a mystery. James noted simply, "They told me he drowned going to Africa." The painful memories of abandonment and loss, as well as his master's unwillingness to allow Coyer Page to purchase his family, understandably left indelible impressions on James Page.[27]

Such events and circumstances helped to mold Page's daily routine and personal outlook as he matured toward adulthood. His master increasingly relied upon him to tend the store while he pursued other interests. But James wanted to play as a child and do things children usually did. According to historian Wilma King, "At early ages, black and white children played together . . . [and] during free moments enslaved children and youth in urban and rural areas used their creativity and imagination for entertainment." In a general sense, boys and girls played together with little regard to gender. By playing with others, Page could develop his leadership and socialization skills. Like for most enslaved children, the free time he spent playing became an avenue for amusement and recreation as well as a way of psychological and physical rest from the travails of servitude.[28]

James's childhood was similar to, yet different from, other enslaved boys and girls of his age. Similar to slave youth in general, he relished playing with neighborhood children. And like thousands of enslaved children in both rural and urban areas of the South, he experienced the sale and separation of loved ones on the auction block. But, unlike most enslaved children who played on the many farms and plantations of the South, the streets of Richmond were Page's playground. "I played in the neighborhood with White boys and Black boys when I was young, and we had a lot of fun playing together." According to historian Marie Jenkins Schwartz, "games and other pastimes could bridge the gulf of race and class that divided black and white children or could emphasize it." Whether Page played with white boys as an equal or whether power relationships existed between him and other children is not known. The only thing we know concerning his white playmates is that, according to Page, "we all got along good." Page's remembrances are silent on the subject of racial prejudice that white children gradually developed toward him as they matured into teenagers and young adults. It would be hard to imagine that Page and his playmates, whether black or white, always enjoyed cordial relationships. Given his urban environment, young Page perhaps did not spend much time swimming in local water holes, climbing trees, or aimlessly wandering in the woods like his plantation and farm peers. In that he liked fishing as an adult, he probably enjoyed fishing as a youngster. Most enslaved children had few material resources to make things for their amusement, but Page did have access to material in his master's store, such as paper, wood, paint, brushes, pens, and other objects, that he could creatively use to make into toys. On occasion, the youngster and his brother got either toys or material to make them from their mother. Later in life, Page recalled that his mother "would always give us little things to play with when she could." The two enslaved lads were more fortunate than most of their counterparts.[29]

Much like other enslaved children in both urban and rural environs, Page remembered playing and fighting sometimes, even with his younger brother, Tom. "I really like[d] the time I spent with my little brother Tom, playing, reading and sometimes fighting a little bit." In occasionally fighting his brother, the elder sibling may have been trying to toughen up the younger lad to fend for himself in a violent society. Page may have participated in games that mimicked the larger society in what Wilma King referred to as "representative play." In these games, enslaved children pretended to be "preachers, mothers, fathers, and auctioneers." At an early age, Page would have lived out his future dream of becoming a minister by playing one in front of his brother and other friends. He may have played the role of a future father with a wife and children but most likely not an auctioneer, given that relatives he loved fell victims to the auction block.[30]

Although boys and girls sometimes played together, many of the games played by children during the antebellum period were gender specific. Like other boys on the farms and plantations throughout the South, Page played male sports like marbles, horseshoes, and ball in the streets of Richmond, while girls played with dolls, played house, dressed up, and jumped rope, among other things. The future minister left little describing his interaction with girls during his youth. But, given that boys and girls sometimes played together, Page may have participated in games similar to what former bondman Charles H. Anderson played as a youth. "[I] used to play games, too. Ring games at play parties—'Ring Around the Rosie,' 'Chase the Squirrel,' and 'Holly Golly.'" He likely played other games that boys and girls played on the farms and plantations of the South, such as hide and go seek, tag, and similar sports. One thing is for sure: Page remembered fondly playing with other children during his youth in Richmond, Virginia.[31]

But some of Page's recreational time was definitely spent in a much different way from the majority of his youthful counterparts. Page amused himself by reading. And because he could read and write at such a young age, he found himself needing greater intellectual satisfaction and personal fulfillment over time. So, the gifted child turned to books and other forms of literature. Books were young Page's window to the world. "I always liked reading anything I could get my hands on," he later observed, "and going to church." He sought comfort in religion. The contents of Parkhill's library can only be speculated upon, so—beyond the Bible and religious tracts—the titles or subjects of the material available to the enslaved lad are not known with certainty. Given the more than four hundred books in his personal library at the time of his death, the young Page likely read books on psychology, history, and sociology. But the picture becomes even clearer on the topic of religion. As a child, one of Page's pastimes was reading the Bible in solitude, which opened the world of Christianity to him. The future minister and race leader noted that "I always like reading the Bible." Reading the Holy Book exposed the enslaved boy to the children of Israel, to the ten commandments, to Job, to David, and to other passages that dealt with morality, triumph over tragedy, hardship, and brutality. We can visualize him reading with intense imagination all or most chapters in the Bible. Reading may not have liberated Page's body, but it could certainly unshackle his mind to dream of a life somewhere else void of slavery. His master also required the youngster to attend the local Presbyterian church with the Parkhill family. Here, from early on Page became particularly intrigued by the Gospel and began to think seriously about religion. The impact proved profound. "When I was a little boy," he reflected, "I felt something every time I went to church with Col. Parkhill." These Presbyterian services were the foundation of Page's future career as a preacher while, with his other activities, they furnished him tools for coping with his enslavement. Overall, Page's deepest memory of his childhood centered on his days as a young boy growing up in Richmond around his father and mother, as well as near John Parkhill and other family members.[32]

Parkhill's actions toward and interest in Page raise one question that should be considered at least briefly. This concerns whether John Parkhill, rather than Coyer Page, might have been the young man's true father. Parkhill had taught Page at an early age how to read, write, and count; came to depend upon his young bondman's acumen to handle business affairs; and guided Page's attention to religion. In Virginia, though, it was not unusual for slaveholders to instruct their "special" bondservants in simple literacy and mathematical skills or to expose them to "safe" religious doctrine. One traveler to Richmond later went so far as to note that "in Richmond, I am informed, almost every slave-child is learning to read." Page became something of a rarity among bondpeople because of the combination of his education and dark complexion at a time when lighter-skinned bondpersons typically received preferential treatment. Certainly, no reliable information suggests that Parkhill fathered the child. Perhaps the most compelling argument to the contrary came directly from James Page, who specified that he knew his biological father to be a "dark" man and identified that man as Coyer Page. Available evidence points to no other possible conclusion.[33]

If the ties between John Parkhill and James Page were not founded in paternity, what did anchor the master-slave relationship? Did Page work productively for his master in hopes of being treated humanely? The enslaved lad understood that his master desired both hard work and obedience from him in exchange for learning to read and write and affording him other privileges. From a young age, Page worked in his master's mercantile business. We do not know from extant sources at what age the enslaved youth began to work or whether he worked alongside any of the white Parkhill children in the Richmond store. But the young lad delighted particularly in Parkhill leaving him alone to manage the business. "I used to like it when he [John Parkhill] left me to take care of the store," he recalled. Page's memory flowed with thoughts of working in his master's general store selling products, taking inventory, cleaning the place, and sometimes closing the business at the end of the day. The master therefore required his bondservant's loyal service to undergird his own prosperity. While Parkhill's outward show of benevolence may have appeared magnanimous to his friends, it provided practical benefit equal to or greater than any advantage gained by Page. With his apprentice capable of handling business chores, Parkhill could leave his understudy for hours, days, and—eventually—weeks, knowing that the store would operate smoothly. Unlike Page's contemporary William Wells Brown, who remained a functional illiterate until nineteen, Page attained his skills at a young age. For Page, managing the store in his master's absence also helped him gain significantly in self-esteem. As he remembered, "The Col. always looked to me to help him." The power equation in the relationship remained lopsided, but the relationship in this instance appeared to benefit both individuals. Page's life says, in fact, a lot about the complex interlocking worlds of the enslaved and the enslaver.[34]

The man who held the power meantime wanted to think of himself as a good and decent man, as illustrated by his willingness to teach his young bondservant to read and write. A major tenet of his ideology of paternalism involved the concept of noblesse oblige. The practice of calling Page and other slaves simply "servants" mirrored his perception of a benevolent master's behavior. Harriet Parkhill claimed that her father "was a kind & lenient Master to his negro servant[s] & they all loved him." Some, if not all, of his bondservants likely would have taken issue with the brand of paternalism displayed by the enslaver. Harriet's general assertion, however, reflected John Parkhill's thinking. Critically, Parkhill's self-interest in educating Page was not repeated when it came to his other bondpeople. The professed

Christian possessed numerous men, women, and children during his lifetime whom he did not educate or choose to know on a truly personal basis. Historian James Oakes found this behavior widespread among men such as Parkhill. "There were people [slaveholders] who could write lovingly, or at least knowledgeably, of a few favored house servants and drivers," he observed. "But these were also people who could not possibly know the hundreds of slaves on their various plantations." This certainly rang true of John Parkhill.[35]

Insofar as is known, John Parkhill managed during the early 1820s—with assistance from Page—to restore the damage wreaked on his finances and social position by the Panic of 1819. During this period he evidenced his renewed prosperity by winning election as a trustee of the Lancastrian Institution, which supported Richmond's Lancastrian School. Illustrating his continued social respectability, he also was selected in 1825 to be a member of the city's elite Amicable Society. Along the way Parkhill dealt in various and potentially lucrative forms of commerce, including that of enslaved human beings. Not until 1826 did his progress stall. That summer New York's Wall Street stock trading exchanges suffered their first corporate governance crisis, an event that triggered the Panic of 1826. Richmond newspapers blamed subsequent business reverses on the "failure of many Insurance Companies and other Institutions in New York" that had been corrupted by "unprincipled speculators who have deeply involved their fellow citizens in such pecuniary distresses." The Parkhill brothers—Samuel and John—were among Richmond's victims. Many friends found themselves in the same position, notably including John and Robert Gamble. Uncertain economic times also adversely affected Page's life and that of other enslaved persons owned by Parkhill.[36]

Other events also changed Page's life, if not directly, certainly indirectly. Family scandal followed for the Parkhills in the economic disruption's wake. On March 19, 1827, John's brother, Samuel, lost control of his temper and cruelly assaulted a salesman named James S. Smithers. "Some remark is said to have been dropt by Mr. P. which touched the feelings of Mr. S.," a report detailed. "Mr. P. made some apology to Mr. S., but the latter was still dissatisfied, and expressed that dissatisfaction. Mr. P. became enraged, struck Mr. S. down, and in that situation is said to have drawn a knife and cut the throat of Mr. S. most dangerously." Samuel, believing that he had killed Smithers, "mounted his horse and made his escape." Lieutenant Governor Peter V. Daniel, a future associate justice of the US Supreme Court, quickly

John Parkhill's brother, Samuel Parkhill, who joined him in frontier Florida in 1827.
State Archives of Florida, Florida Memory

offered a reward for his apprehension. The incident served as fodder for
chatter among the city's social and business elite. "A most horrible transaction took place here a few days since," a correspondent informed a friend on
March 24. "Samuel Parkhill, for a very slight provocation, threw a man down
named Smythers, & cut his throat so much that his life was despaired of
some time; but he is considered at present out of danger." The woman added,
"Parkhill has made his escape, & it is probable he will not be caught." In adding context to such incidences, historian James M. Denham suggested that
such violent altercations were common throughout the antebellum South
where men like Samuel Parkhill sought to maintain their honor with a gun
or a knife.[37]

The Parkhill scandal eventually had a direct impact on the lives of Page, his mother, brother, and other bondservants. It competed as a topic of conversation among the family's friends with excited talk of frontier Florida—what would come to be called the Middle Florida area between the Apalachicola and Suwannee Rivers—and riches to be made there through land speculation and cotton growing. The future of slavery, grounded in its expansion from 1800 to 1860, was assured by slaveholders like John Parkhill. In fact, a Parkhill friend, John Grattan Gamble, Robert's brother, recently had returned to Richmond from a preliminary tour of the Middle Florida region. As Parkhill cheerfully explained to one and all, he was fully satisfied with what he had seen and eager to embark on relocating from the Upper South to a place farther south like Florida. Although the Gambles remained in place through the year, the allure of Middle Florida soon proved irresistible. Joining the brothers in their ultimate move were brothers-in-law William H. Cabell and William Wirt as well as Wirt's son-in-law Thomas Randall.[38]

That John Parkhill shared in the Gamble family discussions appears evident. Twenty-seven days after Samuel's assault on Smithers, Page's master hurriedly embarked on an exploratory trip of his own. "I left Richmond in Virginia the evening of 15 April 1827 in company with William [Copland, his brother-in-law] with the view of visiting in Florida, [and] examin[ing] the land & purchase if found of superior quality & the situation healthy," he confided to his diary. John's brother, Samuel, also had made plans to settle in Florida since surviving correspondence confirms that he and John remained in touch and planned together for their new lives in Florida. Page, then aged nineteen, later confirmed the account. Specifically, he recalled "hearing that Col. Parkhill was going on a trip to buy land in this place called Florida." As will be seen, John Parkhill's dreams of renewed wealth on the newly opened frontier unfortunately and in short order produced nightmares for James Page.[39]

CHAPTER TWO

Forced Migration to the Florida Frontier

I went that day with the Col. when they were sold. I hated watching my mother and brother [being] sold off from me. I cried when I had to leave my mother and brother in Virginny.

—James Page

As was true of many of his contemporaries, John Parkhill's ideology of wealth building had evolved by 1827 to include as an integral element the idea of migration from the Upper South to the Lower South. The inexpensive yet fertile lands he examined on his Florida trip had impressed him, and he purchase 480 acres not far from the new territorial capital at Tallahassee. Accordingly, he opted for a new life away from the comforts of civilized Richmond courtesy of a perilous venture that seemed to promise riches at the end of a shimmering frontier rainbow. The decision made, Parkhill intended to relocate quickly. Back in Richmond, he gathered up members of his white family, James Page, and other enslaved persons for a bold move to the wilds of the peninsular territory. Samuel Parkhill and his extended family either joined in the preparations or else John facilitated his brother's family's relocation to Florida where Samuel awaited. The anticipation, not to say exhilaration, that the white traveling party members felt was palpable, and it was not theirs alone. Numerous other Virginians, North Carolinians, and others either were making or planning the same journey. Prince Achille Murat, Napoleon Bonaparte's exiled nephew, noted as much. Having chosen Middle Florida for his own home, he confirmed the allure: "A planter never comes alone; he persuades some relations and friends to emigrate with him, or at least to come and see the country; the greater part of these visitors settle [sic] there." Murat described quite accurately the desire and need of white families to stick together when traveling. For enslaved blacks, though, preservation of family through mutual relocation by no means was assured. As Page discovered to his lasting pain and regret, those closest to him could be lost even before he took the first step in the planned trek to the wilds of frontier Florida.[1]

An understanding of the dilemma that confronted the enslaved teenager requires closer examination of the master-slave relationship between Page and John Parkhill. Decades ago, historian Eugene D. Genovese popularized the term "paternalism" to describe the master-slave relationship. The concept presupposed a give and take where bondservants produced faithfully and diligently in exchange for their enslavers' protection and generosity. In an abstract sense, slaveholders conceived of the enslaved as extensions of their white families. When it came to James Page and John Parkhill, however, "paternalism" must be viewed with a jaundiced eye. Parkhill clung to an ideology of paternalism, but practice never translated itself into a true and sustained belief put into action. Like most slaveholders, Parkhill could not mask his racist attitudes toward enslaved blacks. He considered them inferior, as Page soon would find out.[2]

Page first learned of his imminent removal from Virginia when listening to his master talk about pulling up roots and leaving the state. He recollected, "I heard my master wanted to leave Richmond to go to Florida." In mid-1827, the nineteen-year-old listened repeatedly to whites' conversations about seeking "a better life" there, in Texas, or in other places. As did many—if not most—household bondservants, Page had become adept at either overhearing or nonchalantly finding out information from owners, their family members, and visitors to glean important information about goings-on that affected him. The thought of leaving the only home he had ever known, at least when it became clear that the move in fact would occur, filled the young man with apprehension approaching panic. To ease his trepidation, the owner made it clear to his skilled bondman that he believed the greater "family" would fare better economically if he left Virginia. According to Page, "The Col. believed we all could live a good life in Florida. Well before you knowed it, the Col. had bought some land in that place and we were going there." What Colonel Parkhill failed to tell the enslaved teenager was that he and other white family members were also fleeing the state of Virginia for Florida to avoid the consequences of Samuel Parkhill's actions.[3]

Shortly thereafter, Page's life was turned upside down as he was compelled to deal with personal tragedy at the hands of his owner. For Parkhill, it turned out, enslaved human beings often were coldly considered mere "walking cash." "It was a very sad time for me because just before we left the

Col. sold my mother and brother. I was told he sold them so he could have money to go to the new place down South. I went that day with the Col. when they were sold," the bondservant recalled. "They stood up on a big platform and was sold as one." Many years later, Page implied in conversations that the worst memory of the situation was not the selling of his loved ones but having to watch them being sold. "I hated watching my mother and brother sold off from me," he lamented. Parkhill's decision was not the act of a compassionate man who cared about the feelings and mental well-being of his "beloved" bondservant. Specifically, why did he sell the mother and brother of his favorite bondservant, given that the enslaver had other bondpeople he could have sold instead? The motive was greed. The enslaver perceived more future value—and more money to be made—in the seven younger bondservants whom he kept. All of the enslaved Parkhill migrants, except one, were nineteen years of age or younger. The answer beckons: John Parkhill made a strictly business decision, untainted by sympathy. Indeed, this supposedly paternalistic master chose to forego an opportunity to show compassion by allowing Page's father to purchase them. Parkhill may have thought that he was "good" to Page, but his deliberate disposal of his bondservant's loved ones plainly evidenced something far different. Page's crying at the sight of seeing his mother and brother sold on the auction block vividly portrayed, from the bondservant's perspective, the fiction of paternalism as practiced by his owner.[4]

For Parkhill, no moral dilemma appeared. The enslaver never attempted at any time to repurchase Page's love ones. The bondservant was compelled, therefore, to cling to the one thing his enslaver could not take from him—the memory of his mother and brother. Page's mother's look, her smile, her words, and her overall appearance were grafted on his memory, subject to fading overtime. The same with his brother. Page at least was able to retain thoughts of the good times that he spent with his mother and brother, memories that slavery could not steal from him.

Other memories were not so positive. The enslaved man further remembered, "I will never forget the street they were sold on was called Wall street." Historian Walter Johnson aptly noted "that the majority of family-separating sales occurred at the behest of upper-South slaveholders [like John Parkhill] rather than lower-South slave traders." At the Wall Street auction, Page saw his mother holding Tom's hand as they were displayed for all to see. Years later, former Missouri slave Bill Simms recalled just such an event: "If he [the enslaver] got hard up for money, he would advertise and sell some slaves, like my oldest sister was sold on the [auction] block with her children." She, Simms reflected, "sold for eleven hundred dollars, a baby in her arms sold for three hundred dollars." Knowing nothing about the health or physical condition of Page's mother, potential buyers would have gathered around Susie. She also could have been taken for closer inspection at this time, for the sexualization of enslaved women such as Susie helped to determine the price. As former bondwoman Millie Simpkins, better known as "Black Mamie," observed, enslaved women "had ter tek all ob ye Clothes off" before the auction bidding started. According to Walter Johnson, a potential buyer "squeezed [the] arms [of slaves] to test their strength and inspected fingers to estimate their dexterity for picking cotton, they probed bellies and hefted breasts to search out histories of childbearing and the promise of reproduction." And the more eyes that gazed upon Susie and Tom, the more they became objects to be acquired instead of human beings.[5]

Page must have seen in Parkhill that day a heart of stone. "I cried when I had to leave my mother and brother in Virginny," he insisted. "But, there was nothing I could do but cry and I cried a lot you know." Page did not learn whether his loved ones were "sold down the river" to places in Mississippi, Alabama, Texas, or the like, a customary practice in Richmond at the time and a harbinger of coming cruelty and inhuman conditions. "I miss them and always prayed that they are doing good wherever they are," he mourned. "I would pray to the Lord for strength. After they left me, sometimes, as a lonely boy I wanted to talk to my mother and father, but I always knew that I could talk to the Lord." Page's memory forever flowed with thoughts of Richmond's Wall Street. One historian observed, "The history of the slave trade is as much the story of those left behind as it is the story of those carried away. It is the story of separated lovers and broken families, of widows, widowers, and orphans left in the wake of the trade." With the loss of both biological parents and a brother, James Page became one of many thousands of enslaved persons separated from loved ones by the auction block. And what he watched at the Richmond auction that day would forever remain a part of his memory of two cherished bodies—two more valuable pieces of flesh—being fed to the carnivorous domestic slave trade for consumption. In such a manner, James Page became another one of slavery's orphans. The auction of his loved ones represented one terrible dimension of racial capitalism during the antebellum period. If any silver lining graced that dark cloud, perhaps—as will be seen—it came through the labors of a race leader who caringly related to people under his charge.[6]

In terms of John Parkhill's intentions, one lesson for Page stood out plainly. As historian Charles Joyner noted, "The auction block was one of the strongest forms of psychological control any slaveholder possessed." Former Virginia bondman William Johnson agreed. "Master used to say," he noted, "that if we [the slaves] didn't suit him, he would put us in his pocket quick—meaning he would sell us." So, Parkhill—as he prepared for the Florida journey—displayed in the bluntest of terms that he held absolute power over Page and all his other bondservants. With whatever degree of consciousness, he instilled fear in the young man. If Page harbored ideas of rebelling or running away, he now knew that what his loved ones had just experienced could well happen to him. It was a common tactic. Former bondservant Acie Thomas, for one, remembered that bondpeople on her Florida plantation who misbehaved would be threatened with sale to "some po' white trash." Walter Johnson amplified the point: "Every slave had a price, and slaves' communities, their families, and their own bodies were suffused with the threat of sale, whether they were in the pens or not." The ploy worked in Page's case. The prospect of being sold haunted him until emancipation.[7]

It must be acknowledged, though, that a second profound and quite different lesson also arose out of the bitter experience. What Page witnessed that day clarified for him that his enslaver was no caring paternalist. In Page's eyes was a man who separated slave families, a symbol of a slave family ruiner, which made slavery for him that much more unbearable and inhuman. It became clear to Page that the material self-interest of his pious Christian master outweighed any real sense of humanitarianism. Although his enslaver was never a physically violent man, Page, however, did not have to be physically whipped to suffer lifelong scars. Parkhill became, in the bondservant's eyes, a psychological abuser, a character flaw that ironically would make him subject to artful manipulation.[8]

~

The bondservant, in line with patterns of behavior expected of him, did not ask his owner questions about the sale of his loved ones or the imminent move. His silence, though, betokened no acceptance. Historians Calvin Schermerhorn and Phillip Troutman noted that enslaved persons who found themselves in Page's position sometimes appealed to a master's sense of religiosity to keep their families intact. Page clearly did not want to leave his mother and brother behind. If he appealed on religious grounds to his Presbyterian owner, though, his pleas fell on deaf ears. The slaveholder seemed to be comfortable with the contradiction of separating families while projecting the persona of a devout Christian. His wealth-building trumped concern for Page's welfare. Despite his familiarity with Parkhill, Page would bear what at least a million other forced migrants were compelled to endure as they set out for distant lands with thoughts of loved ones sold and separated painfully fresh in their minds. His memories of the pain persisted, eventually transforming into an everlasting self-portrait of frustration, anger, and sadness.[9]

Parkhill seemingly believed meanwhile that he had held true to his paternalistic attitudes toward Page and his other bondservants. But did he? The enslaver viewed the relocation to Florida merely as a brief interruption in the lives of his black and white families. That he was acting, in his opinion, to "better" lives in both branches of the family more than justified to him any disruption or dislocation. But there was no give and take between Parkhill and the bondpeople he separated from family members. Parkhill thought less about the welfare of Page and his other bondservants and more about the economic advantages for the white Parkhill family in relocating to the Florida frontier. The enslaver grasped deep within his being that he could not accomplish his goal of becoming a wealthy man without enslaved labor. He had prided himself for years in taking notice of those men who possessed the "negro servants" who made possible the accumulation of wealth on their farms and plantations. So, the money that John Parkhill made from the sale of Page's mother and brother came to him without guilt or second thought because it helped to accomplish the worthy goal of becoming a man of substance. Parkhill's justification satisfied his own conscience about uprooting Page and other bondservants and separating them from loved ones. It also permitted him to continue identifying as a caring and religious enslaver. But Page perceived his "high-minded" Christian master to be a hypocrite, a man who owned enslaved human beings and sold and separated them from family members while keeping his own white family secure and intact. Parkhill's imaginary paternalism, in Page's mind, obviously came second to financial self-interest.[10]

Most slave owners would not have, on the one hand, understood Page's emotions or, for that matter, really cared about them. On the other hand, visitors to Richmond not immersed in slave ideology or awash in the allure of wealth that slavery betokened grasped the pretense and recoiled at the sanctimony. Jack Trammell pointed to this fact in his benchmark study of the Richmond slave trade: "Sometimes, the hypocrisy was so blatant as to stretch the imagination of even a sympathetic critic." He added, "In written histories of the city of Richmond, it is made very clear that citizens of certain social or economic standing did not wish to be seen conducting business in the Wall Street district. Similar to the trading of slaves taking place aboard ships in the James River to hide from prying eyes, there was an element of dirtiness to it that defied apologists' attempts to justify the trade. Many wealthy southerners hired agents or assistants to conduct business along Wall Street on their behalf."[11]

Trammell highlighted English writer Charles Dickens's appalled reaction to visiting the Wall Street slave auctions: "'Cash for negroes,' 'cash for negroes,' 'cash for negroes,' is the heading of advertisements in great capitals down the long columns of the crowded journals. Woodcuts of a runaway negro with manacled hands, crouching beneath a bluff pursuer in top boots, who, having caught him, grasps him by the throat, agreeably diversify the pleasant text . . . all those owners, breeders, users, buyers and sellers of slaves, who will, until the bloody chapter has a bloody end, own, breed, use, buy, and sell them at all hazards: who doggedly deny the horrors of the system in the teeth of such a mass of evidence as never was brought to bear on any other subject, and to which the experience of every day contributes its immense amount; who would at this or any other moment, gladly involve America in a war, civil or foreign, provided that it had for its sole end and object the assertion of their right to perpetuate slavery, and to whip and work and torture slaves, unquestioned by any human authority, and unassailed by any human power; who, when they speak of Freedom, mean the Freedom to oppress their kind, and to be savage, merciless, and cruel; and of whom every man on his own ground, in republican America, is a more exacting, and a sterner, and a less responsible despot than the Caliph Haroun Alraschid in his angry robe of scarlet." Dickens, much like Frederick Douglass and other more radical (Christian) abolitionists, believed that the United States had placed itself on a path to civil war through its wicked pursuit of materialism and profit.[12]

As Trammell also noted, Frederick Law Olmsted, too, cringed at the Wall Street trade and stood indignant at the callous owners who nurtured the business. He especially recalled a conversation overheard one day between strangers on a train, the subject of which was an enslaved girl:

"What are you going to do with her?"
"I'm taking her down to Richmond, to be sold."
"Does she belong to you?"
"No; she belongs to ——; he raised her."

"Why does he sell her—has she done anything wrong?"

"Done anything? No; she's no fault, I reckon."

"Then, what does he want to sell her for?"

"Sell her for! Why shouldn't he sell her? He sells one or two every year; Wants the money for 'em, I reckon."

Many enslaved people knew they could be sold for any reason, real or imagined, by their owners. And Page's master had no discomfort being seen selling human beings on the auction block.[13]

The treatment that Page received stemmed directly from his owner's worldview. Parkhill was comfortable with selling bondservants because he considered slavery to be a biblically sanctioned institution that functioned well when controlled and supervised by "humane" slaveholders like him. He knew also that the peculiar institution had been recognized by the US Constitution, and he entertained no qualms about the situation. John Parkhill knew the Scriptures well. He also became "well versed in the theology of the Bible" as a "deeply pious" man and "elder" in the Presbyterian Church. As described by Johanna Nicol Shields, many other Southerners, including white intellectuals, reflected the same attitudes that Parkhill adopted. They evidenced little or no guilt over enslaving other human beings because they rationalized it as part of a divinely inspired world order. Parkhill in the meantime viewed himself as an unimpeachably humane master. As we have seen, this characterization did not accord with Page's perspective. Especially anxious about the move to Florida, the enslaved teenager understandably feared what lay ahead no matter what his master may have said to him. As Page put it, "I remember wondering how we [bondservants] would be treated when we got to Florida."[14]

This situation illustrated the tricky position in which a "humane" slaveholder could be placed when he attempted to present himself to his peers in one light while acting in a very different one. "An important tenet of southerners' paternalist ideology," Damian Alan Pargas observed, "required benevolent masters to make a genuine effort to protect slave families from dissolution." This Page's master did not do. The idea that he arbitrarily could tear a son apart from his mother and brother necessitated that Parkhill redouble his efforts to show how great a paternalist he really was. So problematic did the circumstances weigh on his conscience that he was compelled to become a consummate actor in order to appear to other slaveholders and the general public as a godly master who truly cared for his underlings. There, his apparent religious devotion came to his aid. As Page cogently recalled, "The Col. would pray over almost everything he did." When his master's prayers received their response from a higher power, however, the message came not from God but from a balance sheet. Bondservants were capital investments to be used and disposed of as the owner saw fit. When it suited Parkhill's purposes, James Page, his mother, and his brother were urged to believe that they belonged to an extended family. At other times they would be counted purely as property in the same manner as cows, horses, or pigs might be evaluated. In the circumstances, his contradictory paternalistic gestures fell far short of protecting and nurturing the enslaved families under his charge. As Page and other bondservants would quickly learn in their move to their future home, their enslaver would focus less on their welfare and more on accumulating wealth through the use of their bodies.[15]

Notably, the ordeal of James Page and the other bondservants' 1827 relocation from Virginia to Florida played out in the context of a huge forced-migration movement that, beginning about 1800 and ending as the calamitous Civil War erupted, transformed the American South. Historians have called the current of humanity "a Second Middle Passage." This "second wave," as historians Pargas and Ira Berlin have labeled it, exceeded the size of the preceding surge that originated in Africa. That development, which occurred between 1680 and the international slave trade's end in 1808, involved the transport of about five hundred thousand uprooted enslaved human beings. Economic historian Lewis Cecil Gray concisely described the second wave's dynamics. An increasing demand for cotton led, he wrote, to a massive "shift of slave populations from the older planting regions—particularly the border states—to the newer planting regions in the lower South."[16]

The second great wave—the one that engulfed Page—eclipsed the first when it came to sheer numbers. Workers in rapidly growing European cities and industrial centers increasingly were demanding greater supplies of cheap yet comfortable cotton cloth and clothing, just as the United States was opening for cultivation millions of acres of prime farmland stolen from Native Americans. Demand prompted supply, as planters giddy over prospects of immense wealth gleaned from cotton or, sometimes, sugarcane production flocked to exploit these regions. Growing staple crops exhausted land, disinherited Native Americans, and brutalized enslaved workers. The military conquest and displacement of Native Americans and their black allies in Florida certainly undermined any appearance of paternalism in Uncle Sam. There was no quid pro quo arrangement between prior occupiers of the land and the United States because the former were either pushed off their property or simply killed to make room for the expansion of slavery. And as these lands opened up for white settlers, more than one million enslaved persons consequently endured relocation to the Lower South or Southwest during the first six decades of the nineteenth century's advent. These men, women, and children formed a part of what some historians called the "migration generations" who were forcibly removed from the historic centers of slavery in the Upper South and Chesapeake between the times of the Revolutionary and Civil Wars. Racial capitalism was at the root of this massive diaspora.[17]

Many, if not most, of the hallmarks that typified the second great wave applied at least generally to John Parkhill and James Page. Parkhill may not have been a speculator in the traditional sense of a man who trafficked primarily in valuable enslaved bodies. Yet he emerged as a hard-headed businessman by moving Page, his other bondpeople, and white family members in order to speculate through enslaved labor and cotton production. The allure of untold wealth promised by the virtually insatiable demand for cotton drew Page's owner, and others, to new homes, situations, and—not insignificantly—risks. The Virginian aimed to reap his fortune in the new territory of Florida. Importantly, he did not act alone. Hundreds of Upper South planters and businessmen left their homes for rich, yet cheap, land in what one day would become the Sunshine State. Among others, the cavalcade included Richmond's John and Robert Gamble; other Virginians of the distinguished Cabell, Eppes, and Brown families; Thomas Randall from Maryland; and Paul Cameron from North Carolina. Page involuntarily joined the phalanx of bondservants whose lives were disrupted and altered dramatically by such men. The teenager found himself an interstate slave migrant much like his counterparts who were driven to the largest importing states of Alabama, Mississippi, Louisiana, and Texas. The tide of enslaved black men, women, and children that swept Page southward, however, should not be considered insignificant: Florida's slave population grew from 15,501 in 1830 to a whopping 61,745 three decades later.[18]

Page did not necessarily typify the era's transported enslaved migrants. Unlike many second-wave victims, he possessed literacy skills, and he was intimate with his enslaver and the enslaver's family. As a result, he could gain a clear idea of his future destination. However, like his fellow forced migrants, he did not desire relocation, and he kept his opinion to himself. The painful memory of his subsequent trial would be etched in his mind. "I did not want to leave my mother and brother and old Virginny," he later confided to a friend, "but I told no one of my sadness." As previously detailed, Parkhill inflicted this bitter experience upon Page at least partly to deter him from flight on the way to Florida. This suggests that Parkhill, despite Page's silence on the subject, sensed the magnitude of his resistance. So, the master could comfort himself that he had acted simply to forestall a looming problem.[19]

The experience that ensued for Page differed noticeably from that of many second-wave migrants. The transported bondservants fell into three broad categories. As historian Michael Tadman noted, between 60 and 70 percent of the total interstate slave migration was a part of the domestic slave trade. These forced migrants were largely the purchases of slave traders who either moved enslaved people from state to state (the long-distance interstate slave trade), within a state (the intrastate slave trade), or locally (usually from rural to urban areas). Within these categories more than 650,000 enslaved human beings were bought and relocated.[20]

Page did not fit any of those three categories. Rather, he fell into a fourth. Within the fourth division, according to Pargas, two categories could be found. Members of the first group were purchased by their new owners during visits to other states and then were moved with them to the Lower South or Southwest. The second group knew their masters personally or had been acquainted with them for most of their lives. In turn, they accompanied those masters on their journey. As a member of this second group Page did not get caught up in the domestic slave trade as such. His master did not sell him or commission him to a slave trader for transport chained in a slave coffle to the auction block, as described by former Kentucky bondman Isaac Griffin: "I saw one hundred men chained, besides women and children, going down south." Instead, Page moved with his migrating owner. As such an emigrant, his 750-mile travel experience from Virginia to Florida differed in significant respects from those of other domestic slave trade migrants. Notably and like most bondservants who accompanied longtime masters to the Lower South, Page—as also was true for his fellow Parkhill enslaved migrants—was not chained or shackled on the long journey to frontier Florida. The future enslaved preacher and overseer recalled, "There was nothing tying me with no one else, we just all walked together." Friends of his owner, such as the Gambles, also brought enslaved laborers with them from Virginia whom they personally knew and who had worked for them for years. They also chose not to chain or shackle their bondservants. Because these men thought they knew their enslaved workers well, owners of this sort felt little need to confine these valuable bodies. Instead, as did Parkhill with Page, they utilized fear of being sold or otherwise punished to avoid escapes or violent reprisals during the long trek to their new wilderness homes.[21]

Besides Parkhill's self-interested dealings and justifications, there were larger issues contributing to this episode that merit due consideration. In the 1800s, economic hard times had befallen Parkhill and many of his fellow Virginia and North Carolina emigrants. Among the causes were the Panics of 1819 and 1826 previously discussed, soil exhaustion in the Chesapeake states from long-term tobacco cultivation, declining tobacco prices, volatile business cycles impacting Atlantic World markets, and possible gradual climate change affecting the Upper South staple crops. But the takeover of Spanish and Native American lands in the Deep South further encouraged those interested in grasping new fortunes, or rebuilding lost or diminished ones, to grow cotton and other crops. The Missouri Compromise of 1820 meanwhile provided the shot in the arm that slavery needed to spark its expansion in the South and Southwest. Given the surplus of enslaved persons for sale in the Chesapeake region during the 1820s, exploitation of the more than 530 million acres acquired through the Louisiana Purchase some two decades earlier now loomed as a very attractive possibility to planters and yeoman farmers. With encroachment into new lands, the peculiar institution's heartbeat grew ever stronger. As became evident, it depended upon a constant infusion of land into its veins to continue to grow and remain strong. This already was well understood by those who chose to be informed, as historian James Oakes pointed out. "Centuries of western history," he observed, "had . . . demonstrated slavery's insatiable urge to expand." Slavery and expansion went hand in hand.[22]

The times and alternatives available to regional slaveowners combined in 1827 to guide Page's future course. A mixture of turbulent economic conditions and prevalent yearnings for a magical solution to the challenge of approaching bankruptcy that afflicted many struggling Upper South planters and businessmen created a ready market for attempts to sell Florida as an unspoiled semitropical paradise filled with opportunity. Thomas Jefferson's grandson Francis Eppes joined the resulting parade south from Virginia. "I see no ties which should bind any of our grandfather's descendants to this state," he exclaimed in defense of his action. Florida's territorial governor

William Pope DuVal, a native Virginian who earlier had represented a Kentucky district in Congress, played a significant role in those efforts. "Governor DuVal," T. D. Allman correctly pointed out, "was a gifted self-publicist." Despite tribulations inflicted by resistant Indians and Maroons whom the governor was attempting to pen within a peninsular reservation, a virtually nonfunctioning territorial government, various catastrophes caused by man and Mother Nature, and lagging popularity at home, the governor brilliantly capitalized on his modest national fame and influential connections to present Florida as a highly desirable locale. He especially took advantage of congressional action in mid-decade that gifted the Frenchman Gilbert du Motier, Marquis de la Fayette, with a township of land adjacent to Tallahassee, by issuing a very public invitation to the Revolutionary War hero to relocate personally to his new lands. By 1827 the Florida Land Agency, headquartered at the territorial capital, aided DuVal in his exertions. Its advertisements, which carried endorsements from Andrew Jackson's aide James Gadsden and Richmond's John Gamble, circulated broadly in Old Dominion newspapers. DuVal became one of the first economic boosters to popularize and to publicize the Florida peninsula. Others bought into the governor's vision.[23]

These and other public relations efforts, when considered in light of Page's literacy skills, allowed him insight about his future home even if the information skewed dramatically positive. One example of the type of account then available was published in 1826 in the form of a letter from a Virginian just returned from a Florida visit. "Since the cession of the Floridas to the United States, much inquiry has been made, and much interest excited with respect to the inducements of emigration in that section of our country," it began. "In the states of Virginia and Maryland particularly, there has been an inordinate interest manifested." The writer's focus quickly narrowed to "that section of the territory called Middle Florida, comprising the country between the Suwaney and the Apalachicola rivers, and which is considered the most desirable part of the territory." The letter continued to weave a tapestry of Edenic bliss: "That part of Middle Florida, now settling, and in which most of the land susceptible of cultivation lies, is elevated about 100 feet above the level of the sea, and is sufficiently undulating to drain off the superfluous waters. Every three or four miles the country is indented with small lakes from three to four hundred yards to five or ten miles in circumference—the water perfectly clear and is never stagnant, as they all have either visible or subterranean outlets."[24]

Having gone on to explore Middle Florida's unmatched fertility and the rich soil's remarkable utility for cotton growing, the man turned to the "delightful" climate and predicted, among other things, the advent of viniculture in a not-too-distant future that would bring to the American South the atmosphere of the most desirable European locales. "The country is yet too young for the development of any extensive experiments in the culture of the Vine," he began. "[Yet,] in St. Augustine some of the European grapes have been reared to great perfection, and from the similarity of the climate of Florida, to that of the South of France, of Spain, Italy and the Island of Madeira, it is confidently believed that the grapes of those countries may be cultivated with entire success in this territory. Vegetables, of almost every kind, grow in Florida, and can be sowed or planted at any season; of some vegetables two crops can be raised the same year." The writer marched in lockstep with Governor DuVal in his idyllic description of the territory. And in case he had failed to convince his readers fully of the awaiting Eden, he waxed, "The society of Tallahassee and neighborhood, is yet small in number, but characterized by sociability and a refinement and elegance of manners not surpassed in any city. The country around Tallahassee, in almost every direction, from the variety of hill and dale and crystal lakes, is extremely beautiful and romantic; and when the hand of art has seconded nature, it will bear a comparison with any other country. The lakes abound with fish of the most delicious flavor, and the large extent of country which will never be cultivated, will always afford a variety of game. In a few years the orange, the fig, and numerous other fruits will be added to the sum of domestic luxuries; nor are the roads to be left out of the class of comforts, they are almost always excellent; the hills are seldom abrupt, and from the nature of the soil, the roads are dry in 24 hours after the longest rains—they are never dusty." Anglos like DuVal, Jackson, Gadsden, and Gamble were among Florida's earliest passionate boosters.[25]

Given his innate intelligence Page likely saw through the puffery that magically transformed a rough frontier into a heavenly oasis; still, the dreams of timely rescue enchanted his owner. Upon Parkhill's return from his first Florida visit in spring 1827, he immediately began preparing for relocation. Admittedly, his haste was encouraged not only by his own precarious financial position but also by the legal problems that dogged his brother, Samuel. A Virginia arrest warrant remained outstanding and threatened a trial for attempted murder or some similar charge. By summer Samuel had ventured to New York City from whence he traveled to England in August. Surviving correspondence confirms that he and John remained in touch and that they planned together for their new Florida lives. A letter dated August 16 also suggests that John had meant to be on the road south by that time. Samuel had directed it to Tallahassee. The Parkhills appeared to be a family on the run.[26]

If John Parkhill's plans called for the Florida expedition to commence as soon as mid-August, his frustrations and anxieties must have been mounting by the day. Not only was he not on his way at that time; months remained before he would be. For one thing, unsnarling his complicated financial entanglements took time and effort. Six years later he still was struggling with Richmond litigation and its consequences. The aspect of the delay that particularly involved Page, however, concerned yet another tough-to-manage problem. The Parkhill estate by 1827 had grown substantially, and the owner needed to find buyers to satisfy creditors. Indeed, buyers needed to be found soon, while the process of organizing and packing alone required an enormous commitment. A rental advertisement run in 1833 provided a description that underscored the task faced by the Parkhills and their enslaved people: "That desirable situation on Church Hill, formerly the residence of John Parkhill, Esq. [is available for rental]. The Lot is a square of two acres, on one of which is the Dwelling House, built of handsome brick, covered with slate and finished in the best manner. . . . On this acre is also a Stable and Carriage House, coal and Wood House, all of brick—a handsome and very productive Garden, two Yards, one of which is entered from the cross street and the kitchen; this yard has on it a well of good water with a pump in it, and is separated from the front yard by a pailing [sic]; the front yard is well covered with grass; the unimproved lot is an oblong square acre, and has produced a good crop of oats."[27]

Doubtlessly, Page found himself occupied for several months helping the family cope with the complex task of leaving such a home, but the delayed departure from Virginia also had a third cause. After their initial fruitful visit to Florida, Robert and John Grattan Gamble, sons of John Gamble, also planned to leave Richmond for their new wilderness home in the fall. In addition to various relations and their bondservants, other Virginia planters such as Thomas Brown and Francis Eppes aimed to head for the territory as well. It appears over the distance of nearly two centuries that all the families planned to travel, if not together, then cooperatively or, at least, roughly at the same time so that they could support one another when necessary. The agreed moment of departure came about November 1, with various parties setting out a few days apart on their nearly two-month trek. This dictated that the travelers deal at times with severe winter weather conditions. For Parkhill, the pain of delay must have felt excruciating as he witnessed his comfortable window of opportunity slipping away. As early as October 17 a heavy frost blanketed northern Virginia, followed by hail and snow on the twenty-sixth. Rain and high winds dominated conditions two weeks later. Once in route, the caravans enjoyed moderate weather at times and harsher conditions at other times. As they traveled through South Carolina, for instance, "oppressive and unsettled heat" preceded "cold and raw [conditions], to a degree of uncomfortableness." Once in Georgia, circumstances fortunately again changed. "To call the present bland weather *Winter*, is a misnomer—it approaches so much nearer the usual temperature of Spring," a Macon newspaper reported. "No Frost has been seen for several weeks, and fire is hardly an article of comfort at any time in the 24 hours; many fruit trees are in blossom, and the woods and fields are putting on a green appearance."[28]

The white Parkhills left no detailed account of the family's journey to Florida, but, fortunately, members of several other clans preserved their memories of the trip. Future governor Thomas Brown's daughter Frances Elizabeth "Lizzie" Brown was one, and her recollections provided an excellent sense of the route followed. Her family's trek commenced northwest of Fredericksburg in Rappahannock County. Brown collected his wife, five children, and 140 enslaved people. "Twenty planter friends" accompanied the party. "Our route to Florida was from Fredericksburg to Danville, Virginia, then through Greensborough and Charlotte, [North Carolina,] . . . then through Chester and Spartenburg[, South Carolina]," Lizzie detailed. "Then Georgia was sparsely settled[,] and days passed when we saw no settlements or people. After we passed into the wilderness [of Georgia] we could get nothing in the shape of provisions and forage until we reached Florida. [Georgia] was long stretch of country with nothing but pine and wire grass, flat and no undergrowth. You could see as far as the eye could reach through monster pine trees. The long leaf pine running up thirty or forty feet . . . before they put out a limb. It was a strange sight to us, coming from that rolling and mountainous country [of Virginia] filled with oaks, hickory and fir trees, to this flat sandy pine country. Well, after a long tedious trip through the wilderness, we bid adieu to Georgia [towns] at Hawkinsville [on the Ocmulgee River south of Macon] and [eventually] entered Florida."[29]

Similarly, Robert Gamble shared recollections of his family's journey. Robert offered details similar to Lizzie Brown's along with a sense of the way the party traveled. "In the Spring and Summer of 1826, my father went to Florida on a prospecting visit with view to ultimate residence there," he commenced. "My impression is that my father secured land not only for himself but for his Brother and also for Uncle [William] Wirt, [and] for his daughter Laura, just married to Thomas Randall." Having obtained the property that they would need for their new life, the Gambles finally set off for Middle Florida in early November 1827. "Our cavalcade consisted of a close[d] carriage or coach in which my Mother & her Sister Charlotte van Courtland Greenup rode," Robert continued. "[Also, we had] a second two horse carriage, a carry all with single horse & saddle horse, two heavy road wagons each drawn by six young mules recently broken for the purpose. Three white drivers for the wagons & the carriage driven by our Servant Isaac Wiggins, the father of Primus, who we all know, and a company of some 12 or 15 negroe servants mostly young women. We carried two large house tents which together with the covered waggons & carriages furnished shelter for all day, or night. On Sundays, we remained in Camp. We reached Tallahassee on Xmas eve 1827 and Xmas day moved on and reached home, having camped the previous night, on the [St.] Augustine road just E of the branch."[30]

Page's journey unfolded similarly—geographically and logistically—when compared to those of the Browns and Gambles. Parkhill, eager to grasp his golden opportunity in the sunshine, necessarily took pains to map out careful plans. Traveling with him were white family members consisting of wife Elizabeth Copland Parkhill and sons Charles and George Washington. His "walking cash" accompanied them. Black members of the party who ended up migrating with the Parkhills included Page, nineteen; Elizabeth, a single girl, age twelve; Sally, a single girl, age thirteen; John, a single boy, age ten; William, a young boy age five, with his mother Mary, age thirty, also with her infant. As mentioned earlier, the enslaved migrants were not handcuffed or chained in a slave coffle, as John Parkhill knew these individuals well enough to feel comfortable that they would not misbehave or run away. His intuition proved correct, for there is no indication that any of the clans had more than ordinary traveling problems. The trip also seems to have gone pretty much as scheduled because on December 4 the *Augusta Chronicle and Georgia Advertiser* noted that, as of the first, a letter had been waiting in the local post office for pickup by John Parkhill. This fit the planned schedule, which would have been disrupted had there been serious trouble such as a slave rebellion.[31]

The 750-mile expedition south from Richmond inevitably required physical and emotional exertion for weeks on end. Although an arduous challenge for all concerned, at least Page and the family's other bondservants did not have to face the potential danger of traveling by water, considering riverboats of the time frequently exploded before reaching their destinations. Instead, the party normally moved an average of twenty miles per day overland. The white Parkhills rode in two wagons with all the worldly possessions they managed to take with them. For the bondpeople, no conveniences were provided. "We walked many days for a long time each day, but I can't remember how many days," Page recorded. "Maybe it was at least 8 to 9 weeks in all." One exception proved the rule. The enslaved mother nursing her baby sometimes struggled to keep up the pace while holding her child in her arms. If she lagged too far behind from exhaustion, white family members might allow her to ride for a time in one of the wagons. "We were always tired I tell you," Page attested. "I even got a little sick along the way[,] but it wasn't too bad." At nightfall, the enslaved migrants set up camp, cooked dinner, cleaned, and entertained. The bondservants, including Page, eventually spent the night in "open tents." Whites "slept in tents with wall and doors." Rest and restoration eluded Page on numerous occasions. "It really got scary sometimes at night," he recollected, "and I was afraid for myself and others mostly at night." Early each morning he and the other enslaved migrants rose early to again cook and clean prior to striking camp. The ritual repeated itself seemingly endlessly. "We all got tired plenty of times," Page acknowledged, "but we kept on walking to our new place."[32]

Page at the least enjoyed the advantage of knowing his traveling companions, whether fellow bondpersons or white Parkhills. This fact encouraged the provision of support from one bondservant to another. It also facilitated communication during each day's walk and, to some extent, socializing each evening. "Sometimes we would have a happy time at night around the camp fire talking about our families and the people we knew," Page recalled. As Pargas noted, most forced migrants faced the "daunting task of completely rebuilding social relationships that had been forcibly torn apart." And, over time, the close relationships developed on the long trip to Florida eventually helped enslaved migrants such as Page reconfigure family units and knit together the slave or quarters community in the new frontier home. This proved especially true for Page and another of Parkhill's single forced migrants. Some years later, he would marry Elizabeth, and the couple would spend the remainder of their lives together.[33]

Given Elizabeth's growing importance to Page, consideration must be afforded to her experience on the journey, especially with respect to one critical issue. Page's recollections did not speak to whether the enslaved girl suffered physical or other sexual abuse at the hands of their enslaver. Their Christian master, in this case, likely did not act in such a manner. His wife was present, and no evidence or insinuation that Parkhill ever exploited his female slaves in such a fashion has become available. Not all female forced migrants were so fortunate. Slave narratives are replete with stories of women raped at the hands of slave traders and owners on the journey from the Upper South. John Brown, also a Virginia forced migrant, recalled the rape of a girl on his party's journey to Georgia, detailing that the young woman was "forced to get up in the wagon with [the trader,] who brutally mis-used her, and permitted his companions to treat her in the same manner." Brown added, "This continued for several days, until we got to Augusta." According to Richard Macks, a former Maryland bondman, "The slave traders would buy . . . well developed young girls with fine physique to barter and sell. At one of these gatherings a colored girl, a mulatto, of fine stature and good looks, was put on sale. She was of high spirits and determined disposition. At night she was taken by the trader to his room to satisfy his bestial nature. She could not be coerced or forced, so she was attacked by him." Parkhill's religion compelled him to take care that the women under his control were not sexually abused. This act of paternalism not only protected the women; it also preserved the enslaver's investment.[34]

A separate issue confronted the party's white and black members. It involved obtaining adequate sustenance during long days of travel in sometimes very remote places. Page recollected that, at times during the extended trip, food became scarce. This necessitated seeking out wild game. He did not mention specific places, but he noted as well that he fished for food while the whites hunted. Sometimes, Parkhill would stop to negotiate with strangers. On occasion, the master also would "buy goods from the general stores along the way." Several incidents stuck with Page. In South Carolina, Parkhill bartered away pieces of household furniture for food. Another time, "[a] man wanted to trade food for one of the horses and the Col. told him no." Page observed that all party members shared the available food: "We always ate the same[,] wild meat and beans mostly[,] as Col. Parkhill and his family."[35]

The toll of extended travel weighed ever more heavily as the party slowly progressed toward Florida. And it certainly did not become easier or more pleasant with time's passage. The farther Page got from Richmond, the more upset he felt. In the circumstances the long journey made for tense moments between master and the enslaved. The first arrived well before the trip had reached its halfway point. "It had been now two weeks on the road," Page reflected, "and I hoped we would turn back to Virginny." Contrary to the suggestion made by Eugene Genovese and Elizabeth Fox-Genovese, the trying nature of frontier travel did not seem to bring enslaver and bondservants more closely together. Instead, it weakened the master-slave relationship, thereby weakening any semblance of Southern paternalism. "I was really sad to have to go so far from home," Page asserted. The enslaved migrant's eyes and those of his master sometimes did not meet for days; "Some days there were few words between me and the Col[.]," he reminisced. Despite raw emotions and repressed resentments, as Page acknowledged, "There was never any talk of hurting anyone or trying to run anywhere." He and other enslaved migrants opted not to resist or run away, as mentioned earlier, because they understood the consequences of doing so. Plus, they were in unfamiliar territory where well-armed white men more uncompromising than their master captured fugitives. And, as a literate man, Page had read about unsuccessful attempts to abscond. He knew that such escapes usually ended in suffering for those who chose the path of a fugitive.[36]

For Page, the journey from Virginia to Florida constituted a crucible from which the man he was to become began to emerge. His memories still filled with emotion when he attempted half a century later to recall its details. "As we traveled I hated the distance between me, my mother, and brother," he declared. "I tried to keep old Virginny in my mind and remember places that looked like her along the way." Understandably, the trip's conclusion produced an outpouring of pent-up sentiments and yearnings. "When I got to Florida I fell on my hands and knees crying and thanking the Lord for a safe journey," Page explained, "but I was also crying for my mother and brother." A fitting end to a long and painful ordeal.[37]

CHAPTER THREE

A New Environment and
Responsibilities as an Overseer

I know if Father had have known the discontent of the negroes, he certainly
would have had them brought back.

—A. H. Nuttall

When James Page arrived in the peninsula territory, he was a young man
who, like millions of other enslaved blacks, had to start his life anew with no
family members to support him. He had to face all of the insecurities of a
young man in a strange land. Page's worldview derived, in part, from his
master, but it also came from his reading and understanding of the Bible. As
a young man who believed in God, the future enslaved preacher needed the
Bible to help him understand why he was forced to move to a strange place
as well as why he had to lose his father, mother, and brother. Ever since he
was a young lad, Page noted, "I always [have liked] reading the Bible." As a
young man searching for comfort in a rapidly changing world, strength to
carry on could be found in scriptural passages that focus on faith and encouragement: Isaiah 41:10, which states that one should not be "dismayed,
for I am your God; I will strengthen you, [and] I will help you"; or Psalm
147:3, when God says he "heals the brokenhearted and binds up their
wounds"; and John 14:1, which declares, "Do not let your hearts be troubled.
You believe in God; believe also in me." Reading the Bible allowed Page to
hope and believe in a better future for himself, and it made the future enslaved preacher more determined to provide spiritual comfort to others in
his new Florida home.[1]

Whatever James Page expected to find upon his arrival in Middle Florida
at Christmastime 1827, reality must have startled him. Having lived his life
of nearly twenty years in the genteel environs of Richmond, Virginia, he now

Early Tallahassee circa late 1820s and early 1830s. State Archives of Florida, Florida Memory

found himself in a landscape not far removed from a howling wilderness. As promised in otherwise skewed promotional pieces in Virginia newspapers and Florida Land Agency advertisements, the countryside itself was lovely and blessed in many places with rich soil. Unfortunately, local society could hardly have been considered polished or sophisticated. Underscoring the point, the region's grand jury recently had detailed prevailing conditions: "We are sorry to find that in Tallahassee, a horrible state of things has existed for some time. The most flagrant breaches of the laws have taken place. The civil authority have [*sic*] in many instances been set at defiance; and the most riotous, immoral and disorderly proceedings have constantly taken place. It is truly lamentable to see such occurrences in any civilized country, but that it has occurred at the capital of our territory, where it is so particularly desirable to establish a character for morality and good order, is the more to be regretted, and shows a culpable neglect of duty of some of the civil officers, and particularly justices of the peace; some of whom appear to have been appointed without due, if any, regard to their qualifications."[2]

As Page quickly learned, the frontier conditions pervaded both town and countryside. Recently arrived settler Laura Wirt Randall described the scene in the territorial capital. "Tallahassee is a miserable looking place, certainly," she informed her father, US attorney general William Wirt. "I expected it to be merely a village, but I thought it w'd have a more agreeable appearance." A scattering of frame homes, three public taverns, and a new—if modest—two-story Capitol relieved the monotony of crude log structures. "[The frame houses] as well as the huts composing most of the rest of the town look old from not having been painted," Laura continued. "I see no stores—at least none that look like such—nor anything else that w'd make it look like a town." The few public accommodations then in operation happened to be overflowing at the time of the Parkhill party's arrival thanks to an ongoing session of the territorial council. Laura commented on her accommodations, "They understand nothing of comfort or cleanliness in this tavern, whilst it is the best in the place, we continue to use our own sheets & towels. At [the] table coffee is served in a *tea-pot* & the cooking *inedible*—I scarcely can prevail on myself, hungry as I may be, to taste the burnt up & dirty food before me."[3]

The countryside possessed virtually no amenities of civilized life, to which condition was added—as the grand jury noted—random and repeated acts of violence and criminality. A few weeks before Page and the other members of his party first trod Middle Florida's ground, for instance, the volatile scene erupted to the detriment of an innocent party of visiting Native Americans: "The Tallahassee Advocate mentions that some Indians being encamped in the neighborhood, selling venison, turkeys, &c[.,] three white men attempted to drive them off—they caught one of the Indian men and attempted to flog him, and, on his offering to defend himself, one of the party discharged a heavy load of buck shot into his back of which he died in a few minutes. Two of the murderers have been arrested and committed." Historian James M. Denham has attested to the persistence of such conditions through the following decades: he labeled the region "a rogue's paradise."[4]

Although the influx of settlers that brought Page to Middle Florida was increasing the area's population seemingly by the day, the density of settlement remained extremely low. When Spain transferred East and West Florida to the United States in 1821, the combined colonies contained only two significant towns. Suggesting the new territory's immense size, those *presidios*—St. Augustine and Pensacola—lay nearly four hundred miles apart. The peninsula's interior rested virtually empty, save for perhaps five thousand Seminole, Creek, and Mikasuki Indians with their Maroon allies and several independent villages of free blacks. Middle Florida previously had offered a home to vibrant Indian communities of Apalachees and other peoples, plus a string of Spanish missions and a stone fortification in St. Marks that guarded coastal access. Now, only isolated villages could be found. Most were temporary or seasonal. Tallahassee, the new territory's capital and the center of social and economic life for Middle Florida, did not exist until 1824 when Governor William Pope DuVal called it into being. He opted for a place situated a short distance from a village once called Tallahassi and the one-time missions of San Luis de Talimali and Purificatión de la Tama. The new town was located less than twenty miles north of St. Marks. To provide for governmental jurisdiction over the capital's vicinity, the council late the same year created Leon County. Early in 1827, the body recognized growth by splitting Leon. Its eastern range became Jefferson, named for Virginia native Thomas Jefferson. Its seat, found twenty-five miles or so east-northeast of Tallahassee, naturally was called Monticello. But the continued growth of Florida with the forced migration of enslaved laborers into the area, settler colonialism, and the unrelenting violent removal and genocide of Native Americans would lead eventually to the second of three race wars between land-hungry whites and the Seminoles and their black allies on the peninsula during the mid-1830s and early 1840s. With white colonists' quest for cheap land upon which to grow cotton, Florida became a microcosm of the South where, as historian Sven Beckert noted, "cotton and slavery would expand in lockstep" until the Civil War.[5]

With the influx of enslaved laborers and white migrants pouring into the territory after 1819, population reports on Middle Florida, indeed, spoke of impressive, if not spectacular, growth. When Leon's tax collector James Cameron canvassed his county in 1825, he found that it contained "996 people: 608 whites, 387 slaves and one 'free person of color.'" Tallahassee claimed about two hundred of that number. Given the movement into the area of planters from the Upper South such as John Parkhill, the numbers rose significantly in the years immediately following. By 1829 enslaved blacks reported for taxation in Leon had increased to 1,116 individuals out of a total population of 1,364 taxable inhabitants. As historian Ira Berlin noted for the South in general during the period from 1800 to 1860, Middle Florida was in the process of transmuting from a society "with slaves" to a "slave society" within ten years of its annexation. Census figures from 1830 bore out that conclusion. Leon then held around 3,300 whites and 3,150 slaves. In Tallahassee, 381 slaves were counted out of a total population of just under one thousand. Notably and as befitted a frontier region, demographics tilted toward men over women. An item published about the time Page reached his new home told the tale: "In the vessels below [in St. Marks] we shall receive a large acquisition to our society, of respectable families from Maryland and Virginia, and some young gentlemen, but we do not hear of any *young ladies*; and we are much surprised at it, for this certainly is the *best market* in the United States. We are quite mortified, every time we go up town, at seeing the heavy groups of long-faced, desponding bachelors, 'Wasting their sweets in the desert air.'"[6]

Page's recollections confirmed undesirable conditions, the rough-hewn quality of Middle Florida life, and the fact that even bondservants of a "humane" enslaver such as Parkhill always were compelled to bear greater burdens and suffer worse conditions than their owners. "When we got to Florida, the Col. and his family stayed with friends until a house was built for them, but we stayed in a little tent which was always cold," he reflected. "I did not like my new home at first and desire[d] to return to my home in Virginny because the ugly place at the time had nothing good to offer nobody. I tell you it was an ugly place to me. It seemed like a scary and mean place sometimes to me too."[7]

Page's stay in Tallahassee proper proved short. The Parkhill bondservants were soon pitched on the lands John had purchased earlier in 1827. They formed the basis of Tuscawilla plantation. The acreage lay along Black Creek twelve miles east-northeast of Tallahassee close to the Jefferson County line. Though crude structures quickly arose on the property, they brought little or no improvement to the living conditions of the extended family members. "So we started building a place to live in when we first got to Florida," Page detailed. "I helped my master drive the wagon. We [the enslaved people] all lived in a small one room cabin with a dirt floor, chimney, and a window on each side." Their new home was similar to the one described by Ohio former bondwoman Sarah Woods Burke: "We lived in a log cabin with the ground for floors and the beds were built against the walls, jus' like books." The Parkhills at first fared little better. One traveler described their new home charitably as a "large hewn log house." Thomas Randall recorded his impression of the residence the next year. "I was how-

A typical Florida cabin during the era of slavery with a chimney fireplace for cooking, heat, and other activities. State Archives of Florida, Florida Memory

ever interested yesterday in stopping to dinner at Mr. [John] Parkhill's," he informed his mother-in-law, "where I found him, his wife, and a large family of children . . . in a miserable log cabin of one room[,] . . . and they I hear left one of the very finest homes in Richmond." A local historian acknowledged, "The log-pen houses of these pioneers [relentlessly] admitted rivers of water and cold blasts of air through their many chinks."[8]

To the toll of crude and unfamiliar living conditions on Page and his fellow slaves could be added the shame of a repeat demonstration of Parkhill's willingness to dispose of or, at least, jeopardize his enslaved laborers to ease his own financial constraints. Upon arrival in Florida, Parkhill mortgaged

James, John, Mary, Sally, William, and Elizabeth, offering them as collateral to his father-in-law Charles Copland for a $2,500 loan. The borrowed money enabled the owner to purchase a 240-acre tract of land. The only family slave to escape the threat of removal by default was Mary's baby. This was not the last time that Parkhill manipulated ownership of his enslaved persons to his immediate financial gain. Ten years later he proved more than willing to trade on their value under even less secure conditions. In that instance Page, with other bondpeople, again was held as collateral. This time, however, the mortgage holder was no family relation of moderate disposition. Rather, Parkhill took out a $38,000 loan from a local bank of questionable stability during a national economic depression. These incidents were simply the beginning. Parkhill mortgaged the valuable bodies of James Page and others several more times in his climb as a cotton planter and banker up Middle Florida's social, political, and economic ladder. For Parkhill, the bondservants existed purely to facilitate his passage along the road to wealth.[9]

Beyond cynical greed, Parkhill's world, actions, and attitudes must be understood within the sphere of racial capitalism. For one thing, a near-mania that clouded perception of status and place in society afflicted many men of his time and place. Men like Parkhill knew, for example, that the more enslaved workers and land they owned, the more they were perceived by others as successful and wealthy, regardless of avowed moral and religious convictions. The condition at its height propelled an irresistible desire simply to own enslaved blacks, and its virulence accelerated with time's passage. Further, to administer the plantation or farm efficiently, an enslaver showed elite status by hiring an overseer to manage enslaved workers. With some exceptions, as will be seen with James Page and other enslaved men, overseers were usually white men, both young and old, who served as middlemen between slaveowners and enslaved workers. They were to manage the plantations profitably while maintaining a cheerful work force. This was simply hard to do. To help accomplish this impossible task, slave drivers, and bondservants themselves, sometimes were assigned by enslavers to help overseers manage other enslaved workers. Specifically, drivers were assigned by overseers, and sometimes owners, to push enslaved workers to accomplish certain tasks, and they also helped to preserve order in the quarters community when enslaved laborers returned from a toiling day's work. But overseers were left with the primary task of running smooth operations on many of the farms and plantations in the antebellum South.[10]

To achieve elite status in antebellum Southern society, an enslaver would have to hire an overseer to manage his or her enslaved workers, at least, that is what one man thought. The masterly storytelling of a pioneer who arrived near Alligator (today's Lake City) as a boy not long after Page settled into his humble log cabin at Tuscawilla highlighted the malady. "We [the narrator and friends whom he considered 'rich men'] would go for three or four days on a camp hunt, having a nigger to drive the wagon, carry the grub and haul in the meat," George Gillett Keen related. "When the day's hunt was over, supper eaten and all seated around the fire, the subject of farming was introduced. One would say, I've got the best overseer I ever had; another would say, my overseer is a worthless fellow, a third would say I am pretty well satisfied with my overseer, and so on. I would sit there like a bump on a log. You bet I never wanted anything worse in my life than I wanted a plantation of niggers so I could talk about my overseer. I had some niggers, but not enough to have an overseer; that's what worried me. When hunting time come round I was in but when overseer talk was the topic of the day I was ten feet above high water mark on dry land. I wanted niggers. How to get them was the question." In such a climate, John Parkhill's veneer of independence would be fabricated upon his overseer, Page, for he lived and prospered through the hard work of his enslaved black plantation manager. In some instances, the enslaver depended more on his overseer for survival than the other way around.[11]

Despite Parkhill's cruelty, Page would have been considered more fortunate than many others. Former bondman Robert Glenn was, for example, "sold three times in one day" during his relocation from North Carolina to Kentucky. Unlike Glenn and thousands of his counterparts who repeatedly were sold and forcibly moved, Page's migration to Florida was a onetime experience. The future enslaved preacher did not become liquid capital or "walking cash" by constantly being resold. Instead, he lived with the same enslaver family until freedom came. When times grew hard financially, Page also did not have to fear that Parkhill would take him, his family, and other slaves to Texas ("Gone to Texas") as did the chattel of some enslavers who hurriedly relocated to avoid creditors seeking to repossess collateral for nonpayment of "slave mortgages." Page's course proved fortunate even within Parkhill's extended family. "Servants were sometimes sold," Page admitted, "but most were able to stay on the place."[12]

However, Page's distaste for his new Florida home turned out to be a sentiment held broadly—at least early on in their residence—by Middle Florida enslaved blacks. Many wanted to return to their former states of residence, and some never identified themselves as Floridians. The Nuttall family bondservants offered an excellent case on point. The family had settled in Leon County, where they built El Destino plantation about the same time as the Parkhills established Tuscawilla. That problems developed among the enslaved workers they had removed from Virginia was evidenced in communications between A. H. and William B. Nuttall. "I know if Father had have known the discontent of the negroes," A. H. Nuttall bluntly informed his brother on one occasion, "he certainly would have had them brought back." The surviving record fails to reveal whether the enslaved people in question ever returned to Virginia, but it is not likely that they did. Much as was true for Page, they probably found themselves compelled to adapt to the new homes and conditions. "Florida would [eventually] grow on me some," Page allowed, "the more I lived in the place."[13]

Several factors complicated the process of adaptation for Page. He and the other Parkhill bondpeople obviously faced adjustment to a new environment that they could not control. Unlike the circumstances confronting the master and his family, they for the most part had to rebuild their lives without the support of parents and family members. Page's father had drowned in West Africa, and his mother and brother had been sold away. Forced migration had disrupted these and other emotional ties, yet no extant documentation suggests that Parkhill ever attempted to alleviate Page's loss or the consequent emotional burdens that he carried. Particularly, the owner made no effort to reclaim James's mother or brother. Within the polite society with which Parkhill identified, a timely attempt to bring them to Tuscawilla would have been a good humanitarian gesture on his part. In one particular case, Thomas Randall notably did what Parkhill refused to do. The future judge had arrived in Middle Florida the same year as had Parkhill. He had purchased in Maryland twelve bondservants for use on his new lands. When the enslaved workers arrived in 1828, a disgruntled male named David was among them. He communicated directly to Randall the misery caused by the sale of his wife and small children to someone else. Because of the bondman's determined pleas, David's owner ultimately reunited the enslaved man with his wife and three of their younger children. "I regret I was not at home to witness the union of David & his wife to give you the interesting particulars," Randall later informed his wife. "They are very happy, I am sure." On the one hand, Parkhill was a rather typical slaveholder, because most people of his ilk saw no economic reason to reunite enslaved family members after they had been sold. But, on the other hand, Randall was atypical in that few enslavers ever sought to reunite enslaved families once they left the auction block.[14]

With little such support to be expected from Parkhill, Page employed his keen intelligence to consider his position and blaze a path forward. He may have believed Florida to be a wild, dreary, and uncertain place devoid of civilization. Yet experience had produced for him certainties regarding his owner. James Page might not be able to predict what would come of his life, but he knew—based upon his master's past behavior and his declared dreams of becoming rich in the wilds of frontier Florida—that by hard work, overt obedience, and generating profits he could make himself indispensable. Those constituted the day-to-day realities with which he dealt. The opportunities that Parkhill perceived for the financial independence he craved meant drudgery and backbreaking work for enslaved persons such as Page. The enslaved overseer knew from bitter experience that working hard did not always guarantee security of family and home. Still, his only available recourse was to hope that it would in his case. "I always wanted to please Col. Parkhill in all [the] things I did," he later observed. By working diligently and prolifically, Page believed that he could please his master and avoid furnishing him pretext for causing him harm.[15]

James's approach responded to Parkhill's self-image and the non-cynical side of his ideological makeup. The cotton planter and putative Christian wanted to be thought of as a benevolent patriarch and not just an enslaver. He envisioned himself the epitome of paternalism. He yearned to be perceived as a good and mild-mannered slaveholder, an image that he endeavored to project to the public. His neighbor Richard J. Mays articulated an ideal formulation of this viewpoint when instructing his heirs on how to tend to his bondservants after his death. He requested specifically that they be treated "not as property, but as human beings, to be cared for as such." He added, "They must not be neglected, it is a duty sanctioned by your interest and [their] welfare." Mays clearly recognized that a reciprocal relationship between bondservants and slaveholders was necessary for the slave system to function smoothly. Mays's words from the grave rang hollow, as he made no effort to free any of his slaves before or after his death. His words simply meant that treating enslaved workers decently will make you a lot of money. Page appealed to that logic. Desirous of building security and enjoying rewards, the enslaved overseer encouraged his master to love him like a son by attempting to run a profitable plantation. This naturally appealed to

Parkhill at the same time as his cynical side appreciated that Page was obligating himself to work diligently. As a heartless enslaver at times, the magnanimity that Page hoped to appreciate in his master unfortunately, as will be see again later, did not always materialize. The absence of physical violence or runaways on Parkhill's plantations during his lifetime, though, suggested two significant things. First, Parkhill's treatment of enslaved blacks on a day-to-day basis, on the surface, appeared tolerable. Second, beneath the surface, bondservants clearly understood that if they refused to work, misbehaved, or tried to abscond, they would be sold and thereby separated from loved ones. Slaves knew also their enslaver could be unfeeling when it came to his own economic self-interest. Indeed, Parkhill did not have to use his hands to punish his enslaved people physically but instead used his mouth to make them stand in fear.[16]

Meanwhile, conflicts of morality, religion, and action bedeviled John Parkhill. It was evident in his personal behavior, and Page tried to turn the situation to his advantage. To some extent these conflicts, more than the paternalistic image he tried to cultivate, ironically marked Parkhill's public persona. As a practicing Presbyterian and elder in the church, his actions contrary to faith vexed and confounded him. Historians have noted the troubles endured by other men as a result of holding enslaved people. Religious historian Terry Matthews discussed the dynamic while considering James Oakes's landmark study, *The Ruling Race*: "Many [slaveholders] became convinced they were going to hell. Yet there was too much money to be made. As a result, they could not bring themselves to give up such a lucrative system. Slavery became a political question that they could not control. One's faith could only be applied to issues of personal morality like drinking, card-play, and sex." Parkhill's daughter Harriet R. Parkhill often commented on her father's obsession with Bible reading. Contemporaries attested to his anxieties about how he lived his life as an enslaver. Some described him as a man unsure of himself. A staunch Bible-toting Christian, the slaveholder knew the Scriptures well. Galatians 6:7–8 particularly may have fortified him: "Do not be deceived: God cannot be mocked. A man reaps what he sows. The one who sows to please his sinful nature, from that nature will reap destruction." Historian Edward E. Baptist noted the dilemma: "Slavery was God's will. To worry about slavery was to doubt God. To oppose it was heresy." But many of the fears and apprehensions experienced by slaveholders like Parkhill did manifest in the widespread emancipation of enslaved persons during the antebellum period. Enslavers such as Parkhill found it more important to project the public persona of a Christian man than to actually live a benevolent life.[17]

As Parkhill's anxieties mounted with the passing years, his dependence on Page also increased. A newspaper published at the time of Parkhill's death referred to him as "so distrustful of himself as to be often disturbed by doubt and fear." The crisis within Parkhill refused to be quelled even when mainstream churchmen strove to offer solace. Many ministers—North and South—in fact defended slavery as an institution sanctioned in the Bible. Yet there were certain white clergymen who went even further by insisting that God sanctioned slavery. And if they did not verbally endorse it, they gave their approval by remaining quiet on the subject. An eyewitness noted that "when I reflect that the ministers of the gospel, for the most part, are as silent on this subject [of slavery] as the dead, I tell you, the blood runs cold in my veins." According to John Hope Franklin, "Slavery had become as much a part of the religious orthodoxy of the South as the Creation in the Book of Genesis or Armageddon in the Book of Revelations. The work of promoting and defending slavery, when entrusted in the southern clergy could not have been in safer hands." Historian David Blight added, "Slavery in America was a national sin with many complicitous institutions, none more so than churches and the clergy." When ministers occasionally switched from preaching about drinking and similar sinful subjects to questions about the morality of slavery, though, slaveholders and their sympathizers saw nothing but troublemaking preachers who had moved on to "meddling." Meanwhile, men such as Page's enslaver hosted an internal war. Devils often won these battles, but angels refused to concede the fight. Those men, as Parkhill, paid with their peace of mind. Perhaps Page's influence on his conflicted master came not through his words or deeds but through his mere presence as an intelligent man held in servitude simply because of his race to exploit his labor. While slaveholders and their supporters used the Bible to sanction slavery, James Page would use the same Holy Book to help liberate enslaved souls.[18]

⌒

Page's living environment naturally influenced his daily life as he campaigned to please his master and thereby secure his own future. At the least it represented a dramatic comedown from one of the finest residences in Richmond. Historians generally have described frontier slave cabins with the adjective "crude." Middle Florida slaveholder John Finlayson's buildings, which were typical for the region in the late 1820s and early 1830s, consisted of one-room cabins built with "whole logs notched together at the corners, with pine straw and mud to close the cracks." On larger plantations, cabins were situated in "slave quarters" that could be seen from the master's home or the house occupied by the overseer. Page did not identify the location of the cabin that he and other bondservants initially lived in upon their arrival. He did remember its single room, dirt floor, chimney, and windows on each side. Historian Julia Floyd Smith reported that roofs at the Finlayson plantation "were covered with wooden shingles and shutters were hung on the windows." She added, "The chimney, exterior to the house, was made of brick or, more frequently, of split sticks, laid horizontally and plastered with mud, and the fireplace opening inside was covered with clay."[19]

Open fireplaces often served as a center of activity for slave cabin residents if the weather permitted. In Florida this meant if the interior temperature had not risen too high to be unbearable. The two windows in the Tuscawilla cabin ensured air flow but likely did little to cool the space or its inhabitants. A breeze in the shade out of doors must have been far more appealing during much of the year. Fireplaces, in any event, were essential. Occupants utilized them, among other things, for cooking, drying clothes, and as light for all activities after sunset and before sunrise. Virginia former bondwoman Georgina Giwebs, recalled that "de only light we had wuz from the fire-place." Page had no other light for reading and writing. Significant risks contrasted with the benefits, however. Constructed of mud and sticks, fireplaces created serious fire hazards when they failed to draw properly. The bigger the fire, the greater the risk. On the one hand, the nature and quantity of furnishings, too, made the dwellings either more or less congenial for occupants. On the other hand, former Florida bondman Claude A. Wilson commented that the furniture he remembered consisted merely of the "cheapest and barest necessities." One student of the subject detailed, somewhat more generously, a typical arrangement: "Furniture inside the cabins was of the simplest, consisting generally of beds, chairs, and boxes. Most of this was home-made. The beds were frequently bunks built into the walls, with bottom solid, slatted, or corded." On a happier note, the dwellings at Tuscawilla became safer and more comfortable over time, while allowing more privacy. At least one Jefferson County bondman's experience suggested as much. As Douglas Parish remembered, his master "gave them comfortable quarters in which to live."[20]

While Page and his fellow Parkhill bondservants needed shelter from the elements, they also required sustenance for their bodies. Customarily, one day a week—what Frederick Douglass called "Allowance Day"—was designated for issuance of food rations. Page substantiated this weekly schedule and specified that distributions came on Sundays after church: "I remember when it came to giving our food and other things [the Col.] gave them out himself." He did not preserve a description of the kind of food or quantity given. But former enslaved preacher Rev. Silas Jackson, who lived in Virginia during slavery, did. He claimed in an interview that "on Saturday each slave was given 10 pounds [of] corn meal, a quart of black strap, 6 pounds of fat back, 3 pounds of flour and vegetables, all of which were raised on the farm." Generally, Southern enslaved people received three to four pounds of pork, usually bacon, a pound of corn meal, and certain vegetables when available, such as sweet and white potatoes, peas, cabbage, collard greens, turnips, pumpkins, water melons, squash, onions, and corn. Under the guise of paternalism, Parkhill attempted to show his magnanimity to bondservants by giving out food himself, as if to suggest his supreme power as the giver of all good things. Most enslaved persons knew this to be a smokescreen since the enslaver did not care to know any of them personally, except, perhaps, the Page family. Most of the plantation's enslaved workers likely held the same feelings toward the master. They knew better than to believe the benevolent image that he projected and had learned by bitter experience his willingness to break up their families if it benefited his financial condition do so.[21]

The weekly distribution that Page received constituted only a portion of the supplies upon which he and other bondservants depended. Without the material conditions and time granted, in large part, by their masters, enslaved people knew that there was not much they could truly do on their own. Specifically, bondservants understood that their enslavers owned the land, the animals, the tools, and other materials they needed to improve their own lives. Yet, within the world that slaveholders had created, enslaved persons sought to create their own world, which focused on interdependence. And within that world, enslaved peopled sought to resist the master's total hegemony over their lives by doing things for themselves and others in the quarters community as much as they could. They did not, therefore, rely exclusively upon the enslaver for sustenance. Exercising agency within whatever latitude they were allowed or assumed, they took charge of their own lives. Historian Philip Morgan pointed out, for instance, that bondservants commonly worked their own garden plots to supplement their diets. Page kept such a plot. He also maintained a small chicken coop near his cabin. Middle Florida bondwoman Mary Minus Biddie recollected that, in similar circumstances, her "Pappy" nurtured "a separate garden" at night by the light of fires mounted upon "huge scaffolds." Uncle Demps at El Destino recalled that each bondservant had access to one-quarter acre for gardening. A Florida overseer asserted that enslaved workers had permission "one day in the Spring to plant [their gardens] and one in the fall to reap" their crops. Bondservants such as Page, who claimed control of gardens or kept animals for food, established a degree of quasi-independence that loosened the total dominance of their enslavers. Additionally, given that most Middle Florida slaveholders focused primarily on cotton production, owners evidenced little or no interest in other agricultural crops. Enslaved blacks who took the initiative to cultivate gardens thus did slaveholders a favor by feeding themselves. Some even sold food in the underground economy. Recognizing the reality of daily life and custom, Florida law, created largely by powerful enslavers, permitted enslaved persons to use tickets when selling their produce. The less money spent maintaining enslaved workers, the more that could go to cotton production.[22]

Page's owner, too, bore responsibility for clothing his workers. With the territory's mild climate, Florida bondpeople may have braved the elements somewhat more easily than could their counterparts elsewhere in the region. Yet, as was true throughout most of the South, bondservants such as Page received clothing twice a year, during the winter and summer. Parkhill purchased most of the shoes from Bainbridge, Georgia. His factor John Daffin, who represented the interests of the slaveholder for a commission, alerted Parkhill on one occasion that he could sell both "cloth and negro shoes delivered to Tallahassee . . . at the following prices—Namby, Negro, Kersy at 30 cents per yard, Negro Shoes at $1.25 per pair." Page detailed the ritual that involved his master giving out clothes and shoes: "Most of the servants would run to the Col. to get the things he was giving out. But I waited until everyone got what he had for them, then I would walk and get what was left. It didn't matter what I got. Elizabeth [by then, his wife] could sew clothes and would make them fit me." The master's "hand-outs" did not overly concern Page and other bondservants since they could supplement their material needs in the internal underground economy.[23]

As personal servants to the Parkhill family, the Pages, in a manner of speaking, became what Frederick Douglass called a part of the "black aristocracy" on the plantation. These were persons who possessed at least some limited degree of independence, mobility, and power in the quarters community.

And Page's degree of power over other enslaved blacks and his general independence heightened as the years passed. House servants, for example, generally tended to fare better than their counterparts in the fields, a fact that made a considerable difference in Page's daily life. His future bride, Elizabeth, worked primarily in the Parkhill home, and over time, he served as his master's overseer, driver, and confidant. Given the perquisites that he gained, many on the plantation perceived him and his family as "special." He came to sit atop what some historians have called a "limited hierarchy within the slave community." Yet bondservants like Page were viewed by some enslaved persons as abusive sell-outs, Uncle Toms, accommodationists, and mouthpieces for their enslavers. Stories are replete with former slaves' descriptions of such figures. Former bondwoman Annie Young Henson recalled that an old "colored man by the name of Peter Taylor" was the mouthpiece for the master. She noted his "orders was [*sic*] law, if you wanted to please Mistress and Master, obey old Peter . . . , [for] the slaves worked from sunup to sundown." Former bondservant Jane Johnson recollected that enslaved workers on her plantation hated their black overseer: "De overseer was a nigger and de meanest man, white or black, I ever see. Dat nigger would strut 'round wid a leather strap on his shoulders and would whip de other slaves unmerciful[ly]." Former slave Liza Jones reminisced that her father, George Price, was the chosen "boss nigger on de place" who gave orders to the enslaved laborers. Page even remembered the built-up frustration and dislike for him during the Civil War years, when he noted that "some of the servants would get up real close to me and tell me I couldn't do anything about them leaving the plantation." Most bondpeople showed some dislike, at times, for black overseers, mammies, and house servants due, in part, to their quasi-independence, power within the black community, and close association with white authority figures.[24]

The flexibility that Page ultimately enjoyed to move unescorted around Florida and the region led some to consider him a "free man." Although not under the constant eyes of his enslaver, the fact remained nonetheless that Page existed under the daily scrutiny of other whites wherever he traveled. The slaveholder expressed care for his special enslaved laborer but controlled his private life as with the other plantation bondservants. "The Col. knew everything I was doing," the enslaved overseer/preacher admitted. So, Page's special status—important as it may have been—ran only so far. He, like other enslaved people, still required permission for keeping a garden and chicken coop, accepting tips from house guests, and selling or giving away food he had produced with his own hands. As Edward Baptist correctly noted, "The literate Page always deferred to white men and women, and never publicly criticized slavery." Living near his owner in fear of saying or doing anything that might upset any member of the white family—or being perceived as too independent, or uppity, or arrogant—would have been traumatic for many men and women in the quarters community. Page clearly understood the parameters of Parkhill's hegemony. The life of the enslaved preacher/overseer says much about the complex interlocking worlds of the enslaved and the enslaver. Understanding his master as he did, Page's ability to withstand the pressures of his position as overseer as well as he did testifies profoundly to his character and strength.[25]

As his owner permitted Page increasing—if not unlimited—mobility, experiences away from home necessarily left impressions on the man and influenced his development. His most common travels involved movement in the plantation's immediate vicinity. Which is to say that, as Tuscawilla expanded and the area's population grew, Page inevitably met fellow bondservants who were not owned by the Parkhills. These occasions afforded all concerned opportunities to assess one another and, possibly, establish ties that might lead to marriage and family. Contrary to findings by historians such as Ira Berlin that "slaves from the North, Chesapeake, and Lowcountry mixed easily," Page at first found such encounters unsatisfying. "The first few black servants we first [met] were not too friendly to us," he insisted. "I wondered why they did not like us." Page could not appreciate that, to many of his fellow bondservants, he—as a literate house servant and experienced store clerk—appeared almost alien and of questionable loyalties. To many enslaved persons in the area, James Page was just different. Former bondman Louis Napoleon attested to Page standing above others because "he could read and write." Former bondservant Amanda McCray, though, may have best stated the case. She remembered Page as a proud man who went about "'all dressed up' in a frock coat and store-bought shoes." Amanda added, "He was more than a little conscious of this and held in awe by the others." Few Middle Florida enslaved blacks of the time enjoyed such benefits or possessed such skills. According to historian Terra W. Hunter, "By 1860, 5 percent of the slave population had defied the laws and learned to read and write." Like some enslaved persons, Page, indeed, considered himself to be a "very special" man. Certainly, there was no black man more recognizable in Florida and other parts of the South during the antebellum period than the enslaved preacher, overseer, and race leader. And Page, for his part, assumed for some time that "no other servant in the territory could read but himself." As he found out over time, he was not. Ultimately, the problem of rapport eased as years passed and area population mounted, or so Page thought. "I didn't feel so lonely when I see so many of them," he acknowledged of the newcomers. The numbers may not have held the key. Rather, it was how Page reacted to their resistance. He soon reached out to those who had held him at arm's length. By the time he no longer felt "so lonely," he was bringing solace to them as their pastor.[26]

Before Page truly could focus on personal concerns such as ministerial aspirations or even rebuilding familial ties torn asunder in his uprooting from Virginia, his circumstances required that he first reciprocate the "goodness and kindness" of his master by agreeing to serve as plantation overseer. Parkhill shrewdly assessed early on that by drafting Page for the work he could save money and, at the same time, obtain the services of a man who could effectively motivate plantation bondservants to work diligently and productively. In a manner, Parkhill also understood clearly that he too was not a free man in the truest sense of the word, for he and his white family depended on the labor of Page and other enslaved laborers for their very livelihood. Without the labor of enslaved workers, the Parkhill family would not have been able to live an ostentatious lifestyle by the late 1840s.[27]

The surviving record does not reveal whether the owner ordered his bondman to take the job. Page recorded, "I agreed to help the Col. run the place." He also once remarked, "I agreed to be the overseer because there was no one else he could trust to get the work done." He had no meaningful choice in the matter. Tallahassee may have been the capital of Florida, but for Page as the overseer, the Parkhill plantation had become the capital of his world. He would join the ranks of thousands of other such managers during the antebellum period. It seems apparent, though, that Page quickly grasped the implications for his own identity, security, and status. He needed, of course, to serve his master well. This meant coaxing enslaved laborers to work hard when they possessed little or no incentive to do so. Plantation profitability demanded efficient management, and the new overseer well understood that his owner demanded profitability. The enslaved overseer quickly learned that he and the enslaved people on the plantation had competing interests. On the one hand, Page needed to grow as much cotton as possible to maximize profits for his enslaver. On the other hand, the bondservants were motivated to do just enough to appease their owner and overseer, while developing private lives that allowed them some independence, agency, and control over their bodies, environs, and time. Page accordingly undertook to exercise power over the lives of his fellow bondservants in the fields and their homes as best he could. He made sure they were up in the morning for work and back in their cabins at a certain time in the evening to rest prior to the next day's toil. He set work assignments and had to take away privileges when cooperation was not forthcoming. All the while, he had to take care not to overly intrude upon personal lives. Circumstances, therefore, constrained Page to project his power astutely—too little would lead to poor production and, consequently, smaller cotton yields. Good management required fine tuning to maximize productivity. "Overseeing was the hardest thing I ever did," Page acknowledged. As overseer, he came to understand clearly that control of workers' labor and private time would ultimately define his success or failure in the eyes of his enslaver. He had, indeed, his work cut out for him.[28]

The greatest challenge may have been that neither Parkhill nor Page knew anything about cotton cultivation, plantation management, or supervision of slave gangs. Parkhill's experience involved merchandizing in sophisticated Richmond. Page had aided him as a clerk and general assistant. At Tuscawilla, in the early going, the blind led the blind. Page as overseer thus had to learn quickly how to grow profitably. The responsibility must have weighed heavily on him, even if his owner was endeavoring to do his part. Page, in his early and midtwenties, had to learn the ins and outs of cotton cultivation as quickly possible, for his life and the lives of the other enslaved workers in the Tuscawilla quarters literally depended upon it. If he did not manage well and the enslaved laborers did not plant and pick cotton as required, all could face the auction block as the owner liquidated his assets to cover otherwise unpayable debts. Page knew as much when he asserted, "I wanted to help the Col. grow lots of cotton." The ramifications for not doing the job well stood out in high relief.[29]

The learning curve turned out to be a steep one. As Page once told a friend, "I knew nothing about growing cotton." Given that the enslaved workers Parkhill purchased or leased likely came from the Chesapeake region where tobacco was grown, they were as uninformed as the overseer and owner. Page's mastery of the subject is yet another sign of his keen intelligence. He left no record as to who taught him. He would have been able to read about workable techniques in agricultural publications. His personal library of more than four hundred books and magazines, held at the time of his death, aided him in this regard. And he learned principally through trial and error. The triumph, in any event, was not one that he savored. "I taught others how to plant and pick cotton after I learn[ed] to do it," he reflected. "But, I liked working in my garden more than working cotton." Some of his approaches varied from traditional practices. For instance, overseers typically pushed laborers to pick an average of 110 pounds of cotton per day in Florida. For example, on the George Noble plantation in Middle Florida, enslaved workers were generally flogged thirty times for picking less. Setting such an arbitrary goal, though, did not suit Page's style. "I tried to get them to pick as much cotton as they could do each day," he explained.[30]

As time passed Page grew more comfortable with his identity and status as enslaved overseer. A part of Page's manhood began to emerge when taking on the task of overseeing fellow bondservants. Eventually, it became a matter of pride. "I did something," he declared, "that no other negro did." Much like his incorrect assumption that he was the "only" or "one of few" literate bondservants in Florida, he again erred in believing that "no other negro" had served as an enslaved overseer but himself. At various times enslaved black overseers labored on plantations as close as adjacent Jefferson County. William Wirt, for one, employed an enslaved overseer to manage his bondservants. His son-in-law Thomas Randall did the same. Their Jefferson County neighbor Sheriff John S. Taylor vested his black enslaved supervisor for years with the responsibility of running his plantation. Relocated from South Carolina to Florida after the Civil War, onetime bondman Randall Lee remembered that his "father and mother were considered lucky. His father was overseer [on the plantation] and his mother was a waitress." On the plantation of Virginia-born Kidder Meade Moore, a bondservant named Bob served both as a wagoner and an overseer who received orders from his master to pass on to other enslaved workers under his charge. In Jefferson County, though, some white residents at one point reacted in alarm to the steadily increasing number of black enslaved overseers. In defying the law by entrusting such responsibilities to enslaved blacks, slaveholders such as Parkhill, Wirt, Randall, and others throughout the South evidenced openly their willingness to serve their own financial interests above all else. Common countrymen may have been upset with black enslaved overseers and drivers running plantations in the region, but it really made little difference what they thought, for slaveholders made the laws and, when to their advantage, enforced them.[31]

Page developed a nervous ambivalence about whom he wanted to please: his master, his fellow slaves, or his own self-interest. It proved a conundrum never fully resolved. His actions, though, demonstrated repeated instances of favoritism or compromise on all sides of the equation. With so many people depending upon him, he grappled constantly with the choices that he faced. "I always tried to do right by the master and my people," he insisted. Although he did not carry a gun or use a whip to make enslaved laborers work harder and faster, the evidence of how bondservants viewed their treatment by Page is sparse, consisting principally of Page's own admission that some bondservants held lifelong grudges against him. Unfortunately, the degree to which such attitudes prevailed cannot be known.[32]

Clearly, at different times and places enslaved workers resented white and black overseers who abused their power in attempts to extract pounds of flesh from their workers. The case of Henry Bibb helps to illuminate the point. "Their [the owners' and overseers'] plan of getting quantities of cotton," he recorded, "is to extort it by the lash." Former bondservant Margrett Nickerson similarly recalled enslavers and overseers, as well as drivers, prodding workers to produce more by whipping or threating to whip them. She recalled particularly a situation involving her sister. Holly would not work harder or faster despite being beaten. Margrett related that her belligerent sibling would resist the overseers' demands by standing up to them, and when they "git behin' her, she'd git behin' dem; she wuz dat subbo'n and when dey would beat her she wouldn' holler and jes take it and go on." At nearby Chemonie plantation the overseer regularly lashed slaves for "coming up short" on their cotton picking.[33]

Contrarily, Page did not employ the more flexible task system utilized in northeast Florida or the South Carolina rice fields. The enslaved laborers he managed worked the cotton fields in gangs, as was true for most of the area's large plantations. As also was true for enslaved workers in much of the cotton belt, Tuscawilla's labor force usually worked from sunup to sundown with a half day off on Saturdays. Sundays, too, usually were spent away from the fields if not from Page. As he recalled, "I would preach to them." While the enslaved preacher may not have misused his power over bondservants who came up short on their work assignments, it remains questionable whether he abused it in coercing them to attend his services on Sundays for fear of punishment or having privileges revoked. Did they believe this was something they simply had to do as bondservants under his control? Regardless of the consequences, some enslaved persons still rejected Page despite his efforts to manage or to Christianize them. As an overseer and preacher, Page lived an excruciatingly complex and nerve-racking life.[34]

Other managers and overseers experienced the same nervousness as did Page. They oftentimes lived a precarious existence because they had to serve as a "buffer between the estate owner and the laborers they were employed to supervise." Historian William Scarborough asserted, "No figure occupied a position of greater importance in the managerial hierarchy of the southern plantation system than did the overseer." As aptly noted by historian Michael Wayne, the overseer "had to produce enough cotton to satisfy his employer while keeping at least a semblance of harmony and order among the slaves." But the greatest anxieties that overseers bore typically grew largely out of attempts to please the plantation owner. A surviving letter from 1836 written by Louis Goldsborough referring to his overseer of about one year highlights the tensions. "W. Barronton, I greatly regret to say, has behaved by no means [well] during my absence to St. Joseph," Louis informed his wife, Elizabeth Wirt Goldsborough. "He has not only neglected his duty, but he gives me strong reason to suspect his honesty. My intention is to dismiss him the moment the crop of cotton is made. . . . I would do it instantly if I knew of any other person I could employ in his stead, as to make the matter short, I am quite satisfied in my mind that he is an arrogant old rogue and a scoundrel, and requires me to watch him with the eyes of an Argus." Nancy DeLaughter meanwhile fired her son Amon because she thought he had been ineffective, but she hired him back a week later. Historian Michael Wayne summed up the predicament most white overseers found themselves in, noting "the high turnover rate for overseers on most plantations proves that this was an almost impossible task for any length of time." Black plantation managers such as Page understood that overseers, regardless of their race, faced very challenging jobs.⁑

CHAPTER FOUR

Challenges, Calamities, and the Ministry

I stop[ped] one day to here [*sic*] this Black man preach. They called him Father Page. I got the Lord that day, and he took me down to the water in a creek.

—Jack Sheppard

James Page began his new Florida life as a man profoundly shaped by his Virginia experiences, but, as of the dawn of the new year 1828, he encountered novel and sometimes persistent problems in a rough Middle Florida plantation region for which he was little prepared. Finding or creating helpful insights and workable solutions to fresh challenges thus became his central focus. The world in miniature that Page would help to build could not, at least for a good while, reflect the one that he left behind in Virginia. Instead, its design had to meet the different demands of a refashioned life within a starkly alternative environment. As a part of a pioneering generation of enslaved migrants who arrived in frontier Florida during the early nineteenth century, he and others had no choice but to rely in good part upon their own wherewithal and ingenuity to survive. The first year alone bested many who tried. Thus, when in March 1829 "two inches" of unusual snow blanketed Middle Florida to remind Page chillingly of his origins, the now-tested overseer necessarily ignored the nostalgic call and continued to direct his attention to the master's affairs. Survival meant focus on the immediate. To the extent that he entertained dreams, they centered now not on a return to the old home but on finding time to pursue a personal agenda that, among other things, allowed him to preach.[1]

Many of the problems that concerned Page in the years that ensued frustratingly stemmed from actions, activities, and personalities with which he was not familiar or else of which he possessed only hazy knowledge. Almost coincidental with Middle Florida's snowstorm in March 1829, for instance, Andrew Jackson began to revolutionize national politics after wresting the presidency from John Quincy Adams. His Indian Removal Act subsequently drove more than sixty thousand Native Americans from their homes. As historian Sven Beckert noted, "The coercion and violence required to mobilize slave labor was matched only by the demands of an expansionist war against indigenous people." The Texas Revolution of 1835 then highlighted the ongoing flood of white migration facilitated also by the forcible movement of Native populations off their lands to make room for slavery's unrelenting growth. European developments meanwhile drove the growth that spurred this migration. The Industrial Revolution was advancing in Great Britain and on the Continent, sparking progress that drew untold numbers of workers to urban centers who, in turn, demanded cheap cotton clothing. In territorial Florida, though, the black/Indian revolt known as the Second Seminole War flared from 1835 to 1842. Also reverberating throughout Florida were dynamics produced by the rise of Tallahassee's unstable Union Bank; the wheeling, dealing, and unbridled cronyism that marked its operations and those of other banks; and fallout of the national economic depression known as the Panic of 1837. These factors and more directly and indirectly affected the lives of Middle Florida slaveholders and the enslaved.[2]

The economic depression especially imposed a chilling effect. Page recorded the sadness that the times evoked: "Sometimes [the master] had to [sell] some servants. I hated to see them leave some of their folks behind." As will be seen, the Union Bank's collapse and ill-advised agreements related to it proved the culprit. Knowing that it would affect bondservants and their families, John Parkhill had forged deals with his brother Samuel and his father-in-law William Copland to "auction off" their valuable bodies in the event any of them ran into financial trouble.[3]

While such circumstances formed a context for the problems with which Page contended, his concerns necessarily kept his attention aimed unwaveringly at his overseer work. In that capacity he bore a plethora of responsibilities. First and foremost, the enslaved overseer had to keep the master abreast of all plantation operations. Page summed up what that meant: "I took care of everything on the plantation for Col. Parkhill." Indeed, his complex managerial duties included, but by no means were limited to, seeing to the overall well-being of his fellow enslaved human beings, tending the livestock, and superintending the workers' labor schedules and performance. The overseer also had to be sufficiently knowledgeable about the medical condition of the laborers to direct treatment or, possibly, consult a physician. Along the way he, with the other enslaved workers, contended with the danger of contracting malaria and other diseases while cultivating cotton. The possibility constituted a real threat, as malaria ravaged Middle Florida during the two years after Page's arrival there. Meanwhile, he executed an essential function for the master and his family that literally came down to a matter of life and death. He protected them from slave violence, unrest, and rebellion.[4]

Given his master's expressed desire to increase his land holdings and enlarge his slave-labor pool on the road to fabled wealth, Page's role as overseer became even more complex over time. At the beginning, at least as indicated by tax rolls from 1829, Parkhill owned six slaves (Mary's baby not included) and 240 acres of land. Whether he leased fields or enslaved laborers at that time is not known. In any event, the totals mounted steadily over the years. Additionally, Page's owner eventually added a second or "auxiliary" plantation half a dozen miles south of Tallahassee near what became the resort community of Bel Air. Parkhill's conspicuous consumption would continue unabated. Of the owner's ultimate holdings, Page later boasted with some exaggeration, "The Col. had a big place with more servants than anyone else in Florida." The consequent increase in responsibilities became a daunting test. All indications, however, point to Page's abilities preparing him well. Parkhill, on his part, evidently recognized with crystal clarity how valuable his bondservant had become and depended on him for growing enrichment. Strong bonds of trust developed between them as Page eventually stepped into the shoes of a confidant, a relationship that the two men maintained until Parkhill's death. With trust came further privilege. "The Col. usually gave me the run of the place," Page acknowledged. The enslaved overseer also gained access to the family's riding horses. "Mr. Parkhill let me use one of two horses anytime I needed one," Page remembered. "He was quite good at letting me use his things." Parkhill plainly sought to manipulate Page by offering him the use of animals, wagons, and farm equipment that cost him little financially. Any real compromise that would have altered his bottom line, such as repurchasing Page's mother and brother, was nonnegotiable. As long as Page did not directly cost Parkhill monetarily and made him prosperous through the production of cotton, he, indeed, had the run of the plantation or could use anything else the enslaver owned for that matter. Page surely came to understand that his master's actions were rarely paternalistic.[5]

Intellectual chores complemented physical ones for the overseer. One of Page's most important duties involved keeping records of daily operations.

He weighed cotton when appropriate and kept a detailed accounting of the amount of fiber picked by each field hand. As Page put it, "I had to write [down] what each hand-picked each day." He made sure that the cotton was properly packed and otherwise made ready for its journey some twenty miles to St. Marks for shipment north or overseas. During the early years before the advent of the rail system, he superintended the hauling of Parkhill's raw cotton to the port. As Beckert noted, the town "had emerged by the 1820s as an important port to export cotton grown" in Middle Florida and South Georgia. The task carried special meaning for Page. "I liked hauling the cotton to [St.] Marks," he later insisted. Since overland transport required substantial expense and effort, Parkhill in time joined other regional slaveholders in financing a primitive railroad from Tallahassee to the coast to get money crops to market more cheaply and efficiently. Whether traveling by wagon or railroad, the unsupervised times away from the plantation were special for Page: "The best time during cotton season was hauling Col. Parkhill's cotton to market and seeing the beautiful and strange places along the way and saying hi to people." He took pride in getting large quantities of cotton to the shipping terminus. The opportunity also allowed the overseer to breathe in new ideas and to keep up with current events by conversing with people along the way. He would have had access to newspapers and other publications not available at Tuscawilla or Bel Air. This relatively high degree of exceptionalism allowed him to travel extensively, which most enslaved people never had the opportunity to do.[6]

As was true in much of the antebellum South, Florida boasted slave codes designed to control virtually every aspect of bondservants' lives and reduce the potential for slave resistance. Owners hoped that these laws, including ones mandating written passes for slave travels, would minimize the number of individuals who absconded from farms and plantations. Understanding the laws, Page necessarily took serious precautions with his personal safety when traveling. Slave patrols and kidnappers naturally concerned him. Without a pass from his master, he could suffer bodily injury at the hands of these roving groups. Former Virginia bondman Charles Crawley reflected what bondservants would face if they were caught roaming away from their home domicile without a pass: "If de Pattyrollers caught you de would wip yo." During the mid-1830s to the early 1840s, though, Seminole Indians and their Maroon allies posed equal, if not greater, dangers.

This period saw the Second Seminole War, "the longest in U.S. history until the Vietnam War," or what historians Paul Ortiz and Anthony Dixon called "the largest slave rebellion in US history," raging on the peninsula. This slave/Indian rebellion reflected, among other things, reaction to President Andrew Jackson's efforts to rid the US territory of all independent persons of color who might attempt to thwart the unrelenting expansion of slavery. Violence, however, was not confined to remote parts of the territory. Raiders repeatedly ravaged Middle Florida. Frightful residents steeled themselves for sudden attacks on farms and plantations. According to Robert Gamble, he and others "lived forted in on the frontier, during that long and bloody Indian War." He added, "The frontier on which we lived was subject to constant inroads on the part of the Indians." Gamble, as was true of others such as Parkhill, resented that there was "no organization in the Territory to meet such an emergency." John Parkhill's brother Samuel served during the conflict as a senior volunteer officer, hoping to address the threats once and for all. According to Gamble, "Col[.] Sam Parkhill of the Florida Volunteers, performed the duties of Adjutant General displaying much military skill and the utmost coolness and courage throughout the whole action." Likely, as he served, Samuel earned for the Parkhill family special, and unwelcomed, notice from those whom he fought. The strained atmosphere prevalent at Tuscawilla grew more tense as the years passed.[7]

The year 1839 particularly boded ill for Middle Floridians when it came to Indian attacks. A November report alerted, "Indians attacked the plantation of Mr. John Johnson, residing on the Ocilla, in Jefferson, and the neighborhood of Mr. Lee's; and killed four negroes and a white lad." The same month, "a party of 10 or 12 Indians attacked the dwelling of Mr. Alfred Oliver, residing on the Oclockonee, about twelve miles from the city. A son of Mr. Oliver was killed by the Indians." December brought news that a "party of Indians had attacked a wagon on the Federal road, near the Ocilla River." Frantic whites meanwhile found it easy to believe that antislavery advocates in alliance with the Indians were influencing them in their rebellion. One resident spelled out the threat: "There are a large number of Negroes amongst the Indians who may be under the influence of Abolitionists of the North whose machinations, are now endangering our safety." While Second Seminole War raids produced occasional injury in Middle Florida, most fighting still occurred in eastern, central, and southern parts of the territory. Despite it all, Page lived to talk about his travels. His recollections reflected little, if any, care in regard to his safety. "I had no problem with anyone when I traveled," he flatly declared, "and I traveled many times alone." Yet Page likely counted his blessings that he met with no hurt, harm, or danger when traveling in a frightful frontier.[8]

Compounding the threats looming over Page's travels, complications on the plantation virtually defined his daily life. Especially given increases in workloads and alterations in assignments aimed at adjusting to Tuscawilla's growth and Bel Air's acquisition, for example, Page faced acute challenges from those whom he supervised. "The workers did their assignments most of the time," Page distinctly recalled, "[but] I had to try and make some people work better by threatening to take their privileges away." As the mouthpiece and representative of the enslaver, Page intimated that, at times, conflict resulted. The enslaved overseer had to manage those under his charge efficiently while living each day as a religious leader as well. He quickly found that the appearance of a smooth-running plantation could be misleading. John Parkhill's clear motive was building wealth by the constant acquisition of land and enslaved laborers. This directly affected allocation of Page's time and energy. And the magnitude of the conundrum swelled over time. By the late 1830s and early 1840s, the enslaver's plantation had grown substantially. In 1839 he reported for taxation thirty-five enslaved workers and 3,570 acres of land, a significant increase from the seven slaves and 240 acres he had owned upon his arrival twelve years earlier. The increase, not coincidentally, paralleled the formation and expansion of Tallahassee's Union Bank, with which John Parkhill maintained intimate connections, having served for six years as cashier. The bank backed slaveholders through shaky loans; it operated, in modern parlance, as little more than a Ponzi scheme. The owners mortgaged their bondpeople to secure loans to add even more enslaved workers and land. The result, they dreamed, would be higher yields of cotton. Parkhill's conspicuous consumption directly affected his favorite bondservant: he mortgaged and remortgaged Page to the bank at least three separate times to raise cash.[9]

The uncertainties created by the financial climate of the late 1830s and early 1840s—combined with Indian war, slave revolt, and John Parkhill's spectacular risk taking—surely caused psychological torture for Page, whose painful memories of separation from his family and friends in Richmond remained fresh. Intimately familiar with plantation issues, he knew moment to moment that he was living in trying, not to say volatile, times. A false step or the arbitrary action of some third party could compel sales of family bondservants. The transactions easily could include Page, his loved ones, and his friends. "I hope the Col. don't have to sale [*sic*] too many servants," he vividly described on one occasion. For Parkhill, though, the potential rewards justified the risk despite the pain inflicted on enslaved people by his actions. Page and other bondservants existed to symbolize for Parkhill wealth and prestige as a slaveholding planter. Page's religious side understood the importance of family as well as God's desire for loved ones not to be separated and alone, when creating Adam and Eve. The enslaved preacher's voice is more evident than enslaved overseer's in the observation, "I would get nervous when servants were sold from the place [plantation]." The uncertainty and insecurity cried out for relief through spiritual comfort and uplift. The process worked both ways. As a man of the cloth, Page tried to live everyday life offering others the fruits of his ministry, for preaching became key to his perception of himself as a religious cleric. In turn, men such as Page were gifted with the knowledge that they had acted, had exercised agency to the extent that they could, for the betterment of their world despite the menacing circumstances with which they contended.[10]

Circumstances tragically brought Page's nightmares to life. After years of turmoil, the Union Bank collapsed in 1843. The fallout proved so profound that, in historian Michael G. Schene's words, "Middle Florida was in a depressed economic condition throughout most of the 1840s." A contemporary newspaper account observed, "A report of the Bank stated the investigation had found the bank in a state of crisis and disarray." Parkhill's yearly salary may have been one of the many reasons the bank was failing. He started at $1,600 annually. By 1840 his salary had swelled to $4,000. Governor Robert A. Reid's compensation of $2,500 per year paled in comparison. Now, the Union Bank's currency was virtually worthless. Reportedly, an Apalachicola barber insisted that he would not take a dollar from a man when he found out "it was from the Union Bank." Criticisms poured in, emphasizing allegations that the bank's problems derived substantially from its treatment of "particular favorites." None of the developments should have surprised John Parkhill. Former governor William Pope DuVal had warned him in 1838 from the port town of St. Joseph, "The merchants here complain loudly of the partiality of the Union Bank. They say none of your exchange ever gets to them—that they hold certificates of deposits on the Bank and when they get to Tallahassee it is all gone. They talk of calling a meeting and withdrawing their deposits and pledging themselves not to receive A Dollar from you." Despite such signals, bank officials failed to take corrective actions. So, the chickens finally came home to roost. Parkhill's reputation was tainted, and his creditors demanded relief and satisfaction.[11]

Thus, many merchants and others who did business with the bank directed their frustrations at Page's master. He had resigned as cashier in March 1840 and, within three months, was shedding assets for cash. The enslaver knew exactly what he could do. He would use the valuable bodies of his enslaved human beings as commodities. This move to liquidate dramatically touched lives in the quarters community. First, Parkhill sold bondwoman Kitty and her daughter Susan for $1,400. The advantage gained was relatively little since he already had mortgaged them two years earlier to the bank. Several other transactions apparently followed given that his total holdings dropped by the mid-1840s to twenty-nine enslaved persons. The desperate measures failed to stem his financial troubles. As early as 1841 bank reports listed him as delinquent on interest due. Accordingly, his shares were "declared forfeited . . . for non-payment of interest upon stocks and are ordered to be sold at the front door of the Banking house." Parkhill desperately treaded water financially in hopes of a better day. Watching these developments, Page could only express regrets: "I felt sad for the Col. when he did not have what he needed to run the place." Remembering the breakup of his own family on the auction block, Page felt regretful, as well, at seeing the breakup of other enslaved families caused by Parkhill's spendthrift behavior. Fortunately for Page, the bank's shaky business practices and Parkhill's uncertain financial status did not have the impact upon his life or the lives of his immediate family that they did for other enslaved persons on the two plantations.[12]

As if financial woes were not enough, Parkhill and Middle Floridians endured a yellow fever epidemic shortly after the slave sales commenced. John Gamble called it the "fatal epidemic of 1841." Page noted, "Yellow fever and lots of bad colds made many servants sick. And when they got sick, they refuse[d] to work." The disease struck most virulently in Tallahassee. "The fear and confusion was [sic] complete and Tallahasseans estimated that only three or four families in town and not more than a dozen individuals entirely escaped the holocaust," local historian Bertram H. Groene reported. "In August one estimate put the death toll at 10 per cent of the city's 1,600 inhabitants, or around 160 people laid in their graves." So fearful did many residents become that circuit ministers began preaching to their congregations that the plague had arrived as God's judgment for members' "sins." During the epidemic, Parkhill lost his brother, Samuel, that August to unspecified causes. One or more of Parkhill's slaves likely succumbed as well, requiring

Page's service in eulogizing these individuals and comforting their loved ones, although history has left no record of them.[13]

The multiple woes of the late 1830s and early 1840s merely compounded the travails endured by enslaved workers conquering and taming still-rough Middle Florida through their labors and sacrifices. Their recitation underscores a range of insights for modern students of the region's experience. Perhaps most importantly, they permit a sense of why so many enslaved human beings craved the comfort of a religion that promised a better life in the next world while yearning for the ministrations of a pastor whose reassurances could be heard and received as credible. By the same token, the ordeals and tribulations reinforced and buttressed Page's intense desire to bring comfort by sharing God's word.[14]

⁓

Page had commenced teaching and preaching in a church without walls during 1828. A longtime deacon of the Tallahassee church that he later established remembered the story as his pastor told it. "He started preaching to those who would listen to him within weeks of his arrival to Florida," Jack Sheppard recorded. "He preached in the woods when he first got to Florida, and many who came to hear him would sit on log seats." Page also left his own recollections: "I started preaching before the Col. knew about it." As religious scholar Albert Raboteau noted, "In the . . . seclusion of the brush arbors ('hush harbors') the slaves made Christianity truly their own." Yet Page voluntarily notified his master of his actions, saying, "But I soon told him what I had been doing. I really think he knew about it all along." Page understood that conducting religious services as soon as possible in the midst of a challenging, if not frightening, new environment would help the migrants better adjust to their new circumstances. His ministrations could serve as well as a balm for the suffering experienced through separation from kinfolk left behind in Virginia. Rather than distract from his outreach, the rustic setting of his services was perfectly appropriate to his listeners, who could worship as they pleased without the inquisitive ears and prying eyes of their enslavers. Former Georgia bondman John Moore recalled, "De slaves would slip out at nite ter private meetin's en turn a pot bottom up on de ground' en leave a little hole under it so de sound ob dere talkin' would go onder de pot en no one would 'year whut de wuz talkin' 'bout." Former bondservant Amanda McCray, for one, warmly remembered enslaved blacks worshipping in such a place. "There was a praying ground," an interviewer related, "where 'the grass never had a chancet ter grow fer the troubled knees that kept it crushed down.'' Former Georgia bondman Andrew Moss echoed McCray's recollection, saying that "way back in 1852—us colored folks had pray[ing] grounds." One respected historian noted a special dimension to the selection of a site. By initiating their church in "brush arbors or woods," he observed, Page and other bondservants "were obeying God's will instead of the slaveholder's will." When speaking to another bondservant about their enslaver, Virginia former bondwoman Jennie Small put it bluntly: "Do not call Mr. McNeal the master, no one is your master but God, call Mr. McNeal, mister."[15]

So, having pleased Parkhill by agreeing to serve as overseer, Page intended from his earliest days in Florida to make the master-slave relationship work as much as possible in his favor. To accomplish his goal unfortunately required him to expose to his master his deepest yearning to become a preacher, risking the secret of what he desired most in life. His priorities did not begin or end with managing enslaved laborers. Rather, he aimed to preach and to live the greater part of his life as a minister of the Gospel: "I wanted to preach more than anything else I did since a little boy in Virginny." For the young man, not preaching signaled failure for he equated his success as a man with his work not as an overseer but as a minister. The ability to preach helped him to legitimize himself in his own eyes. "I [felt] really good when I was preaching," he allowed. The desire to preach illuminated the key dimension of his identity and became the basis for his life's work.[16]

Page accordingly played to his master's religious sensibilities by requesting permission. "I ask[ed] the Col.," he remembered, "what he thought about me preaching some." Page needed for Parkhill to agree publicly with his desire, for this helped to validate him as a spiritual leader not so much within the slave community but more in the outside world among whites. The request should not have surprised Parkhill if he had closely watched the enslaved young man's interest in religion as a boy. As historian Peter Kolchin summarized, the situation was by no means unusual: "Slaves in the antebellum period engaged in a broad range of endeavors. They served their masters in managerial capacities, as drivers and overseers, and cared for their comfort as . . . personal servants. They also attended to the needs of fellow slaves, working as preachers." Additionally, the authentication of worthiness by whites on behalf of blacks already had become relatively common. Men such as Massachusetts governor Thomas Hutchinson, John Hancock of Declaration of Independence fame, Pastor Charles Chauncey of the Tenth Congregational Church, and fifteen other Bostonians had attested to Phillis

Wheatley's poetic abilities. Similarly, white abolitionists lauded Frederick Douglass's writing and oratorical skills. Enslaved preachers including Black Harry and John Chavis also enjoyed such support. Page benefited from the same validation. "[Parkhill] thought it was a good thing for me to do," he recorded. Most particularly, Page did not want skeptical whites to thwart his plans: "I always felt one of the best things I could do for my people was to help them become more Godly." Page strove particularly to forestall white disbelievers of his religious calling and intellectual abilities through the public blessing of his master. And by getting his master's permission to preach, the enslaved minister hoped his life would be more than simply one of toil, exploitation, violence, breeding, and ultimately death.[17]

At the outset, little but personal drive, literacy skills, and a smattering of biblical knowledge served Page's ministry. Historian David Dennard, an authority on the subject, clarified that "slaves who turned to preaching were generally ill-prepared to perform all the duties required of Christian preachers. They had inspiration, often a native wit, and were usually good orators. But the vast majority could neither read nor write." Thus, the benefits of home schooling set Page's ministry apart from the beginning. In fact, his calling—rather than his usefulness as an overseer to the Parkhill family—had afforded him the impetus to study. "I always wanted to learn to read and write so I could become a preacher one day," he told a contemporary. But the accomplishment invited danger. Many whites distrusted blacks who could read and write. Former bondservant Margrett Nickerson spoke to the point when she recalled that literate enslaved persons, including a man on her plantation, could face punishment for no apparent reason: "Dere wuz Uncle George Bull, he could read and write and, chile, de white folks didn't lak no nigger whut could read and write. [So] dey useter jest take Uncle George Bull and beat him fur nothin; dey would beat him and take him to de lake and put him on a log and shev him in de lake, but he always swimmed out." Literacy could imperil those who possessed it. Henry Bibb, for one, became aware that slave patrols broke up Sabbath schools that taught literacy skills to enslaved persons. Much like Uncle George Bull and other enslaved persons who desired to read and write, Page had to exercise extreme caution when preaching in the vicinity of suspicious and potentially violent whites.[18]

The fledgling preacher also confronted the challenge of how to convince doubtful whites not only that he had been called by God to save souls but that blacks possessed souls at all. A Mississippi Methodist enslaved preacher named Pompey faced the same issue. When a white man asked him why he sang hymns all day, he replied that "it makes my soul so happy." The white man responded, "You simpleton, a negro has no soul." For some whites, the lack of a black soul equated to a supposed lack of intelligence. Preacher Jarena Lee encountered such a white man, but one who at least entertained curiosity on the subject. She convinced him to attend one of her sermons to determine for himself whether she could preach, for only people with souls and intelligence could perform that act successfully. Afterward the impressed doubter conceded the argument and acknowledged that blacks did have souls.[19]

As the case of Daniel H. Wiggins illustrated, some—but by no means all—white ministers conceded that blacks had souls to save. Wiggins's observation on the point came during a Florida visit to his friend Judge Thomas Randall: "The soul of the slave is of as much value as the master yet neglected." Enslaved preachers such as Page sought, as Wiggins understood the matter, to save "neglected" souls in the quarters community. Page reflected on the souls of black folk when he declared, "I saved many souls by baptizing them for the Lord." He believed that God had made the world of many different people with "one blood." He did not accept the polygenetic theories that circulated during the antebellum period positing that black and white people comprised different species created separately by God. Page often mentioned his ability to convert souls through his preaching and noted that "we are all the same in the Lord's eyes." He believed that all of God's children—enslaved persons, free blacks, and poor whites—had natural rights given only by God. No man or woman, he thought, should be able to take away those rights. Still, by conceding that bondservants possessed souls, slaveholders and others of their ilk effectively admitted that bondservants ranked equally with them in value in the eyes of God. This proved extremely difficult for many to acknowledge.[20]

Not only did Page face the prospect of resistance from skeptical whites; he also grappled with establishing his credibility among questioning bondpeople. For doubtful congregants, he often talked about his religious conversion to impress upon others that he had been legitimately called to preach and that he had God's and his master's blessings to proselytize members of his race. He noted to listeners that "as a boy around seven or eight, I think, I kept having these same dreams over and over again that God wanted me to preach." He took pride that "I could read a few verses in the Bible as a young boy," insisting that he learned literacy skills specifically to become "a good preacher." He described his personal experience to show that it paralleled the apostle Paul's to prove his conversion authentic. He stressed similarity in the fact that each man had undergone an extraordinary experience that induced him to preach. Finally, Page enjoyed the ability to release his flock from fear of retribution by Parkhill. He always could assert that "the Col. approved of my desire to preach."[21]

The comparison to Paul and his conversion on the Damascus road carried more importance to Page's ministry than at first glance it might appear. The conversion experience became especially important to enslaved persons and free blacks because it allowed them to enter God's kingdom on an equal footing with whites and slaveholders. In telling about his "many dreams," Page meant to impress upon persons who had gone through—or believed that they might go through—a similar Pauline experience that he or she could relate to his experience and calling. Specifically, the enslaved preacher wanted to use the Pauline conversion to overcome skepticism about his call by associating himself with a relevant biblical incident with which most Christians were familiar. Page was not alone in attempting to counter such skepticism. His contemporary Bishop James Hood, for one, combatted skepticism of his call from a superior in the African Methodist Episcopal Zion (AMEZ) Church. His class leader at a quarterly meeting simply did not believe the validity of his experience. As scholar Sandy D. Martin explained, "After informing the minister that he felt the call to preach, the young man found to his surprise that the veteran minister did not inform the quarterly conference. Indeed, the minister was so confident that Hood had not received a call to the ministry that he implied that the young man perhaps had intercepted God's call directed to someone else!"[22]

Page may have referred, on occasion, to the Pauline Epistles; many other enslaved people did not. Former bondservant Nancy Ambrose, a descendant of African enslaved people and Seminole Indians, prohibited her grandson, Howard Thurman, from ever reading certain parts of the Bible to her. Mrs. Ambrose did not like how the slaveholder and his representatives had used one part, the Pauline dictum, to control the attitudes and behavior of bondservants. The Madison County, Florida, woman remembered that "Old man McGhee," her master, "[had been] so mean that he would not let a Negro minister preach to his slaves." McGhee, instead, wanted a white preacher to sermonize that "it was God's will that we were slaves and how, if we were good and happy slaves, God would bless us." Ambrose went on, "I promised my Maker that if I ever learned to read and if freedom ever came, I would not read that part of the Bible." The freed woman clearly understood, like so many other blacks, how certain parts of the Bible were used by proslavery ministers and others to control enslaved persons. Although Page may have used parts of the Pauline doctrine, he offered to his flock, as will be seen in subsequent chapters, a more hermeneutical approach to the Bible by selecting those scriptures and passages that provided hope, happiness, self-reliance, and ultimately freedom in this world.[23]

~

Once Page was called to preach, distant events and far-reaching dynamics influenced his approach, as also proved true for countless others during his era. He had matured as the Second Great Awakening was stirring the nation's consciousness. For many, that landmark development introduced passion and emotional experience into religious practice. Revivals filled with fiery oratory, vivid portrayals of heaven and hell, the witnessing of faith, and the throes of conversion pulled men, women, and children—black and white—together in shared exploration of heart, soul, and conscience. "We use[d] to like going to the big church meetings with Col. Parkhill and his family in the woods," Page confirmed. The clergy meantime increasingly emphasized forgiveness, repentance, and salvation as the tickets to heaven. Baptism and conversion attracted floods of congregants weary of the traditional hard and unattractive fundamentalist teaching of predestination.[24]

But Page was raised from a young lad by his master in the Presbyterian Church. He had a lot to learn about the religious beliefs and behaviors of members of his race before he could become an effective preacher. To add further context, many bondservants clung to the various religious beliefs and practices they brought with them to America during the colonial period. With high death rates and the separation of families and members of the same tribes, preserving African religious traditions as enslaved persons remembered them proved difficult to sustain over time. Plus, enslaved persons found it difficult to maintain their African religious beliefs when enslavers sought to eradicate non-Christian doctrines among their bondservants. By 1808, the United States had ended its importation of enslaved human beings from Africa, with only "illegal" enslaved Africans reaching the shores of America thereafter; this slowed the process of transmitting and preserving African religious practices. The intense religious revivalism during the 1830s, with its emphasis on enthusiastic praying, singing, clapping, dancing, and spirit possession, as well as "equality" before God for all human beings, appealed to enslaved persons, who began to merge their African beliefs with

Euro-Christian tenets into a unique form of black Christianity. It was this religious milieu that Page first confronted as an enslaved preacher in the quarters community.[25]

Moreover, as Raboteau asserted, "[African enslaved people] did not just leave their religious practices on the boats when they set foot in America." So, when they attended camp meetings, enslaved Africans and their descendants adopted their own style of worship, a complex mixture of African religious practices and evangelical Protestantism. Page would gradually accept this brand of worship, which resulted in a highly charged and emotionally gratifying religious experience for his congregants. Over time white ministers also adapted some of the slaves' practices to their services. "The power of African-influenced spiritual practices was too useful for white preachers to resist the temptation to borrow," historian Edward Baptist aptly noted. Thus, the religious practices and services of preachers such as James Page reshaped the religious dynamic for millions of white worshippers. West African and European religious traditions transformed each other. Former bondservant Susie Moss fondly reflected on the intensity of the resulting experience: "[We would] get dizzy and happy and fall out an' roll 'round on de groun.'" Page stated the point somewhat differently: "I like when the people get happy when I preach." As a result, "lively preaching and worshiping services in the woods" marked the atmosphere in early 1828 as his initial church without walls began its mission in Leon County, Florida.[26]

African influences that combined with Second Great Awakening teachings ironically validated Page's mission and those of other enslaved preachers by moving some whites to promote the conversion of bondpeople and acceptance that they had souls. Leon County's Susan Bradford Eppes, among others, reflected an idealistic trend concerning the need to Christianize enslaved blacks. She believed that enslaved persons, like Native Americans, were "heathen souls" who had to be "taught of the existence of a God, [and] not a vengeful Voo Doo [god]." Many men of the cloth came to believe that all people—regardless of race, color, or creed—could seek salvation through good works and faith in God. As one preacher observed, there were "no distinctions . . . made as to age, sex, color, or anything of a temporary nature; old and young, male and female, black and white, had equal privilege to minister the light which they received, in whatever way the Spirit directed." This theology directly challenged the Calvinist doctrine of predestination. Preachers such as Daniel H. Wiggins, Barton W. Stone, and Alexander Campbell sought out people where they were, whether in the city or town or on a plantation or farm. The Protestant faith, as a result, expanded by leaps and bounds. John Parkhill stood among those who embraced ministers who pushed such Second Great Awakening tenets and principles. He therefore found little problem with Page's involvement in such good works.[27]

Page understandably relied on various religious and denominational tools to advance his work once his ministry had been firmly established. He believed fervently, for instance, in the power of baptism, for the rite served to cleanse the soul. To many enslaved blacks whose belief systems reached deeply into African traditions, water already held special mystical meaning. In turn, they perceived the ceremony of baptism as serving a particularly important religious purpose. Water symbolized rebirth. It also suggested life, fertility, and hope. Former bondman Louis Napoleon captured the importance of water to enslaved people when he asserted that those who accepted Christ were "prepared for baptism on the next visit of 'Father Page.'" Page ultimately ministered according to Baptist denominational practices. One of them, immersion in water, paralleled African water rites. Louis Napoleon recalled the process of baptism for those who accepted Christ in the quarters community: "Candidates were attired in long white flowing robes, which had been made by one of the slaves. Amid singing and praises they marched, being flanked on each side by other believers, to a pond or lake on the plantation and after the usual ceremony they were 'ducked' in the water." Onetime Georgia bondman Mack Mullen remembered, "On baptismal day, the candidates attired in robes which they had made, marched down to the river where they were immersed by the minister. This was a day of much shouting and praying." Overseer Jonathan Roberson informed his employer about a baptismal service that he had observed: "Forty-one (41) of your Negroes [were] Baptized last Sunday in the Canal above the Bridge by James Page." Former bondwoman Anna Scott also clarified that "when several persons were 'ready,' there would be a baptism in a creek or river."[28]

No extant document details a typical baptism as performed by Page. A glimpse, though, may be gleaned from Scott's memory. She recollected that, before baptism, a series of questions were asked:

"What did you come up her [*sic*] for?
"Because I got religion."
"How do you know you got religion?"
"Because I know my sins are forgiven."
"How do you know your sins are forgiven?"

"Because I love Jesus and I love everybody."

"Do you want to be baptized?"

"Yes Sir."

"Why do you want to be baptized?"

"Cause it will make me like Jesus wants me to be."[29]

Despite his appreciation of baptism's power, Page did not inaugurate his ministry as a Baptist. Instead, he initially had considered preaching in his master's Presbyterian Church, a denomination that—as scholar David Dennard pointed out—"tended to be more formal and intellectual in character than the Baptist and Methodist sects." Page's choice unfortunately did not appeal to John Parkhill. As Page reminisced, "The Col. never pushed me to be a preacher where he went to church but thought I might make a good Baptist or Methodist Preacher." The prospective minister visited different Richmond churches to sample their approaches, but he resisted shifting allegiances. Perhaps Parkhill truly believed that the less structured approaches of the Baptists and Methodists offered a more supportive environment for Page's religious work. He may, though, have considered his literate bondman and key helper not up to the high standards he expected of a Presbyterian preacher, in keeping with the attitudes of many white Presbyterians. He may also have been swayed by evolving racist ideology that increasingly decried blacks as naturally inferior to whites. Once in Florida, however, Page finally accepted Parkhill's preferences and eventually abandoned his earlier choice. "Col. Parkhill was proud that I had become a Baptist preacher," the enslaved minister recalled.[30]

Page should have considered himself fortunate. He had received permission to start his ministry. Some bondservants did not enjoy such a boon; hard consequences often followed. Without leave to attend worship services or preach, many enslaved blacks chose to frequent or lead secret religious services. Many faced punishments for doing so. Former bondwoman Charlotte Martin remembered her brother taking part in secret religious meetings. When caught by the master, he paid with his life: the master whipped her brother "to death." Former bondman Moses Grandy similarly recorded that his brother-in-law Isaac, an enslaved preacher, "was flogged, and his back pickled." His offense was preaching at unauthorized religious services in the woods. But Page should not have been surprised that his master granted him permission to preach, since it cost him nothing financially. Indeed, the enslaver's actions were not totally magnanimous, for he knew that Christianity could be used as a means of controlling some bondservants as well. And a manageable enslaved worker was a productive slave.[31]

~

As an established and highly recognizable Baptist enslaved preacher, Page with the passing years emerged as a focal figure in the religiosity of bond-people in parts of Florida, Georgia, South Carolina, Mississippi, and Alabama. Merging African and Euro-Christian practices, he sought through his ministry to become the indispensable man who could appeal to the religious sensibilities of most enslaved people. Much as had been true in West African society, Page and men like him became significant figures who exercised considerable leadership on behalf of a large segment of the enslaved population under their aegis. Unlike most preachers, though, Page could read and write. As noted earlier, Page was exceptional, for he stood out among enslaved persons both as literate preacher and overseer. Amanda McCray explained how highly regarded as a minister he was considered on the 116-slave plantation where she resided: "The [Parkhill] slaves had a Negro minister who could hold services any time he chose, so long as he did not interfere with the work of the other slaves He was not obliged to do hard menial labors. . . . He was more than a little conscious of this and was held in awe by others." McCray shared only one facet of the story, projecting onto Page what she, as his admirer, wished to be true. The enslaved preacher rarely walked about the plantation in fancy dress, nor could he hold religious services whenever he desired. With his master's permission, Page would continue over time to gain influence as a preacher among his race during his many travels unescorted throughout Florida and other states of the South. His reality demanded, though, attention to the enslaver and dedicated service as overseer. Those duties necessitated performance before preaching, for they took up much of his time and required hard work.[32]

When his time and energies allowed him to pursue his mission, Page risked much in making the effort. Pursuing a religious calling as an enslaved preacher in the wilds of Middle Florida could prove a perpetually dangerous endeavor. Not so far away in Savannah, Emanuel K. Love claimed a degree of fame as pastor of one of the oldest Baptist churches in the United States. Some whites resented or feared his ministry. Love "was often whipped, and twice imprisoned for preaching the gospel to his people." Former bondman William Bradwell, born in Georgia around 1823 and a man whom Page later came to know well in Reconstruction-era Florida politics, "preach[ed] to his fellow slaves" and endured whippings for his actions. Most whites did not so much fear what such enslaved preachers might do but, rather, what they might say. According to Charles Ball, they feared that the ministers would include in their sermons "notions of equality and liberty" that might encourage bondservants to grow uncontrollable. Enslaved preachers such as Page had only to remember what happened to select Mississippi enslaved ministers in 1835. They were shot dead for sermonizing to fellow bondservants and their severed heads impaled on stakes along the roadside. Slave preaching indeed could become a deadly calling.[33]

The white apprehensions behind such fears arose, at least partly, from incidents of slave revolt and rebellion. Such events provoked owners to suspect and fear enslaved preachers and led to such violent reprisals as just described. They remembered the Denmark Vesey conspiracy, for instance, which started at the black Charleston, South Carolina, Mother Emanuel African Methodist Episcopal (AME) Church in June 1822. Events of late summer and fall 1831, however, stoked anxieties to greater intensity. Whether from overheard conversations, discarded newspapers, or word of mouth, Page and others learned about the self-professed enslaved preacher named Nat Turner and the bloody slave revolt that he led in Southampton, Virginia. Given that his master's father-in-law, Charles Copland, had defended Gabriel Prosser in a criminal case in 1799, the enslaved preacher/ overseer would have been familiar with Gabriel's slave conspiracy, as well as the Denmark Vesey and the Nat Turner rebellions. Speaking specifically about the Nat Turner insurrection, Page recalled, "We knew about that big thing in my old home place[,] but no one ever talked about it." Echoes of the Turner insurrection, which led to the deaths of approximately sixty whites, reverberated around the South. Reaction to it effectively imposed a barrier to many bondpeople undertaking a ministry, as influential whites blamed enslaved preachers. Florida's Zephaniah Kingsley summed up the fears when he noted, "All the late insurrections of slaves are to be traced to influential [enslaved] preachers of the gospel." Concerned about insurrectionary prayers delivered by the enslaved minister on his plantation, Middle Florida's Judge Wilkerson attempted, with little success, to stop secret meetings entirely. As the meetings persisted, so, too, did the fears. Florida governor John Milton as late as 1861 still dreaded the possibility of an uprising propelled by the state's black worshippers. Of course, the very fact that slaveholders despised enslaved ministers furnished a key reason why preachers such as Page appealed to bondservants in the quarters communities.[34]

The author confined in the pillory.

Jonathan Walker, an alleged abolitionist and slave stealer, was branded with an *SS* and confined to a pillory at Pensacola. State Archives of Florida, Florida Memory

On the heels of the Nat Turner revolt, concerns about the activities of abolitionists added to the alarm experienced at times by white Floridians. The press highlighted virtually every rumor on the subject, thus allowing enlightenment for literate enslaved people such as Page. As he reminisced, "I had read many of the master's newspapers." Most white Floridians, and white Southerners generally, believed that antislavery advocates provoked slave unrest. They saw, too, the growth of populations in West Florida and the peninsula where less than enthusiastic support for slavery prevailed. One newspaperman during the territorial era even declared, "We shall have the germ of an Abolition State in east Florida, in less than five years." An Apalachicola newspaper in 1844 alerted readers of "a general massacre" planned by belligerent slaves and their abolitionists allies. Its editor insisted that abolitionists in Florida were inciting "the slaves to discontent and disobedience." In fact, most individuals accused of abolitionist tendencies merely advocated moderate reforms.[35]

The great exception was Jonathan Walker, who sincerely attempted while he was in Florida to aid escapes of enslaved people. If the Apalachicola newspaper did not get the attention of whites concerning the abolitionist threat, the celebrated case of this Bostonian certainly did. Ever since the English outlawed slavery in the British West Indies by 1833, the Bahamas had become another leg of the well-known Underground Railroad. So, the incident centered on Walker's efforts in 1844 to assist seven Pensacola fugitives seeking freedom in the British Bahamas. Unfortunately, the fugitives were caught in the Gulf of Mexico. Following a highly publicized trial, Walker was convicted of "aiding and abetting" the runaways. A judge ordered him branded on the hand with the letters *SS* for "slave stealer," pilloried, and jailed for fifteen days. On his part, Page insisted that abolitionists—whether of Walker's stripe or otherwise—mattered little to him. "I did not have anything to do with those people," he assured. The enslaved preacher obviously found it prudent not to do or say anything on the subject that might alter, restrict, or prohibit his ability to serve as a traveling minister of God.[36]

In trying to assess who James Page was, one must constantly ask, what image did he project to blacks in private and whites in public? Did his personality rest between those of the rebellious clerics, like Nat Turner and Denmark Vesey, and the "good enslaved preacher?" According to Raboteau, religious leaders like Turner and Vesey "used scriptural texts to win supporters for insurrection" or "act[ed] by an omen from God." Turner and Vesey demonstrated, by their actions, that real religious leaders could not support slavery. Given that many whites were strictly against enslaved preachers on their farms and plantations, the fact that Page became and remained a preacher in a hostile Southern environment suggested, to a degree, a rebellious persona. Given the overwhelming power of well-armed whites in Florida and throughout the South, Page, as will be seen in subsequent chapters, sought to rebel within the system of slavery by encouraging agency among bondservants to do things for themselves. Under the material conditions allowed by his master, the enslaved preacher served as an example to members of his race through gardening, fishing, and doing other creative things to care for his family. Page obviously found favor among some whites, who certainly preferred he preach and serve his people within the confines of slavery. Page understood what it took to remain a traveling preacher in a land suspicious of slave religious leaders. In negotiating between his master and fellow bondservants, the enslaved preacher's long life remained, indeed, a complex one.[37]

Remarkably and despite problems that included Indian raiders, whites angry at black literacy, extreme fears of slave uprisings, and abolitionist scares, Page remained steadfast in traveling the Southern frontier and adjacent territories preaching the word of God despite the certainty of being stopped and harassed by slave patrols or vigilante groups. And as long as Page kept up with his work on the plantation, the enslaver evidenced no apparent concerns about his travels or his dedication to his ministry. "I would travel the lonely roads without a pass sometimes from Col. Parkhill," he reflected. "It would be just me, the horse, and the Lord." Page added, "Sometimes I would get stop[ped] by patrollers on the road. They never harm[ed] me like they sometimes did other Negroes." Page was correct; others were not always so lucky. In former bondman Shack Thomas's case, "patrollers . . . gave him a lot of trouble every time he didn't have a pass to leave [the plantation]." Another bondservant, Samuel Simeon Andrews, explained the system: "'Patrollers' were guards for runaway slaves. [We] . . . had to have passes to go from one plantation to another and if one were found without a pass the 'patrollers' would pick him up, return him to his master and receive pay for their service." Sons of slaveholders routinely volunteered for patrol duties. "Frequently slaves would visit without benefit of passes, and as a result some suffered severe torturing," former bondman Taylor Gilbert recollected. "Often the sons of the slaves' owners would go 'nigger hunting' and nothing—not even murder was too horrible for them to do to slaves caught without passes." Frequently, as historian Paul Ortiz noted, "whites who did not own slaves [also] routinely served in slave patrols." Whatever else can be asserted about the traveling enslaved preacher, Page did not let the potential violence from whites stop him from pursuing the calling to preach.[38]

CHAPTER FIVE

Forging Family Ties

I never will give my heart nor hand to any girl in marriage, until I first know her sentiments upon the all-important subjects of Religion and Liberty.

—Henry Bibb

Father James Page's ability to pursue a ministry that eventually saw him travel over a period of three decades thousands of miles through large areas of four southeastern states rested upon many foundations. The supportive attitude of his owner, John Parkhill, formed, from the outset in late 1827 and early 1828, an essential factor in that combination. The young preacher's sincerity, enthusiasm, tirelessness, and daring—especially when combined with keen oratorical skills and adept use of biblical references in combination with African symbolism and religious traditions—aided his cause further. A growing reputation earned over years offered mounting credibility in the quarters communities and also among many whites. Page discovered early on, however, that missing a key component of the needed foundation severely circumscribed his life, one already considerably restricted by slavery's bonds. In common with human beings all over the world, he realized the need for companionship, a home, and a family.

As has been discussed, Page's arrival in Middle Florida revealed a surprising and a hard truth regarding personal relationships. "The few black servants we first [met]," he remembered, "were not too friendly to us." By 1830, though, the number of bondpeople in the Tallahassee area had grown from 400 or so to about 1,100, and Page had begun to perceive the makings of a place where enslaved persons who had been forced to uproot themselves from families and communities elsewhere could start the arduous task of rebuilding their lives. By the early 1830s, too, the increasingly experienced preacher had initiated the expansion of his pastorate from Tuscawilla plantation to the larger vicinity. The success of that early outreach in turn softened initial resistance to him and his fellow Parkhill bondservants. He initiated his own transformation from an object of distrust to a welcomed presence identified with comfort and solace.[1]

Once settled as an up-and-coming minister and overseer, Page understandably sought to recreate kinships previously and capriciously destroyed in Virginia. He knew from personal experience that family afforded strength and support in dealing with the chaotic realities of slavery. When all was said and done, he craved love and a strong connection with someone outside the white race. He found the bond that he sought on Tuscawilla plantation with a young woman he had known since she was a girl. Elizabeth, aged about eighteen in 1832, had traveled the 750-mile journey with him and six other bondservants in 1827 from Virginia to Florida. She worked in the years following as a house servant for the Parkhills. Listed in surviving documentation simply as a single girl, she shared Page's loss of family and isolation. Her parents, Solomon and Amy Saylor, were not Parkhill family property, and she had been torn from connection with them in her forced uprooting from Richmond. So, during 1832 at around age twenty-four, James took Elizabeth as his lifetime partner. No extant sources describe her physical characteristics except that she was, according to Page, "a small frame[d] brown-skinned woman."[2]

Enslaved couples most often sought permission to unite from both their enslavers and their parents. Given that James and Elizabeth's parents were no longer with them, they requested permission only from their master, John Parkhill. Surviving documents offer little illumination as to their courtship. We do not know when the engagement was made or its duration, nor do we know anything about Elizabeth's thoughts on religion and motherhood. For that matter, we remain in the dark about what Page discussed with his future wife concerning his attitudes about fatherhood. Many bondservants, like Harriet Jacobs and Harriet Smith were either not allowed to marry or stay married to the men of their choosing; this was not the case with Elizabeth and James.

Just as with the details of Elizabeth's appearance or courtship, no information survived that described the ceremony that united the two young people. Historian Brenda E. Stevenson offers some sense of the circumstances, though: "From the initiation of a romance, black men and women had to confront and compromise with their masters about control of their intimate lives, aware that their owner typically had the final say about if and when they could marry, and even who." A statement made by Page to a contemporary late in life offered a tantalizing clue as to Page's attraction to his bride and their master's intercession in such ceremonies: "I married Elizabeth as soon as the Col. approved of it. I love Elizabeth and I know she loves me. We are happy together."[3]

Page likely would have married Elizabeth earlier than he did save for his owner's interference. Presbyterian layman Parkhill insisted on postponing any union until the prospective bride had reached what he considered the age of maturity. This was not unusual. Historian Steven E. Brown pointed out, for instance, that enslaved workers in Georgia had to "adhere to rigorous courtship" parameters, which included waiting until they reached an appropriate age. Page put the matter bluntly: "My master did not want me to marry her until she got around eighteen." Florida law, in common with that of other slave jurisdictions, did not sanction slave marriages; Parkhill nonetheless required his bondpeople to abide by a code of conduct concerning enslaved couples "staying together." Many slaveholders did not share such sensibilities. A Mississippi case highlighted the outrageous extremes to which insensitivity could extend. George and a young girl were living as a couple. Circumstances soon compelled his master to decide whether the bondservant should be charged with rape for "violating a slave girl under ten years of age." The matter proceeded eventually to judicial consideration, with the Mississippi Supreme Court ultimately establishing the standard to be applied in that state. The panel first noted that the alleged crime "does not exist in this State between African slaves." It continued by declaring, "Our laws recognize no marital rights as between slaves" and "such cases as this should be dealt with by the owner."[4]

Parkhill, to his credit, would not have tolerated such shocking behavior. At the same time, Page's owner—as mentioned—rarely lost sight of his own pecuniary interest. This applied to the pairing of his enslaved people. The motives of enslavers such as Parkhill were typically self-serving. One thing the slaveholder knew: slave unions, whether legally sanctioned marriages or otherwise, represented economic potential—profits flowed from the children that the "unions" produced. "Most slaveowners encouraged . . . [slave families]," James McPherson explained, "in part because abolition of the African slave trade after 1807 made them dependent on natural increase to meet the labor demands of an expanding cotton kingdom." And although slave families enjoyed no recognition or protection under law, families nevertheless became, in historian James Oakes's words, "essential to slavery's survival." Oakes emphasized, "The 'peculiar institution' could not reproduce itself without slave families." Parkhill clearly understood this fact, as did most other Southern slaveowners. So, enslaved human beings including Elizabeth and James took whatever their master allowed and strove to make life better for themselves and others in quarters communities.[5]

The agricultural calendar influenced the timing of slave marriages. Certain times of the year proved particularly desirable, given the requirements of planting and harvesting cycles. The Yuletide season was perhaps most common, as it offered one of the few occasions when festivities did not interfere with the economic operations of farms and plantations. "Few couples married during the plowing, planting, cultivating or harvest seasons," historian Wilma King observed, "which suggests that there was little time for leisure or festivities." Concessions for rituals and festivities at least recognized that worker morale affected the enslaver's bottom line. Page did not, unfortunately, mention the time of year when he and Elizabeth married. It is possible that James and Elizabeth participated in a wedding ceremony reminiscent of a traditional rite, though the scant available evidence suggests they did not. Some official-looking wedding ceremonies certainly were held despite prevailing laws. Benjamin and Sarah of North Carolina, for instance, received owner permission for a "formal marriage ceremony" because they ranked as the master's favorite house servants. According to onetime Florida bondservant Acie Thomas, enslaved couples were "married properly and quite often had a 'sizeable' wedding, the master and mistress often came and made merry with their slaves." Thomas's observation that "the master and mistress often came and made merry" suggests that James and Elizabeth were not the recipients of similar consideration. As two of Parkhill's favorite bondservants and, therefore, atop the plantation's "black aristocracy," they might have expected a Parkhill presence. Yet, as Page recalled, his owners—for whatever reason—distanced themselves from the event. "I do not think," Page averred, "[that] Mr. and Mrs. Parkhill were on the place when we got married." Similarly, St. Helena Island, South Carolina, planter Thomas Chaplain either did not believe in slave marriages or did not want to be around to witness them. When two of his enslaved women married men on the island plantation, he asserted, "I do not wish to be here to see the tomfoolery that was going on about it." As a religious man, Parkhill may not have wanted to entertain any pretense that a real wedding in the sight of God was taking place. Accordingly, given the laws of the day as well as the owner's perception of James and Elizabeth as property and not as human beings who could legally marry each other, he would have been unlikely to participate in such a charade.[6]

Experiences of other enslaved couples can offer a sense of how the Page nuptials may have played out. Boston schoolteacher Ashton Rice Livermore, who taught in Virginia from 1839 to 1841 provided a helpful glimpse of one set of possibilities: "[I attended] a slave marriage, when the entire slave community gathered in one of the cabins to witness the 'broomstick wedding' of Pompey and Susan." The ceremony was led by an elderly slave called Uncle Aaron who, Rice explained, "was believed to be a man of many gifts,—a conjuror who could raise evil spirits,—and a God-man who wore a charm, and could become invisible at any moment, if anyone attempted to harm him." The teacher continued:

> The broomstick wedding was to take place at Uncle Aaron's house, and under his auspices, and thither we all adjourned.
>
> The bride and groom were in readiness when we arrived at the cabin, both tricked out in the cast-off clothes of their master and mistress, donated for this occasion. Pompey, the groom, wore a pair of embroidered slippers, much too large for him, and Susan, the bride, stout brogans, too small for her. A half-worn maroon-colored merino gown, too small in the waist, with sleeves slashed at the elbow, because they were too tight, and a skirt three inches too long, completed Susan's bridal attire. Pompey wore checked trousers, a white vest, and a brown linen duster, that would have encased two men of his size. But if he had been an Adonis and a Beau Brummel combined, he could not have been happier nor prouder.
>
> "Now stan' up Pompey an' Susan," commanded Uncle Aaron, "an' take ho' o' han's. You git de broom, Lucy an' Sam, and hol' it in de middle 'o de room. Hol' it jess down b'low youah knees,—thar!—so! Now, stiddy! You mus' be very solem', Pompey an' Susan, fo' dis yere is as solem' as a buryin'. Yo's gwine t' jump in t' de married state, an' may God hab mercy on youah souls! Look squar' at de broomstick! I'll count three, an' den you jump. All ready now! One—two—three—jump! Now you is husban' an' wife, an' orter live happy all de rest o' youah days! Lucy an' me wants you t'eat youah first supper heah; an' she'll gib you ash-cake, stewed rabbit, an' lots o' apple toddy.
>
> "De fiel' han's am willin' t' jump de broomstick, but when de house sarvans gwine t' marry, dey wants a white preacher;" said Uncle Aaron; "but de broomstick's jess as bindin' as de preacher." He was right. No marriage was binding

among the slaves, if the master or mistress chose to break it. We remained a
short time after the ceremony. Pompey was a favorite of Uncle Aaron, and he
had arranged for music and dancing, notwithstanding it was Sunday night. His
protégé was to have a good send-off. The company filed in, filling the cabin to
its small capacity, followed by the black musicians with their banjos and fid-
dles, and the singing began.[7]

Other surviving accounts offer similarly useful, if distinctly different,
perspectives and possibilities. One particularly deserves consideration. It involved a prospective union closer to Tuscawilla plantation. Although the
event had a less than desirable outcome for the bridegroom and bride, the
eyewitness record allows an intimate glimpse of an affair planned, if not
conducted, with the owner's blessing and support. The ceremony was to
take place during 1829 or 1830 on the plantation of Parkhill's neighbor
Achille Murat. His traveling friend Francis Tuckett preserved the details:
"The evening I spent with Mr. Murat's friends and had an opportunity of
witnessing for the first time the festivities of a bridal party among the co-
loured population. The different members of the family at whose house I
stayed felt great interest in facilitating the wishes of the party. The wedding
cake was exhibited ornamented with flowers. Friends assembled from a distance of 20 miles around[,] but I am sorry to say the bridegroom was absent,
prevented by his subjection to the caprise [*sic*] of an owner, and the bride
consequently absent herself."[8]

Mercifully, the same misfortune did not mar James and Elizabeth's plans.
They went through their ceremony and were married, even though their
owners were not present. The couple's intentions and desires at the time remain unknown, although the fact of their mutual commitment evidenced
itself through nearly a half century of successful marriage. In their narratives,
former Virginia bondwomen Minnie Fulkes and Georgina Giwebs recalled
jumping over the broom to seal their marriages. It is reasonable to guess
that, having finally gained Parkhill's permission, the young people had a traditional slave marriage of jumping over the broom. In such a manner, Page
and his eighteen-year-old bride would have sealed their union in the eyes of
bondservants in the quarters community if not their owner. In doing so Page
took advantage of the contradictions of "the slave family," which slaveholders did not recognize as legal but which they encouraged to increase ultimately their stock of valuable enslaved property. By marrying Elizabeth,
Page sought to create an institution that would generate support and one

that could make the peculiar institution more bearable for him and his partner.[9]

⌒

The record of James Page's life is the poorer for the lack of insight it affords as to the character, personality, and ambitions of his wife, Elizabeth Page. The facts of her situation—such as they can be understood—suggest that, at a relatively young age and much as was true for countless other enslaved persons, she found herself compelled to do her best to remake broken kinship ties by marrying. Living in isolation from loved ones on a rough frontier, Elizabeth Page possessed few advantages other than native intelligence and perceptive insight, which she used to manage and control her environment as best she could. Historians have claimed that in some cases enslaved women and the wives of their enslavers forged personal bonds of varying degrees when confronting the challenges of a volatile frontier region. Information pertinent to Elizabeth Page and Elizabeth Copland Parkhill unfortunately fails to guide in that regard. Faint allusions from Page's surviving correspondence hint, however, that they did. Perhaps the two women already had drawn closer as a result of their shared migration experience, a dynamic explored sensitively by historian Joan E. Cashin. Thereafter, they lived in close proximity to one another on a daily basis as Elizabeth Page labored as a Parkhill house servant. If such a rapport did grow between mistress and bondservant, the degree of support and even sympathy that accrued to Elizabeth Page is neither known nor measurable. She did express care for her mistress, in any event, as James Page on several occasions conveyed his wife's fervid concerns for the state of Elizabeth Parkhill's health.[10]

Page, in common with the prevailing nineteenth-century ethos, married a woman willing to live through him or, at least, subject to his will. According to historian Daina Ramey Berry, "Gender . . . dictated every bondperson's way of life and influenced all familial relationships." As a woman, Elizabeth had to learn quickly how to be a supportive wife, mother, and laborer in a pioneer society. Page possessed a more than healthy ego. His narcissistic need for her unconditional adoration and support compounded her tasks. Page, just as was true of his master, perceived his wife as a conventionally passive and generally quiet woman. Within two years of the marriage, she gave birth to son Tom, named after Page's only brother, sold on the auction block some eight years earlier. Since Elizabeth did not leave her voice, we do not know much about her parenting skills (nor do we know much about James's). What we know about her comes from the voice of her husband, who was silent about her talents and skills. As a generally quiet woman, designing clothes and serving as seamstress, homemaker, wife, and mother would have numbered among her abilities. Without her contribution to the household, the notoriety and many accomplishments of the enslaved preacher, overseer, and race leader would not have been possible.[11]

Page's reminiscences concentrated on telling his story in context of his relationship with Elizabeth and said little else about her. This portrayal showed her primary role as a spouse lending emotional support and uncritical encouragement to her husband. To her fell responsibility for nurturing and sustaining his ambitions. Page did manage to offer a back-handed compliment when he reminisced that "she never complain[ed] and helped me in everything I wanted to do." Otherwise, what did Page say to recognize the needs, concerns, and interests of his wife? He seemed not to understand or else did not acknowledge many of his wife's needs, because she existed to serve only their enslaver and him. The enslaved overseer and preacher who prided himself on his literacy and knowledge chose not to teach his wife even the rudiments of reading and writing. Throughout her approximate seventy-eight years on earth, she never became, in a traditional sense, a literate woman. Page once noted, "Elizabeth reminds me of my mother in old Virginny," who could neither read nor write since John Parkhill only taught one of his favorite enslaved blacks—Page—literacy. However, Elizabeth, unlike his lost mother, afforded Page greater incentive to look to the future from the comforting base of a growing family.[12]

Assuming that Page perceived Elizabeth's role in such a fixed and limited manner, the question of the nature and tenor of their personal rapport remains open to consideration. Once again, the scarcity of relevant information handicaps any assessment beyond his evident enduring care and affection as a provider of the household. Given his commitment to preaching and use of the Bible as a teaching tool, some further insights, nonetheless, may be gleaned. One of the more popular scriptural passages that Page utilized derived from Paul's Letter to the Corinthians. In 1 Corinthians 14:34–35, the apostle exclaimed, "Let your women keep silent in the churches, for they are not permitted to speak, but they are to be submissive, as the law also says. And if they want to learn something, let them ask their own husbands at home." According to Marli F. Weiner, enslaved women confronted "the ideology of domesticity" every day of their lives. Given Page's strong Christian beliefs, it appears that he confined Elizabeth to the home sphere when he could do so. She occupied her domestic space; he stepped out into the public sphere. He was the learned man, and she assumed the role of the devoted housewife. He lauded her, on occasion, as "a good homemaker." He acknowledged her passion for sewing and insisted that she enjoyed making clothes for their owners' daughter Harriet Parkhill. Much like many slaveholding and enslaved men, Page believed that the subordinate position of the woman in the home was a social construct mandated by God. "I believe," he asserted, "[that] a woman should be a helpmate to her husband like my wife is to me." Their mutually understood arrangement was not one, though, limited strictly to reciprocal rights and responsibilities. "I always wanted to live all my life with Elizabeth," Page related, "who understood me like my mother." In the abstract, Elizabeth would serve, in part, as a surrogate for his lost mother, Susie. Nonetheless, whether it was his mother, Elizabeth, or other women in general, Page lived a lifetime with his idiosyncrasies concerning basic rights of the opposite sex.[13]

Of course, the attitudes held by James and Elizabeth regarding their relationship necessarily should be examined not in isolation but in the context of the world in which they lived. The prevalence of similar views in society resonated from a host of contemporary sources as well as the subsequent work of respected historians. One fascinating example dated to a few years following the Page union. Originally printed in a widely read magazine, the item thereafter was republished repeatedly for decades. It detailed the roles of men and women, as follows:

Man is strong—Woman is beautiful

Man is daring and confident—Woman is deferent and unassuming

Man is great in action—Woman is suffering

Man shines abroad—Woman at home

Man talks to convince—Woman to persuade and please

Man has a rugged heart—Woman has a soft and tender one

Man prevents misery—Woman relieves it

Man has science—Woman has taste

Man has judgment—Woman has sensibility

Man is a being of justice—Woman is an angel of mercy.

Reflecting his master's course and that of countless others, Page in line with patterns of accepted behavior adhered to strict guidelines concerning the roles that his wife could assume in the home and society at large. Foremost, women were to occupy positions that did not threaten the power of men or challenge their masculinity.[14]

While acting in furtherance of that goal, Page invoked biblically inspired authority to fit family rules within societal expectations. He established himself as head of his household within the mainstream of male behavior patterns. Stephanie M. H. Camp found this typical for the times, at least when it came to nineteenth-century marital relationships within the home. As she concluded in her examination of female bondservants, "Women rarely became familiar with the neighborhood geography." Her comments fit Elizabeth Page's situation, comfortably concealing Page's desire to provide a safe environment for his wife. For one thing, Page understood well the culture of violence on Florida's wild frontier. He would have seen planters and poor whites clashing and fighting among themselves, the volatility often sparked or intensified by overindulgence in ardent spirits. He had lived in the world long enough to know that race, kinship ties, and regional loyalty all cemented bonds between slaveholders and their "country-men" or the "plain folk" in opposition to despised outsiders, particularly blacks. Specifically, this quite often included bondservants and meant that physical abuse of bondwomen occurred with regularity and without recourse. Parkhill's treatment of his three wives further shaped Page's perspectives. Parkhill relegated the women in his life to the roles of housewives and plantation mistresses who stayed home and out of the political, economic, and social affairs of men. Elizabeth Page thus served three masters: God, John Parkhill, and her husband, James, but not necessarily in that order. Page believed meanwhile that his wife should practice piety, purity, virtue, submission, and family devotion. Given the cultural values of the antebellum South, he aspired in the domestic realm to live the life of a typical man, one who happened to be black and enslaved.[15]

Page still looked to his wife, however circumscribed her role as a woman, for support and encouragement. She did not disappoint him. "Elizabeth helped me to become the man I am today," he insisted late in life. The strength and resiliency of their bond aided him significantly. Historian Emily West found, for instance, that love between married couples such as James and Elizabeth "increased the psychological distance or 'social space' between bondservants and owners." The distance, in turn, helped enslaved people to endure the vicissitudes of bondage. The open space allowed Page an opportunity to share his secrets with his wife. As a caring spouse, Elizabeth also assisted with things that he considered important. She came to know when her husband was hurting or otherwise needy. "My wife would always help me with anything I needed to do," he acknowledged. Elizabeth undertook and accomplished many more things to support her husband's "career" than will ever be known or credited. That Page would admit only that Elizabeth helped him with his life's work, though, underscored his attitude toward her and other women.[16]

⁓

Among the important contributions that Elizabeth made to her husband's benefit, she gave him a son to treasure, a gift to ensure his legacy. Page deeply loved and attended to the well-being of his son, Tom, evidenced at least by his hard work to support the welfare of his family. Yet just as Page left few details of his relationship with his wife, he said little about his relationship with his only son. We do not know whether Page took an interest in his son's literacy and secular and religious education. He may have taught Tom how to read, write, and count just as John Parkhill had done for him. If so, they would have gone over scriptural passages in the Bible, as well as other temporal things such as how to survive in the world that the slaveholder had made for both of them. Maybe the loss of his mother and brother factored in his reticence. Perhaps Page wanted to maintain emotional distance from Tom for fear that he might lose him to the auction block like his mother and brother, as Parkhill's finances plummeted or his caprices multiplied. As Wilma King suggested, Page seemingly wanted to keep a safe place that sorrow could not touch when and if such a tragedy occurred.[17]

One thing is for sure: James Page disdained household duties. He expressly did not like to cook. Stretching the point further, he did not enjoy performing any "womanly" chores that may have compromised his masculinity and opened to question his status as head of his household. The world as he perceived it demanded that Page stand tall as the family patriarch. He carried responsibility, at least in part, for transmitting the cultural values that would sustain family members through slavery and freedom, including, no doubt, preserving his family history by sharing stories about his father, mother, and brother with his young son. So, Elizabeth performed her womanly duties, and James acted as he thought a man should act, leaving household chores—including cooking, cleaning, hauling water, washing, ironing, knitting, spinning, mending, making clothes, preserving food, and tending the master's domestic animals—strictly to her. Fortunately for Page, Elizabeth proved adept in her management of his home, for she took over many of his "manly" duties during his frequent absences, while making their home a comfortable place to return to after logging many miles of grueling travel.[18]

When at home, how did Page spend time with or support his family? An earlier discussion surveyed his reading habits and efforts to self-educate, especially in biblical matters. The many books he possessed suggest he also spent time at home learning about the illnesses that might afflict his family and the quarters community, and how to treat them. Page also contributed directly to his family's welfare by earning money from tips from Parkhill and his guests, often by driving parties from place to place. He also gleaned a very limited income from preaching on other plantations and farms. His free time often went to gardening or else tending to his small chicken coop. Page often talked about how proud he was of his garden, even in conversation with members of the Parkhill family after freedom came. Page underscored his manhood when he used his crops to supplement family rations as well as when he assisted those in need on the plantation: "I always tried to help those who could not work by giving them vegetables from my little patch." Page could also use the vegetables grown from his garden to barter for other necessities. Fishing added protein to his family's diet. Like Page, Silas Jackson and others fished to supplement their families' food intake. The Maryland former bondman reminisced that "all of the slaves . . . who wanted [to]" could fish. For Page and other men on the Parkhill plantations, these "manly" activities reinforced their image as providers and household heads. This illustrated an agency in taking care of his family and other enslaved families as well.[19]

Above all, Page strove to exhibit the dignity of manhood. He did so in the privacy of his own home and in the glare of public attention. Importantly, though, he did not live out a concept of manhood that focused on violence or revenge, though such goals were common in the area. Nor did he manifest his brand of manhood by directly confronting the evils of slavery or fighting the peculiar institution in the revolutionary manner, as Toussaint L'Ouverture had done in Haiti, or as Nat Turner, Denmark Vesey, Gabriel Prosser, the men and women in the 1811 Louisiana revolt, the Seminoles and their black allies, and others had done in the United States. Page never sought to be a martyr by fomenting what he knew would be an unsuccessful rebellion against slavery in heavily armed Middle Florida. The enslaved preacher's manhood emerged through his own style of race leadership, whether during or after slavery. Many of his congregants looked to him as a man not because of Messianic calls to arms but because of the quality of his preaching and the awe that his literacy skills sparked. "Yes, people like the idea that I can read and write a little bit," he once remarked. As many of those inspired by him

understood, his accomplishments ranged far greater than his modest assertion allowed. Given homeschooling and the large number of books that he
eventually housed in his personal library, the enslaved preacher and future
free leader of his people could read and write far more than just a "little bit."
Page's radical stand at times came not from direct confrontation but from
his words.[20]

Over time, Page matured into a man in his own right. He patiently prayed
to God and did what he could to uplift the lives of congregants spiritually
and temporally within the confines of slavery. For him, manhood went beyond directly resisting slavery. He repeatedly demonstrated his courage, a
key element of masculinity, when he risked his life traveling throughout the
South to bring the word of God to his race. Writing years after the Civil War,
the iconic leader Frederick Douglass knew of the travails of traveling to
places where Page routinely preached during the antebellum period; after
emancipation, he was happy to "live to see the day when I could with safety
to my person, to my liberty, tread the soil of Florida, of South Carolina, of
Georgia." Before, the thought of traveling through these states "sent a shudder through me." During and after slavery, the enslaved preacher appeared
not to fear travel throughout those states or any other place in the South
where people needed to hear his voice. Page also demonstrated daring when
he preached moving sermons to bondpeople that focused on joy, peace,
love, and self-reliance while on earth. His now-worldly sermons provided
for the spirituality of enslaved people and at the same time encouraged
them to provide for the earthly welfare of their families.[21]

To whatever degree he demonstrated his brand of manhood at home or
abroad, Page remained a bondman with deep emotional scars who lived
day to day anticipating the possibility of catastrophe. Likely no area of life
prompted more immediate concern in that regard than protecting Elizabeth
from predators. According to historian Walter Johnson, "Slaveholders used
the well-grooved patterns of plantation life to construct a simulacrum of domestic and agricultural order over sexual predation." The threat of sexual
exploitation constituted a fact of life for enslaved women and their loved
ones. The tragic situation repeated itself time and time again virtually everywhere the institution of slavery touched. "From the beginning of slavery
in the Americas, if not before, white men had believed that when it came to
enslaved women, purchase promised reward," Edward Baptist concluded.
"Male enslavers justified themselves by saying that African-American
women were more sexual, less moral, less beautiful, less delicate." Debra

Gray White observed that many white Southerners conceived enslaved women to be promiscuous by nature, nothing more than "Jezebels" who invited sexual attention.[22]

Owners, owners' sons, owners' nephews and guests, overseers, friends of the family, neighbors, and whoever else attained access posed a threat. To cite an example, North Carolina plantation owner Mary Ruffin Smith, who never married, found out to her surprise that two "race-mixed nieces" had been born to servant girl Harriet. The children, it turned out, had been fathered by her two bachelor brothers, Sidney, an attorney and state legislator, and Francis, a physician. Ella Gertrude Clanton Thomas, the wife of a wealthy slaveholder in Georgia, kept a diary of her life before, during, and after the Civil War. She wrote with frustration about miscegenation between whites and enslaved women, noting, "I know that this is a view of the subject that it is thought best for [white] women to ignore[,] but when we see so many cases of mulattoes commanding higher prices, advertised as 'Fancy girls,' oh it is not enough to make us shudder for the standard of morality in our southern homes." Also in Georgia, Amanda America Dickson shared her history of being the offspring of a rape by the slaveholder's son. As historian Kent Anderson Leslie related the story, David Dickson, a man in his early forties, "spotted a young female slave playing in the fields" of his mother's plantation. He picked up thirteen-year-old Julia Frances Dickson and rode off with her. Nine months later Amanda was born. Similar tales echoed elsewhere. The fact was that Elizabeth Page was vulnerable to sexual interference, try as her husband might to protect her. Julia Frances Dickson did not ask to be raped by a white man twenty-seven years her senior. Neither did another Harriet, Harriet Jacobs, ask to be sexually harassed by Dr. James Norcom, or bondservants Celia, or Ellen Brooks, or the thousands of other victims sexually harassed or raped by those who had control over their valuable bodies. But Ella Thomas said it best when writing particularly about the sexual exploitation of defenseless enslaved girls and women by white men throughout the antebellum South.[23]

Historian Nell Painter noted that "the sexual torment of slave women" has been known by historians for more than a century. Indeed, many studies of enslaved women are replete with stories of violent sexual abuse. But no extant evidence suggests that whites ever sexually abused or even whipped Elizabeth Page. Her success, if she did succeed, in avoiding exploitation counted her among the lucky ones in Florida. Page himself alluded to the fact that "some Negro girls were hurt by their masters." He did not specify exactly what he meant, but instances of sexual abuse within his knowledge certainly would fit within the category of "hurt." As other sources plainly document, numerous Florida slaveholders gained notoriety for their cruel sexual liaisons with enslaved women. The numbers of men who quietly abused women away from public notice were even higher, running rampant through quarters communities. Slaveholders such as Achille Murat, Amon DeLaughter, and Zephaniah Kingsley more or less openly pursued sexual relations with enslaved women. Murat made no effort to keep secret his dalliances with enslaved women. He often laughed when talking about getting "with the slave girls" on his Jefferson County plantation. Amon DeLaughter talked about his "sexual gamboling" on the Madison County plantation that he managed for his mother. Kingsley made known his sexual desires for some of his enslaved women, openly marrying at least one during his lifetime. Some sexual relationships with white authority figures may have been uncontested by the slave women involved. Whether the relationships were consensual, given the unlimited power that slaveholders wielded over these largely powerless women, most, if not all, enslaved women were involved in nonconsensual sex. In fact, many enslaved girls and women were simply raped. If sexual exploitation did not bring pain to the Page household, the tragic injustice befell other slave homes all around.[24]

Whether John Parkhill engaged in the sexual abuse of his enslaved women or men, a reality that would have threatened the Pages directly, deserves consideration. Page's reminiscences and surviving correspondence fail to raise any suggestion that Elizabeth Parkhill ever was compelled to endure such outside sexual exploits from her husband. The enslaved preacher never described his master as a sexual predator or abuser. Nor does Page indicate that his master sexually abused him or other male or female bond-servants by coercing them into having carnal relations with members in the quarters community against their will. Page always remembered his owner as a "Christian family man." And based upon his Christian values, Parkhill appeared not to tolerate sexual abuse of any kind on his plantations. Yet this religious enslaver had no scruples about committing a form of genocide by tearing children from parents and husbands from wives on the auction block, thereby killing off enslaved family units, while maintaining the sanctity of his own family.[25]

Nonetheless, Parkhill does not appear to have lived as a hypocrite, at least when it came to sexual matters. As it particularly related to enslaved women, his behavior stood in contrast to that of Thomas Jefferson, the third president of the United States, who nevertheless proudly proclaimed that a "man must . . . retain his manners and morals." As historian Annette Gordon-Reed aptly noted, "The American public seems willing—almost anxious—to believe that Jefferson and Hemings did have a relationship." And based upon information gathered by the Sally Hemings family, he forced an illicit sexual relationship upon the teenaged enslaved girl. Insofar as the record permits understanding, John Parkhill never approached Elizabeth Page for sexual relations, forced or otherwise. Neither did his sons or his relations. Parkhill reflected Presbyterian norms of the day that frowned on sex outside of marriage, especially with enslaved women. His religious commitments barred him from viewing the quarters community, as did many of his contemporaries, as "a white man's sexual playground." So long as Elizabeth Page performed her duties as a Parkhill house servant and as Page's wife and did not otherwise violate acceptable norms of behavior, her owner protected her, whether from himself or from others. When it cost him nothing financially to do so, Parkhill declined to intrude—and did not allow anyone else to meddle—in the private affairs of James and Elizabeth Page.[26]

If anything, Parkhill's obligation to the Pages grew as time passed. For one thing, the expansion of Tuscawilla in the mid-1830s increased the master's dependence upon Page as overseer. Eventually, more than three thousand acres and scores of enslaved workers came under his owner's control. Parkhill's Union Bank cashier responsibilities, though, limited the time that he could devote to plantation matters during the decade's final six years. His financial crises and legal problems thereafter commanded his attention. Those obstacles necessarily added to Page's work while rendering his efforts ever more valuable to his master.[27]

During the same period, a series of events that carried serious implications and long-lasting consequences for the Page and Parkhill households intervened in life at Tuscawilla. Some were happy ones, and others were tragic. The Second Seminole War, for example, erupted in December 1835 and persisted for nearly seven years. As already has been mentioned, it produced arbitrary, but regular, threats of devastating raids and bloody deaths. Conditions required constant vigilance and, at times, produced extreme stresses. Tragedy of a deeply personal nature for Parkhill preceded that dilemma and cast a pall on family affairs during the war's early years. About two years after Page's marriage to Elizabeth, death turned the Parkhill family's world upside down. On April 10, 1834, Elizabeth Copland Parkhill

Massacre of the Whites by the Indians and Blacks in Florida.

The above is intended to represent the horrid Massacre of the Whites in Florida, in December 1835, and January, February, March and April 1836, when near Four Hundred (including women and children) fell victims to the barbarity of the Negroes and Indians.

Seminole warriors and their black allies waged war from 1835 to 1842 to defend their lands against the encroachment of white migrants in Florida. State Archives of Florida, Florida Memory

passed away at about age forty-six. The circumstances are not known. She left a grieving husband, three daughters, and at least two sons to mourn her. All indications suggest that the loss overwhelmed Parkhill. By the same token, it required James and Elizabeth to devote their energies to buttressing the family. Elizabeth Page turned her attention to the children and the home. Page—preacher, overseer, and confidant—consoled the man who enslaved him. "I sat and spent a lot of time with the Col. when his wife Mrs. Elizabeth passed away," he recorded. "I felt so bad for him." Perhaps referring to those times, a Parkhill family member related, "[James] was also his master's 'body servant,' and helped to nurse him, when ill. They had long talks together, as friends." At times, it seems that the Parkhill family's survival, whether economic or emotional, depended primarily on their bondman, James Page.[28]

The depth of Parkhill's sorrow and the effectiveness of the Pages' care for him can be measured by the fact that Parkhill waited nearly four years to remarry. When he did so it was to a woman with direct connections to one of Virginia's leading families. Lucy Beverley Randolph was born in Bunkershill, Albemarle County, on November 14, 1805. Her father, Thomas Eston Randolph, ranked as Thomas Jefferson's "favorite cousin" and "intimate friend." In recognition of their special rapport, the president named his son mothered by slave Sally Hemings Eston. Reportedly, Sally also maintained close ties with several Randolph family members. Eston Randolph relocated his family, including daughter Lucy and son-in-law Francis B. Eppes, from Virginia to Middle Florida during 1829. They established plantations on Black Creek near John's brother Samuel Parkhill's property. Death took several of the leading Randolph women during roughly the same time frame during which Elizabeth Parkhill was stricken. Those losses, combined with Indian raids and financial fallout from the Panic of 1837, may have encouraged Lucy to consider the older John Parkhill a suitable partner. They married on February 20, 1838, he for the third time and she for the first. A baby girl blessed the union but not until April 5, 1841. That child, Harriet Randolph Parkhill, became the lifelong friend and confidant of James and Elizabeth Page.[29]

One additional occurrence touched directly upon the Page household, although its full weight was not felt for years. Before Parkhill took a new wife, he also acquired an additional plantation, one where James and Elizabeth in time would establish a permanent home. Although the dating of the event remains uncertain, about two to three years prior to his remarriage Parkhill purchased a tract of land a half-dozen miles or so south of Tallahassee. It consisted of approximately seventy-eight acres and was called Bel Air. The vicinity eventually developed into a small, exclusive resort hamlet. One account noted its popularity among "politicians" and insisted that "many questions bearing on the interests of the country had earned discussion in Bel Air." Some considered the area the "best of society in the South." As a man of prestige interested in local, state, and national politics, Parkhill found this second residence very much to his liking. In the early 1850s he moved his remaining family and six enslaved workers to the new locale, and it became his primary residence until his death. Page remained primarily at Tuscawilla, which continued to be the prime cotton-producing site. Page recalled, "I went between Tuscawilla and Bel Air when the Col. moved closer to town with Mrs. Lucy. I lived most of the time with my family on the large place in the country." With occasional assistance from John's son George Washington Parkhill, James Page ran daily affairs at Tuscawilla until the outbreak of the Civil War.[30]

CHAPTER SIX

Intensifying Pastoral Duties and Leadership Responsibilities

We had church wid de white preachers and dey tole us to mind our masters and missus and we would be saved; if not, dey said we wouldn'. Dey never tole us nothin' 'bout Jesus.

—Former bondwoman Margrett Nickerson

Mostly we had white preachers, but when we had a black preacher that was heaven.

—Former bondman Anthony Dawson

Scenes of Father James Page's labors as a veteran enslaved preacher of the 1840s and 1850s are easily evoked. The season and locale necessarily varied, but a typical moment appeared something like this. The beginning of another hot summer sun had begun to come up over the high skies of Tallahassee, Florida, and the air lay heavy on the morning calm. An open-air arbor church, its leafy covering blocking the most intense of the sun's rays, offered a welcomed haven. Dozens of worshipers have gathered to find relief not only from the heat but also from the regimen of an enslaved laborer's daily life. Men wipe their brows with cloths, dripping wet from the sweltering Middle Florida atmosphere. Women gently rock crying babies on their chests, some humming to comfort restless, sweaty children. Older youths lean against mothers and fathers, awaiting a turn to sip from jugs of water being passed back and forth among the families. Before all those who have gathered stands a rather portly, dark-skinned man dressed in a black suit with a graying, wooly head of hair and short-cut curling beard. As he adjusts his clerical collar that he so fondly wears during sermons, his gentle eyes deceptively mask a fiery passion that the audience knows lies beneath his calm, open disposition. Father James Page's confidence as a preacher resounds. The call and response of congregants—as well as the ring-shout that honors African ancestors—provokes participants to get up and move in rhythmic circles as emotions climb. The moment's intensity builds to greater heights as the pastor's oratory booms with the deeds of Old Testament prophets and the hope betokened by baby Jesus, and the promise of rewards awaiting in heaven dazzled many eyes. "When I sometimes preached," Page recollected, "my flock would get happy." He added, "[My desire was] to preach the word of God to my people and they would get happy too when they heard me preach." One enslaved man summed up the attraction of enslaved ministers: "Mostly we had white preachers, but when we had a black preacher, that was heaven."[1]

The power that Page brought to his sermonizing and delivery of pastoral observations, combined with awe of his intelligence and literary skills, worked a profound impact upon his listeners. According to his deacon and friend Jack Sheppard, Reverend Page often would open one of three Bibles that he eventually owned and carefully thumb through the pages for his selected verses. He recognized no need for hurry or to call for the congregants to join him in reading the passage, for no one present was able to. "[When] I got baptized none of us but Father Page knew nothing [a]bout reading or writing," Sheppard recalled, "but he later taught me how to read and write real good." Still, those seated would lend their voices as he slowly bellowed out the words of the Scriptures, providing a chorus of "hallelujahs" and "amens." As Page moved into the heart of the sermon, Sheppard continued, "his preaching was usually met with clapping hands, stomping feet, and crys [sic] of Thank You Lord."[2]

The picture of Page that such accounts paint reflected Parkhill's success and privilege. Fundamentally important to the canvas was his rapport with his owner. Page gained his master's favor to a degree in exchange for obedience, hard work, and compassion. Undeniably, though, by the 1840s the enslaved preacher knew John Parkhill intimately, understood him, and, at times, possessed the means to get most of what he wanted from him. "My master allowed me to travel to Alabama, Georgia, and even South Carolina," Page boasted. But the enslaved cleric had to understand that he served his enslaver's purpose. Typically, men such as John Parkhill wanted enslaved ministers to preach sermons of obedience and social control. Nonetheless, by the mid-1850s the once-fledging preacher had emerged as a servant of God listened to and admired by many Floridians and others through the Southeast.

Page possessed a complex personality; he proved a wizard of deceit who routinely presented two masks to the world. Accounts by contemporaries offer excellent insight into his character. On the one hand, they conjured "the good low-profile slave preacher" who was prepared to manipulate others to obtain his goals. "He was," a friend remarked, "generally a quiet and reserved man of the cloth." As a peaceful and unassuming man, Page would have preached overt obedience to the enslaved that allowed them to receive concessions from their enslavers. But it served the enslaved preacher's purpose as well, for it granted him certain privileges and benefits like traveling and preaching to members of the slave community. On the other hand, the less public persona in the slave quarters suggested something else. In fact, oral tradition insisted that Page could be a fiery preacher "who stirred up his congregations" and that some slaveholders on the peninsula blamed the intransigence of their enslaved workers on his subversive preaching. As the mid-1840s arrived and then faded, Page continued to rebel against slaveholder dominance by discreetly preaching self-reliance and quasi-independence. He argued, "Negroes must learn what they can to help themselves." Here, as elsewhere, constant deceptions marked relations between the enslaved and the enslaver.[3]

A belief that God had called him to shepherd those with no foreseeable path out of bondage guided Page's life as an enslaved preacher. The men and women to whom he preached held little hope of ever meeting a facilitator of liberation such as Harriet Tubman or escaping their bondage through one branch or another of the Underground Railroad. It was even less likely that they would successfully flee to the North on their own as Frederick Douglass had done. Armed rebellion on the model of Nat Turner's 1831 slave revolt remained less than plausible in well-armed Middle Florida. The 1850 Fugitive Slave Act made it even harder for runaways to be hidden by sympathizers. The people in Page's congregations were all born into slavery and, it appeared, more than likely would die as bondservants. Page heard God telling him to aid these individuals in maintaining a sense of human dignity that would permit them to survive the harsh reality of plantation life. "God wanted me to preach to my people," he repeated as if it were a mantra. With Page's ministrations and that of his peers, slaves lived without being broken by despair or a sense of meaninglessness. Each day's survival constituted a victory. The enslaved preacher metaphorically and, sometimes, literally watched over this flock by night, tending to those shackled during the darkest years of Deep South slavery.[4]

Any doubts that Page once had entertained about his ability to discharge his call slowly receded. "I got more comfortable in front of people the more I preached," he remembered. "It made me feel good." His growing pastoral duties also brought him prestige, authority, public recognition, and a sense of power associated with manhood. Preaching from the pulpit to auditors of both races projected him as a competent and intelligent man equal to or better than whites in the audience. By allowing him to preach, white men, by this action, had ceded some of their masculinity, if only for a few hours, to allow Page to exhibit his manhood before the assembly. An embattled Parkhill, who was finding himself increasingly dependent upon Page, allowed him ever-greater mobility to move about. "He . . . would visit all the plantations in Tallahassee, preaching the gospel," former bondman Louis Napoleon detailed. "Each plantation would get a visit from him one Sunday of each month. The slaves on the Randolph plantation would congregate in one of the cabins to receive him when he would read the Bible and preach and sing." Latitude to leave the home plantation offered an important degree of freedom. His pastoral journeys, in turn, opened to him worlds that his counterparts could only dream about.[5]

With the passage of years Page gained renown among enslaved persons who heard him preach or otherwise learned of his ministry. At times, he may have labored as the most recognizable enslaved preacher in the South during the nineteenth century. "Many people knew me when I travel[ed] to so many places," he recounted. "They knew me sometimes more than I knew them." His journeys followed in the tradition of the biblical apostles. His quiet movements through the wilds of frontier Florida and other parts of the South paralleled those of the early missionaries who had pioneered the work of God. Much like the apostles, Page felt compelled to travel far and wide. "I like traveling the lonely roads," he once observed, "with just me and the Lord." The enslaved preacher accepted a moral obligation to travel so that he could convert sinners and save souls. Such missionary work was not easy. Some black men and women preachers asked friends and companions to travel with them for comfort and safety. Page did not. His faith, fortitude, and confidence allowed him to brave frontier Florida, as well as places outside his home region and the peninsula, doing the Lord's work on his own.[6]

As Page's solitary travels expanded beyond Middle Florida, he faced a progressively greater threat of violence to his person. Whites during the 1840s and into the 1850s increasingly feared that religion eventually would lead enslaved blacks to demand freedom. The national secession crisis that led to the Compromise of 1850 and the Fugitive Slave Act added fuel to the flames. Plus, Page's insistence on traveling the lonely roads of the countryside by himself openly defied the belief of Southern whites that a bondservant's place was on his or her master's property. Some whites simply refused to accept that a bondman could leave one of Florida's slave prisons, whether called farms or plantations, for any reason except to fulfill the owner or overseer's express orders. Page evidently did not know or accept "his place."[7]

Beyond general disgruntlement, slave patrols and local law enforcement officers presented persistent obstacles. "They would stop me and ask me what I was doing," Page explained. "Some acted real mean to me at first. I said that Col. Parkhill gave me permission to preach, and sometimes that did not seem good enough for them. I sometimes got guns and rifles being pointed at me. But after a while, when they saw me, they would just wave me on." Given the enforcement of the slave codes, few bondpeople had opportunities to travel beyond the gateposts of their farms and plantations. As one of the most familiar men traveling throughout the antebellum South, Page did what most enslaved people wished they could have done as well. If they were caught off their owners' farms and plantation, they could suffer intimidation or, worse, the loss of life and limb. Former bondwoman Florida Clayton distinctly recalled "nigger hunters" and "nigger stealers" whom bondservants met in travels off the plantation, men for whom intimidation and cruelty came as second nature. Page's own experience, though, had run to less extreme lengths. "I went to Thomasville, Georgia[,] many times during slavery times, and I was only stopped one time by three [white] men," he informed an interviewer. "After that, no one ever stopped me again."[8]

Page's religious belief system, in its mature form, constituted the basis of his philosophy, attitudes, and worldview. Unlike some of his black religious contemporaries, though, Page did not leave a written autobiography or treatise on his principles. But Page grew and matured with age from a rather naïve to a more learned and experienced minister of Christian theology. Bits and pieces of surviving detail and insight aid in discerning nuances generally. In other words, many of his decisions and actions were based upon his evolving understanding of Christian theology. He accepted, for example, the construct of the Trinity: the Father, the Son, and the Holy Spirit. He believed also, fundamentally so, in the existence of one God who was his moral compass in all things that he did. He refused at the same time to embrace polytheism, which is to say that—unlike some of his enslaved brothers and sisters—he afforded no credence to African religious traditions that encompassed many Gods. "I learned from the church and Col. Parkhill," he insisted, "that there was one God." With the belief systems of others, however, he could display some flexibility: "I never bother a man about his religion, but I wanted him to know that there was only one God." Page left no indication as to the spiritual dogma embraced by his biological parents, Susie and Coyer Page. We do not know whether their religious views were rooted in Afro-Christianity or African religious traditions. Sadly, sources remain, therefore, silent as to what, if any, influence his biological parents exerted on their son's religious beliefs.[9]

Although belief in one God may appear to be a relatively unimportant point, Page's firm commitment constituted for some whites the mark of a rebellious nature. Numerous masters, openly or tacitly, led enslaved persons to believe in the existence of two Western Christian gods. One was God the Creator, whom they could not see. The other was the master, whom they could see. Former bondman Douglas Dorsey declared, "The [white] ministers admonished [the enslaved] to honor their masters and mistresses and to have no other God but them as 'we cannot see the other God, but you can see your master and mistress.'" Former bondwoman Della Hilyard recorded in the same vein that bondpeople were "told to honor their masters and mistresses and of the damnation which awaited them for disobedience." Even Page implied that his master acted, at times, like God. At least Parkhill gave out food to his enslaved people in a godlike manner, insisting that he do so himself rather than directing his overseer Page or some other authority figure to do the honors. This practice suggested that the enslaver, much like God, was the giver of all good things. Most owners fervently wanted their enslaved people to fear their ultimate power and, accordingly, acquiesce to their demands. Parkhill already had demonstrated recourse to such an attitude in the sale of Page's mother and brother, and his earlier reluctance to sell the family to Page's father, Coyer, in Richmond. He, with so many of his friends, truly sought various methods of instilling the fear of God in those whom they commanded.[10]

His own creed notwithstanding, Page understood that he had to compete with pre-Christian worldviews among potential congregants. From the beginning to the end of his ministry, he encountered enslaved worshippers who held to West African beliefs in multiple gods, magic, witchcraft, and other cultural and religious practices. Many such people already had suffered bondage for generations. Historian Albert Raboteau underscored that Africans and persons of African descent did not simply drop all that was dear to them and important in their culture when they debarked in the Americas. Page mentioned this challenge to saving souls in one quarters community: "I can't remember now the place in Alabama but I sure remember that some of the brethren did not want to hear what I wanted to tell them." He confided later to a friend that some enslaved people had "their own way of worshipping" and did not need him to preach to them. Such bondservants might have practiced African ancestor worship, adhered to Roman Catholic or Islamic customs, or pursued a variety of other religious paths. Although Page displayed some flexibility when interacting with persons of different religious beliefs, he stood firm in defending Christianity against those who professed voodoo, hoodoo, or Islam. Late in life when asked what he thought about other religions, he responded, "[They] are alright I guess, but just not where I preached."[11]

The "strange practices" of some bondpersons persisted as viable elements of the slave's religious understanding and carried an indelible impact on their cultural experience. Former bondwoman Amanda McCray, for one, attested to the fact that "[slaves] were duly schooled in all the current superstitions, and listen[ed] to tales of ghost[s] and animals that talked and reasoned." Former bondservant Acie Thomas, who lived in Leon County not too distant from Tuscawilla plantation, remembered being taught superstitions "that hooting owls were very jealous of their night hours and whenever they hooted near a field of workers they were saying: 'Task done or no done—night's my time—go home.'" In a metaphoric way, Thomas was also telling enslavers that the time had come for enslaved laborers to stop working for the day. As Page and other enslaved preachers found, these practices and others proved resilient and existed alongside Christian beliefs well past slavery's demise.[12]

Just as confronting African religious and cultural customs occupied Page's attention, so, too, did competition from other religious leaders. This impediment extended throughout Florida and the South. Zephaniah Kingsley, for instance, contended with a religious conjurer called "Gualla Jack or Jack the Conjurer." The mystic had been a high priest in his home country in Africa and was praised and feared on Kingsley's northeast Florida island plantation. Former bondman Henry Bruce recalled enslaved people in Virginia using a slave conjurer to forestall a slaveholder relocating them to Alabama. According to an interviewer, John Henry Kemp "gained the name 'Prophet' from his constant reference to the future and to his religion." The interviewer added, "Kemp claims the ability to read the future with ease; even to help determine what it will bring in some cases. He reads it in the palms of those who believe in him; he determines the good and bad luck;

freedom from sickness; success in love and other benefits it will bring from the use of charms, roots, herbs and magical incantations and formulas." Susan B. Eppes, daughter of a Leon County plantation owner, grew up around those whom she sensed practiced voodoo. She remembered enslaved blacks as superstitious and fearful of the "'de kunjer man' or 'de kunjer o' man.'" Bondservants believed that he could cast or break spells on those whom he liked or disliked. Page met the challenge firsthand. "I had to pray for some slaves who felt they were, I guess, demon filled," he recorded, "but I told them they did not have anything to worry about[;] just pray to the Lord."[13]

The tone of Page's ministry sounded most profoundly in his reverence of and faith in the Trinity's second part. Page believed to his core that "God's son so loved the world that he died for all of our sins." A former bondservant noted, "Father Page believed that we should love one another, and that the Savior died for the sins of man, and those that atone, and followed the ways of God, would enter the gates of heaven." Page preached, consonant with his understanding of Christ's teachings, about loving one's neighbor and turning the other cheek when necessary. He declared, "They should forgive people like God forgave all of our sins and so we should treat people right." Here, the enslaved preacher focused his words on both the enslaver and the enslaved when he implied that forgiving people for their past transgressions and treating others justly was the minimum standard for Christian behavior. Neither abuse nor violence could be condoned. Implying that the son of God died for all humankind regardless of color, Page insisted that "everyone is the same in the sight of the Lord."[14]

Yet that tone resounded with deep and complicated rhythms that derived from a variety of influences. In one example, Page developed—as time passed—a better understanding of, and greater respect for, the meaning and importance of the Holy Spirit. To some extent that fundamental element of the Trinity allowed him to meld his own ways with West African traditions that emphasized spirit possession, the spirts of the gods, the spirits of the ancestors, and the emotional ecstasy that emanated from the spirits during worship services. As a young man in the Presbyterian Church, he had not been exposed to the various meanings and interpretations of the Holy Spirit, nor had he been prepared for the emotional responses that greeted his own preaching. Of those Presbyterian experiences, he claimed that "I sat quietly in the church and heard the minister preach and nobody said nothing but him." So when he initially started preaching, Page had to adjust gradually to the exuberance shown by his various congregations. "At first, I didn't like all the loud hollering when

I first start preaching," he reminisced, "but I got used to it." Page's gradual evolution concerning what constituted religious worship among enslaved blacks continued: "I like[d] when people got happy because many of them were filled with the spirit." Louis Napoleon verified Page's assertion. Many bondservants were touched by Father Page's words, he disclosed, for many were caught up in exhortations, singing, and "much shouting from the 'happy ones.'" Former bondservant Bolden Hall remarked, as well, that enslaved worshippers got "happy" when Page preached to them. Initially rigid in his adherence to Christian ritual, he soon enough began to accept certain West African practices. "The older I got the more I understood [the uniqueness of] how my people worshipped and prayed to God," he explained.[15]

Accordingly, a richness and depth of tradition already ingrained in the minds and souls of congregants and relevant to their experience strengthened the power of his original drive to preach. Attendees at his services likely participated in various Afro-Christian practices such as call and response, the ring shout, and speaking in tongues. An eyewitness to successes achieved thereby, Page step by step encouraged this brand of worship among his fellow enslaved congregants. "Sometimes people shouted and danced for the Lord into the wee hours in the morning," he professed with a degree of pride. Page's instinct that African religious practices could coexist with Christianity continued to develop. By mixing some long-standing African beliefs with Christianity, he molded a unique form of Afro-Christianity in the churches where he preached. This combination increased his membership significantly over time. Once established, the resulting product marked his ministry thereafter.[16]

Underlying the enslaved preacher's ready willingness to elevate his auditors to peaks of emotional joy and physical exuberance was a rock-hard faith that slavery's days were limited. This conviction was rooted in Page's concept of eschatology, one centered—as it developed—on both the afterlife, the other-worldly, and the here and now, or the now-worldly. He trusted teachings he had absorbed as a boy in the Presbyterian Church and had learned from the Bible that heaven and hell were real places. He understood that all humankind one day would face an eschatological day of judgment that would determine whether individuals would enter the pearly gates of heaven or be doomed for all eternity to the fiery pits of hell. Page's embrace of eschatology, as framed by mid-nineteenth-century writings and debates, led him to believe strongly in predestination as it related to his race. He embraced the doctrine of Providence. He did not base his decision strictly on what he had learned from the Bible. Rather he relied upon, in part, what Parkhill had foreseen and conveyed to him. He became convinced, much as did his Calvinist master, that certain events were preordained, such as the second coming of Christ and the eventual end of slavery. "I believed this day [emancipation] would come," he argued, "because Col. Parkhill had visions of Freedom coming for us one day" as well. For a man who firmly believed that slavery was biblically sanctioned, did Parkhill truly believe that slavery would end one day, or was he simply offering cynical hope to Page? Whether he believed his enslaver or not, Page, from an eschatological point of view, used Christian faith to offer hope that slavery would ultimately end one day with the liberation of his race.[17]

Page's sermons on other-worldly topics have been lost unfortunately to posterity, but those frequently found in the literature of the period suggest that the general focus of black preaching throughout the South centered primarily on other-worldly subjects. Raboteau asserted that the imagery of "other-world" sermons sought to give hope to the hopeless. According to religious scholar Wayne E. Croft Sr., "Whatever is distinct about black preaching grew out of an expression of hope in God's liberation of people from slavery." Former Kentucky bondman Arnold Gragston remembered slave ministers preaching about getting "all the way inside of heaven." The fact that some sermons of enslaved preachers focused on the afterlife cannot be denied. As historian David Dennard has aptly noted, numerous scholars have equated slave preachers' lack of revolutionary dogma and focus on the afterlife with complacency and acquiescence. But Dennard cautioned against such a strict interpretation, given the precarious position in which many enslaved preachers found themselves as leaders of quarters communities. He advised that "in order to be clear about what was or was not otherworldly preaching, it is important, first of all, to have some idea of exactly what constituted an otherworldly sermon." He believed the definition used by Benjamin E. Mays and Joseph W. Nicholson explained more clearly what the term meant to most enslaved preachers: "An other-worldly sermon is . . . one that is concerned so predominantly with the hereafter that the practical aspects of life on earth are secondary and submerged, or one in which fear of, not in this life but in the world to come, is the dominant note. It is a sermon that places more on the mysterious, the magical, and heaven than it does on daily living and those things with which the people are familiar."[18]

Bondservants depended upon Page and other enslaved preachers, though, to teach more than the Pauline command of "slaves be obedient to your masters" and the promise of a reward in heaven. Some, in fact, considered white ministers to be "imposters." Many bondservants understood that these supposed men of God acted at the bidding of slaveholders. Former bondman Lucious Lamar Douglas asserted, "De white preacher, he weren't no good. All he preach[ed] about was to serve de white boss, not God. De white boss paid him so he jes come over to de church house an' talk a little to us an' den go by an' git his money and after dat he could go on 'bout his own business. If dey had let de colored preacher do all de preachin' to de slaves we'd of had good services all de time." Former bondwoman Della Bess Hilyard added, "The slaves were not told about heaven; they were told to honor their masters and mistresses and of the damnation which awaited them for disobedience." It did not escape notice that some white preachers owned enslaved people and, therefore, accepted the ideology that all blacks should be enslaved. Historian John Hope Franklin said it best: "Slavery had become as much a part of the religious orthodoxy of the South as the Creation in the Book of Genesis or Armageddon in the Book of Revelations. The work of promoting and defending slavery, when entrusted to the southern clergy, could not have been in safer hands." The basic message of most white ministers to enslaved listeners centered on Ephesians 6:5, which instructed that "servants be obedient to them that are your master according to the flesh, with fear and trembling, in singleness of your heart, as unto Christ." Little wonder that so many enslaved people held the men who spoke such words to be the enemy.[19]

For his part, Page temporized on the subject when confronted with the direct inquiry of a distinguished white minister. The request came at Bel Air plantation. The Rev. Edwin T. Williams, a Presbyterian divine, was enjoying a visit to the Parkhill estate. While present, he had a chance to hear Page preaching at the Bel Air Baptist Church to a black audience. During a friendly conversation that followed, Williams queried Page "about white Presbyterian ministers' missionary work among the slaves." According to Williams's account, Page replied, "Some ministers at first seemed very affectionate and kind, but his people waited to see if this would continue year in and year out and if so, they believed in and loved them." The moderate tone of the response may have reflected a sense of the need for caution or simply good manners. Many white preachers failed to heed Page's suggestions about showing genuine concern for bondpeople's overall religious welfare, since very few of them took quality time to really study the ideas, beliefs, attitudes, and practices of the enslaved. And as a consequence, Page more than likely came closer to agreeing with the historian who asserted that enslaved people

Bethlehem Missionary Baptist Church in Bel Air was started by Father James Page. State Archives of Florida, Florida Memory

refused to concede even that white ministers were "men of good will." In fact, many bondservants considered them to be frauds.[20]

While the "other-world" appeared regularly in Page's sermons, he did not ignore the now-worldly. He comprehended that his sheep required more than just pie-in-the-sky afterlife sermons. They did not want "be obedient to your master" lessons. His challenge was to provide spiritual and worldly guidance, lessons of encouragement and hope for those living on earth. Some of his congregants may have lacked survival skills in the often cruel and sometimes tumultuous world that the enslaver had made for them. They needed inspiration that encouraged them to live another day when, deep inside themselves, they yearned to give up. They ached for the enslaved preacher to illustrate how to inculcate values in children while enlightening them about their history. Bondpeople looked to Page as the balm that would help soothe the aches and pains of daily existence. Page stated the point bluntly: "I wanted to teach my flock how to live while living on earth." His Christology sought to do the work of Jesus Christ in parallel to the worldly work that bondservants had to perform for themselves and their masters.[21]

In pursuit of his now-worldly mission, Page gave considerable attention to the temporal lives of the enslaved people whom he served. He thought that suffering, as such, would continue until the coming of the Lord. Given that fact, he argued that bondpeople should do as much as possible in terms of feeding, protecting, and caring for themselves and their families. He insisted that they not simply wait patiently for someone else to provide. Drawing upon his masculine orientation, Page taught enslaved blacks how to stay alive. As one of his contemporaries put it, "[He] used to tell young boys how to behave themselves in front of white people." Here, Page would have taught self-respect, taking charge of one's own body and life, and helping others in need with encouragement to endure earthly circumstances. Much like for himself, the enslaved preacher was teaching his understudies how to be skillful actors and actresses in front of white people in order to get what they wanted and needed. Teaching bondservants self-sufficiency in the now-world became for Page a subtle path for resisting slavery and rejecting total dependence upon, and the supposed goodness of, his owner and other slaveholders.[22]

As noted earlier, Page consistently wore two masks—a public one and a private one. In front of whites, he was an accommodationist. But when out of sight of white authority figures, his fiery preaching, based on now-worldly precepts, challenged his congregation to confront authority figures. At least, so some influential whites were convinced. When a disturbance occurred on a Jefferson County plantation near Tuscawilla in 1854, for instance, overseer D. N. Moxley complained of slave intransigence and pointed the finger of blame directly at the enslaved preacher. "I have heard since I came to town," Moxley informed his employer, "that Jim Page and his crew bin the cass [*sic*] of all the fuss." The overseer believed that the singing, shouting, and Page's now-worldly preaching lay at the root of the plantation's disciplinary problems. Page, Moxley concluded, was a complex man who could prove unpredictable and, thus, dangerous. The overseer took the only practical action available to him and barred Page from visiting. The incident underscored Page's focus on taking charge of one's life while on earth before turning attention completely to comforts awaiting in the afterlife. This suggests, as well, that Page had become a consummate actor with multiple personas.[23]

As would most effective leaders, Page taught now-worldly concepts of resistance by his own example. With land and materials granted by his master, the enslaved cleric planted a garden to supplement his family's diet and helped others when assistance was needed. "Folks like getting vegetables from my fine garden," he allowed. Because more privileged than most bondservants, he occasionally shared cash tips that he had earned driving his masters' guests with less fortunate members of the quarters community. The bottom line for Page was to lead the life that he preached. His behavior demonstrated to bondpeople firsthand the importance of resisting the total reliance on enslavers' generosity by trying to take care of themselves and their kinfolk in this world while anticipating better times and conditions in the next. Meanwhile, as overseer his task remained inspiring the Parkhill enslaved workers to labor diligently for their master. As the bondpeople's overseer and others' preacher, Page was both hated and liked, for he had to carefully walk a tightrope. He did his best to keep from falling.[24]

Page took utmost care, as he trod the path that he had chosen, not to use the Bible in a context that subordinated blacks to whites. By dint of hard effort, he understood the Bible sufficiently to use passages to articulate who he was and to sidestep those portions, such as the Pauline Epistles, that did not lend themselves to supporting the theology of liberation. Page, as seen, accepted that his congregants hungered for a religious experience filled with meaning, encouragement, and joy. When asked what part of the Bible he liked the most, he smiled and responded, "I like the Moses story of the Children of Israel getting free of old Pharaoh." Page took a hermeneutical approach to the Bible; that is, he selected specific passages that made the Scriptures more palpable to his flock: "I preached what my brethren need[ed] to hear and needed to know to be strong and Godly." Former bondman Henry Clay Bruce remembered his enslaved preacher as even more forthright. That minister boldly preached that his enslaved brethren should be "free, indeed, free from death, free from hell, free from work, free from white folks, [and] free from everything." Talking about slavery more than five decades after it ended, former Alabama bondman Perry Sid Jemisen echoed the minister's words: "I think it's a good thing dat slavery ended, for God hadn't intended there to be no man a slave." Page, in any event, managed well enough to reject oppressive constructs used by white Christians and others to justify slavery. Page knew the members in the quarters community, and he knew also what they expected from him as a preacher if he planned on continuing as their religious leader. While Page certainly faced critics, most of his brothers and sisters adored him. He remained a popular minister until his death.[25]

Some enslaved blacks, however, did not trust enslaved preachers any more than they trusted white ministers. When men like Page faced gatherings, it fell to them to state clearly that they were sent to preach not by the slaveholder but by the Lord. Some individuals additionally required convincing as to the wonders of God and his power to uplift their lives on earth. To accomplish those ends required that Page present himself effectively as the victim—in common with his listeners—of an abusive system. He necessarily shared at times that his master treated him just like any other bondservant, that he had sold his mother and brother on the auction block, that he had mortgaged his body many times, and that he could sell him on a whim. But Page's task meant, as well, persuading his congregants that he did not allow the complete commodification of his body or his soul, either by his master or by society generally. Careful to avoid saying so directly, Page implied that blacks and whites were equal and would end up in the same heaven together. His comment that "all good living Christian people who are save[d] will go to heaven" suggested as much.[26]

As proved true for other preachers of all stripes, Page ultimately had to accept that many enslaved men and women simply did not believe in Christianity and wanted nothing to do with it. The impression that, by the Civil War's end, most enslaved persons were Christians is a myth. Many enslaved blacks never converted. Former bondman Louis Napoleon's attitude toward Christianity and enslaved ministers reflected those of innumerable others in refusing to "accept Christ" at the time of a Page visit to his plantation. Some saw Christianity as the white man's religion. Others did not believe in Christianity if, as Raboteau noted, "a supposedly just God . . . could will or permit slavery." It mattered little to them whether white or black men proselytized Afro-Christian religious beliefs. They just showed no interest in the white God. One South Carolina enslaved worker remembered Sundays as a day to raid orchards for food. Former bondservants Mary Biddie, Margrett Nickerson, and Douglas Dorsey saw it as useful for fishing, cooking, playing, and socializing—anything other than attending religious services to listen to a preacher sermonize. Over his lifetime, thousands of people had heard the word of God through Page's preaching. Some admired his preaching; other did not.[27]

⁓

The needs of bondpersons who were open to hearing Page's message changed over time, a circumstance to which he was required to pay close attention. By way of example, the increasingly adamant arguments by white clergymen, slaveowners, and other whites during the 1840s and 1850s that slaves had no souls created a dynamic that broadly affected the institution of slavery. This trend received attention earlier, as did Page's reaction to the absurd claim. As a by-product of the controversy, Page found himself as a pastor having to reassure fretful congregants that, contrary to what their masters or others had told them, they possessed souls and those souls were worth saving. As early as the 1820s, he had preached about his soulful conversion. He continued to do so through the institution's demise. When asked whether colored folks' souls could be saved, he repeated that "God had no respecter of person." Page regularly comforted shaken black mortals by assuring them that, if their souls were saved, they would "go to heaven like any man," where blacks and whites were equal in the sight of God. Once that principle could be accepted, further reassurance often became unnecessary. Mary Biddie summed up the lesson this way: "Yeah, wese jest as good as deys is only deys white, and we's black, huh."[28]

While absurdities such as arguments about the absence of a black soul could stir Page's ire and oratory, he likely did not directly challenge the evils of slavery through his talks and sermons. Available documentation contains no reference to the subject. Unlike Northern black ministers who spoke against slavery in relative safety and comfort, the enslaved preacher had to exercise great care in offering criticisms. Theologian Stephen Ward Angell confirmed, "Southern antebellum black preachers could never be as outspoken on the matters [of slavery] as those who had found heaven in the North." Eugene D. Genovese characterized the black preacher's dilemma: "He had to be defiant enough in front of his congregations but loyal enough not to raise suspicions from the ruling class." However, Page's recorded words—such as "all men are equal in God's sight" and "people should work hard to help themselves while they are here [on earth]"—suggest that he preached against slavery or, at least, on not succumbing to its devastating effects. He and other enslaved preachers had to pursue a course difficult to maintain as intermediaries between the slaveholder and the enslaved. To retain the trust of both sides, they often had to satisfy the slaveholder as well as appease the enslaved. Page's use of the mask of accommodation as he pursued this difficult task has been alluded to. The fact that many enslaved people expressed joy at Father Page's coming to their plantations indicated graphically that he preached what they wanted and needed to hear as well.[29]

As Page continued to mature intellectually as a minister, he understood better the major principles of Christian theology and utilized its rites to further his mission. While exploiting baptism as a link between his faith and African traditions, for instance, he also grasped the significance of soteriology focused on baptism as a ritual of saving souls. Former bondman Mack Mullen, who grew up on a Georgia plantation, emphasized the importance of baptism to the enslaved. As an interviewer explained, "On baptismal day, the candidates attired in white robes which they had made, marched down to the river where they were immersed by the minister. Slaves from neighboring plantations would come to witness this sacred ceremony. . . . [I]t was a happy scene." "The slave would be there in great numbers scattered about over the banks of the river. Much shouting and singing went on. Some of the 'sisters' and 'brothers' would get so 'happy' that they would lose control of themselves and 'fall out.' It was then that the 'Holy Ghost' had 'struck 'em.' The other slaves would view this Phenomenon with awe and reverence, and wait for them 'to come out of it.' 'Those were happy days and real religion.'" The same elation surrounded Page's baptisms of the converted. The practice mushroomed with time. "I baptized few people at first," he expressed, "but more would come to the Lord the longer I preached." Surviving accounts regularly attested to the fact. A contemporary of Page noted his prowess for baptizing many converts. The *Wakulla Times* reported, for example, that the well-known religious leader had baptized "twelve negroes" in the St. Marks River, some twenty miles from Tallahassee.[30]

Page also conducted other rites for the quarters communities. "I loved being asked to do weddings and funerals," he declared. "De colored preachers, dey 'formed de [marriage] ceremony," former bondman Lucious Lamar Douglas attested. "Jim Page . . . was [one of] our colored preachers." Weddings that involved the African practice of jumping the broom probably constituted the norm but not always. "I did a lot of weddings all over Florida and a few in Georgia and South Carolina," the veteran preacher confirmed, "from the time I started preaching during slavery times to this very day [in 1880]." The total number of such services that Page performed, and exactly where they occurred, cannot be known. "I don't rightly know how many funerals and weddings I did," he admitted, "but I do know I did so many that I can't remember them all." Whenever and wherever they took place, these services reflected a rich mixture of African and Euro-Christian practices. Historian Robert Hall advised that these "were often occasions for celebration, creating an intensely renewed sense of family and communal unity among the survivors." Many funerals focused on West African traditions of leaving personal artifacts at grave sites. "They left little personal things on the graves of their deceased ones," the enslaved preacher recorded. Page may have participated in funeral services similar to those held for Dolly at a location elsewhere in the state. "Her colored friends of all ages then flocked around her, bestowing those peculiar rites which among Southern slaves is

Father James Page experienced African traditions as seen in this photo of an African burial ceremony. State Archives of Florida, Florida Memory

singularly superstitious," a newspaper reported, "but amid incantations, prayers, and day and night watchings . . . at last [came] the grim messenger [with] his inexorable summons, and the spirit of Dolly took wing to the House of Eternal Master."[31]

Page's ecclesiology took on both a "high church" and a "low church" approach. His skillful adoption of emotionalism and soaring oratory illustrated his "low church" leanings. "High church" practices included dress. "The Baptist preacher should always be dressed right before he preaches or perform[s] weddings and funerals," he insisted. Substantiating the claim, in one of the few photos of Reverend Page, he was attired in a black suit with a clerical collar. The enslaved preacher also believed in the sacraments, administering not only baptism rites but also communion. Whether Page considered baptism a form of spiritual regeneration or simply an important ceremony for those becoming Christians is not known. Much like adherents to the African Methodist Episcopal Church, who embraced titles such as bishop, presiding elder, and deacon, Page perceived benefits of rank as well. Specifically, he eventually became known not only as Reverend James Page but also as Father James Page. A contemporary commented that he wore the latter title "proudly."[32]

Several further points are relevant to any discussion of Page—the man and the preacher—during slavery's final decades. For one thing, as a literate person Page—like Frederick Douglass—could have escaped to freedom by himself. Page says nothing about ever taking his wife and son on any of his travels. This may have been by design on the part of the enslaver. By maintaining Elizabeth and later Tom on the plantation as hostages of sorts, Parkhill hedged his bet that Page would return to his family each time he traveled. However, Page possessed, at least at times, sufficient cash resources to attempt an escape with his family.[33]

Several other options were open to him as well. He could have written a pass for himself, his wife, and his son to venture north or to any other place of freedom. Page and his family, like other fugitives, could have used the famed Underground Railroad, thereby self-emancipating themselves ultimately in Montreal, Pittsburgh, El Paso, Haiti, as well as numerous other places in the Midwest or the far Northeast. They might have used another part of the Underground Railroad into Mexico, which had outlawed slavery during the 1830s with the assistance of Mexican abolitionists called "Tejanos." As a literate man, he could have struck out for freedom, saying that he had to perform an errand for his master in Richmond, Virginia. As another alternative, he could have proceeded with his family farther South by water from the leaky Florida coast to the British Bahamas. Scholars recently have documented the success of numbers of fugitives who reached the British West Indies. Within the state, Pensacola stood out as a destination for those seeking release from slavery's bonds. Once there, Page and his family could have boarded one of the many ships headed to a myriad of places in the Atlantic World. No evidence suggests, however, that he ever attempted such a flight. Instead, as a friend confided, Page "never thought about leaving

Florida." His family's safety and what might have happened to them had he successfully escaped to freedom obviously concerned him. Beyond that, the student of his life is left only with the sense that his aim was not freedom but service to God. More than that, his goal of existence was to labor for those who desperately needed his pastoral care and inspiration to continue living in a world where no reasonable chance of freedom existed.[34]

Theoretically, at least, Page could have resorted to physical violence like so many rebellious enslaved blacks before him. No smoking gun appears, though, in any of the Page documentation to suggest that he conspired to rebel or to overthrow slavery in Florida or any other place in the South. Similarly, nothing hints that he advocated violence against those who enslaved him and his family. As a man of God, he did not believe in physical violence, including harm inflicted upon oneself by suicide. The preacher understood that slave resistance came in many different forms on a scale from subtle to violent. Yet the Bible spoke against murder, and the assassination of one's body through suicide constituted murder. "Killing someone and killing yourself," he asserted, "goes against God's commandments." Page knew the Ten Commandments, which made clear his faith's prohibition on murder. Page enjoyed life and loved religion and family. People knew him as a "peaceful man." Chances are that he never gave serious thought to either physical violence or suicide as a form of slave resistance.[35]

Finally, Page lived through one of the great religious movements of modern times, and its influence on him likewise merits attention. It served to wrench organized religion out of cool, intellectual hands and place it squarely within an emotional framework that allowed ordinary men and women to communicate directly with their God. As it progressed, the Second Great Awakening spawned a variety of reform movements that came under the umbrella that historians have named the Benevolent Empire. Among the host of causes embraced by its "do-good" intentions were abolitionism, women's rights, and temperance. Page said little about abolitionism that the record captured except that abolitionists "would face harm from people who did not like them in the South." He said less about women's rights or the role of women within the clergy. It seems safe to say that he did not support preaching by women or an attempt by women to assume high administrative roles in religious circles. Among his peers, individuals such as Henry McNeal Turner and Frederick Douglass disagreed. Within the Baptist denomination, his course represented mainstream opinion. His views likewise agreed with those of most men during the period.[36]

Conversely, the enslaved preacher immersed himself in the temperance movement, as did his master. Unlike his virtual silence on abolitionism or women's rights, he had much to say concerning the evils of alcoholic beverages. Whether on the plantation where he lived or during his various travels, Page confronted enslaved people about the dangers of drinking. "I would tell men that hard drinking destroyed their lives," he thundered. Page's views against alcohol were so strong that he held high the cause's banner well into the postbellum era. He perceived a direct correlation when it came to bondservants' drinking, crime, and violence: "Drinking causes Negro men to commit bad things and hurt the people they love." Consumption of alcohol to Page meant ungodly behavior leading to crime and social problems within the slave community. On the more pragmatic side, the enslaved preacher/overseer clearly also understood that sober enslaved laborers were less troublesome and more productive workers. As the community's pastoral leader, he sought every available means to reduce the possibility of violence and crime among bondpeople. Drastically reduced alcohol consumption was a necessary step.[37]

Page's preaching and other pastoral activities gave his life its meaning and purpose. He willingly undertook personal sacrifice to serve the cause of his mission. The exertions involved in taking the Gospel of the Lord to enslaved persons in South Carolina, Georgia, and Alabama must have taxed his body severely. Absence from the plantation for days or weeks at a time became routine, as did sleeping alongside the road or enduring trying challenges of weather and man. The absences must have taken their toll on Elizabeth and Tom as well. Page once remarked, "I got a little tired of the long trips to South Carolina, Georgia, and Alabama. Some people were used to seeing me and I had my paper from the Col. giving me permission to travel to these places." During a time when there was little field work to do and Page's absence would not negatively affect his financial bottom line, Parkhill allowed his enslaved overseer/preacher increasing latitude to travel. To that point, Page recalled that "I went during the winter time when we could not do very much in the fields. The Col. was always good at letting me use the horse and buggy, and he had trust in me that I would preach the word and return to the place as soon as I could." In any event, the turbulent days that led to Civil War lay ahead. The toll of service then took on new and deeper meaning.[38]

CHAPTER SEVEN

Stepping toward Civil War

At about twelve years old, our family was broken up by the death of my master.

—Former bondman Reuben Saunders

As the nation commenced during the 1850s its inexorable march toward the calamity of civil war, King Cotton produced unprecedented Southern wealth that breathed new vitality into the Parkhill family fortunes and, in turn, touched James and Elizabeth Page in ways that ranged from overt to subtle. As for the Parkhills, the Union Bank's collapse in the early 1840s had struck thunderous blows to a family financial structure based upon loans and slave mortgages. The debacle cost John Parkhill his lucrative and prestigious position as the bank's cashier, portions of his plantation lands, a considerable number of bondservants, and lasting damage to his personal reputation. Threats spawned by its consequences consumed much of his time and energy through the decade as he attempted to stave off complete ruin. With his persistence and the economy's upturn, however, the Parkhill finances eventually improved. During cotton's golden age, slave prices soared, and cotton prices held steady. By 1854, Parkhill owned seventy-four enslaved human beings and 1,500 acres of improved and unimproved land. This marked a considerable turnaround from the dire period that commenced in 1841. Notably, his success was owed in good part to sales of cotton produced and marketed under Page's supervision as overseer.[1]

Page meanwhile found his emotions twisted and his vision confounded by events far beyond his control. No national or local event worked a greater impact on the enslaved preacher and overseer's life than did John Parkhill's death at Bel Air plantation on October 16, 1855. As close confidants of their dying master, were James and Elizabeth at his bedside during the final hours and days of his life? Did Page sit up with Lucy Parkhill during her time of bereavement as he had done in 1834 when his master's first wife, Elizabeth Copland, passed? As was common in elite slaveholding families throughout the South, enslaved persons like James and Elizabeth were probably present to bring household items, carry messages, and do whatever their master needed for his ultimate comfort. Given that Page's life hung in the balance upon the death of his master, he likely wanted to be at the reading of the will, but no evidence suggests any bondservants were present at this momentous event. We do not know whether Elizabeth or James dressed in special mourning cloths to emphasize their close connection to the Parkhill family. Given her skills as a seamstress, Elizabeth along with other female bondservants would have assisted Lucy Parkhill and other family members with clothes worn during the grieving period. One thing is for sure; a whirlwind of uncertainty swirled around the Page family and other bondpeople upon the demise of their enslaver.[2]

At the time of his death, the enslaver was a man of substance who had built his political, economic, and social affiliations on slavery. The enslavement of other human beings for the benefit of him and his family became a way of life that reflected Parkhill success and privilege. Ironically, his obituary published four days later advised, "Mark the perfect man and behold the upright, for the end of that man is peace." Parkhill and Page had interacted with each other since the bondman's childhood but never on equal terms. The relationship with his owner was complicated, at times intimate, and highlighted by the master's occasional perfidy and the bondservant's steadfastness. Page certainly knew well that the deceased qualified neither as perfect nor always as upright. The other enslaved workers knew, as well, their money-conscious enslaver was far from a perfect man. Page understood clearly, with the owner's death, important dynamics could change. Parkhill's passing seemingly foretold the shift of enormous burdens to the enslaved overseer in the form of added responsibilities. Page's words in recalling the moment expressed his ambivalence. "I cried some," he declared, "when Col. Parkhill left this world." Beyond that, the death introduced a new element of uncertainty into Page's life, work, and ministry. Above all else, he would serve a new master who could exert nearly complete control over his activities as well as insufferably intrude into the private lives of the entire slave community. Everywhere, when a slaveholder passed away, such trepidation ensued for the enslaved. "Two events in the 'big house'—

marriage and death—posed the greatest threats to the slave family's security," historian Jane Censer aptly noted. Historian Alice Carter added, "Perhaps no situation presented more uncertainty to the already uncertain lives of slaves than the deaths of their owners." Historian Loren Schweninger similarly commented that enslaved persons often found themselves "caught in the middle" of consequent family disputes.[3]

Page obviously struggled in late 1855. His surviving voice hinted at elements of terror and fear: "I didn't know what was going to happen to us." He and his immediate family faced a potentially unpleasant, if not to say frightful, situation. At the moment in his life, one wonders whether fear owned Page more than his master did. Vital elements of their lives suddenly had become vulnerable to arbitrary and capricious change, and the couple had much to lose. With John Parkhill's permission and blessing, he and Elizabeth for years had enjoyed a relatively privileged life as house servants, coach driver, overseer, preacher, and leader of the quarters community. At Tuscawilla and Bel Air plantations, they rested atop the slave community's hierarchy, the epitome of local black aristocracy. Unlike circumstances for most bondservants in Florida and the South in general, they had experienced social advancement within the slave community's confines. "I began to worry about what would happen to me, my family and the other servants," Page conceded. Parkhill's favorite bondservant faced an abrupt turning point in his life. Indeed, the enslaved cleric had good reason to worry about his future. His family could experience the same tragedy that befell former Georgia bondman Reuben Saunders's kinfolk. "I was the oldest child," he recalled. "There were three brothers and two sisters. At about twelve years old, our family was broken up by the death of my master." Page's anxieties were, therefore, neither unjustified nor unusual. The deaths of enslavers, as historian Peter Kolchin advised, "heightened concern on the part of slaves." That distress could manifest itself in all manner of behaviors, including flight. Perhaps remarkably, Page did not react impulsively. As it turned out, the ordeal paradoxically made him a stronger man and a steadier leader in the years that lay ahead.[4]

Just how much Page had to lose at the time of his owner's death has to be assessed against a relatively recent and important change in his status as a preacher, an event that also had highlighted the ambivalence that had characterized his relationship with Parkhill. In August 1851 Page received regular ordination as a Baptist minister, one of the first black men to be accorded that recognition in Florida. The rites conferred upon him official status in the church's eyes and seemed to bestow an imprimatur of approval, thus easing his way to expansion of his missionary work despite a harshening racial climate and intensified efforts to control slave movement. The ceremony was held in Newport, a small but thriving resort and cotton transshipment point on the St. Marks River a short distance below Tallahassee and Bel Air and a few miles northeast of St. Marks. Although details are difficult to come by, arrangements seemingly were put in place in May after residents organized or, possibly, reorganized a Baptist fellowship under the umbrella of the Florida Baptist Association. They called it the Newport Baptist Church of St. Luke. Rev. William Wallace Maund, a Newport resident and a longtime mainstay of numerous southeastern Baptist churches, already pastored within Wakulla County. He took charge of the Newport congregation as well, apparently convening services in "a vacant dwelling house." This created an opportunity for Page at a time when Bel Air did not host a Baptist church, and the fellowship in Tallahassee—which consisted of only eleven white members—apparently did not enjoy the ministrations of a regularly appointed pastor. That is, as will be seen, a pastor other than Father Page.[5]

Page would have been familiar with events ongoing in Newport because he routinely supervised the hauling of Parkhill cotton there for transshipment abroad. This meant that he was in town several times per year, including a few days each August. Coincidentally, Page learned of a planned "presbytery comprised of Anglo Baptist ministers" scheduled to convene with the town's new congregation about the time in August when he otherwise would be visiting. Concluding that the presbytery would look favorably upon the ordination of a black man, he secured letters of recommendation from his owner, soon-to-be governor James Emilius Broome, and "others of the most respected citizens of Leon County." Lending their support, John Parkhill's wife, Lucy Randolph Parkhill, and her ten-year-old daughter, Harriet Randolph Parkhill, booked rooms in Newport's most fashionable hotel, ostensibly for a vacation stay. For unrecorded reasons Parkhill declined to accompany them. Regardless, the presbytery accepted and ordained Page, presumably with Lucy and Harriet looking on.[6]

John Parkhill stood as one of the most important people in Page's life. The enslaver gave him the opportunity to preach and the use his other property, such as his horse and buggy. But, when spending time with his enslaved overseer, did Parkhill reciprocate Page's importance to him, or did he spend most of that time giving instructions to his enslaved overseer that benefited his plantations? Most specifically, did Parkhill share quality time with Page like he did with members of his white family? It seems that quality time was for white family members only, for Parkhill decided not to be with his closest bondservant when he wanted him most, attending neither, for whatever reasons, his wedding nor his ordination. Whatever Parkhill's absence betokened, Mother Nature quickly foreshadowed less propitious times to come for all concerned when disaster struck Newport.[7]

An intense hurricane nearly destroyed the town. Storm winds swept away bridges spanning the St. Marks and Wakulla Rivers while threatening the lives of everyone nearby. "We had a storm on the 23d of last month that injured our crops very much, and did much damage, hardly left a house standing at St. Marks and injured much goods at Newport, the water rose four feet higher than the gale of 1843, when Port Leon was washed away, it was a dreadful storm," John advised his son Robert. "Your mother & Harriet were at Newport during the whole of the storm, and I here [at Bel Air]," he continued. "You may suppose I was very uneasy about them." Although he was in Newport during the same time as Lucy and Harriet Parkhill, Parkhill made no mention of any concern for James Page or the fact of his ordination.[8]

By late 1855, the dark future that the hurricane presaged appeared close to becoming reality. Indeed, some of the worst nightmares feared by the Parkhill bondservants were about to come true. Over his seventy-two years on earth, John Parkhill had fathered with three wives a total of nine children who grew to adulthood. According to one historian's study of slaveholder wills, "Only eight planters out of the ninety-two [studied], approximately 9 percent, urged the executors of their wills to respect slave family relationships." As we have seen, John Parkhill was not one of those slaveholders who respected the integrity of the slave family. His will, as it turned out, stipulated the breakup of several slave families so that individuals could be allocated to various heirs. Others were to be sold outright. He also had empowered his administrators "to mortgage or sell property [slaves and land] and make lawful conveyances of the same to purchase property for the benefit of my Estate." He bequeathed to Lucy Parkhill all "the home servants." Daughter Ellen F. Maxwell received "the servant Amy"; daughter Virginia, "the servant girl Catharine"; and youngest daughter, Harriet, Eliza's child, "the servant girl Matilda." None of these "servant girls" were bequeathed in company with fathers, mothers, or siblings.[9]

The complications multiplied from there. While Parkhill stipulated that wife Lucy would inherit "the home servants," the bequest extended only

Upon the death of John Parkhill, his son George Washington Parkhill inherited most of the family's enslaved people on the two plantations, and he became Page's second master and was an advocate for the secession of Florida from the Union in 1860. State Archives of Florida, Florida Memory

through her natural life, subsequent to which they might be sold or retained at the option of her daughter, Harriet. Parkhill added, "[If her] servants behaved badly they are to be sold from the plantation." He desired, as well, that the "negro slaves bequeathed to my daughters be delivered to them by my Executors as soon as they see fit to demand them." Youngest son, George Washington Parkhill, meanwhile received the lion's share of the remaining slaveholding. The instrument failed to reflect in any form the care that Page had believed his master held for him; his wife, Elizabeth; or son, Tom. John Parkhill and James Page had spent many private moments together, and the influence they had on one another helped to shape their daily activities and way of thinking. But whatever Page may have said to his master concerning the subject of emancipation obviously fell on deaf ears, for the will did not emancipate any bondservant upon his death or in the future. John Parkhill remained true to the pattern that he had established at least as early as the 1827 sale of Page's mother and brother. When it came to economic self-interest, Page's enslaver looked out for the comfort and wealth of his white family members above all else.[10]

Any frustrations or resentments that Page felt upon learning of the will's contents were ones previously and repeatedly experienced by other bond-persons. By way of example, one of Virginia's most revered enslaved preach-ers of his time dealt with a similar crush of expectations. "John Jasper . . . would seem to have been a prime candidate for manumission by one means or another—through self-purchase, an outright grant from his owner, or by aid from benevolent whites," David Dennard reflected, "[but, he] obviously found all avenues to freedom closed." Dennard added, "He remained a slave until the legal death of American slavery in 1865." Other well-known and highly regarded enslaved preachers, including George and Noah Davis, man-aged to embrace freedom only in death or at the Civil War's end. In the same fashion, Page learned that he would continue to serve the Parkhills. The only silver lining to the repressive cloud was that Lucy Parkhill, who had shown support for him, controlled his destiny for the immediate future. As a result, the Page family continued to live at Tuscawilla plantation. Even that cer-tainty came with a caveat. As objects of personal wealth, each family member theoretically could be sold, if necessary, to satisfy outstanding estate debts. Among the "appraised property," the Page family members as well as other human beings were carefully listed along with farm animals.[11]

Lingering questions about Parkhill's failure to address the hopes of his "special servants" aside, Florida law, it must be acknowledged, made it ex-cruciatingly difficult to free enslaved human beings. An 1829 territorial act regulated the process. Under its provisions, no bondperson present in Flor-ida during that year or previously could be freed under any circumstances. That provision alone would have eliminated James and Elizabeth from pos-sible emancipation. Had it not disqualified them, then the law would have required Parkhill to post a bond equal to their value subject to forfeiture if they did not leave the territory or state within thirty days of manumission. Additionally, the owner was required to pay a $200 fine. Yet, the law's provision—however forbidding its terms were—failed in practice to stop many owners from granting freedom to favored bondservants in a jurisdiction that remained in good part a frontier and in large portions of which little or no effective law enforcement existed whatsoever. At the time of his death, John Parkhill was solvent, and the plantations were doing relatively well. So, should money or price have mattered when manumitting three of the people he allegedly cared so much about? Obviously, it did.[12]

Despite Florida's laxity when it came to law enforcement, Page's owner had declined to give a nod of any kind in the direction of his emancipation. Given Parkhill's professed Christian sensibilities, this appears particularly unusual because he hailed from Virginia, a state with a history of slave manumission dating back to the colonial period. Robert Carter III, the fourth-generation son of a large colonial slaveholding family, manumitted his slaves, for instance, much as his great-grandfather John Carter Jr. had done in his 1669 will. Elite planter Richard Randolph freed his slaves by will in 1796. As an evangelical Christian, he came to view the holding of human beings as a violation of natural rights. Three years later Martha Custis Washington released President Washington's bondservants pursuant to provisions contained in his will. Most of these slaveholders and those who acted in a similar manner also provided for the material conditions of these once-enslaved humans. For example, John Carter Jr. provided livestock, a homestead, and land for his former bondservants. Even the third president of the United States, Virginian Thomas Jefferson, manumitted, among others, three to five of his loyal servants and provided them with land and money to make it on their own. Virginia slaveholders generally retained the right to manumit slaves until the institution finally was crushed in 1865. Parkhill thus was familiar with relevant precedent concerning manumission at the time of his death. As a strong-willed man, he could have countered prevailing Florida law to manumit Page and his family had he so desired. Parkhill's callous actions made clear the incompatibility of paternalism and materialism.[13]

Examples of caring Floridians who acted where John Parkhill proved unable or unwilling are not difficult to find. Zephaniah Kingsley was one of them. The East Floridian, unlike his Middle Florida counterpart, blithely disregarded the stipulations of the law in order to free bondservants. Kingsley probably perceived himself—not so differently than did Parkhill—as the epitome of a paternalist. But Kingsley differed from Parkhill in one significant way. His form of paternalism was not totally based on an ideology but on actions that would truly benefit at least some of his enslaved human beings. Where Parkhill refused to demonstrate true benevolence to his favorite enslaved family by freeing them, Kingsley acted. The East Florida enslaver openly, therefore, thumbed his nose at restrictions on manumission and many other activities barred or regulated by law. As a slave trader, he often bought and sold bondpeople after acquiring them directly from the African coast. He married a young woman who has been described as an "African princess" and had four mulatto children with her. To ensure their rights to inheritance in an uncertain and violent Florida society, he specified his intentions in his will's preamble, dated July 20, 1843: "Whereas I am of sound mind and disposing memory and know what I'm doing, and whereas I know perfectly well that it is against the laws and conventions of life to marry a colored person, and whereas this is my property and it is not anybody's damn business what I do with it . . . and whereas I know that what I am about to do is going to bring down on me tremendous criticism, but I don't give a damn." Kingsley thereupon granted freedom to his wife, Anna Madgigine Jai, and her four children. To them he conferred major portions of his considerable estate. When made public, the contents of Kingsley's will shocked some fellow slaveholders. In East Florida where Spanish traditions prevailed, the emancipation of Anna and her four children and the property she received in the will by no means shocked all white citizens in the region.[14]

Although Parkhill did not free James, Elizabeth, and Tom, one additional point at least should be considered. The less than magnanimous enslaver, intentionally or inadvertently, may have accomplished close to the same end without embroiling any of the three individuals in the tangles and snarls of an increasingly harsh regulatory climate that ultimately governed virtually every aspect of freed persons' lives. As time's passage proved, with Lucy Parkhill as his owner, Page enjoyed very broad latitude for independent action. His behavior even suggested to various persons that he had been manumitted at some time in his life. At least, that is what a number of bondservants believed about him. Louis Napoleon, for one, remembered Page as a "free colored" minister when he came to his plantation to preach the word of God. Amanda McCray implied that he was a free man because he could hold religious "services any time he chose" to do so. Nonetheless, at the end of the day, the enslaved preacher and his loved ones were undeniably valuable property on a ledger book, and they would remain the Parkhill family's chattel until a bloody civil war emancipated them.[15]

With John Parkhill gone, the Pages of necessity picked up the pieces of their world and continued to live their lives. Page still served the interests of the plantations as overseer, often laboring at Bel Air as well as at Tuscawilla. Naturally, he also performed pastoral duties. In addition, he continued to provide food for his family and needy fellow bondservants through fishing, tending his chickens, and working his garden. Whether Parkhill lived or died, Page understood that total reliance upon the generosity of his enslaver relegated him to the true status of a slave, for dependence and slavery went hand in hand. In the meantime, he quietly rebelled against his enslaved status by striving to become increasingly more self-reliant. Ever more intently, he preached to congregants, "You must do for yourself now. God wants you to be good to your family and friends." In matters large and small, he took whatever "freedom" permitted him to help his family and others during insecure and uncertain times. He later confided to a friend, "I like[d] doing things for myself when I could, and I always like[d] fishing . . . [because that is what the] twelve disciples did." His pride in being a capable horticulturalist grew. Denied literal freedom, he endeavored, insofar as he was able, to live as he thought a man should live.[16]

Other developments also factored into his daily life. Particularly, within the year or so after Parkhill's death, Page had faced substantial change in the performance of his overseer duties. As mentioned earlier, Parkhill's will left the lion's share of his enslaved laborers to George Washington Parkhill. Parkhill's wife Lucy may have owned Page, but her youngest stepson wielded the power on both plantations. George accordingly became the "man" who controlled affairs, the person to whom Page reported. George then was still young, aged thirty-three when his father died. His early education had come courtesy of tutors or his parents. Once in Florida, he worked as well as studied. Biographer Donald L. Ivey revealed that young Parkhill had assisted "with the work on the plantation . . . [which] was often also a major part of the child's upbringing, and young George no doubt spent a considerable amount of his time doing chores along with his siblings, while learning to hunt, fish, ride a horse, and tend crops and livestock as well." At age six, the Parkhills enrolled him in a one-room elementary schoolhouse with his other siblings and neighboring planters' children. He later attended the Grammar School of Centre College in Danville, Kentucky. Minor but potentially troubling signs revealed themselves there. "I have all reason to believe his conduct is unexceptionable," the principal reported, "but in school or about the school room, he is sometimes a little disorderly, and when reproached shows an unwillingness to submit to authority."[17]

Fortunately, young Parkhill's developing intransigence evolved into mature judgment and intellectual depth by the time he entered medical school at age twenty-two. George attended the College of Physicians and Surgeons of New York City, later renamed the Columbia University School of Medicine. Upon graduation he returned to Middle Florida to establish a medical practice and to be near his parents. He treated patients both black and white. John Parkhill's death also had transformed him into a planter of stature. In that capacity he willingly took time away from his practice to support his overseer. "I could count on Mr. George for helping me around the place when he could," Page acknowledged. Profoundly influenced by his father, the now-grown man held unequivocally to a Southern way of life built around the institution of slavery. In his expression of those beliefs, hints of the problematic personality traits of his youth reasserted themselves. Where his father's sedate demeanor maintained a civil tone in public discourse, the young man ardently and fiercely defended slavery and the right of the South to uphold the institution. He kept his heated rhetoric away from his relationship with Page, in any event. They continued to work cooperatively.[18]

The cooperative spirit that overcame heated political rhetoric facilitated, in turn, Parkhill prosperity. Thanks to his father's legacy of acquiring enslaved human beings and land as well as Page's management skills, by 1856 George Washington Parkhill had become, in Florida terms, a wealthy man. Although the dollar figures may seem small at today's rates, they represented huge amounts at the time. While the young slaveholder possessed other chattel, the seventy-nine bondservants that he inherited alone represented $35,050, or approximately $1 million in 2019 US currency. For reporting purposes, James, Elizabeth, and Tom were included in that total. The venerable enslaved preacher—now forty-eight years of age—was appraised at $600. No value was accorded to his literacy or to his position as the overseer. He remained in family accounting terms nothing more than a piece of property that was depreciating with age. Elizabeth was listed at $400. Tom, who had grown toward adulthood and had become a prime laborer with high market value, ranked at $900. James Page's life gave credence to the reality of social death when he, his wife, son, and other bondservants were listed on an inventory roll along with horses, cows, and other farm animals.[19]

Page's new owner's fortunes leapt again in 1858. This time, though, the cause was marriage. That July, Parkhill took as his bride Elizabeth (Lizzie) Brooks Bellamy. Aged nineteen, she was the daughter of William and Emmala

(Simkins) Bellamy of neighboring Jefferson County. The Bellamys came to Middle Florida during the late 1820s from Edgefield, South Carolina. By the 1850s they possessed one of the largest Florida plantations in terms of enslaved laborers and land. The family stood in the upper tier of the first families of Middle Florida. The union understandably elevated Page's status as well. The elegant ceremony took place in the bride's hometown of Monticello. Shortly afterward, physician and planter George Parkhill erected a fine home for Lizzie at Tuscawilla. Elizabeth Page worked there. Within eleven months, the newlyweds had their first son. They named him Charles Breckinridge Parkhill.[20]

The bondservants who accompanied the bride into her new life proved the factor that worked the largest impact on Page. Clearly understanding that the political economy of the South rested largely on the backs of enslaved workers such as James Page, William and Emmala Bellamy gave their daughter Elizabeth "100 slaves to [take to] Tuscawilla as a part of her dowry," a descendant recalled. "And with the slaves that George Parkhill inherited from his father (72)," she noted, "he now had about 172 slaves, hereby making him one of the wealthiest men in the South." As a result, the increased responsibilities afforded a serious challenge for Page. "Mr. George had the biggest plantation of any other man in Florida," he insisted with a degree of exaggeration, "[and] I had so much more work to do on it." The experienced overseer and manager rose to the occasion, both at Tuscawilla and at Bel Air, where Lucy Parkhill continued to live. "The prospect for a fine [cotton] crop is far better than it has been for several years," he soon informed Harriet Parkhill. "The servants are in better spirits. I shall endeavor to try and keep everything in order as near as I can."[21]

Despite the greater burden of his on-plantation duties, Page kept up or even increased the pace of his ministry. In that regard a surprising historical evolution increasingly manifested itself. Despite a trend away from whites worshipping alongside the enslaved, Page experienced an increase in the number of whites willing to worship openly with blacks during the 1850s and early 1860s. The First Baptist Church of Tallahassee, for example, started in 1849 with seven white and 258 black members. Coincidentally, the same year the *Christian Index*'s editor challenged white "Christians to teach and worship with their slaves." He urged, "Indifference toward the colored man is a great obstruction that clogs the wheels of the missionary chariot." To some extent this reversed dynamic came into play because of the Nat

Turner insurrection during the early 1830s. Fears spawned by the revolt had resulted in heavy restrictions on the ability of enslaved blacks to preach. Accordingly, white clergymen had intensified efforts to instruct bondservants with a message of God-sanctioned slavery and the slaveholders' best interests. "They tried to get all the servants to visit with them," Page explained. "And sometimes they [the white clergy] would come to them [the slaves]." The stilted message delivered directly to black-only congregations produced mixed results in the quarters communities, mostly weighted toward skepticism and rejection. Redoubled efforts resulted, as Edward Baptist discovered: "They would henceforth work harder than ever to make Christianity into a tool that would help . . . [them] govern [slave] society [better]." Page privately scorned what he saw as an ungodly message but otherwise had little to say about his white clergy colleagues.[22]

His accelerated rate of activity did not deter Page from continuing to gather knowledge of ongoing events in the world around him, especially incidents and trends that seemed likely to touch the lives of bondpeople generally or him and his family particularly. He proudly acknowledged his practice of reading carefully the "many . . . newspapers around the place as often as I could." He perceived that changes were rushing by at a dizzying pace during the decade's final four years, and he knew especially of the continued uneasiness of whites concerning attacks on the institution of slavery. One report published in Tallahassee in late 1856 represented many others of a similar sort that found readers during the period: "A gentleman writing from Quincy over the anonymous signature of Floridian, informs us that a bloody conspiracy is now ripening with a certain class of this State, against the lives of our citizens and that the development of the plot is to occur sometime between the morning of the 25th inst., and the first day of January next, ensuing." The editor attempted to tamp down fears of such a calamity by declaring halfheartedly that he did not believe the report: "We frankly confess that we place but little confidence in the statement, yet such a thing is possible, and suggests very forcibly the propriety of organizing an active police force in every neighborhood to guard against the improbable contingency." The same year bloodshed instigated by or directed at John Brown, his associates, and others smeared Kansas Territory. Two years later came Brown's raid on the arsenal at Harpers Ferry, Virginia (now West Virginia), aimed at confiscating arms to free enslaved people. "I read many things in the newspapers during slavery times that seemed to upset the white folks a lot," Page recalled. "Nothing ever really happened to them that I can remember." The enslaved preacher obviously perceived the world around him much differently than did the whites who lived all around him.[23]

Still, nagging fears of antislavery conspiracies persisted. When asked years later a direct question about abolitionists in Florida, Page asserted, "I would never want to come in contact with [any of] those people and I wouldn't have talked to them had I did." His words suggested a belief that nothing really happened one way or the other when antislavery advocates frequented the state. Few abolitionists in fact penetrated Middle Florida, but challenges to the peculiar institution from the likes of Dred Scott, John Brown, and, later, Abraham Lincoln kept Middle Floridians and many Southerners generally uneasy. Through these years leading up to national division, Page—working daily under the direct supervision of a rash but wealthy young man intent upon defending his Southern way of life at all costs—selected his words very carefully. Even after freedom came, Page did not appear comfortable talking at length to a contemporary about abolitionists, abolitionism, or slave revolts—real or imagined—that he may have heard about or discussed during his travels through Florida and the Southeast.[24]

Page felt little compunction, however, discussing the emergence at Tuscawilla of a more complex, if also more viable, slave community. The scores of enslaved people who accompanied Lizzie Bellamy Parkhill added new dimensions to life in the quarters community and created new and sometimes unusual challenges for Page. "My grandmother brought a hundred slaves to Tuscawilla as her dowry," recorded Genevieve Parkhill Lykes. "She built a church for them and had her house servant, Uncle Jeems Page, educated to read the Bible and preach to them." The granddaughter also correctly detailed that Lizzie facilitated Page's ability "to preach to the new servants." And with the large number of enslaved human beings brought to the union by Lizzie, Page was amazed that "so many of them want[ed] to marry after Mr. George added more people to the plantation." So, could the cheerier disposition displayed by bondpeople mentioned earlier by Page been more due to the possibility of finding mates than anything he did or did not do? And given his worldview about male dominance, Page crediting George Parkhill rather than Lizzie Bellamy Parkhill was mistaken but not surprising. But as the quarters community evolved Page grappled with new challenges and realities, for it constituted no utopia. The portion of his time required to mediate disputes between disgruntled persons swelled. The same applied to those who abused spouses and loved ones. "Some of the people would fuss and fight all night long and I hated what some of them did," he reflected, "and in the morning they would sometimes want to talk to me, but some would go and do it again." These challenges were not unique to the slave community at Tuscawilla but reflected human relations wherever people lived and worked. Generally speaking, enslaved people on the plantations and farms throughout the South fought and had conflicts. Sometimes, competition between or envy among young men resulted in altercations. "The boys would fight a little over the girls they liked," Page clarified. Although the slave family anchored the quarters community, Page unceasingly endeavored to resolve conflict. He continued to perform the job even after freedom came.[25]

A separate issue involved what Page termed the "strange practices" of some of the newly arrived bondservants. The enslaved preacher did not go into detail about the actions that troubled him. Likely, some arrivals practiced religions other than Christianity. For that matter, one or more may have considered themselves competitors to Page in the religious realm. Certainly, conjurers elsewhere occupied the same space as did enslaved preachers. Such leaders may have esteemed themselves as being just as important in the quarters community as Page. Not inconceivably, conjurers may have appeared at the site of altercations either to place a "hinx" to hurt someone or protect someone else. Had there not been abrasive social relations between bondservants, it might not have been necessary for anyone to exhibit "strange practices." Page nonetheless coped with the issue and generally felt positive about social and religious interactivity at Tuscawilla. He went so far as to insist, years later, that many of his race acted in a better manner before freedom came than afterward.[26]

By the time the 1860s dawned for Page, heady times swirled around him. Dramatic state and national events aside, Bel Air and Tuscawilla plantations continued to grow and prosper. George and Elizabeth Parkhill's 172 bondpeople by then carried a value of $133,000 and their real estate added another $36,000 to their overall wealth, which would have been worth about $5 million in 2019 US currency. Much of the burden of maintaining operations, however, by then had fallen upon the back of James Page. Events had altered Parkhill's flexibility in the allocation of his time. For one, his medical practice now took him to domiciles throughout the state of Florida, and at times out of state. The absentee slaveholder was away from the plantations for weeks on end. Additionally, Middle Florida residents anticipating Abraham Lincoln's election to the presidency chose George as one of Florida's two state militia major generals to protect the interests of slaveholders like him. In General Parkhill's absence, Page managed the estates essentially by himself.[27]

By November 1860, many leading Middle Florida residents had decided that with the election of "abolitionist" Abraham Lincoln, they ultimately would have to compel the state's secession from the Union. John C. McGehee, a large slaveholder from Jefferson County and president of the Florida Secession Convention, reflected the basic attitude of many Floridians: "At the South, and with our People of course, slavery is the element of all value, and a destruction of that destroys all that is property." In his annual message to the General Assembly the month of Lincoln's election, Governor Madison S. Perry said as much: "The crisis, long expected by men of observation and reflection, has at length come. The only hope the Southern states have for domestic peace and safety, or for future respectability and prosperity, is dependent on their action now; and that the proper action is secession from our faithless perjured confederates." Perry added, "I most earnestly recommend a call of a Convention of the people of the State at an early day, to take such action as in their judgement is necessary." Floridians and white Southerners in general feared Lincoln would destroy their precious "peculiar institution." Following South Carolina's move to secede in December, an election for statewide delegates to Florida's secession convention took place on the twenty-second. George Parkhill attended as one of five Leon County delegates.[28]

As a Leon County delegate to the Secessionist Convention, Parkhill represented the attitude of many Southerners concerning the sacredness of slavery, for he, and others like him, had too much wealth to lose with its abolition. He was, therefore, delighted to accept the position. He publicly and firmly "believed in the wisdom of a separate government for the slave and free states" and was prepared to act in furtherance of that end at the direction of Florida's white people. He had come to sense that secession from the Union offered the South its only hope of protecting the institution of slavery and ridding the region of "abolitionist tyranny." Parkhill perceived himself and other Southerners like him as victims of Northern aggression, which had to be stopped at the point of a gun. Unfortunately, the enslaver remained blind to the facts that enslaved human beings were victims of a brutal system that would lead to an eventually horrific, bloody, and long-lasting confrontation with the North. In defense of his way of life built on the foundation of slavery, Parkhill would become a Confederate officer to his peril.[29]

Despite the overwhelming responsibilities on his shoulders in his master's absence, Page somehow found enough time and energy to travel during 1860 to perform the Lord's work. In fact, extant documentation evidences him traveling widely immediately prior to secession and the war's outbreak. His auditors included at times members of all-white congregations, including during a notable visit to Georgia. As the *Baptist Encyclopedia* reported, "He visited Thomasville, Ga., in 1860, and, by invitation, preached acceptably to the white congregation." The era coincided, though, with the establishment of numerous black Baptist churches, congregations that would continue to operate after slavery ended. "I still tried traveling all over Florida to help my friends with their Godly work just before and during the Big War," Page confirmed. When asked to explain what he meant by helping "friends with their Godly work," the cleric responded, "I am old and can't remember many things, but I help[ed] establish Baptist churches all over Florida, and some in Alabama, Georgia, and even a couple of them in South Carolina too. Now, don't ask me some of their names because I forgot most of them." His critical guidance aided in the establishment of other Baptist churches during his travels. Those travels may have encompassed more than religious outreach, permitting conversations about the impending war with those he met during his many travels and networking for eventualities that might occur.[30]

Most available details concerning Page's peregrinations during this period involved trips into East and South Florida. He helped, for example, establish black Baptist churches such as Library Chapel Baptist Church in Ocala, the Philadelphia Baptist Church of Waldo near Gainesville, the Falling Creek Missionary Baptist Church of Lake City, and Mount Olive Baptist Church in Kings Ferry, Nassau County. Closer to home in Leon County, Shiloh Baptist Church benefited from his leadership. "I helped to start over 100 churches in Florida and throughout the South during my lifetime," Page proudly averred. He reportedly offered assistance that included terms of policies, advice on procedures, practical input, and general encouragement. Page felt particular urgency, given descriptions of the current state of his denomination in Florida. One newspaper item, for instance, highlighted the small number of Baptists in the state and declared the Baptist faith to be the weakest wing of "the professed Christian Army." The veteran pastor thus found it crucial to spread Christianity by assisting the formation of congregations and, sometimes, erection of churches. Despite and, likely because of, the looming Civil War, Page remained steadfast in pursuing his religious obligations in building the kingdom of God.[31]

Through 1860, Page's presence also continued to be felt in Middle Florida. In one example, persons interested in St. Peter Primitive Baptist Church in Leon County and Concord Baptist Church of Greenville in Madison County requested that the enslaved preacher assist in establishing and organizing their churches. At St. Peter Baptist, Page found himself interestingly engaged in friendly competition with a bondman named Henry Griffin. As with Page, Griffin had been educated by his white master. Whatever the nature of the competition, Page's status guaranteed him eventual recognition as the senior man of God on the scene. Middle Florida whites agreed. At the eighteenth annual session of the Florida Baptist Association—held with Liberty Church on October 19, 1860—leading clergymen recognized Page by including in the association's table of statistics his name as the only "regular" black pastor. It added that "[Reverend Page] preaches at Bel Air to colored members." The recognition, begrudging as it may have been, marked a milestone in the antebellum experience of the Baptist Church in Florida.[32]

CHAPTER EIGHT

The Civil War Years

When the war started, my master sent me to work for the Confederate army. When the Union army came close enough I ran away from home and joined the Union army.

—Former bondman Bill Sims

Abraham Lincoln's election as president in November 1860 set in motion dynamics that led in short order to secession and years of frightful civil war. Those consequences of Republican ascendancy, in turn, altered and then revolutionized James Page's world. Onlookers—including the Middle Florida enslaved preacher—initially anticipated few of the dramatic changes that occurred, and persons touched by them often found themselves little prepared to respond when called upon. Perspectives on the issue of slavery, for instance, altered with time and experience. When inaugurated on March 4, 1861, the sixteenth president of the United States made it clear that he would not disturb the peculiar institution where it already existed. Within less than one year, however, Lincoln had become convinced that men required a higher purpose than maintaining the Union if they were to go willingly onto battlefields of unimaginable horror. Following the Battle of Antietam in mid-September 1862, he issued a preliminary emancipation statement, with a formal declaration to become effective January 1, 1863. On December 1, prior to issuance of the final proclamation, the president explained to Congress the compelling need amid the great national struggle to rethink old ways: "The dogmas of the quiet past are inadequate to the stormy present. The occasion is piled high with difficulty, and we must rise—with the occasion. As our case is now, so we must think anew, and act anew. We must disenthrall ourselves, and then we shall save our country."[1]

The disenthralling ordeal that was the Civil War era opened for Page with his de facto master clamoring for disunion. White Floridians on December 22, 1860, elected delegates to a convention to determine the state's course of action. George Washington Parkhill easily secured one of five seats allocated to Leon County. When the delegates convened at the State Capitol on January 3, 1861, a majority favored immediate secession. Parkhill quickly offered motions for withdrawal, although his plan required approval by voters. Senseless of the calamities that lay ahead, he prepared to put lives on the line to protect from Northern aggression a privileged Southern way of life. The culture's cherished institutions and traditions, he believed, were worth dying for. The convention concurred with all of his message but the referendum. On January 10, the delegates endorsed immediate secession, making Florida the third state to do so. When advised of the action, former governor Richard Keith Call, an old friend and political ally of George's deceased father, John Parkhill, expressed his disgust. "You have opened the gates of Hell," Call bellowed, "from which shall flow the curses of the damned which shall sink you to perdition." The *New York Herald* labeled the newly created republic "the smallest tadpole in the dirty pool of secession."[2]

Parkhill soon demonstrated his willingness to put words into action, a course that carried profound consequences for Page. Some historians have traced the opening of Civil War fighting to the bombardment of Fort Sumter in Charleston Harbor, South Carolina, on April 12. At about that point George resigned his major general's commission in the Florida militia and began planning to organize a company of men to support the military forces of the newly created Confederate States of America. In May he traveled to Richmond to seek President Jefferson Davis's permission to raise an independent company for the South. Davis agreed and commissioned Parkhill a captain with authority to enlist the required men for service as directed by the army. Dependent on Page's administrative ability, Captain Parkhill required the skillful bondman's cooperation in the task. "Me, and the Parkhill family, and some of the servants worked to help all the soldiers and the Captain outfit with the supplies they needed," Page recollected. "I remember a lot of young men wanted to follow him." The unit's tents and uniforms, according to a family source, boasted "green trim in honor of the Parkhill family's Irish heritage." The family showed all the spirit of the fighting Irish.[3]

The exhilaration that surrounded organizing Parkhill's company and that was exuded by George himself quickly enough collided with grim reality. Transferred to Virginia, he and his men had entered combat by August.

Glorious Southern victories at the outset quickly led to stalemate or worse. By late October, his spirits had dampened. George admitted to wife Lizzie, "War is a dreadful thing." Most of his men agreed. Union forces already occupied Florida's largest town, Key West, and were expected to take Pensacola, St. Augustine, Fernandina, and Jacksonville at their leisure. Anxious that occupation of Middle Florida might soon follow, they petitioned Governor John Milton late in the year to request that "President [Davis] . . . return us to Florida." The instigators took care that Parkhill "did not see" the correspondence. When Parkhill did learn about it, the captain adamantly disagreed despite his own disenchantment: "I suppose the Company knew I would not sign it & did not like to hear me talk. If my State need[s] my services I will go to her aid, but until I know she needs me I will remain where the War Department places me." Page would have recognized the reasoning. "I can remember master George saying he would do whatever the South wanted him to do when the Big war started," he recorded, "and that he would do whatever for them to win it too." In any event, Parkhill and his men remained distant from Florida. Coincidentally, General Robert E. Lee recommended the withdrawal of most Confederate soldiers from the state, having concluded that it was not defensible.[4]

During his early tour in Virginia, Captain Parkhill continued to write letters to his wife expressing his concern for her well-being. As the person who probably brought the letters to Lizzie Parkhill, Page must have known about them. If the enslaved preacher and overseer had asked his female master whether her husband had inquired about him or other bondservants on the planation, she would have had to tell him no. Page's absentee master differed from other Florida Confederate slaveholding officers like Rabun Scarborough and Winston Stephens, who asked their wives constantly about the bondpeople on their respective plantations. Perhaps George Parkhill knew that the affairs on the properties he owned were in good hands with Page, or perhaps he was interested in the welfare of only his white family during these tumultuous times. As a second-generation slaveholder, the absentee planter expressed much less concern, compared to his father, about the goings-on within the quarters community.[5]

Meantime, several other significant events occurred in the white Parkhill family that touched James and Elizabeth Page directly. George's wife, Lizzie, gave birth to their second child in March 1861, with Elizabeth Page attending both mother and daughter. They named the baby girl Emmala Ann Simkins Bellamy Parkhill. As George and his company prepared to depart for Virginia, Lizzie grew distraught. "I had to help out Mrs. Lizzie sometime[s] and talk to her when Captain Parkhill was off to the Big War," Page commented. To ease her fears, Lizzie insisted that she accompany the unit on its journey north. The children went with her. A descendant explained, "The Captain's wife and his two babies went with the company as far as Richmond and stayed there until the end." Their departure left Bel Air and Tuscawilla plantations in Page's charge. For the time being at least, he worked now without direct supervision from either his male or female masters.[6]

In 1862 the Parkhill family faced tragedy, an outcome that Page had dreaded. "I prayed for the safety of the Captain that he would return to us safe one day," Page recorded. One can only surmise that Page prayed also for the safe return of those blacks who had left family members on the Parkhill plantations during the war to fight on the side of the Union military for their freedom. The enslaved cleric's prayers for the safe return of his master fell, nonetheless, on deaf ears. As Page recalled, "Something really bad happened." In late June, Union forces were pressing westward to Richmond. Confederate defenders countered the drive in what history has dubbed the Seven Days Battle. Superiors dispatched Captain George Parkhill's unit to the front on the conflict's first day. "The Captain [was] leading his men when, in the early dawn, a bullet pierced his noble Christian heart," a biographer detailed. It was left to George Parkhill's body servant Lewis to recover the remains, which were buried in Richmond. "I remember that a servant went with Captain Parkhill to the Big War," Page related. "I understand he took real good care of the body." Men like Lewis were common among the many bondservants who assisted their Confederate masters during the war. But sometimes enslaved women accompanied their enslavers to the battlefront as well. Former bondwoman Harriet Barret remembered, for example, that her master "carry me to war with him, 'cause I's de good cook." Body servants proved to be instrumental in the Confederate war effort. With his job done on the battlefield, Lewis returned to Tuscawilla. George Washington Parkhill's death meanwhile dealt his widow's emotional state a severe blow. "When the Captain was killed, Mrs. Lizzie took it real hard," Page recalled, "and would not talk to nobody for a long time." Awash in her grief, she soon returned with the children to Tuscawilla. "I did not want to disturb her until she wanted to talk to me," Page added.[7]

For the Civil War's remainder and in the years that followed, Lizzie Parkhill built up an extreme dependency on James Page. Now the sole master of more than 170 bondservants, she relied upon his management of the plantation, as well as his advice and prayers. As an immediate matter, Page continued as best he could to operate Tuscawilla and Bel Air plantations as she mourned. It would have fallen to Elizabeth Page to aid in caring for her children. As he admitted, "Mrs. Lizzie knew little about running the place." The need for regular attention to chores continued, as did the making of key management decisions. Keeping the workforce occupied posed an especially important challenge. By the time of Captain Parkhill's death, Union naval forces had imposed a more or less effective blockade of Florida's panhandle coastline. This meant that, for practical purposes, cotton could not be shipped. By summer 1862 also, despite early expectations that the war would be short lived, virtually everyone accepted that the conflict would endure for years. Governor John Milton in the circumstances strove to limit cotton production while encouraging cultivation of daily necessities. Always a practical man, Page assessed the situation pragmatically and adjusted focus as appropriate. As a result, cotton production plummeted on the Parkhill properties, while attention to food crops intensified. However, "all they wanted to do was tend to their own little gardens," Page recollected of his charges. "They didn't care about planting or picking cotton. For those servants who stayed on the place, it seemed like all they wanted to do was hear about the War. I remember a servant once had a newspaper with soldiers on the front and wanted me to read to him about the War, so I did." Page reflected Governor John Milton's sentiments. In a letter to the Confederate secretary of war, he noted that without consistent supervision, enslaved workers in the state "will not only fail to make the crops, but will destroy the Stock, necessary to the very existence of the country [Confederacy]." Milton was right. In their not-so-quiet boycott, bondservants on the Parkhill plantations, much like the army of bondpeople throughout the South, were destroying the Confederacy from within by their refusal to work for their enslavers.[8]

The task of managing the Parkhill family's "restless servants" grew ever more complicated with the passing months. News of Union victories circulated in Middle Florida with increasing regularity as 1862 evolved into 1863 and 1864. Throughout the state, and many other areas of the South, individual bondservants and families began to slip away from farms and plantations toward freedom and security behind Union lines. "Some servants got mean to me and some of them got up real close to me and said that there was nothing I could do to them," Page related. Many men found a welcome embrace in the ranks of the US Army, most specifically in regiments of the US Colored Troops. Their rolls included men from Tuscawilla and Bel Air.

Fugitive slaves who left the Parkhill plantations to join the Union army wore uniforms similar to that of the soldier shown here. State Archives of Florida, Florida Memory

"It seems that every couple of days during the War I would lose a servant or two," Page noted. "They would usually leave at night time. It was hard stopping them from leaving." He continued, "Now for some of the servants, well, most of those who left the plantation joined I [guess] the Union Army. At least that is what they told me. Most of those who left the plantation were young boys who went off to the Big War. . . . And like I said before, I am pretty sure the boys who left the place joined the Union Army mostly. I

JEREMIAH ROLLS, 1st Sergt., Co. I.   ABRAM C. SIMMS, Corp., Co. I.
GEORGE LIPSCOMB, Corp., Co. I. THOMAS BOWMAN, Sergt., Co. I.
ISOM AMPEY, Pvt., Co. K.   JOHN H. WILSON, Sergt. Major.

Soldiers of the Massachusetts Fifty-Fourth Regiment who fought at the Battle of Olustee. State Archives of Florida, Florida Memory told them I could not help them if they got caught." He added proudly, "I believe those servants who ran away from the place helped the Union a lot to win the war." It appeared that Page made no strong effort to stop anyone from leaving Tuscawilla. And in not earnestly trying to contain bondservants who went to fight for the Union, Page showed his more rebellious side.[9]

~

What was James Page's son doing during the war years? Much like Elizabeth Page, the lack of extant information on Tom's childhood and adult life leaves a gaping hole in the James Page story. But, by the time of the Civil War, Tom was at least twenty-eight years old, and he could have fought in the war. Frederick Douglass encouraged his two sons, Lewis and Charles, at ages twenty-two and eighteen, respectively, to enlist in the Union army's Fifty-Fourth Massachusetts Regiment. What did Page tell his son in the private of their home about the Civil War, and what did Tom proceed to do during this period? The record gives nothing.[10]

The slow drain of slaves from Middle Florida farms and plantations at times kindled or rekindled a volatile climate of fear, contributing yet another new concern that Page had to factor in his planning. Remarkably, most whites preferred to cling to the myth that enslaved laborers remained loyal servants out of unconditional love for those who owned them. Page ensured that no harm came to the Parkhill women and children. According to historian Martha Hodes, "White women were not necessarily engulfed by sexual alarm when white men went off to war and left them alone with slave men." Given that no white men resided at or near Tuscawilla or Bel Air during the war years to protect their white women, the enslaved preacher/overseer succeeded, nonetheless, in protecting the Parkhill women from black rage, for they were not brutalized or raped. His loyalty to the Parkhills arose from complicated attitudes crystallized at the intersections of his personal experience, moral tenets, and religious beliefs. Yet those who received his protection sadly found little reason to articulate their own emotional ties to him, despite James's actions to spare them from grim realities feared, if not felt, by many other slave mistresses. Virginia's Mary Ann Whittle was one of those who believed that, if bondpeople ever got a chance, they "will sho[o]t us in our beds." Similar concerns may have prompted apprehension in Middle Florida that enslaved people were growing unmanageable and becoming potentially violent. Alarmed that many fleeing bondmen intended to commit crimes up to and including murder, a Tallahassee editor encouraged whites as early as May 1862 to arm themselves for impending catastrophe. Panicked civilians even demanded that the governor proclaim marital law to thwart possible slave violence. A Georgia newspaper editor claimed that an "insurrectionary plot" and conspiracy ran rampant in his state. Elsewhere in the South similar fears echoed broadly. Some Southerners lived convinced that they were fighting two enemies, the North and their own restless slave populations. They were right.[11]

Despite the rumors and fears, no major uprisings among bondpeople occurred in Florida during the Civil War years. Still, Middle Florida remained an armed camp, a circumstance that sometimes impeded Page's mission as well as his ability to manage the Parkhill estates efficiently. Whites occasionally shot enslaved fugitives on sight, a dreadful state of affairs with which Page was all too familiar. As he remarked, "Many of those boys took their lives in their own hands by running away." Because of the region's distance from areas controlled by the Union, relatively few bondservants fled Middle Florida farms and plantations as compared to the runaway rates in the Pensacola region and the peninsula. Tuscawilla was an exception, since young men frequently left the plantation to join the Union military. Numerous bondservants from outside Middle Florida, however, absconded to the Union. Over a thousand bondpeople in North Florida fled, for example, to the federal military. "We learn that a few days ago all the negro men from the plantation of Hon. Philip Dell, about 18 miles west of Waldo [in Alachua County], stampeded on mules to the enemy at Jacksonville," declared a not unusual report from the war's final years. Most Middle Florida bondmen, though, understandably stayed near their loved ones and awaited the arrival of Union armies. W. E. B. Du Bois argued that they and others like them throughout rebel-controlled areas of the South resisted in their own quiet but effective way, doing what they could to aid the Union cause. Echoing Du Bois's claim, historian Paul Ortiz went further, saying "the mass exodus of slaves from South plantations [constituted] the first national general strike [of workers] in US history." Although Page stayed on the Tuscawilla plantation and protected Lizzie Parkhill and her children until freedom came, as overseer and minister he stood in the way of no one who planned to leave. He never attempted to retrieve a fugitive after he or she had absconded.[12]

As rumors suddenly comprised a principal means of imparting news, Page was confounded and off balance as he sought to provide insightful leadership. For example, rumors dampened the ardor of some young men who might otherwise have fled Parkhill properties, perhaps surprisingly so. At a time when communications had become problematic and printed reports were unreliable, for good or ill, rumors counted for much and had to be taken seriously into account. So it was with Union policies regarding black refugees. During the war's early months, many Union officers declined to accept escapees into their lines, much less the military's ranks. Politics and controversy swirled around the professed reluctance of President Lincoln to accept their service. "I heard Mr. Lincoln did not want Negroes fighting in the Big War," Page insisted. Indeed, the president feared that he might alienate Southern Unionists by arming onetime bondmen. He was also concerned that border states such as Maryland, Kentucky, Delaware, and Missouri might secede.[13]

Thus, in the case of enlistments, the initial rumors that reached Page carried more than grains of truth. He did not err in placing trust in them. In relatively short order, though, that status quo changed without him knowing or understanding the new policies. As it happened, after a long-awaited major Union victory at the Battle of Antietam on September 17, 1862, the president was more comfortable with allowing blacks, free and enslaved, to enlist. His initiative went hand in hand with military-enforced emancipation. The North needed more soldiers to fight for the Union cause at the same time as it desired to drain the South of its human resources. Lincoln accordingly hoped that both his preliminary emancipation statement in September and, later, the formal Emancipation Proclamation would entice blacks to abandon the South to aid in the struggle for freedom. According to a biography of former Virginia bondman Charles Gandy, "The news of war, and the possibility of Negroes enlisting as soldiers was truly a step closer to the answering of their prayers for freedom. Upon hearing of this good news Gandy joined a few of the others in the break for freedom. One night, he and a close friend packed a small quantity of food in a cloth and set out about midnight to join the northern army." The participation of blacks willing to fight for the Union, according to historians Bob Luke and John David Smith, "made clear that after 1863 Lincoln had transformed the war from a constitutional struggle over states' rights to a war of black liberation." The strategy worked, because approximately 200,000 black men fought on the Union side before the war's end. Of the approximately 750,000 soldiers who died in the conflict, more than 40,000 were African American. With so many black men fighting against their former enslavers, historian Steven Hahn characterized this large swell of blacks joining in the war effort as "the largest slave" uprising in America. How many more of those brave fighting men might have enlisted from Tuscawilla or Bel Air had communications allowed Page to understand such policy changes in a timely and reliable manner can never

Black Union soldiers at Olustee, 1864. State Archives of Florida, Florida Memory

be known. Literate as he was, he shared believable relevant news whenever it came to him with members of the quarters community.[14]

Twice during the war Union armies drew close enough to Leon County and the Parkhill plantations to compel Page to anticipate critical eventualities. Not only did the possibility of Union victories in these drives require attention but so, too, did the possibility of the family's enslaved blacks losing loved ones serving in the military. Rumors flew around each of the forays, as he prepared in a chaotic atmosphere. The first incursion originated at Jacksonville and led to the Battle of Olustee on February 20, 1864. The aims of this major foray have never been detailed conclusively, but the capture of Tallahassee loomed a possibility in the minds of some of its leaders. If so, those ambitions were crushed when Confederate authorities successfully interposed their forces a dozen or so miles east of Lake City at Olustee. Vehement abolitionist Colonel Thomas Higginson, among others, praised the valor of black soldiers—possibly including enlistees from Tuscawilla or Bel Air— during and after the fighting. Another officer, as historian David J. Coles found, declared that the black warriors "fought like devils." Olustee long has been heralded as Florida's largest engagement of the war. More recently, Luke and Smith pointed out that it also constituted only the second major battle, after the ill-fated clash at South Carolina's Fort Wagner, where black soldiers had the chance to meet the Confederate rebels in mortal combat.[15]

The second of the two engagements that drew Page's rapt attention took place just before the war's end at and near a familiar locale of great sentimental value to him. Union forces from Key West, many of them black troopers, landed in early March 1865 at the St. Marks Lighthouse south of Tallahassee. Despite the inability of naval support vessels to ascend the St. Marks River, about a thousand troops quickly advanced on Newport, the site of Page's ordination as a Baptist minister thirteen years earlier. Their initial goal involved capture of Tallahassee, although some accounts have suggested an aim of freeing Union prisoners notoriously held at Andersonville, Georgia. Preliminary fighting at Newport's bridge over the St. Mark's River led on the sixth to a larger engagement eight or so miles north at Natural Bridge. There, a ragtag collection of older men, reinforcements hurriedly rushed to the scene, and boys from the local academy that ultimately became Florida State University managed to frustrate the advance. Union officers decided that the potential cost of pressing ahead outweighed any possible gain from Tallahassee's seizure and withdrew their forces. Confederates trumpeted the outcome as a great victory. Still, even Confederate reports conceded, "The enemy fought very stubbornly." Union accounts gave additional detail. "The blacks are highly spoken of for their conduct in charging," one correspondent asserted, "which seems to be their *forte*."[16]

The landing, subsequent clashes, and ensuing deflation of expectations thrust Page onto an emotional roller-coaster ride. He did not need rumors this time to judge the nature of events close at hand, although reports he received exaggerated Union strength. Alarms literally rocked Tallahassee, as well as other county seats in the vicinity. "On the following Sunday morning—March 5th, the Alarm cannon began firing at 4 o'clock A. M.; an hour or more before daylight," recorded a physician at Tallahassee who knew Page well. "It was still very dark—; no sign of daybreak—the first person I met was Will Gunn, who was going homeward with a lantern—I hailed him, and asked him what was to pay—; he answered in his profane style—'H——s to pay—5000 Yankees have landed at St. Marks, and are advancing on Tallahassee.[']" The physician added, "This was alarming intelligence to be sure."[17]

Just as reverberations of Tallahassee's cannons would have reached Bel Air plantation, the exchange of fire at Natural Bridge—a very short distance southeast of that Parkhill property—thundered across the landscape. As it happened, Page had been dispatched to a nearby plantation to retrieve a young woman who had been summoned to Bel Air from the front by her mother. "An old colored preacher, Uncle James Page, was waiting outside in his buggy to take me home," Susan Archer remembered. "The roar of cannon could be distinctly heard. As we neared Bel Air, the din of musketry, with one volley after another, greeted my ear, causing cold chills to run through me." At the outset, an elated Page must have believed that salvation day had arrived at last. Union retreat, though, collapsed dreams of immediate freedom into a crisis of fear as vengeful Confederates, headquartered at Camp Randolph near Bel Air, combed the vicinity for fleeing Union soldiers. The brutal and speedy execution of two Union scouts who were accused of being rebel deserters struck abject terror into hearts already grappling with disappointment. "I was thoroughly shocked to witness the extent of cold blooded want of feeling in the soldiers," the physician admitted. "I heard them claiming the hats, clothing & boots of the poor men, before the shooting took place, and as they fell, there was a rush from all sides, and all of the clothing was stripped from their bodies." He added, "By and bye some negroes were made to dig two holes, and the naked bodies were tumbled in and buried like two dogs."[18]

Despite the dashed hopes and worker resistance that increasingly inhibited crop production on the plantations, Page's responsibilities for all residents required that he ensure certain work was accomplished in an acceptable and timely fashion. One of the areas that compelled his attention, a critical chore that became universal in Middle Florida as the war ground on, concerned the production of salt. The availability of an item simply taken for granted in peacetime meant nothing less than the difference between the capacity to preserve food and possible starvation. Page left no description of his efforts to ensure an adequate supply, but facts generally available indicate the nature of the challenge that he faced. Salt's production posed real difficulties; it could not be manufactured at Tuscawilla or Bel Air. Page's principal option—when he could not purchase supplies—was to take crews to the coast to boil seawater over extended periods of time in huge, open pans. The process left salt as a residue. It was, however, a risky one. Fires and smoke drew the attention of naval blockading vessels, the crews of which specialized in destroying production facilities and seizing any bondservants found present. Plus, competition for suitable sites also limited options. As historian Robert A. Taylor discovered, "Most of the lower counties in southwest

Georgia eventually operated saltworks in north Florida." The coast immediately south of Tallahassee and Bel Air, roughly the site of the Union landing in March 1865, constituted a prime and bustling salt manufacturing
center. By November 1862 warships already were striving to disrupt operations there.[19]

A member of one area plantation family helpfully detailed the situation
almost exactly as it confronted Page. "A year ago salt began to get scarce but
the people only had to economize in its use, but soon there was no salt and
then Father got [a cousin] to come down from Georgia and take charge of
some salt works he was having installed on the coast," Susan Bradford Eppes
related in October 1863. "He had plenty of hands from the plantation[,] but
they had to have an intelligent head and then, too, it is a rather dangerous
place to work, for the Yankee gunboats can get very near the coast and they
may try shelling the works." The industrial labor, as she discovered, had to
continue despite the perils involved. "The great big sugar kettles are filled
full of water and fires made beneath the kettles," Eppes continued. "They are
a long time heating up and then they boil merrily. Ben and Tup and Sam keep
the fires going, for they must not cool down the least little bit. A white foam
comes at first and then the dirtiest scum you ever saw bubbles and dances
over the surface, as the water boils away it seems to get thicker and thicker,
at last only a wet mass of what looks like sand remains. This they spread on
smooth oaken planks to dry. In bright weather the sun does the rest of the
work of evaporation, but if the weather is bad fires are made just outside of
a long, low shelter, where the planks are placed on blocks of wood. The shelter keeps off the rain and the fires give out heat enough to carry on the evaporation. The salt finished in fair weather is much whiter and nicer in every
way than that dried in bad weather, but this dark salt is used to salt meat or
to pickle pork. I think it is fine of Father to do all this. It is very troublesome[,] and it takes nine men to do the work, besides [our cousin's] time;
and Father does not get any pay whatever for the salt he makes." Eppes could
have also added, neither did the nine enslaved workers who were made to
brave military gunfire to make it.[20]

Such dangerous and taxing efforts ironically grew less pressing for Page
as the war neared its conclusion. According to a Parkhill descendant, no enslaved people remained at Bel Air or Tuscawilla in the closing months of
the conflict except for Page and his family. While that blanket statement almost surely distorted the true picture, it does suggest that a significantly
diminished number of bondmen and bondwomen were present. One thing

appears certain: a considerable number of Parkhill enslaved workers emancipated themselves over time by departing the estates, thus lessening the demand for food and salt. Whether Page had the capacity to put in a crop for 1865 or attempted to encourage the remaining workers to do so is not known. Chances are that, save for garden production, he did not go to the trouble. Page never wanted to be a warrior in the Union military; the enslaved preacher was a man of words and not a man of war. He seemed, nonetheless, to have had no problem with other enslaved persons fighting to destroy slavery. His lackluster effort to retrieve fugitives heading to the Union lines to fight for their own freedom suggested so. The enslaved preacher/overseer did not clearly describe his feelings about the Civil War. But his nuanced statements clearly suggest that he was on the side of the Union and the liberation of enslaved persons in the United States.[21]

~

Throughout the conflict Page persisted in his responsibilities as a pastor, offering comfort, consoling the aggrieved, baptizing the converted, marrying the hopeful, and interring the dead. If anything, calls upon his pastoral care expanded through the stresses, tragedies, separations, and inconveniences of wartime. The geographical scope of his duties, wartime complications notwithstanding, remained immense. Conditions compelled this range, a circumstance easy to understand given the standing that Page enjoyed at the war's beginning. Ordained in 1851, he had expanded his work over the decade to include church organization and support in many areas of the Southeast. In the process he earned widespread regard for his contributions and effectiveness not only from fellow bondpeople but also from many whites, including denominational leaders. By 1860, he stood in a unique position for the region, as illustrated by events that occurred in Thomasville, Georgia, on March 18. The town's principal white Baptist minister, Tennessee native and venerable churchman Rev. William Nowell Chaudoin, broke precedent that day. Chaudoin hosted Page's participation in a three-member presbytery for the ordination of white deacons on an equal basis with him and a second white minister. Page preached the service's sermon and administered the charge to the new deacons. "It was impressive beyond the power of those who saw it to express, or of the reader to conceive, to see that venerable man, Page, his head white with age, and face expressive of manly dignity, and christian humility, and tears, giving advice to his brethren," a correspondent reported. "Yes, brethren, and that not in name, but in reality and feeling, though one of them the owner, perhaps of a hundred slaves." He added, "It was new and impressive to see master and slave, under the hands of the same Presbytery, at the same time."[22]

Page's unique position afforded him latitude to pursue his mission energetically despite wartime dislocations, disruptions, suspicions, and confusion. "I still did some traveling during the War," he recalled. "I remember traveling and I could see that the Confederacy was using servants every where I went. I remember seeing servants loading and unloading for the Confederates. But I was more interested in doing work for God. I am proud to say that I helped people all over Florida build nice Baptist churches as I traveled during the War." Accordingly, congregations sprinkled throughout the region proudly retain memories of ties to Father Page. In March 1862, for instance, the Union Baptist Church of Molino in Pensacola received a visit. Six months later, the enslaved preacher returned to Escambia County to assist in the founding of New Hope Primitive Baptist Church in Cantonment. Among other religious visits, Page ventured to Nassau County in July 1864 to assist the establishment of the first black Baptist church in Fernandina. "You know I still traveled many places to points north, east and west," he confirmed, "preaching the word of God and helping to build churches for our Savior."[23]

The legacy of Page's mission travels during the war extended well beyond church organizations and edifices. He converted, during times of arduous trials and intense stress, hundreds if not thousands of individuals who became mainstays of influential congregations, including a considerable portion of the rising generation of black Baptist preachers. Two examples help to illustrate the point. John Jamison, a Leon County native, credited not only his denominational affiliation but also his ministry to Father Page. Later prominent as a layman at Jacksonville's Bethel Baptist Church and as a pastor in that city and St. Augustine, Jamison pursued a highly successful ministry well into the twentieth century. Still, his 1912 obituary reflected back over fifty years to note carefully, "He was converted when a boy 14 years old, and baptized by the Rev. James Paige [sic]." Rev. John A. Potter, too, cherished his association with the venerable cleric. A South Carolina native who long associated with the Monticello church, he was preaching before the war's end with Page's encouragement. Shortly after the peace, a Union officer heard him give a sermon at Bel Air. He recorded, "On Sunday I visited the church of Rev. Mr. Page and heard two very interesting sermons— one in the morning by Rev. Mr. Potter, and in the afternoon by the pastor."

Doubtlessly reflecting Page's influence, at least in part, Potter's obituary noted, "He was one of the old time Christians and was a gentleman."[24]

Exactly what Page meant when he referred to "preaching the word of God" during wartime remains a mystery beyond the basics of pastoring and church building. His own words, as mentioned, have suggested that he kept his fellow bondpeople at Tuscawilla and Bel Air apprised of news, but whether he went further in his yearning for delivery at the hands of the Union army is not known. Page's capacities for fighting slavery were not in directly rebelling against the institution or joining the Union military but preaching words of encouragement to bondservants as they endured servitude until freedom came. Other enslaved ministers prayed, however, for the North to win the war. Former bondwoman Amanda McCray, who spent most of her life on a Middle Florida plantation, saw this as a routine practice. She insisted that her enslaved preacher "held whispered prayers for the success of the Union soldier." At the least, Page would have passed on news and information as he traveled. Amanda McCray's minister did so. Former bondman Acie Thomas easily remembered doing the same on his Middle Florida journeys. A slave wagoner on the Kidder Meade Moore plantation in Jefferson County shared news of the war as well. A steady flow of information about current events circulated thanks to literate bondservants like Page.[25]

Did Page endeavor to move beyond mere exchange of news? Explaining how enslaved blacks knew so much about the war in northeastern Florida, Confederate general Joseph Finegan argued, "There was a communication network between negroes within Union lines in east Florida and the slaves behind Confederate lines. Many slaves have escaped, because messages were conducted through the swamps and under cover of the night and could not be prevented." Enslaved fugitives even carried information to the Union military in West Florida. According to a Confederate sailor, "We captured a negro man making his way to Fort Pickens [Pensacola], in a boat. He was carrying information to the enemy." After the Union army had taken control of the battle at Gettysburg, General Robert E. Lee blamed the loss on the intelligence of a black spy. He bemoaned that "the chief source of information to the enemy is through our Negroes." President Lincoln even asked about a "grapevine" network that could be used among bondservants to inform them to leave their masters for the protection of the Union military. Former bondwoman Julia Ward King confirmed, "The slaves used to get together in their cabins and tell one another the news in the evening." Slave communication systems similarly operated nearby in Georgia, Alabama, and South Carolina. Page easily could have participated in such a network. Given that he failed to note such activities in later years and his deeply held desire not to jeopardize his privileged status, however, any such behavior—if, indeed, it occurred—was conducted in complete secrecy with utmost discretion.[26]

Other intriguing questions about Page's Civil War–era experiences also elude definitive answers. His engagement with enslaved congregations and his nurturing of black preachers are evident from his own testimony and surviving documentation, but the frequency and quality of his contacts with white congregations and denominational leaders has defied reliable characterization. For that matter, Florida Baptist historians even have proved shy about analyzing church activities during the conflict, to the point of asserting that the Florida Baptist Convention did not meet during the era. This simply was not the case. In 1863, for instance, the convention met on November 20 in the Baptist Church at Madison Court House. Delegates convened the next year during the same month at Leon County's Indian Spring Church. Harriet Parkhill, for one, adamantly believed that the enslaved preacher attended these and the other annual meetings. "He [James Page] always attended the Baptist Convention of the white peoples' organization," she insisted, "taking his place among them as one of the ministers and brethren." In the absence of accurate minutes, though, the facts remain inconclusive.[27]

What is certain is that the war dealt profound blows to Florida's Baptist Church insofar as white membership, attendance, and support were concerned. In fairness, the same dynamic applied to the white Methodists. Once the glory of early Southern victories had begun to fade and notices of killed and wounded began to pour into the state, enthusiasm for those who had instigated secession—the Florida Baptist Convention included—faded. As Douglas S. Hepburn reported, "In December [1860] the fledgling State Convention meeting in Monticello approved a resolution by F. C. Johnson expressing sympathy for the Southern cause and supporting the destruction of all political ties with the Union." Veteran Methodist minister John C. Ley described the consequences. Although he was referring to his denomination, the words applied equally to the Baptists: "This large decrease in our membership [as of December 1862], the general state of the country, the disorganized condition of the Church by the absence of nearly all the white men in the army called upon those who remained for more than ordinary faith." Revivals held at times of extreme uncertainty or imminent threat sometimes produced temporary membership advances. What irony if Page had been called upon on such occasions to lift white spirits and bandage denominational wounds.[28]

During a time when travel was more complicated because a rail system had not yet been built between Georgia and Florida, the Florida Baptist Association (FBA) met in Georgia where travel to and from meetings was less challenging. Members of Baptist state conventions in both Georgia and Florida looked forward to attending the larger and somewhat more prestigious FBA. Father James Page had a greater opportunity at the larger FBA meetings to interrelate with white peers, and its gatherings would have tended to be held in closer proximity to Tuscawilla and Bel Air than were typical Florida state convention assemblies. Only minutes from the 1860 session at Liberty Church in Brooks County, Georgia, survive to attest to his presence during the period. He had been ordained by the association a decade earlier, and they listed him in the same manner as other white clergymen were enumerated. The association continued to assemble through the war years. This included gatherings at Indian Springs in October 1863 and at Friendship Church twelve miles northwest of Thomasville one year later.[29]

The war surprisingly ended melodramatically for Page, at least if Parkhill family legend can be believed, with the loyal overseer defending the property of his owners from Yankee aggression. Genevieve Parkhill Lykes asserted that Union soldiers came to one of the Parkhill plantations—presumably Tuscawilla—searching for food and meaning to ransack the place. "It was not long before the Yankee troops foraged through middle Florida. When news of their approach came, all the hams and bacon, along with silver and valuables, were buried for preservation. The slaves hid—all but Uncle Jeems Page. He stood his ground with his mistress. So the Yankees found an empty smoke house. When Uncle Jeems refused to tell them where the stores were hidden, they hung him up by his thumbs. Grandmother took the carving knife and cut him down; then she told the marauders, 'You can burn the house, but you cannot mistreat my slaves.'" Lykes added, "Her courageous gesture impressed the Commanding Officer. The troops left, doing no harm."[30]

The tale of defiance is impossible to verify. The first Union forces to arrive on the scene came, however, with General Edward M. McCook, who entered Tallahassee on May 10 to accept the surrender. Ten days later he publicly read the Emancipation Proclamation there before a mass audience, notifying all enslaved persons that they were free. There is no reason to suppose that Page was not present on that occasion. A black trooper described the atmosphere: "The rebs here seem to die very hard at the idea of having black troops to guard them, but they keep very quiet, and do not have much to say. How true is the saying that we know not what a day may bring forth! Great changes are being wrought." Reports of the time suggested that the Union soldiers treated the defeated Floridians most courteously. "The arrival of Union forces in Tallahassee meant a new life for the citizens of Florida as well as the end of the Confederacy," John E. Johns concluded. "In general they sought to accept this new situation in a peaceful and normal manner. Civilians and Federal soldiers accepted each other freely, and unpleasant incidents were unusual." In the meantime, Page remained with the surviving Parkhills until slavery ended. And despite the manipulation, exploitation, and sometimes mistreatment experienced by Page from Parkhill family members during the antebellum period, the venerable minister continued to maintain a close rapport with them as a free man.[31]

CHAPTER NINE

Emancipation and Congressional Reconstruction

It just like dis, I believes it was intended from God for de slaves to be free.
—Former bondwoman Sallie Paul

After de war, a man came along on a red horse; he was dressed in a blue uniform and told us we was free.
—Former bondwoman Adeline Jackson

The Civil War's end arrived in stages for James Page over several months, beginning on March 6, 1865, with the nearby defeat of US forces at the Battle of Natural Bridge. The Union repulse dealt a crushing blow to the enslaved preacher's hopes for immediate freedom for him, his loved ones, and his remaining charges on the Parkhill plantations. Less than one month later, though, signs of cessation of hostilities began to reappear. An early and clear indication came on April 1. Florida governor John Milton, driven to despair by the frustration of his secessionist dreams of chattel slavery safeguarded by the Confederate States of America, had retreated to his Sylvania plantation in Middle Florida's Jackson County less than seventy miles northwest of Tallahassee. "While his daughter prepared his 'homecoming' meal," writer Gary Loderhose explained, "the governor retired to his chambers and fired a shotgun blast into his head."[1]

Events then began to tumble one upon another. Eight days after Milton's suicide, Robert E. Lee surrendered the Army of Northern Virginia to Ulysses S. Grant at Appomattox. Within the following week the coward John Wilkes Booth ended Abraham Lincoln's life, and Southerner Andrew Johnson of Tennessee became president. Meanwhile, Florida remained in the war under the jurisdiction of General Joseph E. Johnston and the Army of Tennessee. The one-time US Army quartermaster general's forces were shadowing General William T. Sherman's triumphant advance northward from Savannah to the Chesapeake Bay following his heralded March to the Sea from Atlanta.

On April 26 near Durham, North Carolina, Johnston, too, conceded the fight. The Confederate States flag nonetheless continued to fly over Florida's Capitol. It remained in place until May 10 when General Edward M. McCook arrived to claim the state for the victors. "I remember for the first time in my life when I actually saw Colored Troops in Tallahassee helping to raise the Union flag," Page remembered warmly. Another ten days then elapsed before McCook publicly proclaimed freedom for Page and the state's other bondpeople. Unlike Frederick Douglass, Henry Box Brown, William Wells Brown, Harriet Tubman, and other fugitives who self-emancipated, social and historical forces freed Page.[2]

So far as is known, Page waited to hear of freedom after the Natural Bridge debacle at Bel Air plantation south of Tallahassee. There, he quietly bided his time. Rev. Edwin T. Williams, a Princeton graduate and onetime Presbyterian missionary to Africa, visited him at the recreational resort village on April 9, delivering a sermon at Page's church to what may have been a racially mixed congregation. "I went to the Baptist Church, James Page, pastor," Williams recorded. "Bro. [Jefferson] Hamilton [a refugee Methodist minister then assigned to Mobile] present. My heart enlarged. A large audience. I preached from Heb. 2.3. How shall we escape if we neglect so great salvation. Speaking of the inefficacy of the work of the Father and Son, in Redemption, without the additional applying work of the H[oly] S[pirit]. It occurred happily to me in the way of attenuation, in connection with the parcel offerings, that it is not enough for the blood to be in the basin, it must be put on the doorposts, and lintels—so Christ's blood of [body] must be applied to the soul by the Spirit in faith." Williams added of the occasion, "A large and attentive audience."[3]

Such occasions promised for Page a happy future of helpful cooperation and easy interaction between the races. Other signs unfortunately hinted strongly of division and troubles to come. A black Union soldier recorded details of an encounter that occurred soon after McCook's reading of the Emancipation Proclamation at Tallahassee. "In the morning . . . we had plenty of visitors, and among them was the most inhuman and brutal man that ever lived, in the person of the *Hon.* Benjamin Chaires, of Tallahassee; and if ever there was a demon in human form, he is one," related William B. Johnson of the Third Regiment, US Colored Troops. "The day before we came up, he took one of his slaves, a boy of twelve years, and laid upon his naked back *Three Hundred Lashes!* But, thank God, to-day he stands awaiting his trial." The war had neither chastened nor transformed Chaires, a condition that he shared with many others. His racism and greed for profits through continued cheap labor manifested themselves in the treatment of his former slave. In fact, another war in the South started after the Civil War ended. As the scholar W. E. B. Du Bois aptly noted, this second conflict "became a labor war, an attempt on the part of impoverished capitalists and landholders to force laborers to work on the capitalist's terms." The now-emancipated twelve-year-old wanted to work as a free man under his own terms, but Chaires assumed that he retained authority to force submission in the most brutal manner. As during slavery, Page understood that whites like Chaires throughout the South would continue to use the whipping post as the chief method of brutality and as a symbol that the attitudes and the behavior of some former slaveholders had not changed with the end of the Civil War or with the liberty of former bondservants. Page thus found himself trapped in the middle of a labor battle between former slaveholders and former enslaved workers. This duel for labor control, as Du Bois described it, would come to define the Reconstruction era and beyond. Page had his work cut out for him in this brave new world.[4]

Page, the veteran pastor and counselor, chose to believe that Reverend Williams's visit, rather than Benjamin Chaires's inhumane cruelty, betokened the future. "I am happy that slavery is now over with the loss of the South to the North and the Colored people are now free," Page declared. "Col. [John] Parkhill told me this would be so one day." As a man of the cloth and a prophet of sorts, Page had seen the coming of Providence with the freedom of blacks from bondage: "I also knew it in my heart that the Lord would free Black folks one day like he did the Children of Israel. We just needed to have faith in God that it would happen one day." Doubtlessly, he sympathized with former bondman Claude A. Wilson, who recalled that, when a Union soldier asked his mother whether she knew that she had been freed, she replied, "Yeh Sir . . . I been praying for dis a long time." By all accounts, Page received the news of emancipation with equanimity. "Some of the Colored folks really started acting up when they heard they were free," he remembered in words suggesting the intensity of his own restraint. The Baptist minister and leader did not want to be alone in dealing calmly with his newly acquired freedom; he wanted members of his race to react peacefully to their hard-fought liberty as well.[5]

There was no significant transformation in Page's basic attitudes and behavior toward whites after blacks gained their liberty. Harmony of action characterized his behavior just as harmony between the races became his goal during Reconstruction. As a man who firmly believed in working with all people as well as all religious denominations, Page would help lay the foundation for black economic, educational, and political progress during the Reconstruction era. Given that freedmen and women had few material possessions after the Civil War, the cleric wanted magnanimous whites to work cooperatively with blacks in obtaining a solid footing in the political economy of the state and the South: "I hope now that White folks and Black folks would live and work together in peace."[6]

Yet Page had to reconcile his thoughts about the magnanimity of most whites with the truth that many of them, like Chaires, perceived blacks only as workers or property to be exploited rather than as human beings who deserved decent pay for a hard day's labor. In fact, some former slaveholders did not want to live after learning their former bondpeople were free. According to freewoman Sarah Ross, "many plantation owners took their own lives in desperation" after the Civil War. Sallie Paul echoed Ross's sentiments, claiming "den when de colored people was freed, heap of de white folks died cause dey grieve demselves to death over de loss of dey property." Anna Miller recalled her former master saying "he don' want to live in a country whar de niggers am free. He kills hisself 'bout a year after." Whites had developed such a dependency on the free services of blacks that many would rather die than be without their exploitable laborers. So, the fight between freedmen and women and their former enslavers for absolute authority over workers' labor and time would largely define the political economy of the South during the Reconstruction era. A black minister summed up the matter: "It has been said that the Negro here will not work, that they are becoming indolent and vicious. The facts are, they have become tired of working without pay.... [T]hose who have considered it their God-given right to swindle the negro out of the hard earn money due him are without help."[7]

As events and circumstances compelled Page's leadership during this new era, he faced the daunting task of dealing with these two very different and conflicting realities. He had plenty of company in facing this quandary. Many blacks after the war were full of hope and unrealistically high expectations. As historian Paul Ortiz rightly noted, "African Americans believed [after the war] that access to inexpensive farm land, the right to bargain with employers, free public schools, and the elective franchise were keys of liberty." But fears, leftover frustrations, uncertainty, and, in the case of some whites, downright nastiness meanwhile made it difficult for the newly freed men and women to perceive and act in their own best interest. For more than four million emancipated blacks, including Page, the war's end sparked not only joy but also degrees of apprehension, if not dread.[8]

Page continued his work at Tuscawilla and Bel Air plantations, and his positive attitude toward Parkhill family members remained the same even though his legal status had finally changed. Knowing that they had come to depend on his generosity, the Christian cleric felt an obligation to support Lucy, Harriet, and Lizzie Parkhill after the war just as he had aided John Parkhill for decades and George Washington Parkhill before the war. So, he continued to look after the interests of the three single women, now as plantation manager rather than as overseer. If anyone possessed postwar paternalistic sensibilities, it was James Page, the former bondman, and not the Parkhill family. So, high on the newly freed man's list of priorities came ensuring that his onetime owners could count on a reliable workforce. The plantations' worker populations already had diminished by war's end. Emancipation hastened the process. "Most of them left the plantation when they found out they were free," Page observed. Page strove to stem the tide on the home plantations as well as to encourage freedmen and women to remain at other locales where he pastored: "Some of them wanted to leave their places, but I told them to stay if they could get along with Whites until they could do better. But some left anyway, and once the folks left their places they never came back. [They knew that] whites looked at me as a leader of my race. They wanted me to tell them what to do. I told them to work for good people if they could. And I always wanted my people to do what was best for them." As he would come to learn, Page tended to place too much confidence in the sincerity of whites.[9]

His encouragement to freedpeople to remain at Tuscawilla or Bel Air or to move for employment brought positive results, but the challenge required more than his good name in the way of incentives. His response, as it turned out, proved highly effective. Page's vision of institution building became a main goal in his life after slavery and during Reconstruction. More than aware that many persons recently held in bondage yearned to gain literacy, he first opened a school at Bel Air. "We have to start our own schools to let the white folks know we are serious about educating our people," he later remarked. "I believed with a little education, Black people would really be happy because they could help themselves. They would act better if they could get good jobs and own a little something of their own."[10]

Page believed in the concept of black self-help with a caveat. As a pluralist, he held that blacks should pave their own way. But, possessing only the clothes on their bodies at the war's end, they needed help. So, the cleric sought to solicit the support of individual whites while looking, as well, to the US government to help them achieve goals of racial uplift and black community progress. He believed in building black institutions for freedmen and freedwomen just as he previously had urged fellow bondpeople to undertake whatever efforts they could to reduce their dependence upon their former owners. "We must work hard to build our own," he explained. "And it's not a shame to ask others for a little help sometimes." Page believed in an interventionist national government that would guarantee and protect the basic human rights of newly freed men and women as they sought to become educated and self-sufficient. As he had done while a bondman, he looked to his former owners for assistance in reaching that goal. Particularly, he asked Harriet Parkhill to set aside land on the Bel Air plantation to organize the Bethel Baptist Sunday School to teach children and adults how to read and write. Page understood Parkhill well, sensing that she would assist the school if it started out as a religious institution. Once it was in operation, he could expand it into a regular day school. With the aid of individuals and governmental institutions, Page comprehended that black land and business ownership as well as education had become possible and would improve the chances that members of his race could live a more independent and productive existence.[11]

With the approval of the Parkhill family, Page moved quickly on his plans to build an educational institution. The Bethel Baptist Sunday School soon operated in one of the first buildings in Florida erected specifically for the education of black children and adults. As construction proceeded in spring 1865, though, local dynamics had brought new realities into clearer focus for Page. Onetime bondpeople were learning that landowners possessed little or no means to pay them for work or even to advance them goods and supplies. They often responded by fleeing the land for what seemed a more welcoming environment at Tallahassee and other county towns. The old plantation world had collapsed, and no one knew in the immediate postwar months what would replace it. Page found himself among those forced to adapt to the new circumstances. "For years before the Civil War, he was not expected to do any work, only controlling and guiding the other servants," Harriet Parkhill explained. "Afterwards when he had to earn his living, (we had lost everything), his knowledge of reading and writing became most useful, as it enabled him to open a school in Tallahassee, whither he went and came daily in his buggy." Page's former master had underestimated the serious-ness of his duties and his worth as the Parkhill's overseer for at least forty persistent years. As in years past, Father Page sought to rely on his own in-genuity to make a living for himself while helping members of his race. So, in July 1865, the Tallahassee school he started greeted its first students. A visitor that month noted, "There are three schools, one of whom the princi-pal teacher is Rev. Mr. Page (a freedman; how strange!), and although I did not visit it, I was informed it was conducted very well, reflecting great honor on the reverend gentleman."[12]

At Tallahassee, Page encountered friendly competition from black Meth-odists, a fact that bothered him not at all. "I believed in the education of everyone," he insisted. "I believed in the children of God who needed an ed-ucation and that meant White folks and Black folks." He added, "I was a Baptist man, but like I told you, I had some good Methodist friends." One of those friends, Robert Meacham, had preceded Page in offering lessons to lo-cal people. During the war if not earlier, according to a biographer, "he [had] carried [his] education to the other slaves secretly and by night, using the dim glare of a candle for light." By summer 1865, Meacham's policy of education by stealth had given way to operation of a regular school. "School number two [of three freedmen's schools in Tallahassee] has for its teacher a Mr. Robert [Meacham], also a freedman," the July visitor to Page's school observed. "Oh, wonder of wonders, how can all this be?" Meacham also had undertaken the guidance of a substantial block of black Methodists formerly associated at Tallahassee with the Methodist Episcopal (ME) Church, South. Under his tutelage, the group in late 1865 and early 1866 transferred its denominational allegiance to become the Bethel African Methodist Epis-copal Church. Meacham thereafter emerged as one of Florida's leading AME ministers as well as one of the state's most influential political leaders of the Reconstruction era. As Jefferson County state senator in 1869, he shepherded passage through the upper chamber of the measure that created Florida's public school system. Both the black Baptists and the black Meth-odists understood clearly that a strong state-supported education system would produce independent citizens among their race.[13]

Rev. James Smith also competed with Father Page and his Tallahassee school. The black Methodist preacher's conservative philosophy and per-spectives more closely aligned with Page's than did Meacham's more radical views. The American Missionary Association's Rev. Gorham Greely found Smith "an intelligent Colored man" and harkened to his urgent pleas born of the "great want of Teachers and Books." In summer 1865, though, Smith labored in the shadow of the work being done by Page and Meacham. The July visitor, for instance, commented only, "School number three is taught by a freedman. Well, this caps the climax." Where Meacham quickly found a pastoral home with the AME Church, Smith remained for the time being a "junior preacher . . . to the colored charge" under the local white ME, South, minister. Within a few years, however, he helped to pioneer creation in Florida of the Colored Methodist Episcopal Church (now Christian Methodist Episcopal Church). Tallahassee's St. James CME Church yet stands as an enduring legacy of his ministry.[14]

In those early times following emancipation, Page created a problem for himself by continuing to seek white acceptance while striving to aid and enjoy the black community's approval. Understanding clearly that the material conditions of the newly freed men and women neared the point of desperation, he principally enlisted, therefore, the financial assistance of former slaveholders and other whites to support the self-reliance goals of his race. In exchange for their financial assistance, whites believed that a man such as Page could be utilized as an agent of social control, one who could contain an increasingly restless, frustrated, and unanchored tide of former bondservants by keeping them in "their place." To the extent that the teacher and pastor counseled accommodation or what appeared to be accommodation, he encountered degrees of resistance. Even with the financial support Page received from whites, some blacks understandably refused to work for former enslavers. They wanted to own land, hold jobs, and pursue educational opportunities. Into the gap rode men such as Meacham and his AME mentor, Presiding Elder Charles H. Pearce. Pastor of the Tallahassee AME congregation after he transferred Meacham to Monticello, with the advent of Congressional Reconstruction in 1867, Pearce transformed into a powerhouse of Florida politics. In that role he became somewhat of a nemesis to the more conservative Father Page. The AME titan, unlike Page, eagerly pushed for state legislation granting the newly freed blacks opportunities to buy land, start their own businesses, and enjoy the fruits of schooling—including higher education—on an equal basis with whites. Paul Ortiz aptly summed up that "members of the African Methodist Episcopal Church play[ed] an important role in rural communities by promoting small farm ownership, independence, and the dignity of labor."[15]

To his credit, Page understood why so many freedpeople refused to listen to his admonitions or, for that matter, the teachings of his God. Unwilling to change his core beliefs and reluctant to take important steps necessary to adapt them to shifting political and social realities, he faced serious questions concerning the relevance of his leadership in this new and uncertain world. His quandaries stemmed from events at many different governmental and societal levels. Abraham Lincoln's assassination in April 1865 and its consequences stood out. The tragedy thrust Vice President Andrew Johnson into power and vested him with responsibility for leading a war-torn nation. Johnson at first appeared desirous of working with congressional Republicans to transform the South and the country into a place of equal opportunity for blacks and whites. His Southern lineage soon prevailed, however, as the president quickly began to espouse racist policies related to the affairs and condition of newly freed men and women. Instead of working with Congress to decide jointly how the South would be reconstructed, he fought Republicans in order to ease the return of the conservative South to Congress and the nation. Against the wishes of most Republicans and in a conciliatory gesture to powerful former slaveholders, he returned most Southern states into the hands of former slaveholding Confederates. Many Republicans viewed Johnson ultimately as one of the worst presidents to ever occupy the White House.[16]

The process of returning Florida to the Union commenced in July with Johnson's appointment of former federal judge William Marvin as provisional governor. By the time the New Yorker reached the state in early August, chaos reigned. "Florida is full of terrible elements," a journalist declared that month. "In the breast of nearly every man you meet a conflict is raging. Old ideas, old convictions, revered customs, traditional habits, and everything related to civil, social and business life are uprooted, torn to pieces, scattered, thrown down, confused, reduced to chaos and at war with each other. Their sovereign State has fallen, and over its ruin and darkness but the faintest glimmer of light, from the new order of things, has yet dawned." The correspondent proved astute enough, despite prevailing chaotic conditions, to discern that a core leadership had been at work planning the state's future: "Already projects and plans are under discussion for restoring the substance of slavery, though another name may have to be given to the creature in its new garb." Having detailed several of the options under consideration, he added, "Each of these plans, it will be seen, contains an essential element of Slavery, and contemplates the continued degradation of the African race. It is sickening to think that men of intelligence, and claiming to be civilized, should resort to such heartless devices for the purpose of defrauding a weak and inexperienced race out of its hard and honest earnings." Indeed, whites used terroristic tactics to control a disadvantaged working class of former bondservants who, largely, could not defend themselves in American courts. As one historian correctly noted, "racial capitalism" was at the root of whites' desire to exploit former bondpeople, for they needed to make money from the abandon lands after the Civil War, and forcing poor blacks to work much like enslaved people was the answer to their labor shortage problems.[17]

Marvin's arrival, though it brought Page and other race leaders some initial heartening news, quickly produced despair. From Jacksonville in the east to Marianna in the west, the governor addressed racially diverse assemblies. "He preached the prompt acknowledgement of the abolition of slavery, the annulment of the secession ordinance, the repudiation of the war debt, and the admission of blacks as witnesses and litigants in the courts," William Watson Davis explained. "To the native white he counseled an acceptance in good faith without question of the clear issues of the war. To the black he counseled the acceptance of the white man as political and social superior." The new governor also threw cold water on hopes that a beneficent federal government would intervene by providing an economic leg up for freedmen and freedwomen. At Marianna he told the crowd, "There has been a story circulated in Middle Florida that on the first day of January next the land and mules will be taken from your former owners and divided among you. Such a story, I suppose, you have all heard. Have you? Speak out if you have and tell me. ('I'se hearn it! I'se hearn it!' say all.) Well, who told you so? (An answer: 'The soldiers.') . . . I want you to understand me. The President will not give you one foot of land, nor a mule, nor a hog, nor a cow, nor even a knife or fork or spoon. (A voice: 'Dar, ole man, you hear dat!')." President Johnson had no intention of giving lands owned by former slaveholders to the former bondservants. AME elder Charles Pearce said it best: blacks "cannot get homes very well; the lands are owned by large land owners who are unwilling to sell their lands." In these circumstances, James Page quickly understood that members of his race could not depend on the federal government to defend their newly acquired rights as free people.[18]

Page, if quietly, doubtlessly joined other race leaders at Tallahassee and elsewhere in hoping for a prolonged administration by Marvin before he called a convention to perform those acts necessary to return Florida to the

Union. Some may have dreamed that he would allow adult black men to vote. All were disappointed. On August 25, the New Yorker called an election for delegates to be held on October 10. The convention was to assemble at Tallahassee fifteen days later. The president's man limited suffrage rights to "free white male person[s] of the age of 21 years and upward." His proclamation contained a charge to delegates: "The freedom intended [for the former slave] is the full, ample and complete freedom of a citizen of the United States. This does not necessarily include the privilege of voting; but it does include the idea of future possession and quiet enjoyment." To the extent that any question existed on Marvin's stand on black suffrage, he clarified the point when addressing the overwhelmingly pro-Confederate convention when it met. "Shall the elective franchise be conferred upon the colored race, and if so upon what terms and qualifications?" he queried rhetorically. "I am not advised that the President has expressed his views or wishes on this subject, and I know no more of the views or wishes of the members of Congress than is generally known. I cannot think, however, that, if the convention shall abolish slavery and provide proper guaranties for the protection and security of the persons and property of the freedmen, the Congress will refuse to admit our Senators and Representatives to their seats because the freedmen are not allowed to vote at the State and other elections."[19]

The governor had shown his prejudiced hand. Frederick Douglass was not alone in noting that black voting rights equated with freedom: he "looked upon suffrage for the Negro as the only measure which would prevent him from being thrust back into slavery." As historians John Hope Franklin and Alfred A. Moss Jr. added, "African Americans believed that the right to vote was an indispensable vehicle in the long and difficult road they would have to travel to gain true freedom." This meant to Page, unfortunately, that black men would have to wait a little longer, and women much longer, to see the day when they could exercise true citizenship by voting.[20]

Taking Marvin's cue, the convention set the stage for election of state officials and a legislature by white voters only. After the General Assembly convened toward year's end, the body performed as expected and enacted "black codes" that imposed restrictions on black life and action so severe that they came close to reimposing slavery in all but name. Most black leaders condemned the measures as "very diabolical and oppressive." Unfortunately, Page had not yet recognized that the times had overwhelmed his more passive leadership style. Even years later he could only lament that "no Colored man was invited to attend Marvin's convention." He added, "To show that things were changing for the good, some Colored men should have been invited." Where Page declined forceful public advocacy, others proved far more outspoken, increasingly so as anti-black race riots grew, for example, in Memphis and New Orleans during 1866 and early 1867. Notably, leading race advocates, included Presiding Elder Pearce, Reverend Meacham, and other AME stalwarts, fought relentlessly to get full civil and political rights for blacks. "The Baptists were sadly losing out to the [African] Methodists in the state politically," Page acknowledged of the times.[21]

As Page discovered, his saving grace in reestablishing his credibility and relevance in Florida's new social and political worlds, came in the form of the Freedmen's Bureau. Created under the leadership of Union general Oliver O. Howard, who had served in Florida during the 1850s, it was intended to operate as a middleman between newly freed persons and their former masters. The bureau provided tangible assistance to former bondpeople and even some poor whites. Its agents negotiated and supervised labor contracts. It also furnished to some individuals and families necessities such as food, clothing, housing, education, and health care. Thomas W. Osborn headed the Florida bureau during its early operations. By no means a radical, the colonel came to know Father Page at Tallahassee and recognized in him and his mission a conservative individual—and denomination—with whom he could work to fulfill the bureau's goals and, eventually, his own ambitions. At Osborn's encouragement, Page worked directly with Capt. George B. Carse, who became the Leon County agent during 1866. The local Baptist icon proved invaluable to Carse's work, providing him with not only helpful advice but also insight into local affairs and key contacts within the ranks of both races.[22]

The bureau's work notwithstanding, it appeared to many freedpeople as 1866 evolved that they could count on few friends, Northern or Southern, to stand up for their rights. In Washington, President Johnson was battling Radical Republicans, because he believed the Civil Rights Act of 1866 favored "the colored against the white race." During the same year, their conflict even involved whether the existence of the Freedmen's Bureau should be prolonged. The army and the bureau accordingly received mixed signals concerning how to deal with the "Negro problem." Despite his proximity to bureau operations at the state capital, even Page grew leery of the agency's effectiveness: "I like[d] the Freedom's Bureau, but it didn't have much power to do anything for the Colored People or the White people. I always hoped the Bureau could help Black people get some land. I prayed that Black people could own some of their own land one day. It's only through owning a piece of land can Colored folks try to make it on their own." He continued, "During that time, things were not changing for Black folks much after the war. Former masters did not want to work with the former servants as free people. They treated them real mean at times. I saw and read about a lot of violence done to Black people for a long time over this state and throughout the South after slavery ended. Yes, some of the Whites did not want to work with Black folks in a Godly way, but I had no problem working with them." Page's larger point of the impotence of the Freedmen's Bureau rang loud and clear. In many places, including some in Florida, the agency essentially became a sociopolitical arm of Southern whites and sought to keep blacks dependent on them.[23]

This dynamic brought Osborn, Carse, Page, and others secretly into a cooperative relationship that within a year or so began to work a significant influence on the course of Florida politics and government. John Wallace, a black Union army veteran, future lawyer, and officeholder-to-be, told the story: "Thomas W. Osborn, the Commissioner of the Bureau for Florida, stationed at Tallahassee, through his servant, a freedman, requested a meeting of three or four of the most influential colored men at the house of a colored man whose name I do not care to mention. He met them there and informed them that it was the desire of the government that they should form a secret league to prevent their being again returned to slavery. This was sufficient to bring out the old and young, the halt and the blind. In order to deceive and allay any apprehension in regard to the purpose of the gathering, they were instructed to answer any questions by saying that the assembly was for the purpose of forming a benevolent society. At the appointed time several hundred freedmen assembled, but only seventy-five or eighty were initiated the first night, as it was deemed wise to impress them with an air of deep solemnity and great formality."[24]

The Lincoln Brotherhood's Tallahassee chapter stood as the "parent lodge" of branches throughout the state, creating a potent network ripe for exploiting its membership numbers when the timing was right. Although Page parsed his words on the subject, he qualified as one of the "three or four . . . most influential colored men" at Tallahassee. As such, he probably attended Osborn's initial meeting and many related conferences thereafter. "The fraternal men would have meetings at my church," he would say, "but I never joined any of them." John Wallace confirmed Page's approval of the local Lincoln Brotherhood chapter because the religious leader allowed the

JOHN   WALLACE.

John Wallace, Father James Page's sometime Republican political ally during Reconstruction, fought with the Second US Colored Infantry at the Battle of Natural Bridge in Florida in 1865. State Archives of Florida, Florida Memory

organization to meet at Bethel Baptist. Much like Booker T. Washington, who would succeed him, a part of Page's persona meant keeping a low profile while discreetly fighting for the rights of his race. No activity would have been allowed at his church without his blessing. And with Page's nod, the black fraternal organization proved instrumental by forging strategies to help protect the rights of freedpeople. "The lodge at Tallahassee became so large that it became necessary to remove from the private house where it was first organized to the lower colored Baptist church, in a part of the town seldom visited by the whites," Wallace detailed. "The freedmen considered this league a great thing, and their meetings at the church were carefully guarded by armed sentinels, who halted anyone who came into the vicinity of the church, requiring the countersign under penalty of the contents of the old musket." So successful was the wedding of Osborn and his white associates with Page and Tallahassee's black Baptists that they created a pattern repeated throughout Middle Florida.[25]

It should be remembered meanwhile that, when the Lincoln Brotherhood began its organizational activities at Tallahassee, Page already had attained the age of fifty-eight. Life expectancy at that time ran considerably lower than in the modern era, and Page had labored hard for nearly four decades and had traveled extensively, often in extremely poor conditions and under significant stress. Now, his health began to register the toll already taken. "I have been suffering ever since I saw you," he informed Harriet Parkhill on February 17, 1866, "with a very bad cough." His appearance and likely his stamina reflected the trials that he had withstood. John W. Alvord of the American Missionary Association visited his school early the same year and left a helpful, if brief, word portrait of a schoolmaster he described as "an old negro preacher with spectacles": "Here, in the capital of the State, we still find the same self-supporting efforts [as seen at Fernandina and Jacksonville]. No white man with any aid has come near them. They have 'no one to consult with,' as one of the colored preachers told me; and yet six schools, with an average of thirty pupils each, are hard at work with such books as are within their reach,—a motley, torn miscellany indeed. One of the teachers,—a venerable old negro,—many years since brought from Virginia, and the coachman of his master while a slave, said to me with great emphasis, 'I try to teach them everything good.' His first classes read to us in easy lessons with commendable accuracy."[26]

Regardless of questions of aging, health, and stamina, Page persisted in fulfilling his numerous responsibilities beyond teaching, tending his flocks at Bel Air and Tallahassee, counseling the Freedmen's Bureau, and facilitating the Lincoln Brotherhood's development. Although production had diminished considerably on the Parkhill lands, he continued to superintend operations there. "I am trying to make a crop or have it made," he informed Harriet in March. "I hope to make a good crop of corn and a little cotton." The task grew even greater after Harriet and her mother, Lucy Randolph Parkhill, relocated to Jacksonville early in 1866, though he corresponded with them regularly. Still, he found time to maintain the personal garden in which he had taken so much pride for decades. In all of this, Page's commitment to self-sufficiency stood out. He may have struck a respectful pose for the Parkhills, but by no means did he rely on them to take care of him or his family. Page clearly understood, though, that self-reliance and governmental interventionist support and protection were necessary if blacks were to become full-fledged productive citizens.[27]

Page in the meantime persisted in his drive to address his expanded duties as a pastor, on the road and at home. In the latter category the performance of marriages emerged beginning in January 1866 as a matter of high priority. On the one hand, Florida's slave codes had forbidden, among other restrictions, bondpersons to legally marry. The legislature that established the state's "black codes," on the other hand, required all free couples who were cohabiting to marry within nine months or, if they remained together at the expiration of that time period, be considered wed as a matter of law. Although they had lived together during slavery as common law partners, many free men and women still looked forward to getting legally married. Accordingly, Page soon found himself called upon to perform appropriate rites by the scores. The first came on January 15, 1866, when he united Charles Taylor and Susan Bond at Tallahassee. Four days later, Robert Beard and Polonia Rivers took their turn. Charles Gorham and Ann Johnson followed the next day. For months dozens of such rites occupied the pastor's attention and required a significant portion of his time. Nearly one hundred couples benefited during the year from his ministrations. Page later insisted that nothing had changed: "I remember I started doing a lot [of] weddings when I first got to Florida to this very day." He added, though, "I liked it when I started marrying Colored folks after the War."[28]

James and Elizabeth Page, too, came under the law's provisions, although they delayed their ceremony until April 10. Surviving recollections fail to provide details, other than his assertion: "I even got married again although I always believed we were always married to each other in the sight of God no matter what other people thought." Page was not alone. Other enslaved couples believed their antebellum marriages were sanctioned by the Almighty but still legalized them. "After the war, when they were made citizens with civil rights," former Kentucky bondman Carl F. Hall recalled, "many former slaves who had been married in this way, hastened to legalize their union by obtaining licenses and having a legal ceremony performed."

As far as the religious leader was concerned, his marriage and the others he performed were legal in the sight of God, but after the Civil War they needed legalization in the eyes of whites. Interestingly, Page chose not to be married by a black minister, Baptist or Methodist. Instead, Rev. William W. Childers, longtime Tallahassee Baptist Church pastor, performed the ceremony. The selection spoke volumes about the close relationship that the two men had established over the years. It also underscored a stark reality of the postwar era. Childers's congregation prior to the war had overwhelmingly consisted of enslaved worshippers. Several hundred of them now had withdrawn from his supervision and transferred their allegiance, principally, to Father Page. A handful of white members were all that remained to the white pastor, including Page's onetime ordination sponsor, Gov. James E. Broome.[29]

The veteran missionary preacher occasionally continued to travel the region's highways and byways sharing the word of God, although age and nagging health issues complicated his mission. He had planned in early 1866, for example, to accept an enticing invitation to visit Key West, Florida's largest and southernmost town, located 435 miles southeast of Tallahassee. During a trip to Newport in March, though, he learned that an epidemic had broken out in that island community. "I have nearly given over the Idea of going to Key West[,] hearing so much about the yellow fever being theare," he informed Harriet Parkhill. "Several of my friends Both White and Black think that I ought not to go at this Season of the Yeare at all." The disappointment of the Key West venture aside, Father Page still preached at and assisted the establishment of churches other than his own: "I continued my traveling to help build God's kingdom. I helped to start quite a few more Churches after the War in Florida, Georgia, and South Carolina, too. I even helped those Colored Methodists start a few of their churches, too. When I felt ok, I would travel all over Florida preaching. I evened traveled [in 1867] to a Colored Baptist Church in Alabama to preach a word or two. Now, I can't remember what I preached about because that was a long time ago. But, I can tell you I know it was good." The venerable minister gave himself credit for his preaching prowess whether others did or not. Page's outreach even to "Colored Methodists" included his AME rivals. "The corner stone of the first African Methodist Episcopal church was laid in the city of Tallahassee, Florida, on Duval street, on Monday, Feb. 20th, 1866," a local newspaper proclaimed, "by the Rev. Robert Meacham, assisted by the Rev. James Page." The black leader had to admit to others, if not to himself, that the

AME church throughout the South "played an important role [during much of the Reconstruction era] in rural communities by promoting small farm ownerships, independence, and the dignity of labor."[30]

While Father Page filled his days with activity into 1867, national events reached a crisis point. President Johnson had maintained his support for white secessionist Southerners over the rights of newly freed blacks. Ever-larger numbers of congressmen grew determined to reduce his power and alter Reconstruction policies. Elections held late in 1866 ratified the new direction, and by January 1867 actions were proceeding aimed at neutralizing the president. As a result, the national legislature developed a new reconstruction plan. Passed over the president's veto, the Reconstruction Acts became law in the spring. Florida's political climate, as was true for most of the former Confederate states, altered dramatically. Congressional (or Military or Radical) Reconstruction, as it became known, divided the South into five military districts. General John Pope initially commanded Florida, along with Alabama and Georgia. He held responsibility for calling new constitutional conventions, and for the first time, black men were permitted to vote. James Page subsequently recruited blacks to vote the Republican ticket. Also a staunch Republican all his life, national leader Frederick Douglass believed accurately that freedom and black voting rights went hand in hand. Given the few party options available to them, both leaders believed that black political progress could be achieved only through the Republican Party.[31]

The First Reconstruction Act passed in March 1867 signaled to former bondpeople and poor whites in Florida and the South a glimmer of hope for improving their lives. The Freedmen's Bureau, for example, became somewhat more effective in delivering services. Significantly, it convened bureau courts in areas where blacks were not treated justly by the local legal system. Its primary purpose focused, however, on negotiating and supervising contracts between onetime enslaved blacks and masters. Even with the added power of the bureau courts, Capt. Carse in Leon County avoided whenever he could interference in the relationship between landowners and their employees. Instead, he used powers of persuasion to get both sides to live up to their contracts. His approach pleased many whites but found few admirers in the black community.[32]

Carse's approach fit within parameters that Page might have set. Although Page never indicated whether he personally attempted to serve as a middleman for white landowners and their black employees, it is implied in his vivid recollection of the refusal of some whites to deal with black people "in a Godly way." He had not yet abandoned his strong desire for white approval and support, however, so his actions remained informal, low key, and confidential. Pressures were building in any event. The advent of Radical Reconstruction, combined with demeaning racism and discrimination on the local level, not to mention occasional violence, was generating forces that soon would compel change. The question in spring and summer 1867 centered on how long Page could resist.[33]

Not without a degree of irony, at that very point Page became a landowner. He had demonstrated well back into the antebellum era a knack for earning and saving money. His school and some of his church work, plus the bounty of his garden, maintained him in the war's immediate aftermath. Now, he purchased sixteen acres for one hundred dollars. This meant more for him in a pecuniary sense than might first appear to be the case. Under what became known as "circular 3," which had been introduced previously by the Freedmen's Bureau, blacks who could prove they owned or rented at least ten acres would be provided with rations until the first crop could be harvested. The money could be applied to the purchasing of additional land. Thus, at a time when most of those to whom he ministered remained landless and subject to labor contracts the bureau refused to enforce, Page had begun to establish a foundation for his own economic independence. He wanted to lead by example. The race leader also understood that landownership by blacks would help them to become more self-reliant as well as help them stave off oppressive working conditions inflicted by unscrupulous white employers.[34]

The unfortunate timing and context of the land purchase illuminated the quandary that bedeviled Page in spring 1867. He increasingly felt isolated and in need of guidance. His positions appeared unhelpful or irrelevant to many of his potential flock, while his association with the Freedmen's Bureau failed to result in meaningful action demanded by local freedpeople. Beloved as a pastor and regularly called upon for marriages and funerals, his ministry otherwise floundered as the AME Church gathered strength in numbers and influence within the race. Coincidentally, with the departure of Lucy and Harriet Parkhill for Jacksonville, he felt alone and without anyone to serve as his sounding board. Page remained a man of many contradictions. He maintained a loving relationship with his wife, Elizabeth, but he did not perceive her as an appropriate source for advice on matters outside the household. Yet he sought the counsel from a white woman, his former enslaver, when dealing with post–Civil War issues. As an example, just before the Reconstruction Acts passed, he poured out his angst to Harriet: "I am getting along at this time tolerable well. But I have no one to go to to tell all of [my] affairs to as when you and Mistress and Miss Mary was here. That perturbs me often. There is no one that I would take the Liberty of telling all of my matters to as I would to you all[,] and I dont know of any person that would take the pains to Be troubled with me as you would." If Page did not depend on his former masters' monetary support, the free black leader relied, nevertheless, on their emotional support and intellectual advice.[35]

~

However, things were about to change for the better with Congressional Reconstruction, and Page was about to change with them. Beginning in April and May 1867, black Floridians found themselves increasingly thrilled about the prospects of participating in the political process as voters. Elections for constitutional convention delegates loomed in the fall, and steps already were being taken to identify qualified electors. Plans called for a voter registration process composed of three registrars in each county, one of whom had to be a black man. Florida's leading white Southern Loyalist, Ossian B. Hart of Jacksonville, headed the state's registration drive. From a family of longtime political influence in East Florida, Hart easily could have encountered Page as early as 1845 when he represented St. Lucie County in the last territorial house of representatives. However they came to know one another, Hart turned to the Baptist preacher to serve alongside Ozias Morgan and James S. Wilson as Leon registrars. Yet the very act of signing up freedmen to vote constituted a political act that endangered Page's standing among the county's more conservative white residents. When called upon to choose, Page reconsidered past ways and opted to adapt, a decision that may have come more easily in the Parkhills' absence. He discovered now that he recognized no irreconcilable conflict between religion and politics and that, furthermore, he needed to be a part of the political changes sweeping the country. In the months that followed, he eagerly pursued his duties, assisting in registering more than 3,000 voters. About 1,800 of the registrants were black. Suddenly, Page had found relevant purpose within the swirl of revolutionary times.[36]

That was not all. In late March prior to Page's appointment as a voter registrar, Hart had presided over organization of the Florida Republican Party in his Jacksonville law office. Subsequent to that event, he had issued a call for a state convention to be held in Tallahassee during July. Preliminary to

REV. CHAS. H. PIERCE,
Founder of the A. M. E. Church in Florida.

AME presiding elder Charles H. Pearce was Father James Page's powerful religious
rival as well as his political opponent. State Archives of Florida, Florida Memory

that gathering, a "Grand Mass Meeting of the Colored Citizens of Jacksonville" convened on May 25. "Proceeded by a drum corps," an account noted,
"the procession marched through the streets, presenting a very neat and
creditable appearance." Once at the place of gathering, master of ceremonies
Samuel Spearing asked Father Page to come forward. The venerable pastor
opened the occasion with a prayer, thereby effectively extending his personal blessing. His Baptist colleague Cataline B. Simmons then accepted
election as chairman by acclamation. Simmons declared the gathering to be
"a Radical Union Republican mass meeting" before introducing Hart for extended remarks. AME presiding elder Pearce soon spoke as well, in words

that Father Page could have voiced himself. Raising the promise of black representation in upcoming legislatures, Pearce exclaimed, "We are hunting for education, that will give us a name and position in the nation. I love that old flag, and under it I know we have a glorious future before us. We have a right to aspire to and claim position with education. We will send to the legislature men who are qualified. We need not ask who our friends are—we known [sic] them.—Lincoln's name will never die in the memory of the colored people, and the Republican party was the instrument in the hands of Providence in giving us our liberty."[37]

At the July state Republican convention, Page represented Leon County as a delegate. Most blacks who attended the gathering made clear their feelings about the Democratic Party and its members, including their former masters. "If the Southern whites had been our friends," they queried, "why did they not anticipate President Lincoln's Proclamation?" Where until recently he would have shied away from public political pronouncements, Page—notwithstanding his moderate tone—stood forthright at the dais as a Republican: "We [have] come here for the purpose of laying a plot from upon which to build up a free party, and I hope that all prejudices will be laid aside and the plain truth guide each man." One Democratic newspaper reported, "The colored portion of the convention was invited to talk, four or five of them talked[,] and they used big words, spoke grammatically and in a loud tone of voice; they were all statesmen and would have appeared to better advantage in Congress. Old man James Page [sixty years old at the time] of Leon County made a very good talk and wanted to know the right thing to do, he was not extreme in his views, he was probably the best man in the concern."[38]

Page's words at the state convention were not heeded. The new Republican Party quickly divided into factions. The more moderate segment consisted of men such as Hart and white Freedmen's Bureau personnel including Thomas W. Osborn, Marcellus L. Stearns, and William J. Purman. Osborn and his associates, of course, already controlled an organizational network of potential black voters, the Lincoln Brotherhood. From its headquarters at Father Page's Tallahassee church, the secret society set out to grasp party control through the influence of black Baptist ministers. As voter registrar, Page shied away publicly from the very movement that his sanctuary sheltered. The long-standing tie could not be denied, however. A more radical wing of the party, called the "Mule Team," meanwhile enjoyed the backing of national Radical Republican leaders. "Their political agenda bespoke a far

Reverend Robert Meacham of the Florida AME Church, Father James Page's Tallahassee friend. State Archives of Florida, Florida Memory

greater equalitarianism than that of the moderates," Canter Brown explained, "and they preached widespread social and political changes." While the Baptists under Page's leadership called for gradual progress, AME leaders found that they had far more in common with the Radicals.[39]

In this heated atmosphere Page strove to stay above the worst of the fray as individuals and factions jockeyed for position in the electorate and a presence at the constitutional convention. The bitter divisions formed in the process scarred the state generally and the Republican Party specifically. A frustrated Lake City resident spoke for many of his fellow whites: "This is a white man's government, and the sooner the negroes [*sic*] understands and appreciates his position the better for him. This country is settled by Anglo Saxons, and he who contends that the negro shall govern it, is either a knave or the most consummate of fools." Sentiments hurled between Republican factions hardly improved upon the tone or quality of these remarks. Unlike his AME counterparts Pearce and Meacham, Page did not strive for election as a convention delegate. Surviving evidence indicates that blowback from his summer activism and the effectiveness of his registrar's work had brought more problems than he had anticipated. A clue to his reasoning can be found in a letter that he sent Harriet Parkhill a year later: "The People Bother me Sometimes so much about these Political affairs that I think very often of moving to Jacksonville and teaching [in] a Little two-Bit School."[40]

⌒

The end of 1867 and the beginning of the new year found Florida's economy devastated. Bad weather, incessant rain, and labor shortages had resulted in small or ruined crops. Concerned about economic survival, many freedpeople turned with fevered hope to the constitutional convention, set to convene at the State Capitol in January 1868. Even with the persistent pressure former enslaved people and their allies put on the US government to grant blacks full citizenship, the constitutional amendment still would not pass until almost seven months later. In the meantime, many freedmen and women continued to push to revise the Florida state constitution to recognize their full-fledged citizenship rights. Once the convention opened, turmoil unfortunately prevailed as Radicals battled the more moderate party wing with which Page was identified. AME elder Pearce took over as the temporary chairman, and an ally soon won election as president. Yet the moderates eventually seized control. Page absented himself throughout. Living so close to the action, however, he witnessed at close hand the eventual triumph of Hart, Osborn, and their allies. Although on the losing side and signing the revised constitution in protest with other "Mule Team" members, Robert Meacham acknowledged the progress represented by the final document. "It is true," he admitted, "that our Constitution was made for the people, not for a few individuals; for the whole State, not for several counties; to be the charter of a Government, not for the white man, nor for the black man, but for the people."[41]

With the convention's end, the effort to gain approval for the new charter and to elect state officers and legislators ensued. "I was a Republican and I supported the Republican party plain and simple," Page recalled. He also embraced the new constitution despite persistent opposition from some Mule Team rivals: "I told you about that first political Convention [in 1865]. Well, they had a second one. Black people participated in that one and it was better than the first thing they passed. We had to try and get a document that both White and Black people would be willing to live with. I believe it was the best thing we could get at the time." Page decided not to run for any office that year, and his advocacy for party and constitution appeared lackluster. Whether he could have won in the climate then prevailing appears doubtful. This was not, however to be the case forever. Presiding elder Pearce, for one, would discover that fact to his chagrin in the not too distant future.[42]

May polling sadly failed to squelch the intraparty feuding. In the end, most blacks voted in favor of the moderates' version of the state constitution over objections from Pearce and other Radicals. Harrison Reed, a moderate Republican of spotty character from Wisconsin who had represented President Johnson in the state as head of post office operations, won the governor's election by a vote of almost two to one over his principal opponent. The newly elected governor turned out to be one of Florida's largest and most significant boosters—and no true friend of Father James Page or members of his race. In large part, he joined with former slaveholders and businessmen to form a party that would serve to boost Florida's overall economy by advocating low wages for blacks. With Reed's gubernatorial election, voters also overwhelmingly approved the state constitution. June and July saw Republicans, black and white, take control. Within days, though, the once-cordial alliance between Osborn and Reed fractured. Page witnessed the ultimate breakup of the alliance and rued its portent. Years later he reflected, "There is too much fighting in the Political Affairs of this state today just like back then." When the dust settled, Osborn went to the US Senate while his new nemesis ran the state government. Reed quickly found that he needed Page's support to counterbalance the weight of African Methodists who backed Osborn. The former enslaved preacher may have understood the dubious qualities of Reed's character. Still, as will be seen, he felt compelled to support him.[43]

CHAPTER TEN

Radical Reconstruction
and Its Aftermath

Soon after the smoke of the cannon had died down and people began
thinking of the future, the Negroes turned their thoughts toward
education.

—Former bondman Willis Williams

I vot de 'publican ticket, as I try to show my 'preciation, and dat gits me
in bad wid de Klu Klux.

—Former bondservant Bill McNeil

The congressional passage of the Reconstruction Acts in spring 1867 over
President Andrew Johnson's vetoes led in 1868 to political and social revolution in Florida. James Page witnessed it all. As Radical Reconstruction ensued in Florida, delegates elected in good part by black voters rewrote the
state constitution and installed a Republican administration to redefine the
role of state government and its attitudes toward freedmen, freedwomen,
and their families. As of summer 1868, seventeen black Republicans sat in a
house of representatives controlled by their party. The Republican state senate's three black members—Charles H. Pearce, Robert Meacham, and Jacksonville's William Bradwell—meanwhile highlighted by their presence the
emergent power of the African Methodist Episcopal Church in politics as
well as religion. Their demonstration of political might came at the expense
of rival Baptists. Unfortunately, the two men whose careers Page especially
had supported and whom he had considered his friends and political allies,
Governor Harrison Reed and US senator Thomas W. Osborn, quickly fell to
fighting one another. With Osborn away in Washington, however, Reed enjoyed closest proximity to the respected preacher and teacher who could influence thousands of black Baptist voters.[1]

Page's introduction to this brave new political world found him embroiled
in public scandal for the first time and hardly prepared to meet the challenge. He had served during the May 1868 polling as an election manager at
Tallahassee. Democrats quickly jumped upon minor irregularities that oc-

curred during and after the voting to allege widespread fraud. To counter the attack, Republicans solicited Page to sign two affidavits, dated June 3 and July 1, that denied any impropriety. His political opponents, led by the state's principal Democratic newspaper, picked the statements apart. Careful not to accuse Page directly, its editor mourned the manipulation that Page had suffered at the hands of wily carpetbaggers. "James Page has grown gray and venerable in this community—enjoying its confidence at all times," Tallahassee's *Weekly Floridian* proclaimed. "He still enjoys that confidence, and his many white friends feel regrets, long and deep, that in his old age it should be left to his pretended friends of Radicalism, to give him the deepest, the deadliest stab of his life."[2]

Having spent most of his life in service to whites and receiving their magnanimity in return, Page reeled from the attack. Throughout his life he had dealt persistently with an internal issue of wanting their approval. Always, he had fought to balance that yearning with an external effort to improve the lives of fellow bondpeople and freedmen. He ached for their affection and respect as well. These two concerns continued to clash without clear or final resolution. To calm those from whom he needed to garner financial support for building black religious and educational institutions and to reduce white fears that as a free black man he had changed significantly, Father Page distanced himself from certain potentially controversial activities. Particularly, he declined leadership roles in black civic and fraternal organizations. Instead, in the same manner as he had supported the Lincoln Brotherhood, he eased the path of black organizations to utilize the facilities at his Tallahassee Baptist church. He participated quietly as a member in activities of organizations such as Prince Hall Masonry and the Knights of Pythias. Page clearly understood the agency of these organizations in protecting and fighting for the rights of black citizens.[3]

Although Page's surviving reminiscences do not directly mention the subject, Bethel Baptist Church, like many other Southern black churches, enjoyed during the period the services of women. In fact, the dynamic role played by the women of Bethel in the 1960s civil rights movement reflected and reinforced patterns that dated at least to the Reconstruction era. As one of the church's historians noted, "The women of Bethel helped the men fight for their voting rights during Reconstruction even though they were denied the suffrage until the 1920s." Historians Evelyn Brooks Higginbotham and Glenda Gilmore detailed the active political role played by African American women in the various churches throughout the United States. Higginbotham notes that African American women of the black Baptist Church were "duty-bound to teach the value of religion, education, and hard work" by actively participating in the political process equally with men. By supporting the political rights of black men during Reconstruction, African American women, Gilmore asserts, began to fight for "woman suffrage," which ultimately lead to the passage of the Nineteenth Amendment granting them the right to vote. Historian Elsa B. Brown aptly showed the participation of African American women in various aspects of public life including the fight for citizenship rights immediately after the Civil War. Further, black women at Father Page's church were never invisible actors or participants. "Although the Bethel Baptist church became known for its masculine presence as personified by men like James Page, it was, nonetheless," history enthusiast Samuel Dixie Jr. noted, "a religious institution where a majority of its original members were women, and they made their presence known." Clearly understanding their presence and strength in the church, Father Page gave a nod of approval to the participation of women in educational and political meetings at Bethel without publicizing the fact. The cleric also appreciated that his goal of institution building was not just for the present age but for future generations. And for that to happen, women would have to play a viable role in laying a firm foundation for black economic, political, and educational progress.[4]

However, when it came to religious, moral, and educational causes, "I always stood out front," he once remarked, "for the religious, political, and educational rights of my people." To women, the assertion likely rang hollow. In any event, Page's own political involvements soon brought their rewards. On June 16, 1868, for instance, the newly installed state senate, upon the motion of Osborn associate and white Union veteran Alva A. Knight, elected Page senate chaplain for service through the session's end on August 6. Leon County senator Charles H. Pearce apparently consented to the action, evidencing an attitude of cooperation that was about to change.[5]

～

As the divide between Osborn and Reed widened in the months that followed, the governor, too, courted Page's continued favor. Reed soon placed him on the Leon County Board of Commissioners, a body that, thanks to the governor, held a Democratic majority. Thereafter, Reed's impeachment by disgruntled party factions and equally riled Democrats appeared increasingly likely. The governor then left the state temporarily, effectively leaving his rival, Lieutenant Governor William H. Gleason, as acting governor. Closely allied with Osborn, Gleason eagerly grasped the reins of power and began removing Reed appointments and replacing them with his and Osborn's men. Two Democrats on the Leon County Board of Commissioners were among those who lost positions. Gleason selected Senator Pearce and a second Republican leader to take their places. This handed control of the Leon board to Republicans. At that point, Pearce and Page crossed swords. A three-man board majority, which included Page, convened on October 21. Its members rejected the acting governor's interference and recognized the continuing authority of the removed commissioners. Gleason thereupon discharged Page in favor of a Pearce friend. The struggle continued for several weeks until Reed managed to regain control of affairs. "C. H. Pearce, Noah Graham and O[zias] Morgan, whom Lt. Gov. Gleason appointed county commissioners, for Leon County, in the absence of Gov. Reed, have resigned," Jacksonville's *Florida Union* advised on November 18, "and three of those removed have been reinstated, viz: Dr. Hawkins, James Page, and Mr. Avery." Not so coincidentally, the newspaper's omission of any handle of respect (Mr., Rev., or Father) for Page similar to his colleagues showed the prevailing attitude of some whites toward black leaders during the period, whether they were literate or not. Reverend Page should have gradually gotten the message that some whites regarded him as no different from other blacks.[6]

Whether Page even wanted to serve as a county commissioner remains open to question; if anything, his appointment created a stumbling block to his true ambitions. Page already maintained a hectic schedule and bore the weight of numerous responsibilities. To those, he added an enormous new challenge in 1868. His Tallahassee congregation, as mentioned earlier, had withdrawn from the white-led Tallahassee Baptist Church. Already several hundred members strong in 1865, it had grown sufficiently in three years to convince Page that it required a new sanctuary. Given the economic calamities that marked the times, the pastor required the financial support of affluent whites. The longtime religious leader applied well-honed fundraising skills to the task, astutely encouraging giving by stressing the inspirational value of a new sanctuary in elevating standards of religion, morality, and good behavior among people of color. The white-owned *Tallahassee Sentinel* supported him. "We cordially invite our white friends to come and aid us in a good cause," it proclaimed prior to a fundraising concert and festival held February 1, 1869. In April, the newspaper again advertised Page's needs and encouraged attendance at a series of upcoming events. Many Tallahassee whites already were comfortable supporting the black minister and had been since slavery days. Now, they felt able to continue investing in an institution that would instill a sense of "acceptable behavior." As the *Sentinel* assured, "They have been raised to the dignity of fellow citizens and we may rest assured that we shall have to build for them churches and schools or jails and prisons. Let us help to educate them, and thus encourage them to be good and peaceful citizens." Page's actual intentions, of course, varied from the *Sentinel*'s take on things. "They would act better if they could get good jobs," he recorded, "and own a little something of their own." Dating back to slavery days, Page was a leader who consistently espoused the concept of self-reliance among members of his race. Now, he wanted to promote black self-sufficiency with the aid of national, state, and local government as well as philanthropic whites.[7]

Thanks to Page's leadership, the fundraising efforts proceeded fruitfully. Spring 1869 found the pastor and his trustees—J. W. Toer, Elijah S. Sheppard, John N. Stokes, Agrippa Sutton, and Henry Cook—prepared to purchase land. The prime lot cost them the considerable sum of $250. The new sanctuary had progressed sufficiently by fall 1870 to house the congregation. Despite whatever frustrations he felt from failing to raise sufficient funds to complete the structure, he took pride in what he had accomplished. In the meantime, he savored the process of once again separating whites from their money to support his vision: "It . . . made me proud to get money from some very rich people in Florida, Georgia, and even Alabama to help start churches. They all knew I would do right with the money for my people." Even the *Sentinel* recognized his extraordinary ability to raise funds during "hard times." The record fails to reveal exactly when Bethel Baptist congregants finally witnessed the ultimate fulfillment of their dreams for the sanctuary. Clearly, the task occupied Page for years. "The colored Baptists of Tallahassee will give a festival this evening," the *Savannah Morning News* reported on January 23, 1873, "for the purpose of raising funds to complete their new church."[8]

While pursuing the dream of a new sanctuary in Tallahassee, Page took time as well to address key organizational and leadership issues among Florida's black Baptists generally. By 1869, "some five or six thousand" members attended Baptist churches headed by African American pastors. "Black Baptists were to be found in large numbers in those sections of the state where the slaveholders found cotton-raising most profitable," denominational historians George Patterson McKinney Sr. and George I. McKinney explained. "These were chiefly the counties beginning with Columbia and extending

Tallahassee Bethel Baptist Church during the 1870s. State Archives of Florida, Florida Memory

west as far as Jackson, and south as far as Marion. There were, however, an appreciable number in such cities and towns as Jacksonville, St. Augustine, Fernandina, Key West, Tampa, Apalachicola and Pensacola." The congregations, though, lacked an organizational structure to help guide and coordinate them while facilitating the projection of strength in the state's new political climate. What the AME Church could achieve easily given its episcopal framework, the Baptists struggled to accomplish.[9]

Given his preeminent standing within the denomination, Page took upon himself responsibility to find an answer to the problem. He extended a general invitation for pastors to gather on October 7. "In the Summer of 1869, Rev. J. Page . . . issued a statewide call of the churches to send their Pastors and messengers to a convention to meet at the Bethel Baptist Church in Tallahassee," Altermese Smith Bentley detailed. "The purpose of this meeting centered on forming the twenty-eight known black Baptists churches into an Association." Nineteen churches responded to the overture. "I told them to forget about what they did or did not do during slavery," he recorded. The McKinneys

Reverend Cataline B. Simmons, Baptist minister and friend of Father James Page. State Archives of Florida, Florida Memory

observed that, of the meeting's participants, Father Page "was best prepared intellectually." They added, "He was the only member who could write well enough to [record] the proceedings of the meeting." Accordingly, the members of the Florida Bethlehem Baptist Association, as the new organization was called, elected Page as their clerk. His Jacksonville friend Cataline B. Simmons presided as moderator. Page retained the clerk's assignment for years. He soon held the additional office of treasurer. Worthy of note, Page's outreach extended well beyond his fellow black clergymen. Northern Baptists and white Southern Baptists also received invitations. Given his personal commitment to public schooling, he additionally invited Jonathan C. Gibbs, Florida's first black superintendent of public instruction, to a seat at the conference table. Not surprisingly, the association's constitution—in line with Page's views—expressed as a principal purpose "to encourage among our brethren, by all Christian means, education, industry, self-reliance, general improvement, and especially spiritual elevation."[10]

The five-day organizational session of the Florida Bethlehem Baptist Association attained the goals that Page had envisioned, and he quickly capitalized on the achievement. On October 11, the pastor escorted a representative selection of attendees to the Capitol to announce to state government leaders that black Baptists had arrived at an advanced state of association and were prepared to act together thereafter to further their mutual interests and positions. "On Monday a delegation of fifteen ministers, with Rev. James Page and C. B. [Simmons], called upon His Excellency the Governor [Harrison Reed], and Secretary of State [Gibbs]," a report observed. "His Excellency being absent, the Secretary of State addressed them as follows: 'Permit me, gentlemen, in behalf of His Excellency the Governor, who is unavoidably absent, to say that this mark of your appreciation and abiding confidence is gratifying, and also may be regarded as a pledge of your loyalty to the government, and your undying attachment to those truths and principles by which he was raised to the Executive Chair of the State; and also to reassure you of His Excellency's intention to foster, by all legitimate means, the spiritual and material prosperity of the people of the entire State.'" Gibbs continued, "And for myself, permit me to say that I thank you for this token of regard and here pledge myself anew that you shall have my best efforts to sustain and make sure in Florida the principles and doctrines of the National Republican Party of the Union, and I ask your earnest cooperation, as Secretary of the State of Florida. In a short time you will be scattered over distant points in this State, and I wish you to assure the people that the government will use its utmost diligence to protect and defend all law-abiding citizens, and in all difficulties that may arise to look to the legally constituted authorities for redress, and in no case to permit themselves to be compromised by mob violence. Encourage schools, and teach the people to enter upon homesteads of their own as quickly as possible, and thus build up a thrifty, intelligent people in this State." In the area of education, Page and other black Baptists had a lot of work to do to catch up with their AME rivals, for by late 1870

Jonathan C. Gibbs, both secretary of state and superintendent of public instruction during Reconstruction. State Archives of Florida, Florida Memory

and early 1871, the latter had organized "forty-eight Sabbath schools across the peninsula responsible for educating over 2,500 children."[11]

Page then took a highly controversial step to further project newfound organizational influence. In 1870 he challenged Senator Pearce directly by running against him for his seat. Page claimed later that the move came by popular demand: "People wanted me to run for a seat in the senate. I didn't want to do it at first, but [I] decided to try it anyway." The encouragement likely derived from three sources. The first included Baptists in his Tallahassee congregation who esteemed him highly for moving ahead with construction of their sanctuary and others excited by the Florida Bethlehem Baptist Association's creation and the potential to extend Baptist influence as far as that of the AME Church The second and probably crucial source was Governor Reed, who once again found himself locked in political combat with Pearce and his allies. Finally, Leon County's white Democratic leadership—its members were calling themselves conservatives—also nudged their longtime friend into the race. Subsequent events suggest that they did so by making clear that they would not offer their own ticket. To the contrary, they would support Page.[12]

The opening salvos of what evolved into an epic political battle came during the summer. On July 11 Republican activists, including Page, convened at the Leon County Courthouse to select the party ticket. Stark divisions immediately surfaced between Pearce's more radical delegates (mostly African Methodists) and Page's traditionalist allies (mostly Baptists). Tumult ensued. Pearce's men ultimately prevailed, leaving the Page forces frustrated and unwilling to concede. They gathered late the same afternoon at the same location and named their own ticket. Page headed the slate as nominee for the state senate. His friends Henry Sutton, Andrew DeCourcey, Gadsden Twine, and John E. Proctor accepted nods for the legislative seat in the state house. The resulting clash between the two factions quickly escalated to the point that party chairman Noah Graham attempted on September 17 to reconcile the two sides at a mass meeting held on the Capitol grounds. However laudable the effort, it accomplished nothing as the rhetoric mounted and party divisions widened. Remarkably, Page and Pearce retained a dignified bearing and accorded each other respect. "[Reverend Page] spoke in a very sensible, calm, and dignified manner," a newspaperman expressed after one appearance. "He denied strenuously that he was a Democrat; he would not suffer such a base imputation upon his character, as he never had anything to do with a disreputable party. Mr. Pearce, at the conclusion of Mr. Page's address, came forward, and expressed the liveliest sense of respect and deference for Mr. Page's character and principles." Thanks in good part to coverage in the conservative organ the *Weekly Floridian*, Page and many whites believed his chances to win were high. "The friends of both tickets are equally confident," the paper reported on November 1. "If they divide the colored vote between them or nearly so, the conservatives will hold the 'balance of power,' and can elect whichever ticket they may vote for."[13]

Election day found voters crowding the polls only to discover that the county commission, on which Page continued to serve, either had failed to plan properly for the turnout or else had acted to impede voting. The Tallahassee precinct especially encountered problems, ones that bear chilling resemblance to modern electoral issues. "Those electors allowed to vote at each box had to take their place in line, white and colored promiscuously, and await their turn," a report detailed. "And how they were jammed and crammed! We never saw anything like it. It took from an hour and a half to two hours to get to the entrance up to the ballot-box, the voter during that time being crowded almost to suffocation. Such a trying ordeal incensed even many of the colored voters, who declared that they would never vote again if they had to work that hard for it. In the morning the whites were disposed to stand off, hoping that the crowd would soon diminish sufficiently to render voting easy, but alas! the number of voters seemed to increase instead of lessen, and towards evening they had to go in and take their chances with the balance or lose their vote. The voting continued without cessation from eight o'clock to sunset, when the polls were promptly closed, leaving between one hundred and fifty to two hundred voters on the ground who could not reach the boxes in time." Given that some whites and blacks who identified with the Radical wing of the Republican Party found it so difficult to vote, this may have been the first organized attempt at voter suppression in the state of Florida.[14]

If Page and his fellow commissioners meant to stifle the Radical vote, their initiative failed miserably. Page enjoyed support from white conservatives and some black Baptists, but he badly misread the attitudes of other voters of his race. Some of the disaffected perceived him as an instrument of Southern planters and other whites. Others believed that the minister's white friends were using him as a wedge to split and, therefore, dilute the Republican Party. More than a few simply believed that whites led Page by the nose and he could not be trusted. Many rejected his political philosophy outright. For these and other reasons, final tallies found voters spurning Page by greater than a two-to-one margin. Countywide, he received a mere 650 votes. Among those finally coming to grips with political realities in the vote's aftermath was Reed. The governor now realized that he needed the support of Senator Pearce and his friends far more than he required Page's assistance. Accordingly, he granted a boon to the AME presiding elder by refusing to renew the Baptist preacher's appointment to the county commission. Before Thanksgiving, Page found himself out of office. Page had misread Reed and should have more closely analyzed his motives. He was, above all, a Florida booster who identified more with the interests of former slaveholders and prominent businessmen than with former bondpeople. As evidenced by his quick shift of allegiance from Page to Pearce, the governor was willing to act arbitrarily and capriciously to maintain his position and direct his power to the benefit of his white backers.[15]

The political wounds of the 1870 Leon County senate race endured for years, with Baptists and African Methodists distrusting one another and often refusing to cooperate in the Republican Party's best interests. A telling example of these dynamics occurred in July 1871, one year following the disastrous nominating convention at the county courthouse. Page now enjoyed enough free time to escort his congregation members from the bucolic environs of Tallahassee to urbane Savannah for several days of entertainment and relaxation. First African Baptist Church members met the arrivals at the railroad station and led them through the streets to the church and a sumptuous luncheon. Sightseeing and further festivities followed. "Our monuments and tall steeples, few and insignificant as they are, afforded much comment and astonishment to the unsophisticated," a local newspaper related. "Our beautiful buildings and squares, the fine paved streets, and the street cars [thrilled them]. Innumerable objects of interest and curiosity met their astonished gaze. But, most of all, they admired and wondered at the Park, the fountain, and the nice seats, the beautiful smooth walks, green grass and shade trees." A party of Tallahassee whites rode the same train, although they sat apart from the black Baptists. "From the gentlemen [in the white group] we learn that there were two excursion parties," the reporter added, "one representing the extreme wing of the Republican party, the Methodists, went to Jacksonville, and the other, representing the conservative element of the party in Florida, the Baptists, came here."[16]

Page traveled to many places in and out of the state of Florida after slavery ended. During these interstate and intrastate trips, he had to be careful about how he conducted himself. As a well-known leader of his race in the peninsula state, he faced potential harm and even death. Other black leaders in Florida and elsewhere became targets of terrorism for encouraging members of their race to vote and to be as independent as they could through the ownership of businesses and land. This did not sit well with some white segments of the population. And from 1868 to 1871, they used any means necessary, including the services of the Ku Klux Klan, to control black workers and suppress their right to vote. Father Page knew about the racial conflict then ongoing in nearby Jackson County. According to historian Daniel R. Weinfeld, this "war" of intimidation, violence, and terrorism inflicted on blacks by whites became a common method of keeping blacks in their place. Secretary of State Jonathan C. Gibbs estimated that 153 black Floridians were assassinated in Jackson during this three-year period. Page recalled the terrible situation in Jackson County and all over the state: "I saw and read about a lot of violence done to Black people for a long time over this state and throughout the South after slavery ended. It wasn't right than [sic] and it is wrong to this day that people hurt other people because they want to vote and live a Godly life." With little protection from the federal government on the horizon, violence inflicted by whites on blacks would endure decades beyond Reconstruction.[17]

Although he admired Jacksonville native Ossian Hart, who sought the governor's seat in 1872, there were those who still tried to encourage Page to run for the state's highest office as well. According to a descendant of the Parkhill family, "The 'Carpetbaggers' rule the State. They thought it would aid to the humiliation if they put a Negro Governor in the State Capitol. They chose Uncle Jeems because he could read & write and speak well." But, despite the patronage the Parkhill family members extended to the black minister, they could not dismiss their basic prejudices, like so many whites during the nineteenth century, that a black man or woman, educated or not, should assume such a dynamic role as governor in reshaping the economic, political, and educational institutions of the state. Given the violent climate of the times, a basically noninterventionist federal government approach to protect the basic rights of blacks, and his previous unsuccessful foray into officeholding, the black religious leader ultimately declined to run for governor in favor of his friend Hart. A century and a half would pass before a

Ossian Bingley Hart, Florida's Loyalist governor during Reconstruction and friend of James Page. State Archives of Florida, Florida Memory

mainstream party would nominate a black candidate for Florida governor, with the 2018 campaign of Andrew Gillum.[18]

Page's unfortunate 1870 state senate campaign may have created persistent cracks within his party and muted Page's political ambitions, but the misadventure little diminished respect held by the black community for the man personally or in his capacity as a pastor. As noted, Senator Pearce even attested to his "character and principles" amid the party infighting. The distinction is worthy of careful note and highlights special and enduring qualities that Page brought to public and private notice. His contemporary Jack Sheppard spoke for many when he declared, "Father Page is a great and powerful preacher. He is a very intelligent man and he has earned the respect of both White and Black people." Unfortunately, the distillation of written history too often eliminates such subtle distinctions, creating lines of black and white where complex shades of gray had prevailed as lives in question were lived. Inhabitants of Page's world yearned for the warm and protective embrace of his care, compassion, and behavior. He might be conservative, but he was fair and honest. The question of whether they agreed with his political leadership was, insofar as most of them cared, beside the point.[19]

In that context, Page returned to public office in 1872 in a position that called for just the qualities so generally admired about him. Governor Reed once again was floundering politically, fending off renewed impeachment attempts and struggling in his quest for reelection. Needing friends badly, he turned to Page and the Baptists. The position that Reed offered Page was that of justice of the peace. In today's world, the job usually is considered one of lesser importance. Then, it represented the principal trial court for most offenses charged against black defendants despite the informality of its proceedings. Page accepted and thereafter served agreeably for four years until Democratic governor George F. Drew ironically and unceremoniously unseated him in January 1877. Page's allegiance to Governor Reed and to the Republican Party were probably genuine, but it could have also been motivated by personal gain. The black race leader identified with the Republican Party because of its instrumental role in the liberation of former enslaved human beings. His affiliation with the Grand Old Party, though, had brought lucrative jobs as a Leon County commissioner, voter registrar, chaplain, and justice of the peace, raising the question of whether Page's loyalty to the Republican Party stemmed more from the largess he received than to a strong belief in its overall philosophy. Motivations aside, Page's rulings as justice of the peace sometimes enjoyed less than unanimous popularity within the black community.[20]

One incident arose in late winter 1873 when Lewis Wilson, a local black resident, decided to racially integrate Tallahassee's roller-skating rink. Florida's new governor, Ossian B. Hart—the same man who had appointed Page a voter registrar six years earlier—had pressed for passage of a civil rights act as his administration's first legislative accomplishment. Approved in

January, the law provided that "no citizen of this State shall, by reason of race, color, or previous condition of servitude, be excepted or excluded from the full and equal enjoyment of any accommodation, advantage, facility, or privilege furnished by inn-keepers, by common carriers, whether on land or water by licensed owners, managers, or lessees of theatres or other places of public amusement; by trustees, commissioners, superintendents, teachers, and other officers of common schools and public institutions of learning, the same being supported or authorized in the same way: Provided, That private schools, cemeteries, and institutions of learning established exclusively for white or colored persons, and maintained respectively by voluntary contributions, shall remain according to the terms of the original establishment." Because of the new law and for reasons related to character and principle, Page particularly admired the new governor: "I liked Mr. Hart for the good things he tried to do for the state. Governor Hart was a good man to the White and Black people of the state."[21]

The civil rights law seemed to Wilson and others to apply directly to the roller rink as a "place of amusement," and so he set out to test the measure's strength. In early March he approached the establishment's entryway where he encountered the owner, a Mr. Charles. Lewis attempted to enter, whereupon Charles "refused admittance." In the days that followed Charles offered a variety of comments on his rights. The remarks interestingly echoed those sounded by some of Charles's counterparts in the same town nearly a century later, as the modern civil rights era, thanks to protests led in part by Page's Bethel Baptist successor Charles Kenzie Steele, finally brought lasting change. Charles went so far as to mention opening a separate rink for the "exclusive enjoyment of the Black people." His legal argument came down, though, to this: "The Skating Rink is nothing more or less than a private school, and the proprietor, just as the manager of any other private establishment, has a perfect right to decide what classes of persons shall be admitted." In the face of such rationalizations, Wilson complained to Judge Page. James Page having heard the matter to his satisfaction, summarily ruled in Charles's favor and dismissed the complaint. According to a report, "Rev. Mr. Page, justice of the peace, . . . held that it was a private institution, and that the proprietor had the right to admit who he pleased." Page's social accommodationist stance would serve as a precursor to the social segregationist approach popularized by the iconic black leader Booker T. Washington and some of his lieutenants, such as Charles Banks and James E. Shepard, a quarter century later. In matters social, Page stayed his course as an accommodationist all his life.

But, when it came to educational, political, or economic rights, he pressed for racial progress.[22]

⌢

Although demands on the sixty-four-year-old man's time grew with his appointment as justice of the peace, he had actively participated in a variety of efforts since his senatorial debacle and abrupt loss of his county commissioner's job. Teaching and the cause of education, for example, continued to engage him, although his focus returned to Bel Air from Tallahassee. The Bel Air Free School, erected by the Freedmen's Bureau a few years earlier, still operated with bureau support and Page's cooperation. The facility stood out for its successes. In April 1870 the school held a fair to showcase its work and attract support, and the occasion offered a good example of Page's philosophy in action: "[It] started around 8:30 when the crowd assembled to about 11:30. In fact the whole affair reflects much honor upon all parties concerned, and gives the most convincing proof and undoubted assurance of the rapid progress of this portion of the community in all the qualities that adorn and promote the best interest of society." Page, as was his practice, strove to demonstrate the self-reliance of blacks while assuring whites, as he once said, that "good things" were emanating from this school.[23]

By year's end Page's involvement at Bel Air had become even more time consuming. The Freedmen's Bureau, pursuant to congressional direction, had begun closing its operations in Florida and elsewhere. Accordingly, in October Director Oliver O. Howard transferred the Bel Air school to a local board of trustees that included Page, Marion Wilson, and Edward Shakespeare. The transaction referred to "the frame building erected for educational purposes by the Freedmen's Bureau on 1 acre owned by the Trustees in Bel Air." Terms reportedly specified, "The building and proceeds of rental or sale to be perpetually devoted to education purposes. Pupils [are never] to be excluded because of race or previous condition of servitude." Within months a local white minister was aiding Page in the search for a qualified teacher. "We have a school four miles from Tallahassee (Black) about 60 pupils and a New School House and comfortable," E. A. Edwards detailed. "Teacher can board with Rev. James Page, price of board $20.00 per month. There is a large Sabbath School where a teacher can make herself a very useful Salary [of] $50.00 per month." For two years, under Page's direction, the school prospered. Then, in September 1873, a killer hurricane swept up from the Gulf of Mexico to ravage the Tallahassee region. The town itself emerged "an appalling sight." Similar conditions prevailed in Page's vicinity. "In every direction, fences and trees are prostrate, as in the city, and many gin houses are badly injured," an observer recorded. "At Bel Air, the church and school-house are gone, and a building in the lot of Father James Page has fallen. An old colored woman, named Mary Dudley, was killed in the building."[24]

Despite recurring colds and respiratory problems likely associated with the elements, fatigue, and aging, Page devotedly pursued his church work as well. For one thing, he focused on kingdom building and growing the Florida Bethlehem Baptist Association. "I [went] to Gainesville to our Association which convened on the 6th of this month," he informed Harriet Parkhill on October 14, 1870. "I intended to go to Jacksonville on my return. I was not well when I left home and being very much exposed whilst in Gainesville, I had a fever and very bad cough which I am suffering with at this time." He added, "I will not be able to go to Tuscawilla if I live until the Third Sabbath in December." Page's generally poor health would remain a challenge for him until death.[25]

Yet the venerable cleric kept up his godly work by focusing on the evils of intoxicating spirits. Page remembered that Harriet's father had preached to him about the evils of alcohol and the necessity of temperance. At the Second Annual Session of the Florida Bethlehem Baptist Association, Page proved his devotion to Parkhill's principles by accepting the Temperance Committee chairmanship. "Our members abstain from the use of intoxicating liquors as a beverage of common drinking," the veteran pastor proclaimed, "believing the habitual use of intoxicating drinks is hurtful to soul and body, and contrary to the word of God, which declares that no drunkard shall inherit the Kingdom of God." Page understood, as well, that excessive drinking made for abusive husbands and fathers as well as truant workers.[26]

Increasing the number of Baptists in the state ranked as a principal goal for Page and the association. "The Baptists were losing out to the Methodists in this state politically," he remarked, "and we tried to do something about it." The *Christian Index* found in 1871 that "there were about 5,000 members each" in Florida's white and black Baptist and Methodist churches. By contrast, the year before thirty-two churches had reported to the Florida Bethlehem Baptist Association with a total membership of nearly six thousand. While those numbers reflected significant growth, they represented only the beginning of an impressive upward curve. "The colored Baptists of Florida number some seven or eight thousand, gathered in about fifty churches," Boston's *Christian Era* heralded in September 1873. "They reject *in toto* the 'new gospel' which some other colored churches preach so zealously, and discard shoutings, wonderful dreams, etc., from their services and forms of expression. The ministers, as a rule, keep to the pure Word of God, and work in their legitimate sphere." The item perceived the state's black Baptist clergy as a worthy bulwark against Roman Catholic advances: "The best channel for meeting Romanism in the South among the freedmen is through the Baptist churches. The plain, colored Baptist preacher . . . with his testament in his hand, would be more than a match for the gorgeously-robed priests of a religion which has very little of the gospel in its creeds."[27]

It quickly became apparent to Page and other associational leaders that a training facility for clergy was essential to the building of the denomination. Page's longtime colleague John N. Stokes first promoted the idea in 1871, at which time the association named a board of trustees to manage the project. The following January a special association meeting concluded in the naming of a three-man "Board of Education for the Baptist Association of the State of Florida." Page headed the list of its members, which also included J. W. Toer and Daniel Hall. Three months later the new board purchased the Tallahassee "Mansion House" of planter George W. Walker, a former lieutenant governor who had died five years earlier, located in the hills immediately south of town. Page likely made the connection that led to the transaction because the Walker family for decades had maintained a second residence at Bel Air. For whatever reason, within another year the board had reconsidered its action and decided to locate the school at Live Oak, then an important railroad connection, in "an unfinished two story building, 60 by 40 feet, originally intended for a court house." Final arrangements were agreed to at Jacksonville in October 1874, with Page moving the selection of Rev. William F. Wood as first principal. One newspaper correctly reflected the thoughts of many Floridians: "Rev. James Page, of Bel Air, is said to have started the first colored church in Florida." So, there were early discussions of naming the institute after Father James Page. But for unknown reasons, this did not materialize. The institution initially carried the name Theological Institute for Ministers and Teachers, but the board soon altered it to the Bethlehem Baptist Theological and Literary Seminary. Fundraising posed serious obstacles, but the accomplishment, once in place and ongoing, meant much to Father Page. "We were mighty proud of helping to get that

College in Live Oak started, but we needed a lot of money to make it a reality," he declared. "It was a College to teach men how to [be]come educated Baptist ministers."[28]

As preparations for locating and opening the seminary took their course, Page reveled in other successes while coping with several especially painful losses. On the positive side, his exertions on behalf of Bethel Baptist Church had paid substantial dividends. By mid-1873, according to the *Christian Era*, its congregation had swelled to "over fourteen hundred members." Little wonder, then, that three years earlier Page had presided there over no less than 177 baptisms. It had become clear to Bethel's pastor, as well, that Florida's black Baptists required a statewide organization to embrace all denominational adherents. Accordingly, at the 1873 Bethlehem Baptist Association meeting, he proposed a general convention to be held at Bethel Baptist in March 1874. At that time, the venerable pastor guided representatives of fifty-six congregations in the creation of the Florida Bethlehem Baptist State Convention. At Live Oak in February 1875, delegates changed the title to Convention of the Missionary Baptist Churches of the State of Florida.[29]

~

All tidings were not so happy for Page. For one thing, Governor Hart passed away on March 18, 1874, at Jacksonville. Compounding that loss, the death left Lieutenant Governor Marcellus Stearns, a man of questionable integrity and intentions, running the state. A greater blow lay in store for Page, however. On August 14, 1874, Superintendent of Public Instruction Jonathan C. Gibbs died suddenly of apoplexy at the age of forty-seven. Gibbs had become Page's friend, and Page, in turn, had become convinced that the cause of education for the race, as deeply personal as the issue remained for the pastor and teacher, was safe in the superintendent's accomplished hands. "I . . . liked Mr. Gibbs," Page reflected. "He did right by both White and black folks, too. The Honorable Mr. Gibbs wanted education for both Whites and Blacks in the state. He and [Florida's black congressman Josiah] Walls will always be remembered fondly by me and members of the church." The memory of those two men who sought to uplift former bondpeople politically, economically, and educationally remained with Page for the rest of his life.[30]

The loss side of Page's ledger for the period also included the impacts of a deep economic depression that lasted for years. This calamitous phenomenon—the Panic of 1873—commenced on September 18 of that year with the failure of New York City's Jay Cooke & Co. The reverberations built to a financial tidal wave as banks, insurance companies, and industrial and manufacturing companies collapsed with mounting consequences. Page's vaunted fundraising abilities could not stem the tide. In turn, the reduced flow of contributions frustrated many of his educational and religious ambitions. Most personally, however, he felt the sting with the fall of the Freedmen's Savings Bank. Organized by the Freedmen's Bureau to aid onetime enslaved people and the institutions they created subsequent to emancipation, the bank's deposits represented life savings for many, even though most accounts ran to fifty dollars or less. Page remembered the bank as a "good idea for helping people to save, but not so good when I and other people lost money in it." He declined to state how much money he lost with the institution's failure. When pressed, he replied simply, "Not too much." But, given that the deposits in the Tallahassee Branch of the Freedmen's Bank totaled $40,207.00 before it closed, the possibility cannot be discounted that his losses were considerable. Those potential losses paled, however, in comparison to Frederick Douglass's. Douglass, who had served as the bank's president for a short time, stood to lose more than $10,000. Unfortunately, Page and Douglass were not alone: nearly seventy thousand other depositors throughout the South also stood to lose their life savings, which came collectively to a whopping $57 million before it finally closed in 1874. On a bright note, biographer David Blight noted that "Douglass's $10,000 was eventually repaid, but most depositors never saw much more than sixty cents on their dollar." It is unclear whether Page recovered any money he had deposited in the Freedmen's Bank.[31]

The financial blow that Page incurred thanks to the Panic of 1873 and the Freedmen's Bank closure may have explained his hectic travel schedule in 1874. Despite the needs of his congregation members and the call of his duties as justice of the peace, he found time to preach and participate in religious services in Georgia and South Carolina because he needed the money to sustain his family. As he acknowledged, "I sometimes received a little piece of money for my preaching." The traveling took its toll. At age sixty-seven in 1875, Page's health began to fail on a regular basis. This fact understandably curtailed his teaching and ministry. His ability to support himself independently, a circumstance of such vital importance to him for so long, suffered accordingly. "I am not nearly as able to help myself as I have been," he informed Harriet Parkhill in April. "If I could not Preach or Spell, I don't know what I would do for a living." He added, "I am happy to say to you that I have not had a very bad cold this winter."[32]

In such a dispirited state of mind, Page witnessed the collapse of Republican Reconstruction dreams in 1876 and early 1877. Marcellus Stearns's tenure in the executive office had proved as problematic as Page had feared. In discussing "the hard labor of his plundering career," John Wallace ascribed these faults to the governor: "the packing of juries, the prostitution of the public schools, the disfranchising of whole counties, mob conventions, planned irregularities in elections, the public money expended to get possession of railroads, and the wholesale stuffing of ballot boxes." Given that Stearns was also a Florida booster to the detriment of black residents, divisions racked the Republican Party again as they had under Governor Reed. This time, however, the GOP could not count on all or even most of the Baptists. Various congregations spawned Conservative Clubs to back the Democrats, and several ministers openly changed parties. For his part, Father Page mostly stayed aloof from the fray. He did not attend the Republican State Convention held at Madison, so his fellow pastor John N. Stokes represented Leon's Baptists. Violence flared, schemes were hatched, and deals were consummated, all without his participation or apparent interest. He insisted afterward, though, that he always stayed true to his party.[33]

The Republican loss of Florida's governorship and Democratic legislative majorities as of January 1877 struck deeply at the remarkable advances that had been made in the state by former bondpersons in only one decade, many of which—such as the public education system—Page had backed heartily. Now, black influence at the State Capitol no longer commanded serious attention. Black leadership, as historian Canter Brown has argued, increasingly found itself thereafter confined within growing towns where its representatives made signal contributions to the development of urban Florida. In winter and spring 1877, though, future directions appeared far from certain. The quandary prompted the call of a "colored convention" at Tallahassee in July. Page attended as a delegate, although he does not appear to have participated in a leadership role. He did speak briefly to the assembly, urging that "Black people needed to be treated fairly and have the right to vote if they wanted to." He would have approved heartily of the gathering's call for "education, securing land, and homesteads."[34]

His active political involvements now essentially a thing of the past, Page immersed himself in religious and educational work from 1877 to 1879. Governor George F. Drew quickly relieved him of his duties as justice of the peace, and no other public office came his way. As Democrats approved cuts in educational funding, particularly for black schools, he grumbled that "the

Black schools did not get the same money as the White schools." Still, he persisted. The Bel Air school had been rebuilt from the ravages of the 1873 hurricane, and along with the Tuscawilla school it remained open under Page's aegis despite the deepening funding crisis. The term, though, now ran only for six months each year. Meanwhile, the Bethel Baptist school at Tallahassee flourished in a relative sense. With his longtime connections within the conservative community, Page managed to hold its public funding to within five dollars of the amount allocated by the county for each white pupil. "The White schools always received $25.00 per student for each year as long as I could remember," he noted.[35]

The tough economic and political climate also hampered development of and operations at the Live Oak school. The adverse conditions further militated against incorporating critically needed teacher training into the curriculum. The *Christian Index and Southwestern Baptist* highlighted the dilemma during 1878, underscoring the importance of training black teachers who would "lift their people to a higher plan of religious thought and feelings." At the time, much educational and religious work in the freed community had been done by the Northern Home Mission Society and the American Baptist Home Mission Society. The article added that the "Black Baptists of the State . . . have not been idle, but with commendable zeal have been stirring for years to build up themselves a school. They have purchased, and we believed paid for, a property at Live Oak, in this state, which cost about two thousand dollars." The next year, at Father Page's urging, Floridians directly petitioned the American Baptist Home Mission Society for assistance. The body found that black Baptists "greatly need such a school, on account of the imperfect school system of the State, and their remoteness from other schools of this character in the South." Enough funding in hand from the Home Mission Society, the Bethlehem Missionary Baptist Association in 1880 opened the rechristened Florida Institute under the presidency of J. L. A. Fish.[36]

The affairs of the Florida Baptist State Convention, as it was called by decade's end, meanwhile continued to draw Page's interest and contributions. In October 1879 at Live Oak, for instance, he presided at the age of seventy-one over one of its key sessions, after which members demonstrated their continuing respect by electing him to the executive board and as the organization's clerk and secretary. The preachers further enlisted his service on the finance subcommittee of the convention's constitutional revision committee. The aging churchman also accepted responsibility for reporting on those ministers and deacons who had passed away since the prior association meeting. When he completed his memorial report, according to the minutes, "Elder James Page [having] concluded the service, sung 194 Hymn, 'Behold the Sure Foundation Stone, which God in Zion says.'" Page remained in advanced age the indispensable man.[37]

Lamb of God though he may have been during sessions of the Florida Baptist State Convention, teacher Page presented a starkly different visage to his pupils. What with the discriminatory racial overtones that hovered over Florida's leadership circles and step-by-step debasement of school funding and educational exposure, the gentle schoolmaster of the immediate post–Civil War era had, in his senior years, evolved into the stern taskmaster. His approach fit neatly, though, within guidelines established by Leon County's school board. Its minutes, recorded in 1879, detailed that "corporal punishment shall be inflicted when other means fail to correct offenders." Given that Page did not tolerate misbehavior in his classroom, he wholeheartedly endorsed the policy. "I had no problems teaching the children," he explained. "I believed that if you spare the rod you will spoil the child, and we had no spoiled children in our schools." Rev. James Page continued his life's work of leading his race as the decade of the 1870s ended and the decade of the 1880s began.[38]

Epilogue

May the Works I've done speak for me.
. . . .
May the Life I live speak for me.

—The Consolers

The journey's end came for Father James Page in the early 1880s. Three years before his death, time had taken its toll on the old man. In 1880, he reached his seventy-second birthday. Still, he continued unabated his religious, community, and civic activities. Little seemed amiss with his body and mind. He traveled the lonely roads of Florida, Georgia, Mississippi, Alabama, and South Carolina almost as if he were a young man. As one of the most recognizable African Americans in the Deep South during the nineteenth century, he expanded ministries in his own church while assisting with the establishment of other churches throughout the South up to the time of his death. Even through aches, pains, and chronic bouts of poor health, he lived for his ministry. "Over the years," the cleric admitted, though, "I got a little tired of the long trips to Alabama, Georgia, and South Carolina."[1]

In old age, Page took a nationalist view of the country. He understood that the nation as a whole was changing and that the Reconstruction era that helped to guarantee the basic rights of the newly freed men and women was declining by the late 1870s and early 1880s. Still a Republican, he had lived long enough to see the approval and later erosion of the Thirteenth, Fourteenth, and Fifteenth Amendments. He had witnessed, as well, his party subsequently betray black citizens in favor of economic boosterism throughout the South.[2]

Even more disconcerting, Page viewed the ongoing increase of lynchings, racism, and violent terrorism up close. He understood the place in society to which whites now sought to relegate blacks to during the nadir period. Not surprisingly, Page faced insecurity and fear. With few material resources to aid his cause, he sought to lead by convincing his race that working cooperatively with whites offered the most pragmatic path forward in violent and uncertain times. He confronted, as well, the attempt to reinstate slavery in all but name that came in the guise of the emerging convict-lease system. Blacks who refused to work willingly for whites were jailed, often on trumped-up charges, and then leased to exploiters as cheap labor. More specifically, scholar Douglas A. Blackmon correctly noted that convict leasing became "a system in which armies of free [black] men, guilty of no crimes and entitled by law to freedom, were compelled to work without compensation."[3] In many respects, the convict-lease system stood out as worse than slavery. Where enslaved persons had been valued as property, leased convicts—whether working on railroads, mines, farms, or at other jobs—simply were objects to be worked virtually to death. Historian Matthew Mancini characterized the conditions as "debilitating, and occasionally fatal." If a black convict died or was killed, landowners and capitalists would simply lease another one until he or she died. Page knew about the cruel and abusive convict-leasing system as well as the turbulent and extremist times when he stated, "I saw and read about a lot of violence done to Black people for a long time over this state [Florida] and throughout the South." The cleric still held out hope "that White and Black folks would live and work together in peace." As Page eventually learned, most white capitalists remained determined to maintain blacks as a cheap source of labor.[4]

Despite the uncertainty of the times, Page ventured out on dangerous and lonely roads in Florida and other places in the Deep South teaching, preaching, and leading his race. He managed to maintain a pace and bear a load of responsibilities that would have humbled many other men. In January 1880, for instance, he hosted the Florida Baptist State Convention at Bethel Baptist Church in Tallahassee, Florida. Convention minutes recognized 8,776 members of black Baptist churches. At the same time, 8,410 white members of the denomination in Florida were noted. A main agenda concerned the opening of the long-anticipated Florida Institute thanks to outside funding, mentioned earlier, that Page had helped to secure. "We expect to have the College open," the minutes proclaimed, "by next fall in Live Oak." Page, of course, sat on the institution's board of trustees. February saw him continue his travels on church business. In the early part of the month, he attended the Bethlehem Baptist Association State Convention held in Madison, Florida. There, he served as one of three delegates, corresponding secretary, chairman of the ministerial education committee, and member of several other panels. During the latter part of the month, he ventured to Thomasville, Georgia, to work with the church there and soon extended his trip to Eufaula, Alabama. He took immense pride that, at his age, he still could exert himself in such a manner: "I was about 72 years old when I went to Madison [Florida], Thomasville [Georgia], and Eufaula [Alabama] for church business."[5]

With age, Father Page continued to be fascinated with his African roots, reflecting a growing sense of his own mortality. He had become interested in Liberia early after learning that his father, through support from the American Colonization Society in Virginia, had sailed some sixty years earlier to drown under murky circumstances attempting to disembark in his new home country. Rev. Edwin T. Williams had noted as early as 1860 that Page "had many questions to ask about Liberia to which I answered . . . before he left Savannah for Liberia." No extant documents indicate Page ever visited Liberia, but illustrative of his deep interest, he organized a special appearance at Bethel Baptist Church during August 1880 by a highly educated African speaker. "We understand that 'Professor [Jacob C.] Hazeley' who is said to be a full-blooded native African, educated in the colonial schools of Liberia," an announcement declared, "will lecture on civilized Africa at the Missionary Baptist Black Church this evening." The speech focused on Westernizing Liberia and Africa through Christianity. Hazeley's appearance came as the back-to-Africa movement crested in many areas of the South. Page, though, seemingly extended the invitation for more personal reasons. Hazeley was thus linked in the minister's mind to dreams of Liberia that allowed Reverend Page to revive memories of his long-gone father.[6]

During the months that followed, thoughts of Africa continued to command the minister grown weary in the service of his mission. During summer 1880 he traveled again to Alabama. This time, Page took part in a new organization called the Foreign Mission Baptist Convention. The event, held at the First Baptist Church in Montgomery, focused on "giving Africa the Gospel of Christ." Of the 151 delegates present, Father Page alone represented Florida. The convention had as its mission "to send missionaries to West Africa." Members recognized Father Page's special status in the black community of the Southeast by selecting him as a vice president of the new organization. Page convinced Bethel Baptist Church to contribute to the cause, though the gift was a small one, given the hardships of the times. He remained a part of the state executive committee of the organization until his health completely failed him.[7]

The next year started with Page burying longtime friend and church member Thomas Mason, an act that epitomized the pastor's steadfast nature. That the two men had remained close may have surprised people who did not know them well. During Page's controversial 1870 state senate campaign, Mason had openly rejected both Republican candidates and joined the Democratic Party. He then had supported the white nominee for the senate. Given that Page and Mason were close friends, some onlookers had linked the two politically and argued that Reverend Page sympathized with the goals and objectives of the Democrats. The black minister vehemently challenged the whispering campaign, but, in some eyes, he stood guilty by association. Even such a political betrayal, though, failed to damage the personal and longstanding rapport that the two men had enjoyed. "[Thomas Mason] was buried on Friday from the Missionary Baptist Church," a Tallahassee newspaper reported, "the funeral services being conducted by Rev. James Page, pastor, who paid a fervent tribute to the sterling qualities of the deceased." Father Page had many professional relationships with individuals but few truly personal friends. But the cleric remained both a close friend to the deceased and his staunch supporter to the end.[8]

By the early months of 1882, the toll of time and mortality began to hang heavily for Father Page. Sensing decline, he began taking actions to get his house in order. For instance, the preacher of more than five decades and his wife, Elizabeth, conveyed to "William Richards, Edward Gross, Isaac Verdier, Caesar Reese, and Isaac Reese, Trustees of the Missionary Baptist Church in the town of Bel Air, one and half acres" of ground upon which stood his Bel Air church. The Pages had paid eight dollars for the property. The transaction represented a passing to safe hands of an important portion of the pastor's legacy.[9]

Age and infirmities notwithstanding, an often-ailing Father Page at age seventy-four kept up his ministry. "Last Sunday morning Rev. James Page, pastor of the Missionary Baptist Church, baptized, in St. Augustine branch, thirty-two persons who had recently joined his church," Tallahassee's *Weekly Floridian* reported on April 30, 1882. "When the baptismal ceremony was concluded, the congregation formed a procession and proceeded to the church, singing one of the familiar hymns as they filed down McCarty Street [now Park Avenue]. Mr. Page is one of the oldest colored ministers in this city, and it must be very gratifying to him in his declining years to see his labors so abundantly blessed in the conversion of sinners." The minister by then had baptized thousands of individuals. On the subject, Page once commented, "I always like baptizing people for the Lord. I don't know how many people I baptized but plenty of them though. Now, they all had to live good lives for him [God]."[10]

⁓

Father James Page's life journey ended March 14, 1883, the year that African American abolitionist and women's rights activist Sojourner Truth died, the year that the US Supreme Court declared the 1875 Civil Rights Act unconstitutional, and the year during which race riots erupted in his home state of Virginia. Father Page's indefatigable role as a preacher of the Gospel and minister of God extended until five days before his death. As noted by the *Christian Index*, he continued his life's work of preaching "at one of his outstations in the morning and again at home [at Bel Air] at night. But on that following Friday, the elderly minister took sick with a chill, and died at home on March 16 at the age of 75, or nearly so." Besides scant information contained in one newspaper account, no full description has survived as to the cause of Page's death. Elizabeth Page obviously stood at his side, heartbroken at the loss of her husband of fifty years. The extent of her grief, given that her voice was not documented, cannot be known. The couple likely had known that the elder's days were numbered. It seems logical that they would have spoken about relying on Lymus F. Johnson, their longtime boarder, to serve as the administrator of the estate upon his death, as Elizabeth could not read or write.[11]

By 1883, Father James Page had become one of the most highly visible persons in the black South. Individuals of both races, though, paid tribute to one of the South's greatest and most traveled ministers of the Gospel and leaders of his people. The white press complimented him. The Tallahassee *Weekly Floridian*, by then the strongest Democratic editorial voice in the state, summed up his life and spoke to its meaning to the community: "Rev. Jas. Page, the aged and venerable pastor of the colored Missionary Baptist Church, last Friday evening quietly and peacefully passed from the scene of his earthly labors to that rest prepared for those who doeth the Master's will. For more than half a century he had been a faithful laborer in the Master's vineyard, was a man who had great influence with his race, which was always exerted for their well-being, and was respected alike by white and colored people."[12]

According to the newspaper, "The funeral took place from his church on Sunday morning." Within minutes of opening Bethel's doors, the church filled to capacity with standing room only. An overflow of people wishing to view the iconic leader and minister one more time stood outside. Besides Elizabeth and son Thomas, we do not know how many members of the extended Page family attended the funeral. The *Christian Index* reported that, in all, "nearly three thousand thus beheld for the last time the face of their father in Israel, and with strong crying and tears bade him good-by." Prominent men and friends of Christendom attended the service. Rev. John A. Potter of Monticello offered prayers. Jacksonville's Cataline B. Simmons, John Jamison, and Roger D. Dunbar followed. J. L. A. Fish, principal of Live Oak's Florida Institute spoke. Tallahassee's John N. Stokes detailed for those assembled the remarkable events and achievements of Father Page's life and noted that the deceased pastor had had occasion to work with governors, congressmen, state legislators, and businessmen. Father Page was, indeed, one of the few blacks to rise from a bondservant to a man who touched the lives of both prominent and common people. "After these most impressive services, the community, Societies, Sabbath school, church and relatives took their final leave of the remains," the *Index* observed. Men from various fraternities and organizations such as the Odd Fellows, Good Templars, and Good Samaritans were present to pay their final respects and to serve as honorary pallbearers. Afterward, Father Page's casket was taken to the segregated section of Tallahassee's Old City Cemetery where he was laid to rest on Sunday, "the Lord's Day," only a few miles from his beloved Bethel Missionary Baptist Church.[13]

Recognition of the worth of Rev. James Page's life and ministry was not confined to Tallahassee. Memorials services quickly ensued in Baptist congregations in various parts of Florida—and, likely, Georgia, North and South Carolina, Alabama, and Mississippi. A typical occasion was held on June 17, 1883, at Mt. Moriah Baptist Church in Ocala, Florida. Five hundred people assembled that day to pay tribute. Samuel Small opened the services before Pompey Summers preached "from the text 'Lord now lettest [sic] thy servant depart in peace, for mine eyes have seen the salvation.'" Teacher and senator Henry W. Chandler, a graduate of Bates College and the Howard University law department, believed "the sermon was able, and deeply affecting, and made an impression not soon to be forgotten." He noted that Reverend

Small then "made some very eloquent and touching remarks on the life, character and death of Elder Page whom he fitly called the Father of the Baptist Church of Florida." In reflecting upon the occasion and the man, Chandler closed his observations with these words: "Thus young and old united to honor the memory of the great and good man who had spent half a century in the active ministry of God."[14]

Father James Page had, unfortunately, not prepared a will before his death, so all of his worldly possessions reverted to his wife Elizabeth after debts had been satisfied. Although never a truly affluent person, Page managed nonetheless to accumulate more worldly possessions than was true of the majority of his race at that time. The estate was valued at between $250 to $500 dollars. Based upon the inventory, Elizabeth inherited the land, the house, more than four hundred books and magazines, and other miscellaneous items. After settling her husband's debts, she retained the house, his books, and other items, as well as $35 in cash. No record documents son Tom's inheritance. In fact, Page's reminiscences imply little about Tom during his waning years. Tom appeared on the census records during the 1870s and 1880s but disappeared thereafter. The question of what Father Page's son did during the Reconstruction era remains shrouded in mystery. Similarly, little is known about Page's other blood relations, if any. He knew who he was, and he knew who his parents were. Unfortunately, after his traumatic and fearful involuntary uprooting from the Upper South and removal to the Lower South in 1827, Page did not appear to have ever reunited with any of his kin. No evidence suggests that Page ever tried to find out the mysterious circumstances surrounding his father's drowning off the coast of Liberia. However, as his contemporary Jack Sheppard remembered three years before the cleric's death, "Father Page never forgot his mother [and] brother." Nothing comes to us that would suggest he sought to find or attempted to reunite with them during slavery or after its demise. Meanwhile, as the black Page family seemed to have evaporated during the mid-1880s, the white Parkhills prospered. Some relocated to Tampa, Florida, and enjoyed wealth thanks in good part to profits from the world-spanning Lykes hot dog corporation.[15]

Unfortunately, within two years of Father Page's death, the closest human being to him, Elizabeth Page, passed away. Next to nothing is known about her homegoing. No extant newspapers recorded her passing. We do know that she was laid to rest beside her husband. What happened thereafter to her husband's books, their land, or other possessions also remains a mystery.

Public records fail to mention the subject. His personal papers, at least those that still exist, remain in the hands of individuals and are not housed in a central repository. "The most effective way to destroy people is to deny and obliterate their own understanding of history." In such a manner, the weight and meaning of Father James Page's life and works have virtually been erased from history.[16]

~

Fortunately, recently discovered sources that project Reverend Page's own voice tell us a good deal about his life, attitudes, and worldview. He grew to be an old man whose core values and philosophies were formed by his faith, parents, master, enslaved and free black communities, and the times in which he had lived. He identified always with his original home of Virginia. "Although I am old," he announced on one occasion, "I still possess the Virginia Spirit." He then performed the "ole Virginia shuffle" for his audience. He gradually came to identify with his new state of Florida. At times, Page stood at odds with himself and with a rapidly changing world. Overall, though, his ideology shifted little. He never transitioned from pacifism to a more militant leadership style in his words or deeds. Unlike some of his Christian colleagues such as AME bishop Henry McNeal Turner and AMEZ bishop M. D. Clinton, he persisted as a traditionist in his worldview. In slavery as well as in freedom, he remained basically conservative, a tradition that one of his successors, Booker T. Washington, followed in terms of whites and blacks maintaining their distance in all things social but working cooperatively in all things educational and economic. In a sense and almost a century later, Martin Luther King Jr. pursued Father Page's nonviolent philosophy to advance the cause of full justice, freedom, and equality for African Americans.[17]

A conservative or traditionalist perhaps, Rev. James Page also was a multidimensional and complicated man. He wore at least two hats. As an enslaved preacher, he presented one guise to the enslaver and other authority figures. The other he offered to his enslaved brothers and sisters. The cleric's personality displayed a number of contradictions. On the one hand, he believed in the basic constitutional rights of all Americans; on the other hand, he did not encourage women's equality at the ballot box or in the house of the Lord. Page spoke little about women's rights, but his actions bellowed when he chose to teach literacy skills to men but not to women, including his wife. In certain respects, he treated Elizabeth as a subordinate instead of his equal. In doing so, however, he reflected the attitudes of most men concerning the role and position of women in society during the nineteenth century. Page obviously loved and cared for Elizabeth, but he also believed that the rightful place for women was the home. "She is a good woman and she is a good helpmate to me," he observed. "She would never complain[,] and she helps me in everything I wanted do. She stays at home and sews for the Parkhills and us and other servants too. Elizabeth understands all the things I had to do as a preacher." So, like most men of the era, Page expected women to remain quiet in most pursuits of life.[18]

During his climb up the ladder from the fiery depths of slavery to a heaven of freedom, individuals had both revered and hated Father Page. Most loved and respected him, but some distrusted the cleric because of his close affiliation with whites. Jack Sheppard spoke to the point: "Most Black and White people liked Father Page while a few thought he was quiet about things like violence against Black people and their problem with trying to vote in the South." Some even hated and distrusted him because of his religion or because of his onetime power as an overseer. Others disliked him because of his success at securing government jobs and acquiring land for himself when few members of his race could. Some blacks may have thought of Page as a selfish man who looked out only for his own welfare. He was, however, without question a quite magnanimous man. In fact, he shared vegetables from his garden as well as money he had earned as tips when he possessed little to share. Meanwhile, he could not resist the limelight. As he put it, "I always stood out front for the religious, political and educational rights of my people." Some female activists of his time may have disagreed with Page's willingness to truly stand up for the overall religious, political, and educational rights of women. He came also to understand, however reluctantly, that he had to share power with such AME Church rivals as Robert Meacham, Charles Pearce, and William Bradwell.[19]

As a literate man, Page believed that he served as an example of how black people, especially black men, could learn, achieve, and prosper if given the opportunity. In fact, the spiritual leader wanted to be perceived, in large part, as a self-made man. Yet that perception was only partially true. Indeed, the onetime enslaved overseer/preacher and later free leader of his race did become over time a man of letters, the builder of schools, and the owner of land. Yet behind that façade at times, hid an insecure man who sought to lean on others. He depended far more than he could articulate on the unconditional support of his devoted wife, Elizabeth, the calculated benevolence of his masters, the support of postbellum white philanthropists, and loyal men and women in the black church community who believed in him. The aid and sometimes intervention of a reluctant US government in protecting the rights of blacks contributed as well to his becoming an effective and iconic leader.[20]

~

One of Father James Page's greatest legacies perhaps, above all else, involved institution building. He sought not only to construct churches and sanctuaries but to leave a firm foundation for the continued growth of the Baptist denomination for future generations. He erected a religion based on faith, hard work, mutual aid, caring, and self-reliance. Religious institution building dominated his spiritual and everyday life. The legacies of his efforts to increase the presence of the Baptist denomination in the Deep South, especially in Florida, remain evident today. Based on the foundation that he laid, historic Bethel Baptist Missionary Church established in 1870 became, some eighty-five years later, the epicenter of the black freedom struggle in Florida during the civil rights movement of the late 1950s, 1960s, and beyond. The Southern Christian Leadership Conference and the Tallahassee bus boycott took root there. Page assisted other ministers despite their differing approaches. These activities helped to pave the way for future civil rights activists like Mordecai Johnson, Howard Thurman, Rosa Parks, Fannie Lou Hamer, Charles K. Steele, Martin Luther King Jr., and others to take up the banner of justice, freedom, and equality for all Americans. Christianity started out for him as a religion that his enslaver tried to use to control him. Despite the shackles he and other enslaved preachers contended with, he and they made "black Christianity" a religion that over time offered meaningful faith, solace, self-reliance, and encouragement to its converts.[21]

Although Reverend Page spent 75 percent of his life as an enslaved human being, he never spoke of himself as a victim. In the end it mattered less what Parkhill did to Page than how the cleric responded to his enslaver's actions. Father Page grappled as best he could with very complicated and, in some instances, heartbreaking challenges. He gave no direct indication that he considered his enslaver to be a villain or that Parkhill treated him inhumanely in a physical sense. Yet Parkhill's actions spoke volumes about his true attitude toward his enslaved overseer. They reflected a callous master who cared little about the bondservant's welfare or peace of mind. Parkhill's brand of Christian racial capitalism allowed him to separate families and sell human beings while remaining in good standing in his faith and with his church.[22]

⌒

So, who was Father James Page? He was a man who sought to navigate the treacherous waters of slavery and the uncertainties of Civil War and Reconstruction by offering hope, inspiration, humanity, dignity, and self-reliance to his race. He was a committed father and husband, a teacher, a sexist, a segregationist, a moralist, a pluralist, a pragmatist, an overseer/manager, and a conservative political leader. Most of all, Father Page was an iconic leader whom future generations will remember as a religious builder through the thousands of people whom he converted to the Baptist denomination and the many churches he helped to establish over a fifty-year period. As a religious man, Providence guided Father Page's life from cradle to grave. Through his many trials and tribulations, the cleric's faith in God, the hereafter, the now-worldly, and service to others remained steadfast. One of his successors might have concluded in this manner: Father Page may have gone in body, but he still remains alive today in the memories of those who recall and celebrate his many contributions. A long and difficult climb leading to a life well lived![23]

Introduction

1. Department of the Interior, Census Office, *Statistics of the Population of the United States at the Tenth Census, June 1, 1880* (Washington, DC: US Government Printing Office), 118; "Rev. James Page," *Christian Index* (Atlanta), May 14, 1883; "Rev. Jas Page," *Weekly Floridian* (Tallahassee), March 20, 1883.

2. Jack Sheppard interview with James Page, January 21–22, 1880, Bethel Missionary Baptist Church Library, Tallahassee, FL; "Old Family Cemeteries Scattered over Area," *Tallahassee (FL) Democrat*, March 28, 1974; "Patriarch's Spirit Lives On in Bethel Baptist," *Tallahassee (FL) Democrat*, October 15, 1978; "Restored Church Is Window to Past," *Tallahassee (FL) Democrat*, February 1, 1986; "Marker Inscriptions Have Been Preserved," *Tallahassee (FL) Democrat*, November 20, 1986; "Remembering the Black Hands That Built Florida," *Tallahassee (FL) Democrat*, January 2, 1996; "Standing on the Shoulders of a Giant," *Tallahassee (FL) Democrat*, February 22, 1997; "Bethel Missionary Baptist Church: The Page Era (1870–1884)," and "History of the Bethel Baptist Church (1865–1870–1979)" (undated manuscript), Bethel Missionary Baptist Church Library, Tallahassee, FL.

3. Sheppard interview.

4. See for example, Charles V. Hamilton, *The Black Preacher in America* (New York: William Morrow, 1972); William Edward Burghart Du Bois, *The Negro Church* (Atlanta: Atlanta University Press, 1903); W. E. B. Du Bois, *The Gift of Black Folk: The Negroes in the Making of America* (New York: AMS Press, 1972); W. E. B. Du Bois, *The Souls of Black Folk: Essays and Sketches* (Chicago: A. C. McClurg, 1903; repr. ed., Greenwich, CT: Fawcett, 1961); Milton Sernett, *Black Religion and American Evangelicalism: White Protestants, Plantation Missions, and the Flowering of Negro Christianity, 1787–1865* (Metuchen, NJ: Scarecrow and American Theological Library Association, 1975); James Weldon Johnson, *God's Trombones: Seven Negro Sermons in Verse* (New York: Viking Press, 1927).

5. Eugene D. Genovese, *Roll, Jordan, Roll: The World the Slaves Made* (New York: Pantheon Books, 1974), 1, 255; Joshua A. Licorish, *Harry Hosier: African Pioneer Preacher* (Philadelphia: Afro-American Associations, 1967), 1; Carter G. Woodson, *The History of the Negro Church* (Washington, DC: Associated, 1921); W. P. Harrison, *The Gospel among the Slaves* (Nashville: Publishing House of the M.E. Church, South,

1893), 1; Mason Crum, *The Negro in the Methodist Church* (New York: Methodist Church, 1951), 23; Charles H. Wesley, *Richard Allen: Apostle of Freedom* (Washington, DC: Associate, 1935), 30; Elmer T. Clark, J. Manning Potts, and Jacob S. Payton Asbury, eds., *The Journal and Letters of Francis Asbury*, 3 vols. (New York: Abingdon Press, 1958), 1:357; David Dennard, "Religion in the Quarters: A Study of Slave Preachers in the Antebellum South, 1800–1860" (PhD diss., Northwestern University, 1983), 16–22; John A. Oates, *The Story of Fayetteville* (Charlotte, NC: Dowd Press, 1950); Hamilton, *The Black Preacher in America*, 12–31; Carol V. R. George, *Segregated Sabbath: Richard Allen and the Emergence of Independent Black Churches, 1760–1840* (New York: Oxford University Press, 1973), 73; Joseph R. Washington, *Black Religion: The Negro and Christianity in the United States* (Boston: Beacon Press, 1964), 190; Charles C. Jones, *The Religious Instruction of the Negroes* (New York: Negro Universities Press, 1969); B. F. Riley, *A History of the Baptists in the Southern States East of the Mississippi* (Philadelphia: American Publication Society, 1898), 312; John H. Franklin and Alfred A. Moss Jr., *From Slavery to Freedom: A History of African American* (New York: Alfred A. Knopf, 1988), 160; Ira Berlin, *Slaves without Masters: The Free Negro in the Antebellum South* (New York: Pantheon, 1974), 38–41; Nancy Bullock Woolridge, "The Slave Preacher—Portrait of a Leader," *Journal of Negro Education* 14 (Winter 1945): 28, 28–37; Isaac Lane, *Autobiography of Bishop Isaac Lane* (Nashville: Publishing House of the Methodist Church, South, 1916), 47; John W. Blassingame, ed., *Slave Testimony: Two Centuries of Letters, Speeches, and Autobiographies* (Baton Rouge: Louisiana State University Press, 1997), 666; William J. Simmons, ed., *Men of Mark: Eminent, Progressive and Rising* (New York: Arno Press and the New York Times, 1968); R. E. Randolph, *The Life of Rev. John Jasper* (Richmond: R. T. Hill, 1855), 12–38; William E. Hatcher, *John Jasper: The Unmatched Negro Preacher* (New York: Fleming H. Revell, 1908), 10–17; Austin Steward, *Twenty-Two Years a Slave, and Forty Years a Freeman* (Rochester, NY: W. Alling, 1857), 51–52; Lawrence W. Levine, *Black Culture and Black Consciousness: Afro-American Folk Thought from Slavery to Freedom* (New York: Oxford University Press, 2007), 8.

6. Stephen Ward Angell, *Bishop Henry McNeal Turner and African-American Religion in the South* (Knoxville: University of Tennessee Press, 1992); Sandy Dwayne Martin, *For God and Race: The Religious and Political Leadership of AMEZ Bishop James Walker Hood* (Columbia: University of South Carolina Press, 1999).

7. John W. Blassingame, *The Slave Community: Plantation Life in the Antebellum South* (New York: Oxford University Press, 1979); Hamilton, *The Black Preacher in America*; Genovese, *Roll, Jordon, Roll*; Kenneth M. Stampp, *The Peculiar Institution: Slavery in the Ante-bellum South* (New York: Alfred A. Knopf, 1956; repr., New York: Vintage Books, 1964); Ira Berlin, *Many Thousands Gone: The First Two Centuries of Slavery in North America* (Cambridge, MA: Belknap / Harvard University Press, 1998); Michael Gomez, *Exchanging Our Country Marks: The Transformation of African Identities in the Colonial and Antebellum South* (Chapel Hill: University of North Carolina Press, 1998); Edward Baptist, *The Half Has Never Been Told: Slavery and the Making of American Capitalism* (New York: Basic Books, 2014); Steven Hahn, *A Nation under Our Feet: Black Political Struggles in the Rural South from Slavery to the Great Migration* (Cambridge, MA: Belknap / Harvard University Press, 2005); Annette Gordon-Reed, *Thomas Jefferson and Sally Hemings: An American Controversy*

(Charlottesville: University of Virginia Press, 1998); Eric Foner, *The Fiery Trial: Abraham Lincoln and American Slavery* (New York: W. W. Norton, 2015); Sven Beckert, *Empire of Cotton* (New York: Vintage, 2015); Jeff Forret, *Slave against Slave: Plantation Violence in the Old South* (Baton Rouge: Louisiana State University Press, 2015); Sterling Stuckey, *Slave Culture: Nationalist Theory and the Foundations of Black America* (New York: Oxford University Press, 1987); John David Smith, *Black Voices from Reconstruction: 1865–1877* (Gainesville: University Press of Florida, 1997); Jane Landers, *Atlantic Creoles in the Age of Revolutions* (Cambridge, MA: Harvard University Press, 2011).

8. Dennard, "Religion in the Quarters," iii.

9. Randolph, *Life of Rev. John Jasper;* Licorish, *Harry Hosier;* Hatcher, *John Jasper.*

10. Stanley Elkins, *Slavery: A Problem in American Institutional and Intellectual Life;* (Chicago: University of Chicago Press, 1959); Genovese, *Roll, Jordon, Roll.*

11. Albert J. Raboteau, *Slave Religion: The "Invisible Institution" in the Antebellum South* (New York: Oxford University Press, 1978); Albert J. Raboteau interview by Maya Berkley, June 27, 2008, Center for Interfaith Relations, Louisville, KY; Albert J. Raboteau, "The Secret Religion of the Slaves," *Christian History,* January 1992, accessed April 10, 2019, https://www.christianitytoday.com/history/issues/issue-33/secret-religion-of-slaves.html.

12. Raboteau, "The Secret Religion of the Slaves"; Peter Kolchin, *American Slavery: 1619–1877* (New York: Hill and Wang, 1993), 144.

13. Raboteau, *Slave Religion;* Betty Collier-Thomas, *Daughters of Thunder: Black Women Preachers and Their Sermons, 1850–1979* (New York: Jossey-Bass, 1997); Chanta M. Haywood, *Prophesying Daughters: Black Women Preachers and the Word, 1823–1913* (Columbia: University of Missouri Press, 2016); "Waycross Colored Woman Now a Noted Evangelist," *Jacksonville (FL) Times-Union and Citizen,* September 24, 1900.

14. David T. Shannon Sr., Julia Frazier White, and Deborah Van Broekhoven, eds., *George Liele's Life and Legacy: An Unsung Hero* (Macon, GA: Mercer University Press, 2013).

15. Patricia Griffin, ed., *The Odyssey of an African Slave* (Gainesville: University Press of Florida, 2009); Larry Eugene Rivers, "Baptist Minister James Page: Alternatives for African American Leadership in Post–Civil War Florida," in *Florida's Heritage of Diversity: Essays in Honor of Samuel Proctor,* ed. Mark I. Greenberg, William Warren Rogers, and Canter Brown Jr. (Tallahassee, FL: Sentry Press, 1997), 42–53; Leslie Ashford, "Loyal to the End: The Life of James Page, 1808–1883," *Journal of Negro History* 82 (Winter 1997): 169–79.

16. Eric Foner, *Freedom's Lawmakers: A Directory of Black Officeholders during Reconstruction* (Baton Rouge: Louisiana State University Press, 1996), vii.

17. Joe M. Richardson, *The Negro in the Reconstruction of Florida: 1865–1877* (Tallahassee: Florida State University Press, 1965); Canter Brown Jr., *Florida's Black Public Officials, 1867–1924* (Tuscaloosa: University of Alabama Press, 1998); Larry Eugene Rivers and Canter Brown Jr., *Laborers in the Vineyard of the Lord* (Gainesville: University Press of Florida, 2001); Canter Brown Jr. and Larry Eugene Rivers, *For a Great and Grand Purpose: Beginnings of the AMEZ Church in Florida, 1864–1905* (Gainesville: University Press of Florida, 2004).

18. Sheppard interview; Linda Kay Kneeland, "African American Suffering and Suicide under Slavery" (master's thesis, Montana State University, Bozeman, March 2007), 8–102. See also the suicide attempts of James Williams, Henry Bibb, and Charles Ball, who grieved over their separation from loved ones: James Williams, *Narrative of James Williams: An American Slave*, annotated ed. (Baton Rouge: Louisiana State University Press, 2013), 29; Henry Bibb, *Narrative of the Life and Adventures of Henry Bibb, an American Slave, Written by Himself* (New York: published by the author, 1850; Mnemosyne, 1969), 66; Charles Ball, *Slavery in the United States: A Narrative of the Life and Adventures of Charles Ball, a Black Man, Who Lived Forty Years in Maryland, South Carolina and Georgia, as a Slave, under Various Masters, and Was One Year in the Navy with Commodore Barney, during the Late War, Containing an Account of the Manners and Treatment of Slaves, with Observations upon the State of Morals amongst the Cotton Planters, and the Perils and Sufferings of a Fugitive Slave, Who Twice Escaped from the Cotton Country* (New York: John S. Taylor, 1837), 35; James Lindsay Smith, *Autobiography of James L. Smith: Including also, Reminiscences of Slave Life, Recollections of the War, Education of Freedmen, Causes of the Exodus, Etc.* (Norwich, CT: Bulletin, 1881), 19–20; John Joseph, *The Life and Sufferings of John Joseph, Etc.* (Wellington, NZ: J. Greedy, 1848), 7.

Chapter 1 • Early Life in Virginia

1. Jack Sheppard interview with James Page, January 21–22, 1880, Bethel Missionary Baptist Church Library, Tallahassee, FL; George Patterson McKinney Sr. and Richard I. McKinney Jr., *History of the Black Baptists of Florida: 1850–1935* (Miami: Florida Memorial College Press, 1987), 357; William Cathcart, ed., *The Baptist Encyclopedia: Dictionary of the Doctrines, Ordinances, Usages, Confessions of Faith, Suffering, Labors, and Successes, and the General History of the Baptist Denomination in All Lands, with Numerous Biographical Sketches of Distinguished American and Foreign Baptists, and a Supplement* (Philadelphia: Louis H. Everts, 1881), 878; "Letter from Dr. Randolph," *Christian Watchman* (Boston), December 18, 1873.

2. W. E. B. Du Bois, *The Suppression of the African Slave Trade to the United States of America, 1638–1870* (Cambridge, MA: Harvard University Press, 1890), 94.

3. Steven Deyle, *Carry Me Back: The Domestic Slave Trade in American Life* (New York: Oxford University Press, 10); Jeffrey A. Frankel, "The 1807–1809 Embargo against Great Britain," *Journal of Economic History* 42 (June 1982): 291–308; Merrill D. Peterson, *Thomas Jefferson and the New Nation: A Biography* (New York: Oxford University Press, 1970), 874–921; David Waldstreicher, *Slavery's Constitution: From Revolution to Ratification* (New York: Hill and Wang, 2009), 107–52; James Oakes, *Slavery and Freedom: An Interpretation of the Old South* (New York: Vintage Books), 34–35, 147; Peter Roberts, *The Anthracite Coal Industry: A Study of the Economic Conditions and Relations of the Cooperative Forces in the Development of the Anthracite Coal Industry of Pennsylvania* (New York: FB&C, 2015), 10–43.

4. William C. Davis, *Jefferson Davis: The Man and His Hour: A Biography* (New York: Blackstone, 2018), 23; William G. Copper Jr., *Jefferson Davis, American* (New York: Vintage Books, 2001); David Herbert Donald, *Lincoln* (New York: Simon & Schuster, 1995); Michael Burlingame, *Abraham Lincoln: A Life*, 2 vols. (Baltimore: Johns Hopkins University Press, 2008); Frederic Bancroft, *Slave Trading in the Old*

South (New York: Frederick Ungar, 1931), 223. Unfortunately, the international slave trade continued up to the Civil War; see, for example, "On the Coast of Africa," *Daily Republican* (Savannah, GA), November 8, 1848; "Another Slaver Captured," *Florida News* (Fernandina), November 8, 1858; "A Slaver Captured," *Florida News* (Fernandina), September 9, 1858; "Rumor of the Arrival of a Slaver," *Florida News* (Fernandina), December 16, 1858.

5. Sheppard interview.

6. Harriet R. Parkhill, "A Biographical Sketch of John Parkhill, October 1915," folder 14, John Parkhill Papers, 1813–1891, Southern Historical Collection, University of North Carolina, Chapel Hill; Lucy Beverly Randolph Parkhill, "Brief History of John Parkhill and His Family, February 8, 1859 and October 17, 1866," folder 14, John Parkhill Papers; Genevieve Parkhill Lykes, *Gift of Heritage* (Tampa, FL: priv. pub., 1969), 1–15; Sheppard interview.

7. Parkhill, "Brief History of John Parkhill," 3; Virginius Dabney, *Richmond: The Story of a City*, rev. and expanded ed. (Charlottesville: University Press of Virginia, 1990), 50–139. On Richmond, also see Marie Tyler-McGraw, *At the Falls: Richmond, Virginia, & Its People* (Chapel Hill: University of North Carolina Press, 1994), 2–9; Myrtle Elizabeth Callahan, "History of Richmond as a Port City" (master's thesis, University of Richmond, 1952).

8. Harriet Parkhill, "Biographical Sketch (1915); Lucy Parkhill, "Brief History of John Parkhill," 3; Frank J. Byrne, *Becoming Bourgeois: Merchant Culture in the South, 1820–1865* (Lexington: University Press of Kentucky, 2006), 61; Michael Durey, ed., *Andrew Bryson's Ordeal: An Epilogue to the 1798 Rebellion* (Cork, IE: Cork University Press, 1998), 1–17; William Henry Foote, *Sketches of Virginia, Historical and Biographical*, 2nd ser. (Philadelphia: J. B. Lippincott, 1855), 324; "Just Received," *Virginia Argus* (Richmond), September 13, 1808.

9. Durey, *Andrew Bryson's Ordeal*, 82–83; Christopher McPherson, *A Short History of the Life of Christopher McPherson, Alias, Pherson, Son of Christ, King of Kings and Lord of Lords: Containing a Collection of Certificates Letter, &c. Written by Himself* (Lynchburg, VA: McPherson, 1855), 13, 15–16.

10. Sheppard interview; Richard Channing Moore Page, *Genealogy of the Page Family in Virginia*, 2nd ed. (New York: Press of the Publisher's Printing, 1893), 71; John Page entry, 1810 Federal Census, Richmond, VA, Henrico County, 123A.

11. Parkhill, "Brief History of John Parkhill"; Lykes, *Gift of Heritage*, 1–15; James Oakes, *The Ruling Race: A History of American Slaveholders* (New York: W. W. Norton, 2013), 23–34; John B. Boles, *Black Southerners, 1619–1869* (Lexington: University of Kentucky Press, 1963), 3–69.

12. Eva Eubank Wilkerson, *Index to Marriages of Old Rappahannock and Essex Counties, Virginia: 1655–1900* (Richmond, VA: Clearfield, 1953), 187; Nellie West Dobbs, "Quarles and Dobbs Bible Record," *Virginia Magazine of History of Biography* 39 (July 1931): 263–66; Conley L. Edwards, comp., "Partially Proven Wills: Henrico County," *Virginia Genealogical Society Quarterly* 18 (July 1980): 87.

13. Orville Vernon Burton, *In My Father's House Are Many Mansions: Family and Community in Edgefield, South Carolina* (Chapel Hill: University of North Carolina Press, 1985), 75–79, 99–103. On the modern women's rights movement including the present-day Me Too movement see, for example, Rebecca Solnit, *Men Explain Things*

to Me (New York: Haymarket Books, 2015); Karen Karbo, *In Praise of Difficult Women: Life Lessons; 29 Heroines Who Dared to Break the Rules* (New York: National Geographic, 2018), 1–29; Cherrie Moraga and Gloria E. Anzaldua, eds., *This Bridge Called My Back: Writings by Radical Women of Color* (New York: State University of New York Press, 2015); Alida Nugent, *You Don't Have to Like Me: Essays on Growing Up, Speaking Out, and Finding Feminism* (New York: Plume, 2015); Jenny Zhang, *Sour Heart* (New York: Lenny, 2017); Anne Helen Petersen, *Too Fat, Too Slutty, Too Loud: The Rise and Reign of the Unruly Woman* (New York: Plume, 2017); Audre Lorde, *Sister Outsider: Essays & Speeches* (New York: Tantor, 2016), 1–17.

14. Katharine Gates, "Mystery Parkhill Graves in Richmond, Va.," accessed February 7, 2019, genealogy.com/forum/surnames/topics/parkhill/293/; Eleanor W. Parkhill and Samuel Henry Parkhill tombstone, Brook Hill Graveyard, Henrico County, VA; Annette Gordon-Reed and Peter S. Onuf, *"Most Blessed of the Patriarchs": Thomas Jefferson and the Empire of the Imagination* (New York: Liveright, 2017), 25–39.

15. Foote, *Sketches of Virginia*, 324–35.

16. *Virginia Patriot* (Richmond), August 31, 1813, 4; Foote, *Sketches of Virginia*, 325–26; "The Bible Society," *Newport (RI) Mercury*, September 25, 1813; *Virginia Argus* (Richmond), June 12, 1816, 3; Sheppard interview. On the American Bible Society, see John Fea, *The Bible Cause: A History of the American Bible Society* (New York: Oxford University Press, 2016), 1–13; George Rawick, ed., *The American Slave: A Composite Autobiography*, vol. 16 (Ohio narratives) (Westport: CT: Greenwood Press, 1972), 54.

17. Herbert Aptheker, *American Negro Slave Revolts* (New York: Columbia University Press, 1938), 11, 15, 65, 81, 83, 98, 106–7, 154, and 268; Eugene D. Genovese, *Roll, Jordan, Roll: The World the Slaves Made* (New York: Pantheon Books, 1974), 202, 257, 259, 271–72, and 593–97; Larry Eugene Rivers, *Rebels and Runaways: Slave Resistance in 19th Century Florida* (Urbana: University of Illinois Press, 2012), 5, 96, 122–23, 133, 139, and 142; Douglas R. Egerton, *Gabriel's Rebellion: The Virginia Slave Conspiracies of 1800* (Chapel Hill: University of North Carolina Press, 1993), 50–53 and 179–81; Douglas R. Egerton, *He Shall Go Out Free: The Lives of Denmark Vesey* (Madison, WI: Madison House, 1999), 97–121; Eric Foner, ed., *Nat Turner* (New York: Prentice Hall, 1971), 39–61; Stephen B. Oates, *The Fires of Jubilee: Nat Turner's Fierce Rebellion* (New York: Harper and Row, 1975), 29–38; Daniel Rasmussen, *American Uprising: The Untold Story of America's Largest Revolt* (New York: Harper Perennial, 2012), 97–111.

18. *Virginia Argus* (Richmond), October 11, 1813, 3; "Cast Iron Foundery," *Enquirer* (Richmond, VA), May 11, 1814; "The Richmond Union Air Furnace," *Virginia Argus* (Richmond), July 9, 1814; *Virginia Patriot* (Richmond), July 20, 1814.

19. Stuart L. Butler, *Defending the Old Dominion: Virginia and Its Militia in the War of 1812* (Lanham, MD: University Press of America, 2013), 157, 282; "Richmond, (Virginia) July 2," *Gettysburg (PA) Adams Centinel*, July 14, 1813.

20. Alan Taylor, *The Internal Enemy: Slavery and War in Virginia, 1772–1832* (New York: W. W. Norton, 2013), 285–86; Sheppard interview.

21. "War in the Potomac," *Pennsylvania Gazette* (Philadelphia), August 10, 1814; "Private Correspondence," *Savannah (GA) Republican and Savannah Evening Ledger*,

August 18, 1814; "To Arms! To Arms!," and "By the Governor," *Enquirer* (Richmond, VA), August 27, 1814; Helen Kay Yates, comp., "Abstracts from the John K. Martin Papers, War of 1812," *Virginia Genealogical Society Quarterly* 17 (April 1979): 72. Among numerous excellent works on the War of 1812, see, for example, Walter R. Borneman, *1812: The War That Forged a Nation* (New York: Harper, 2004); Donald R. Hickey, *The War of 1812: A Forgotten Conflict*, bicentennial ed. (Urbana: University of Illinois Press, 2012).

22. "Marriages," *Virginia Patriot* (Richmond), February 4, 1815; Harriet Parkhill, "Biographical Sketch (1915)"; Lucy Parkhill, "Brief History of John Parkhill"; Lykes, *Gift of Heritage*, 2; Anna Melissa Graves, comp., "Extracts from Diary of Charles Copland," *William and Mary College Quarterly* 14 (July 1905): 44–45. See the excellent explanation of the John Parkhill family tree by Donald Ivey, *The Life and Times of George Washington Parkhill (A.D. 1822–1862): A Chronological Biography* (St. Petersburg, FL: Pinellas County Historical Museum, 1996), 38.

23. *Virginia Commercial Compiler* (Richmond), October 15, 1818, 3; Charles Poindexter, *Richmond: An Illustrated Hand-Book and Guide with Notices of the Battle-Fields* (Richmond, VA: J. L. Hill, 1896), 16–17; Egerton, *Gabriel's Rebellion*, 32 and 38; John T. O'Brien, "Factory, Church, and Community: Blacks in Antebellum Richmond," *Journal of Southern History* 44 (November 1978): 521–23; see Paul Ortiz, *An African American and Latinx History of the United States* (Boston: Beacon Press, 2018), 20.

24. "Dry Goods," *Virginia Argus* (Richmond), December 9, 1815; "Directors of the Farmers' Bank of Virginia, and Its Branches," *Enquirer* (Richmond, VA), January 4, 1816; Notice, *Virginia Commercial Compiler* (Richmond), July 9, 1817, August 17, 1818; "Stock of Dry Goods at Auction," *Virginia Commercial Compiler* (Richmond), November 25, 1817; *American Beacon* (Norfolk, VA), January 20, 1818, 3; *Enquirer* (Richmond, VA), March 10, 1818, 1; "John and Samuel Parkhill," *Virginia Commercial Compiler* (Richmond), September 24, 1818; Andrew H. Browning, *The Panic of 1819: The First Great Depression* (Columbia: University of Missouri Press, 2019), 209–11.

25. Sheppard interview; Rawick, *The American Slave*, vol. 16 (Ohio narratives), 1–3; Wilma King, *Stolen Childhood: Slave Youth in Nineteenth-Century American* (Bloomington: Indiana University Press, 1995), 21–41; Marie Jenkins Schwartz, *Ties That Bound: Founding First Ladies and Slaves* (Chicago: University of Chicago Press, 2017), 7.

26. Michele Mitchell, *Righteous Propagation: African Americans and the Politics of Racial Destiny after Reconstruction* (Chapel Hill: University of North Carolina Press, 2004), 20–50; Marie Tyler McGraw, "Richmond Free Blacks and African Colonization, 1816–1832," *Journal of American Studies* 21 (1987): 207–24; Bell I. Wiley, ed., *Slaves No More: Letters from Liberia: 1833–1860* (Lexington: University of Kentucky Press, 1980), 100–105; Charles I. Foster, "The Colonization of Free Negroes in Liberia, 1816–1820," *Journal of Negro History* 38 (January 1953): 41–66; George F. Adams, *A Brief Sketch of the Life and Character of the Late William Crane of Baltimore* (Baltimore: John F. Weishampel, 1868), 11–14; Claude A. Glegg III, *The Price of Liberty: African Americans and the Making of Liberia* (Chapel Hill: University of North Carolina Press, 2004), 29–44; Edward Baptist, *The Half Has Never Been Told: Slavery and the Making of American Capitalism* (New York: Basic Books, 2014), 193; Richard

Wade, *Slavery in the Cities, 1820–1860* (New York: Oxford University Press, 1964), 329;
Lisa Lindsay, *Atlantic Bonds: A Nineteenth-Century Odyssey from America to Africa*
(Chapel Hill: University of North Carolina Press, 2017), 45–51; Ortiz, *An African
American and Latinx History*, 28; David Blight, *Frederick Douglass: Prophet of
Freedom* (New York: Simon and Schuster, 2018), 369; "Baltimore: From Liberia,"
Mercantile Advertiser (Richmond, VA), December 19, 1822; "Arrival of the Shark,"
Mercantile Advertiser (Richmond, VA), December 16, 1822; "American Colonization
Society," *Mercantile Advertiser* (Richmond, VA), November 2, 1822; "Liberia,"
Commercial Compiler (Richmond, VA), April 16, 1823; "Colonization Society,"
Commercial Compiler (Richmond, VA), February 24, 1825, and November 11, 1828;
"From Africa," *American Commercial Beacon and Norfolk and Portsmouth Daily
Advertiser* (Norfolk, VA), September 3, 1823; "African Colony," *American Commercial
Beacon and Norfolk and Portsmouth Daily Advertiser* (Norfolk, VA), September 19,
1823; "The African Colony," *American Commercial Beacon and Norfolk and Portsmouth
Daily Advertiser* (Norfolk, VA), December 27, 1823; "African Colony," *American
Commercial Beacon and Norfolk and Portsmouth Daily Advertiser* (Norfolk, VA),
January 10, February 18, June 17, and June 30, 1824; "Norfolk Colonization Society,"
American Commercial Beacon and Norfolk and Portsmouth Daily Advertiser (Norfolk,
VA), January 13, 1824; "Liberia," *Nile's Weekly Register* (Baltimore, MD), June 16, 1827.

27. Sheppard interview; Harriet Parkhill, "Biographical Sketch (1915)"; Works
Progress Administration Federal Writers' Project, *Slave Narratives: A Folk History of
Slavery in the United States from Interviews with Former Slaves*, vol. 3, *Florida*, 279–84,
Bethel Baptist Church Library, Tallahassee, FL; McGraw, "Richmond Free Blacks
and African Colonization," 212–15; B. S. White, *First Baptist Church Richmond
1780–1955* (Richmond, VA: Whittet and Shepperson, 1955), 1–30; Mechal Sobel,
Trabelin On: The Slave Journey to an Afro-Baptist Faith (Westport, CT: Greenwood
Press, 1979), 399–413; Lindsay, *Atlantic Bonds*, 45–51; Carle Patrick Burrows, *Black
Christian Republicanism: The Writings of Hilary Teage* (Bomi County, LR: Know Your
Self Press, 2016), 12–17; "Colonization Society," *Niles' Weekly Register* (Baltimore,
MD), November 29, 1828. Colonization would be a constant issue up to the Civil War:
"Wouldn't Go," *Florida News* (Fernandina, FL), May 19, 1858; L. Maria Child, *Linda
Brent Incidents in the Life of a Slave Girl: An Authentic Historical Narrative Describing
the Horrors of Slavery as Experienced by Black Women* (New York: Harcourt, Brace,
1973), 3–4.

28. King, *Stolen Childhood*, 44–45; David K. Wiggins, "The Play of Slave Children
in the Plantation Communities of the Old South, 1820–1860," *Journal of Sports
History* 7 (Summer 1980): 21–39.

29. King, *Stolen Childhood*, 48–43; Sheppard interview; Rawick, *The American
Slave*, vol. 16 (Ohio narratives), 29; Marie Jenkins Schwartz, *Born in Bondage: Growing
Up Enslaved in the Antebellum South* (Cambridge, MA: Harvard University Press,
2001), 94; Anna Mae Duane, ed., *Child Slavery before and after Emancipation: An
Argument for Child-Centered Slavery Studies* (New York: Cambridge University Press,
2017), 2–10.

30. Sheppard interview, 2–3; King, *Stolen Childhood*, 48;

31. Sheppard interview, 2–3; Desiree Lee, "Childhood in Slavery," in Maryland
State Archives, *Legacy of Slavery in Maryland: An Archives of Maryland Electronic*

Publication, accessed July 17, 2017, slavery.msa.maryland.gov.html.antebellum/essay1 .html; Rawick, *The American Slave*, vol. 13, parts 3 and 4 (Georgia narratives), 56, 67, vol. 16 (Maryland narratives), 34–35, 8. Schwartz, *Born in Bondage*, 75–106 and 119–23; King, *Stolen Childhood*, xx and 45; Herbert Gutman, *The Black Family in Slavery and Freedom, 1750–1925* (New York: Pantheon, 1976), 65–70; Rawick, *The American Slave*, vol. 16 (Kansas narratives), 1–3, vol. 16 (Kentucky narratives), 32, 113–14, vol. 14 (North Carolina), 74.

32. Sheppard interview, 2.

33. Lillian Hiscock, "Florida's Religious Syncretism: How Black Africans Interacted with Florida's Diverse Religious Background" (senior seminar paper, Florida State University, 2016), 3–35; Peter Kolchin, *American Slavery: 1619–1877* (New York: Hill and Wang, 1993),142; James Sterling, *Letters from the Slave States* (London: John W. Parker and Son, 1847), 295; John H. Franklin and Loren Schweninger, *Runaway Slaves: Rebels on the Plantation, 1790–1860* (New York: Oxford University Press, 1999), 19, 118–19, and 215; Sheppard interview; Rawick, *The American Slave*, vol. 16 (Kentucky narrative), 23, vol. 16 (Tennessee narratives), 48, vol. 16 (Maryland narratives), 35.

34. Sheppard interview, 2; Ezra Greenspan, *William Wells Brown: An African American Life* (New York: W. W. Norton, 2014), 3; Byrne, *Becoming Bourgeois*, 61–65; Wade, *Slavery in the Cities*, 33; Sheppard interview. For an interesting comparison with Page's experience, see Lee H. Warner, *Free Men in the Age of Servitude: Three Generations of a Black Family* (Lexington: University Press of Kentucky, 1992), 23–49.

35. Troy L. Kickler, "Urban Slaves a Little Recognized Part of the South Economy," *North Carolina History Project*, accessed March 12, 2019, northcarolinahistory .org/commentary/urban-slaves-a-little-recognized-part-of-the-southern-economy/; see also David S. Ceceleski, *The Waterman's Song: Slavery and Freedom in Maritime North Carolina* (Chapel Hill: University of North Carolina Press, 2012), 3–34; John H. Franklin and Alfred A. Moss Jr., *From Slavery to Freedom: A History of African American* (New York: Alfred A. Knopf, 1988), 39–149; Alan D. Watson, *African Americans in Early North Carolina: A Documentary History* (Raleigh: North Carolina Office of Archives and History, 2005); Christopher Rose, "Urban Slavery in the Antebellum United States," episode 54, *15 Minute History* (podcast), University of Texas at Austin, accessed March 12, 2019, 15minutehistory.org/2014/09/17/episode -54-urban-slavery-in-the-antebellum-united-states/; Lucy Parkhill, "Brief History of John Parkhill"; James Oakes, review of *Masters of the Big House: Elite Slaveholders of the Mid-Nineteenth-Century South*, by William K. Scarborough, *Journal of Southern History* 71 (May 2005): 447.

36. "Lancastrian Institution," *Family Visitor* (Richmond, VA), November 16, 1822; deed, 1823, of Thomas Atkinson, William Mayo Atkinson and Alexander Fulton to Edward Carrington Mayo and John Parkhill for African American Slaves and Personal Property, mss 2F9599b37, Virginia Historical Society, Richmond; Samuel Mordecai, *Richmond in By-Gone Days* (Richmond, VA: George M. West, 1856), 184–85; Eric Hilt, "Wall Street's First Corporate Governance Crisis: The Panic of 1826," *Richmond (VA) Whig*, August 22, 1826, 1–2; Edward Baptist, *Creating an Old South: Middle Florida's Plantation Frontier before the Civil War* (Chapel Hill: University of North Carolina Press, 2000), 22.

37. "Richmond, March 21," *Alexandria (VA) Gazette*, March 24, 1827; "By the Lieutenant Governor of the Commonwealth of Virginia, a Proclamation," *North-Carolina Star* (Raleigh), April 12, 1827; Elizabeth Ann Macon Heath to Sarah "Sally" Tate Steptoe Massie, March 24, 1827, Massie Family Papers, Virginia Historical Society; James M. Denham, *"A Rogue's Paradise": Crime and Punishment in Antebellum Florida, 1821–1861* (Tuscaloosa: University of Alabama Press, 1997), 25–105.

38. Michael G. Schene, "Robert and John Grattan Gamble: Middle Florida Entrepreneurs," *Florida Historical Quarterly* 54 (July 1975): 61–62; John Foster Jr. and Sarah Whitmer Foster, *Contentment and the Pursuit of Ambition: The Grattans and Their Remarkable Women* (Tallahassee, FL: Rose Digital, 2011), 54–59; Ortiz, *An African American and Latinx History*, 23; David McCullough, *John Adams* (New York: Simon and Schuster, 2001), 628.

39. Baptist, *Creating an Old South*, 17; Sheppard interview; Samuel Parkhill to John Parkhill, August 16, 1827, folder 2, John Parkhill Papers; "Loss of the Ship Aurora," *Spectator* (New York), November 13, 1827, *New York Daily Advertiser*, November 13, 1827, 2; On the early development of the Middle Florida plantation belt, see also Sidney Walker Martin, *Florida during the Territorial Days* (Athens: University of Georgia Press, 1944), 1–35; Julia Smith, *Slavery and Plantation Growth in Antebellum Florida, 1821–1860* (Gainesville: University of Florida Press, 1973); Bertram Groene, *Ante-bellum Tallahassee* (Tallahassee: Florida Heritage Foundation, 1981); Mary Louise Ellis and William Warren Rogers, *Tallahassee and Leon County: A History and Bibliography* (Tallahassee: Florida Department of State, 1986); Larry Eugene Rivers, *Slavery in Florida: Territorial Days to Emancipation* (Gainesville: University Press of Florida, 2000), 120–24; David H. Jackson Jr. and Kimberlyn M. Elliot, "African Americans in Florida, 1870–1920: A Historiographical Essay," *Florida Historical Quarterly* 95 (Fall 2016): 152–93.

Chapter 2 • *Forced Migration to the Florida Frontier*

1. Edward Baptist, *Creating an Old South: Middle Florida's Plantation Frontier before the Civil War* (Chapel Hill: University of North Carolina Press, 2000), 16–18; Achille Murat, *A Moral and Political Sketch of the United States of North America* (London: Effingham Wilson, 1833), 65. On the tide of southern planter emigration and experiences of such emigrants, see Walter Johnson, *River of Dark Dreams: Slavery and Empire in the Cotton Kingdom* (Cambridge, MA: Harvard University, 2013); Walter Johnson, *Soul by Soul: Inside the Antebellum Slave Market* (Cambridge, MA: Harvard University Press, 1999); Sven Beckert, *Empire of Cotton* (New York: Vintage, 2015); Edward Baptist, *The Half Has Never Been Told: Slavery and the Making of American Capitalism* (New York: Basic Books, 2014); William Warren Rogers and Erica R. Clark, *The Croom Family and the Goodwood Plantation: Land, Litigation, and Southern Lives* (Athens: University of Georgia Press, 2016); Jeff Forret and Christine E. Sears, *New Directions in Slavery Studies: Commodification, Community, and Comparison* (Baton Rouge: Louisiana State University Press, 2015); Bonnie Martin and James Brooks, eds., *Linking the Histories of Slavery: North America and Its Borderlands* (Santa Fe, NM: School of Advanced Research Press, 2015); Walter W. Jenson, *Cultivating Race: The Expansion of Slavery in Georgia, 1750–1860* (Lexington: University Press of Kentucky, 2012); David E. Paterson, "Slavery, Slaves, and Cash in a Georgia Village,

1825–1865," *Journal of Southern History* 75 (November 2009): 799–930; Ira Berlin, *Generations of Captivity: A History of African-American Slaves* (Cambridge, MA: Harvard University Press, 2003), 160; Michael Tadman, *Speculators and Slaves: Masters, Traders and the Slave in the Old South* (Madison: University of Wisconsin, 1989); 133–37; Stephanie Yuhl, "Hidden in Plain Sight: Centering the Domestic Slave Trade in American Public History," *Journal of Southern History* 79 (August 2013): 593–624; Antonio Rafael de la Cova, *Colonel Henry Theodore Titus: Antebellum Soldier of Fortune and Florida Pioneer* (Columbia: University of South Carolina Press, 2016), 1–2.

2. For an overall discussion of paternalism, please see Eugene D. Genovese, *Roll, Jordan, Roll: The World the Slaves Made* (New York: Pantheon Books, 1974), 195–234; James Oakes, *Slavery and Freedom: An Interpretation of the Old South* (New York: Vintage Books), 137–94; Peter Kolchin, *American Slavery: 1619–1877* (New York: Hill and Wang, 1993), 111–20; Eugene Genovese and Elizabeth Fox-Genovese, *Fatal Self-Deception: Slaveholding Paternalism in the Old South* (New York: Cambridge University Press, 2011), 36–79; David Brion Davis, *Inhuman Bondage: The Rise and Fall of Slavery in the New World* (New York: Oxford University Press, 2008), 193–200; William Dusinberre, *Them Dark Days: Slavery in the American Rice Swamps* (New York: Oxford University Press, 1996), 35–49; Charles Joyner, *Down by the Riverside: A South Carolina Slave Community* (Urbana: University of Illinois Press, 1984), 69, 231–32. For studies that challenge paternalism as a theoretical framework for analyzing the master-slave relationship, see Stephanie M. H. Camp, *Closer to Freedom: Enslaved Women and Everyday Resistance in the Plantation South* (Chapel Hill: University of North Carolina Press, 2004), 39–41; Stephanie M. H. Camp, "The Pleasures of Resistance: Enslaved Women and Body Politics in the Plantation South 1830–1861," *Journal of Southern History* 68 (August 2002): 533–72; Kathleen M. Brown, *Good Wives, Nasty Wenches, and Anxious Patriarchs: Gender, Race, and Power in Colonial Virginia* (Chapel Hill: University of North Carolina Press, 1996), 328–34; Michael A. Gomez, *Exchanging Our Country Marks: The Transformation of African Identities in the Colonial and Antebellum South* (Chapel Hill: University of North Carolina Press, 1998), 4–69.

3. Jack Sheppard interview with James Page, January 21–22, 1880, Bethel Missionary Baptist Church Library, Tallahassee, FL.

4. Sheppard interview.

5. Sheppard interview; George Rawick, ed., *The American Slave: A Composite Autobiography*, vol. 16 (Kansas narratives), 8–17, vol. 16 (Tennessee narratives) (Westport: CT: Greenwood Press, 1972), 13 and 66; Walter Johnson, "The Slave Trader, the White Slave, and the Politics of Racial Determination in the 1850s," *Journal of Southern History* 87 (June 2000): 13–38; Johnson, *Soul by Soul*, 25, 26–41, 133–61, and 214; Peter Wood, *Black Majority: Negroes in Colonial South Carolina from 1670 through the Stono Rebellion* (New York: Alfred A. Knopf, 1974), 41.

6. Sheppard interview; Anne C. Bailey, *The Weeping Time: Memory and the Largest Slave Auction in American History* (New York: Cambridge University Press, 2017), 1–30; Dylan C. Penningroth, *The Claims of Kinfolk: African American Property and Community in the Nineteenth-Century South* (Chapel Hill: University of North Carolina Press, 2003), 88–89; see William Johnson narrative, 29–30, in *A North-Side*

View of Slavery: The Refugee; or the Narratives of Fugitive Slaves in Canada, ed. Benjamin Drew (Boston: John P. Jewett, 1856, 1st repr., New York: Johnson Reprint, 1969); Marie Jenkins Schwartz, *Born in Bondage: Growing Up Enslaved in the Antebellum South* (Cambridge, MA: Harvard University Press, 2001), 88–99; Rawick, *The American Slave*, vol. 16 (Kansas narratives), 8–17, vol. 16 (Tennessee narratives), 66; Johnson, *Soul by Soul*, 161; Lester B. Shippee, ed., *Henry Benjamin Whipple, Bishop Whipple's Southern Diary, 1843–1844* (Minneapolis: University of Minnesota Press, 1937), 69; Richard Follett, Sven Beckert, Peter Coclanis, and Barbara Hahn, *Plantation Kingdom: The American South and Its Global Commodities* (Baltimore: Johns Hopkins University Press, 2016), 39–60.

7. Rawick, *The American Slave*, vol. 17 (Florida narratives), 327; Charles Joyner, "The World of the Plantation Slaves," in *Before Freedom Came*, ed. Edward D. C. Campbell Jr. and Kym S. Rice (Charlottesville: University Press of Virginia, 1991), 61; Johnson, *Soul by Soul*, 214; Tadman, *Speculators and Slaves*, 133–78; Steven Deyle, *Carry Me Back: The Domestic Slave Trade in American Life* (New York: Oxford University Press, 10), 246–47.

8. Kolchin, *American Slavery*, 59–62, 111–35, 142–46, and 153–54; Joyner, *Down by the Riverside*, 32–33, 50–57, 66–67, 69–70, and 137–38; Ira Berlin, *Many Thousands Gone: The First Two Centuries of Slavery in North America* (Cambridge, MA: Belknap / Harvard University Press, 1998), 40–41, 172–73, and 318–19; Larry Eugene Rivers, *Slavery in Florida: Territorial Days to Emancipation* (Gainesville: University Press of Florida, 2000), 85–105; Larry Eugene Rivers, *Rebels and Runaways: Slave Resistance in 19th Century Florida* (Urbana: University of Illinois Press, 2012), 90–105; Baptist, *Half Has Never Been Told*, 100–107.

9. Sheppard interview; Damian Alan Pargas, *Slavery and Forced Migration in the Antebellum South* (New York: Cambridge University Press, 2015), 57; Baptist, *Creating an Old South*, 67; Calvin Schermerhorn, *Money over Mastery, Family over Freedom: Slavery in the Antebellum Upper South* (Baltimore: Johns Hopkins University, Press), 4–5 and 13–16; Phillip Troutman, "Correspondences in Black and White: Sentiment and the Slave Market Revolution," in *New Studies in the History of American Slavery*, ed. Edward E. Baptist and Stephanie H. M. Camp (Athens: University of Georgia Press, 2006), 214; Johnson, *Soul by Soul*, 41–65; Steven F. Miller, "Plantation Labor Organization and Slave Life on the Cotton Frontier: The Alabama-Mississippi Black Belt, 1815–1840," in *Cultivation and Culture: Labor and the Shaping of Slave Life in the Americas*, ed. Ira Berlin and Philip D. Morgan (Charlottesville: University of Virginia Press, 1993), 155–69; Brenda Stevenson, *Life in Black and White: Family and Community in the Slave South* (New York: Oxford University Press, 1996), 3–71 and 200–226; Francis Fedric, *Slave Life in Virginia and Kentucky; or, Fifty Years of Slavery in the Southern States of America* (London: Wertheim, MacIntosh and Hunt, 1863), 14; Baptist, *Half Has Never Been Told*, 2, 176.

10. Sheppard interview. On paternalism, see Pargas, *Slavery and Forced Migration*, 7–12. Although the majority of owners who transported their slaves to new locations were men, women slaveholders also brought bondservants to places such as Florida. Mary DeLaughter, for instance, brought her slaves from Edgefield, South Carolina, during the late 1820s. Amon DeLaughter journal, collection of Elizabeth Sims, Madison County, FL; Stephanie E. Jones-Rogers, *They Were Her Property: White*

Women as Slave Owners in the American South (New Haven, CT: Yale University Press, 2019); Marie S. Molloy, *Single, White, Slaveholding Women in the Nineteenth-Century American South* (Columbia: University of South Carolina Press, 2018); Kirsten E. Wood, *Masterful Women: Widows from the American Revolution through the Civil War* (Chapel Hill: University of North Carolina Press, 2014); Lorrie Glover, *All Our Relations: Blood Ties and Emotional Bonds among the Early South Carolina Gentry* (Baltimore: Johns Hopkins University Press, 2000); Drew Gilpin Faust, *Mothers of Invention: Women of the Slaveholding South in the American Civil War* (Chapel Hill: University of North Carolina Press, 1996); Stephanie McCurry, *Masters of Small Worlds: Yeoman Households, Gender Relations, and Political Culture of the Antebellum South Carolina Low Country* (New York: Oxford University Press, 1997); diary of John Parkhill, 1821–1827, 1:38–43, John Parkhill Papers, 1813–1891, Southern Historical Collection, University of North Carolina, Chapel Hill; for an interesting story of enslaved family separation, please see the account of Henrietta Wood in W. Caleb McDaniel, *Sweet Taste of Liberty: A True Story of Slavery and Restitution in America* (New York: Oxford University Press, 2019), 5–75.

11. Jack Trammell, *The Richmond Slave Trade: The Economic Backbone of the Old Dominion* (Charleston, SC: History Press, 2012), 70–71.

12. Charles Dickens, *American Notes for General Circulation and Pictures from Italy* (New York: CreateSpace, 2015), 89; Trammell, *Richmond Slave Trade*, 74–75.

13. Trammell, *Richmond Slave Trade*, 76–79; Rawick, *The American Slave*, vol. 16 (Virginia narratives), 13, vol. 16 (Tennessee narratives), 12–13.

14. Sheppard interview; Baptist, *Half Has Never Been Told*, 48; Donald Robinson, *Slavery in the Structure of American Politics* (New York: Harcourt Brace Jovanovich, 1970), 330–31; David Brion Davis, *Slavery and Human Progress* (New York: Oxford University Press), 162–63; Pargas, *Slavery and Forced Migration*, 58; Johanna Nicol Shields, *Freedom in a Slave Society: Stories from the Antebellum South* (New York: Cambridge University Press, 2012), 1–29 and 289. See also Travis Glasson, *Mastering Christianity: Missionary Anglicanism and Slavery in the Atlantic World* (New York: Oxford University Press, 2012), 230–32; Jeffrey Robert Young, *Domesticating Slavery: The Master Class in Georgia and South Carolina, 1670–1837* (Chapel Hill: University of North Carolina Press, 1999); "Obituary," *Floridian* (Tallahassee), November 3, 1855; Lucy Beverly Randolph Parkhill, "Brief History of John Parkhill and His Family, February 8, 1859 and October 17, 1866," and Harriet R. Parkhill, "A Biographical Sketch of John Parkhill, October 1915," folder 14, John Parkhill Papers.

15. Pargas, *Slavery and Forced Migration*, 8 and 58; Peter N. Moore, "Family Dynamics and the Great Revival: Religious Conversion in the South Carolina," *Journal of Southern History* 70 (February 2004): 35–62.

16. Damian Alan Pargas, ed., *Fugitive Slaves and Spaces of Freedom in North America* (Gainesville: University Press of Florida, 2018), 8; Pargas, *Slavery and Forced Migration*, 18, 115; Lewis Gray, *A History of Agriculture in the Southern States to 1860*, 2 vols. (Washington: Carnegie Institution, 1993), 2:650; Berlin, *Many Thousands Gone*, 1–19; Berlin, *Generations of Captivity*, 21, 96–97; Phillip D. Morgan, *Slave Counterpoint: Black Culture in the Eighteenth-Century Chesapeake and Lowcountry* (Chapel Hill: University of North Carolina Press, 1998), 23–39; Deyle, *Carry Me Back*, 41–46; Robert William Fogel, *Without Consent or Contract: The Rise and Fall of American*

Slavery (New York: Norton, 1989), 63; Herbert S. Klein, *The Atlantic Slave Trade* (New York: Cambridge University Press, 1999), 41–45; Phillip D. Curtin, *The Atlantic Slave Trade: A Census* (Madison: University of Wisconsin Press, 1969), 231–64. The illegal international slave trade would continue in Florida up to the 1860s; see "Another Slaver Captured," *Florida Home Companion* (Ocala), March 16, 1858; "Slaver Captured in St. Joseph's Bay," *Floridian and Journal* (Tallahassee), March 26, 1859; "The Slaver at Apalachicola," *Floridian and Journal* (Tallahassee), April 9, 1859; "Chase of a Slaver—Terrible Result," *Florida Dispatch* (Newnansville, Alachua County), May 11, 1860; "Capture of Another Slaver," *Floridian and Journal* (Tallahassee), June 2, 1860; Rivers, *Slavery in Florida*, 253; *Population of the United States in 1860: Compiled from the Original Returns of the Eighth Census* (Washington, DC: US Government Printing Office, 1864), 225; Greg Grandin, *The Empire of Necessity: Slavery Freedom, and Deception in the New World* (New York: Metropolitan Books / Henry Holt, 2014), 3–85.

17. Pargas, *Slavery and Forced Migration*, 18–20, 115; Berlin, *Many Thousands Gone*, 1–19; Deyle, *Carry Me Back*, 41–46; Berlin, *Generations of Captivity*, 21, 96–97; Fogel, *Without Consent or Contract*, 63; David L. Lighter, *Slavery and the Commerce Power: How the Struggle Against the Interstate Slave Trade Led to the Civil War* (New Haven, CT: Yale University Press, 2006), 5–8; Johnson, *Soul by Soul*, 6–7; Jonathan D. Martin, *Divided Master: Slave Hiring in the Antebellum South* (Cambridge, MA: Harvard University Press, 2004), 6–7; Kolchin, *American Slavery*, 18–24, 96–98; Peter McClelland and Richard Zeckhauser, *Demographic Dimensions of the New Republic: American Interregional Migration, Vital Statistics, and Manumissions, 1800–1860* (New York: Cambridge University Press, 1982), 118–19; Gerald Horne, *The Deepest South: The United States, Brazil, and the African Slave Trade* (New York: New York University Press, 2007, 1–3; Enrico Dal Lago, *American Slavery, Atlantic Slavery, and Beyond: The U.S. "Peculiar Institution"; An International Perspective* (Boulder, CO: Paradigm, 2012), 41–45 and 63–65; Sean K. Kelley, *Voyage of the Slave Ship* Hare: *A Journey into Captivity from Sierra Leone to South Carolina* (Chapel Hill: University of North Carolina Press, 2016), 1–35; Thomas Pettigrew, *A Profile of the Negro American* (Princeton, NJ: Van Nostrand, 1964), 15–34; Paul Ortiz, *An African American and Latinx History of the United States* (Boston: Beacon Press, 2018), 58; "Runaway Maria 20$ Reward," *Pensacola (FL) Gazette*, December 19, 1829.

18. A. B. Cabell to My Dear Laura, March 26, 1827, and Thomas Randall to William Wirt, December 3, 1827, William Wirt Papers, Maryland Historical Society, Baltimore; John Parkhill journal, #1826, 1821–1827, John Parkhill Papers; Rivers, *Slavery in Florida*, 16–33 and 229; Baptist, *Creating an Old South*, 1–45; *Population of the United States in 1860*, 225; see also Sidney Walker Martin, *Florida during the Territorial Days* (Athens: University of Georgia Press, 1944); Julia Smith, *Slavery and Plantation Growth in Antebellum Florida, 1821–1860* (Gainesville: University of Florida Press, 1973), 3–39; Thomas Randall to William Wirt, December 3, 1827, William Wirt Papers.

19. Sheppard interview; John Parkhill journal, #1826; Pargas, *Slavery and Forced Migration*, 5, 30; Robert H. Gudmestad, *A Troublesome Commerce: The Transformation of the Interstate Slave Trade* (Baton Rouge: Louisiana State University Press, 2003), 43; Deyle, *Carry Me Back*, 246; Joshua D. Rothman, *Flush Times and Fever Dreams: A Story of Capitalism and Slavery in the Age of Jackson* (Athens: University of

Georgia Press, 2012), 13–17; Matthew Pratt Guterl, "Slavery and Capitalism: A Review Essay," *Journal of Southern History* 81 (May 2015): 405–20; Johnson, *River of Dark Dreams*, 14; Beckert, *Empire of Cotton*, 109–11.

20. Tadman, *Speculators and Slaves* 44–45; Pargas, *Slavery and Forced Migration*, 40; Kenneth M. Stampp, *The Peculiar Institution: Slavery in the Ante-bellum South* (New York: Alfred A. Knopf, 1956; repr. New York: Vintage Books, 1964), 239; Stanley Elkins, *Slavery: A Problem in American Institutional and Intellectual Life* (Chicago: University of Chicago Press, 1959), 209, 211; Frederic Bancroft, *Slave Trading in the Old South* (New York: Frederick Ungar, 1931), 3–35; Winfield H. Collins, *The Domestic Slave Trade of the Southern States* (New York: Broadway, 1904), 61–77; Stanley L. Engerman and Eugene D. Genovese, eds., *Race and Slavery in the Western Hemisphere: Quantitative Studies* (Princeton, NJ: Princeton University Press, 1975), 173–210; "Slave Trade," *Florida Advocate* (Tallahassee), May 10, 1845; "Another Slaver," *Ocala (FL) Home Companion*, May 16, 1858.

21. Pargas, *Slavery and Forced Migration*, 49–50; Sheppard interview; Benjamin Drew, ed., *A North-Side View of Slavery: The Refugee; or The Narratives of Fugitive Slaves in Canada* (Boston: John P. Jewett, 1856, 1st repr., New York: Johnson Reprint, 1969), 284.

22. Baptist, *Half Has Never Been Told*, 47, 147–48; Oakes, *Slavery and Freedom*, 134–35; Follett et al., *Plantation Kingdom*, 47.

23. Cythina A. Kierner, *Martha Jefferson Randolph, Daughter of Monticello: Her Life and Times* (Chapel Hill: University of North Carolina Press, 2012), 233; Martin, *Florida during the Territorial Days*, 53–68; T. D. Allman, *Finding Florida: The True History of the Sunshine State* (New York: Atlantic Monthly Press, 2013), 122; Bertram Groene, *Ante-bellum Tallahassee* (Tallahassee: Florida Heritage Foundation, 1981), 44–45; "Florida Land Agency," *Alexandria (VA) Gazette*, August 18, 1827. On William Pope DuVal, see James Denham's excellent *Florida Founder William P. DuVal: Frontier Bon Vivant* (Columbia: University of South Carolina Press, 2015).

24. "Florida," *Alexandria (VA) Gazette*, April 6, 1826; "Florida," *Niles' Weekly Register* (Baltimore, MD), September 22, 1827, and November 29, 1828; "Florida," *Commercial Compiler* (Richmond, VA), May 27, 1828.

25. "Florida," *Alexandria (VA) Gazette*, April 6, 1826; "Florida," *Niles' Weekly Register* (Baltimore, MD), September 22, 1827, and November 29, 1828; "Florida," *Commercial Compiler* (Richmond, VA), May 27, 1828.

26. Samuel Parkhill to John Parkhill, August 16, 1827, folder 2, John Parkhill Papers; "Loss of the Ship Aurora," *Spectator* (New York), November 13, 1827; *New York Daily Advertiser*, November 13, 1827, 2.

27. Richmond, VA, tax receipt, John Parkhill, debtor, August 27, 1827, folder 2, John Parkhill Papers; "For Sale or Rent," *Daily Richmond (VA) Whig and Public Advertiser*, January 21, 1833; "Virginia," *Daily Richmond (VA) Whig and Public Advertiser*, March 7, 1833.

28. Groene, *Ante-bellum Tallahassee*, 44; Bertram Groene, "Lizzie Brown's Tallahassee," *Florida Historical Quarterly* 48 (October 1965): 155–56; John Gamble to James Monroe, October 25, 1827, James Monroe Papers, Library of Congress, Washington, DC; Nicholas War Eppes, "Francis Eppes (1801–1888), Pioneer of Florida," *Florida Historical Quarterly* 5 (October 1926): 5–96; Michael G. Schene,

"Robert and John Grattan Gamble: Middle Florida Entrepreneurs," *Florida Historical Quarterly* 54 (July 1975): 62; "Meteorological Observations," *Alexandria (VA) Gazette*, November 2, 1827; "The Weather," *City Gazette* (Charleston, SC), November 22, 1827; "The Season," *Macon (GA) Weekly Telegraph*, December 24, 1827.

29. Groene, "Lizzie Brown's Tallahassee," 155–56.

30. Robert Gamble Jr., notebook (photocopy), 55–56, Jefferson County Historical Society, Monticello, FL; Shelia L. Martin, "Leaving Virginia and Coming South from the Notes of Major Robert Gamble (1813–1906)," *Tallahassee Genealogist* 20 (Fall 2000): 9–10; Schene, "Robert and John Grattan Gamble," 62; Baptist, *Half Has Never Been Told*, 32.

31. Terri L. Synder, *The Power to Die: Slavery and Suicide in British North America* (Chicago: University of Chicago Press, 2015), 7–12; Baptist, *Half Has Never Been Told*, 32; "List of Letters," *Augusta Chronicle and Georgia Advertiser*, December 4, 1827; see also Charles Ball, *Slavery in the United States: A Narrative of the Life and Adventures of Charles Ball, a Black Man, Who Lived Forty Years in Maryland, South Carolina and Georgia, as a Slave, under Various Masters, and Was One Year in the Navy with Commodore Barney, during the Late War, Containing an Account of the Manners and Treatment of Slaves, with Observations upon the State of Morals amongst the Cotton Planters, and the Perils and Sufferings of a Fugitive Slave, Who Twice Escaped from the Cotton Country* (New York: John S. Taylor, 1837).

32. Sheppard interview; Edward Baptist, "The Migration of Planters to Antebellum Florida: Kinship and Power," *Journal of Southern History* (August 1996): 536; Baptist, *Half Has Never Been Told*, 2; Baptist, *Creating an Old South*, 67–72; see also Frances Elizabeth Brown Douglass memoirs, folder 19, Florida State University, Strozier Library Special Collections, Tallahassee; Thomas Brown memoir, Florida folder 1, Ambler-Brown Papers, Duke University, Durham, NC; Joan Cashin, *Family Venture: Men and Women on the Southern Frontier* (Baltimore: Johns Hopkins University Press, 1991), 57; Johnson, *River of Dark Dreams*, 14.

33. Pargas, *Slavery and Forced Migration*, 114–15; Sheppard interview. See also Johnson, *Soul by Soul*, 41–65; Jonathan B. Pritchett, "Quantitative Estimates of the United States Interregional Slave Trade, 1820–1862," *Journal of Economic History* 61 (June 2001): 467–75; Jonathan B. Pritchett, "The Interregional Slave Trade and the Selection of Slaves for the New Orleans Market," *Journal of Interdisciplinary History* 28 (Summer 1997): 57–85; Steven Deyle, "The Irony of Liberty: Origins of the Domestic Slave Trade," *Journal of Early Republic* 12 (Spring 1992): 37–62; Laurence J. Kotlikoff and Sebastian Pinera, "The Old South's Stake in the Inter-regional Movement of Slaves, 1850–1860," *Journal of Economic History* 37 (June 1977): 434–50.

34. John Brown, *Slave Life in Georgia: A Narrative of the Life, Sufferings and Escape of John Brown* (London: L. A. Chamberovzow, 1855), 16–19; John S. David, *The American Colonization Society and the Founding of the First African Republic* (Bloomington, IN: Universe, 2014), 46; Alexandra Finley, "'Cash to Corinna': Domestic Labor and Sexual Economy in the 'Fancy Trade,'" *Journal of American History* 104 (September 2017): 410–30.

35. Sheppard interview.

36. Pargas, *Slavery and Forced Migration*, 112; Sheppard interview.

37. Sheppard interview.

Chapter 3 • *A New Environment and Responsibilities as an Overseer*

1. Jack Sheppard interview with James Page, January 21–22, 1880, Bethel Missionary Baptist Church Library, Tallahassee, FL.

2. "Domestic," *Pensacola Gazette and West Florida Advertiser*, November 2, 1827. On Middle Florida conditions at the time of the Parkhill party's arrival, see also Edward Baptist, *Creating an Old South: Middle Florida's Plantation Frontier before the Civil War* (Chapel Hill: University of North Carolina Press, 2000); Julia Smith, *Slavery and Plantation Growth in Antebellum Florida, 1821–1860* (Gainesville: University of Florida Press, 1973); Sidney Walker Martin, *Florida during the Territorial Days* (Athens: University of Georgia Press, 1944); Clifton Paisley, *The Red Hills of Florida, 1528–1865* (Tuscaloosa: University of Alabama Press, 1989). On regional conditions for slaves, see Larry Eugene Rivers, *Slavery in Florida: Territorial Days to Emancipation* (Gainesville: University Press of Florida, 2000).

3. Laura Wirt Randall to William Wirt, September 30, 1827, reel 9, William Wirt Papers, Maryland Historical Society, Baltimore; James M. Denham, *Florida Founder William P. DuVal: Frontier Bon Vivant* (Columbia: University of South Carolina Press, 2015), 127–28; "Florida Legislature," *Pensacola Gazette and West Florida Advertiser*, January 18, 1828; "General Description of Middle Florida," *Recorder* (Boston), December 11, 1828;

4. "Tallahassee, Florida," *Daily National Intelligencer* (Washington, DC), December 28, 1827, 3; James M. Denham, *"A Rogue's Paradise": Crime and Punishment in Antebellum Florida, 1821–1861* (Tuscaloosa: University of Alabama Press, 1997), x–xi.

5. Martin, *Florida during the Territorial Days*, 1–37; Bertram Groene, *Ante-bellum Tallahassee* (Tallahassee: Florida Heritage Foundation, 1981), 13–21; Paisley, *Red Hills of Florida*, 10–56; Canter Brown Jr., *Florida's Peace River Frontier* (Orlando: University of Central Florida Press, 1991), 1–27; Canter Brown Jr., "The Sarrazota, or Runaway Negro Plantations: Tampa Bay's First Black Community, 1812–1821," *Tampa Bay History* 12 (Fall/Winter 1990): 5–19; Allen Morris, comp., *The Florida Handbook, 1991–1992* (Tallahassee: Peninsular, 1991), 426–28.

6. Larry Eugene Rivers, "Slavery in Microcosm: Leon County, Florida, 1824–1860," *Journal of Negro History* 66 (Fall 1981), 235–45; Rivers, *Slavery in Florida*, 16–33; Larry Eugene Rivers, *Rebels and Runaways: Slave Resistance in 19th Century Florida* (Urbana: University of Illinois Press, 2012), 131–45; Groene, *Ante-bellum Tallahassee*, 23, 33–34; Mary Louise Ellis and William W. Rogers, *Tallahassee Favored Land* (Norfolk, VA: Donning, 1988), 36; Ira Berlin, *Many Thousands Gone: The First Two Centuries of Slavery in North America* (Cambridge, MA: Belknap / Harvard University Press, 1998), 10; *Vermont Republican and American Journal* (Winsor), January 19, 1828, 3; "Snow in Florida," *Daily Georgian* (Savannah), March 6, 1829; Sven Beckert, *Empire of Cotton* (New York: Vintage, 2015), 103, 105–8.

7. Jack Sheppard interview.

8. Genevieve Parkhill Lykes, *Gift of Heritage* (Tampa, FL: priv. pub., 1969), 2; Baptist, *Creating an Old South*, 16; Thomas Randall postscript to "My dear Madam," in Laura Randall to "My Dear Mother," May 25, 1828, box 818, Wirt Papers; Paisley, *Red Hills of Florida*, 88.

9. Leon County, Florida, deed and mortgage records, Book A, 389; Book E, 602, Leon County Courthouse, Tallahassee. By 1829, John Parkhill owned 240 acres, six

slaves, and one carriage. John Parkhill entry, 1829 Leon County tax rolls (microfilm), State Library of Florida, Tallahassee; George Rawick, ed., *The American Slave: A Composite Autobiography*, vol. 16 (Kansas narratives) (Westport: CT: Greenwood Press, 1972), 8.

10. William K. Scarborough, *The Overseer: Plantation Management in the Old South* (Baton Rouge: Louisiana State University, 1966), 3–19; William L. Van Deburg, *The Slave Drivers: Black Agricultural Labor Supervisors in the Antebellum South* (New York: Praeger, 1979), 3–35; William E. Wiethoff, "Enslaved Africans' Rivalry with White Overseers in Plantation Culture: An Unconventional Interpretation," *Journal of Black Studies* 36 (January 2006): 429–55.

11. James M. Denham and Canter Brown Jr., eds., *Cracker Times and Pioneer Lives: The Florida Reminiscences of George Gillett Keen and Sarah Pamela Williams* (Columbia: University of South Carolina Press, 2003), 46; Rivers, "Slavery in Microcosm," 235–45; Larry Eugene Rivers, "A Troublesome Property: Master-Slave Relations in Florida, 1821–1865," in *The African American Heritage of Florida*, ed. David R. Colburn and Jane L. Landers (Gainesville: University Press of Florida, 1995), 104–27; Larry Eugene Rivers, "Dignity and Importance: Slavery in Jefferson County, Florida—1827 to 1860," *Florida Historical Quarterly* 61 (April 1983): 404–30; Larry Eugene Rivers, "Madison County, Florida—1830 to 1860: A Case Study in Land, Labor, and Prosperity," *Journal of Negro History* 78 (Fall 1993): 233–44; Larry Eugene Rivers, "Slavery and the Political Economy of Gadsden County, Florida: 1823–1861," *Florida Historical Quarterly* 70 (July 1991): 1–19; Carol R. Osthaus, "The Work Ethic of the Plain Folk: Labor and Religion in the Old South," *Journal of Southern History* 70 (November 2004), 745–82; Edward Baptist, *The Half Has Never Been Told: Slavery and the Making of American Capitalism* (New York: Basic Books, 2014), 350; David Blight, *Frederick Douglass: Prophet of Freedom* (New York: Simon and Schuster, 2018), 46.

12. Leon County, Florida, deed and mortgage records, Book A, 389, Book E, 603; Damian Alan Pargas, *Slavery and Forced Migration in the Antebellum South* (New York: Cambridge University Press, 2015), 12–13, 218–53; Baptist, *Half Has Never Been Told*, 287; Sheppard interview; Rawick, *The American Slave*, vol. 14 (North Carolina narratives), 330.

13. Kathryn T. Abbey, comp., "Documents Relating to El Destino and Chemonie Plantations, Middle Florida, 1828–1868, Part 1," *Florida Historical Quarterly* 7 (January 1929): 206, 208–9; Sheppard interview; Pargas, *Slavery and Forced Migration*, 113; Susan Eva O'Donovan, "Changing Places, Changing Lives: A Review of Pargas's *Slavery and Forced Migration in the Antebellum South*, *Southern Spaces*," May 10, 2016, accessed March 28, 2019, southernspaces.org/2016/changing-places -changing-lives; Keith D. McCall, "*Slavery and Forced Migration in the Antebellum South*: A Review," *Essays in History: The Annual Journal Produced by the Corcoran Department of History at the University of Virginia* (2016): 49; Robert Gudmestad, "Gudmestad on Pargas, 'Slavery and Forced Migration in the Antebellum South,'" H-History: The History of Slavery, accessed March 20 2019, https//networks.h-net .org/h-slavery.

14. Thomas Randall to William Wirt, December 20, 1828, and November 20, 1829, Wirt Papers; John W. Blassingame, *The Slave Community: Plantation Life in the Antebellum South* (New York: Oxford University Press, 1979), 178; Rivers, "Dignity and

Importance," 414; Herbert Gutman, *The Black Family in Slavery and Freedom, 1750–1925* (New York: Pantheon, 1976), 11–18, 128–33, 285–90, and 354–59; James Oakes, *The Ruling Race: A History of American Slaveholders* (New York: W. W. Norton, 2013), 176–79; William Warren Rogers Jr., "As to the People," *Florida Historical Quarterly* 75 (Spring 1997): 441–46; Damian Alan Pargas, "In the Fields of 'Strange Land': Enslaved Newcomers and the Adjustment to Cotton Cultivation in the Antebellum South," *Slavery and Abolition* 34 (2013): 562–78.

15. Sheppard interview. For helpful insight into conditions of slavery in Middle Florida, see Achille Murat, *America and the Americans*, trans. Henry J. Bradfield (Buffalo, NY: G. H. Derby, 1851); Achille Murat, *The United States of North America: With a Note on Negro Slavery* (London: Effingham Wilson, 1833); Achille Murat, *A Moral and Political Sketch of the United States of North America* (London: Effingham Wilson, 1833); Alfred Jackson Hanna, *A Prince in Their Midst: The Adventurous Life of Achille Murat on the American Frontier* (Norman: University of Oklahoma Press, 1946).

16. Pargas, *Slavery and Forced Migration*, 174–75; Smith, *Slavery and Plantation Growth*, 6–7; Leon County, Florida, Will and Estate Records, Wills and Letters Testamentary, Book BB, 85–87, Leon County Courthouse, Tallahassee; Rivers, "Madison County, Florida," 233–44; Eugene D. Genovese, *A Consuming Fire: The Fall of the Confederacy in the Mind of the White Christian South* (Athens: University of Georgia Press, 1998), 3–33.

17. Terry Matthews, "Lecture 8: The Convenient Sin," *Controversies over Civil Rights Series*, accessed March 28, 2019, www.liberalslikechrist.org/Believable /slavery&southernchurches.html; John Parkhill, 1826 to 1827, 1:23–51, John Parkhill Papers; Baptist, *Half Has Never Been Told*, 211; Cooper C. Kirk, "A History of the Southern Presbyterian Church in Florida, 1821–1891" (PhD diss., Florida State University, 1966); Barbara Rhodes, *At First: The Presbyterian Church in Tallahassee, Florida, 1828–1938* (Tallahassee: First Presbyterian Church, 1994), 141–42; Life Application Study Bible: New International Version; Genovese, *A Consuming Fire*; Carl Stauffer, *God Willing: A History of St. John's Episcopal Church, 1829–1879* (Tallahassee: St. John's Episcopal Church, 1984), 239; "Ruling Elders of Presbyterian Church in Tallahassee," *Democrat* (Tallahassee, FL), April 29, 1938.

18. Sheppard interview; Blight, *Frederick Douglass*, 126; "Obituary," *Floridian and Journal* (Tallahassee), November 3, 1855; see also Claudia L. Bushman, *In Old Virginia: Slavery, Farming, and Society in the Journal John Walker* (Baltimore: Johns Hopkins University Press, 2002), 81–97; "Blessings of Slavery in Baltimore Maryland!," *Freedom's Journal*, October 31, 1828; Paul Ortiz, *An African American and Latinx History of the United States* (Boston: Beacon Press, 2018), 23; David T. Moor Jr., "Southern Baptists and Southern Men: Evangelical Perceptions of Manhood in Nineteenth-Century Georgia," *Journal of Southern History* 81 (August 2015), 563–606; Donald G. Mathews, *Slavery and Methodism: A Chapter in American Morality, 1780–1845* (Princeton, NJ: Princeton University Press, 1965), 3–61; Donald G. Mathews, *Religion in the Old South* (Chicago: University of Chicago Press, 1977), 1–38, 123, and 135; Bertram Wyatt-Brown, "The Ideal Typology and Ante-bellum Southern History: A Testing of a New Approach," *Societas* 5 (Winter 1965): 1–29; Bertram Wyatt-Brown, *Southern Honor: Ethics and Behavior in the Old South* (New York:

Oxford University Press, 2007), 99–105; Bertram Wyatt-Brown, "God and Honor in the Old South," *Southern Review* 25 (April 1989): 283–96; Bertram Wyatt-Brown, *The Shaping of Southern Culture: Honor, Grace, and War, 1760s-1890s* (Chapel Hill: University of North Carolina Press, 1982), 84–174; Rhys Isaac, *The Transformation of Virginia, 1740-1790* (Chapel Hill: University of North Carolina Press, 1998), 245–48 and 308–10; Christine Leigh Heyrman, *Southern Cross: The Beginnings of the Bible Belt* (New York: Alfred A. Knopf, 1997), 92–94, 138–39, and 155–56; Cynthia Lynn Lyerly, *Methodism and the Southern Mind, 1770–1818* (New York: Oxford University Press, 2006), 69, and 153–56; William F. Quigley Jr., *Pure Heart: The Faith of a Father and Son in the War for a More Perfect Union* (Kent, OH: Kent State University Press, 2016), 2–3, 9, 23–28, and 43–46; Luke E. Harlow, *Religion, Race, and the Making of Confederate Kentucky* (New York: Cambridge University Press, 2014), 45–75; Genovese, *A Consuming Fire*, 25, 3–33; Eddie S. Glaude Jr., *Exodus: Religion, Race, and Nation in early Nineteenth-Century Black America* (Chicago: University of Chicago Press, 2000), 34–43, 61, 65–67, and 128–32; John H. Franklin, "The Great Confrontation: The South and the Problem of Change," *Journal of Southern History* 38 (February 1972): 10; Jennifer Oast, *Institutional Slavery: Slaveholding Churches, Schools, Colleges, and Businesses in Virginia, 1680–1860* (New York: Cambridge University Press, 2016), 97–108; Alfred L. Brophy, *University, Court, and Slave: Pro-slavery Thought in Southern Colleges and Courts and the Coming of Civil War* (New York: Oxford University Press, 2019), 40–41.

19. Rivers, *Slavery in Florida*, 134–35; Smith, *Slavery and Plantation Growth*, 90; Ira Berlin, "Slaves' Changing World," in *A History of the African American People: The History, Traditions and Culture of African Americans*, ed. James Oliver Horton and Lois E. Horton (Detroit, MI: Wayne State University Press, 1997), 48–49; Ira Berlin, *Slaves without Masters: The Free Negro in the Antebellum South* (New York: Pantheon, 1974), 252; John Brown, *Slave Life in Georgia: A Narrative of the Life, Sufferings and Escape of John Brown* (London: L. A. Chamberovzow, 1855), 191; Austin Steward, *Twenty-Two Years a Slave, and Forty Years a Freeman* (Rochester, NY: W. Alling, 1857), 19; John Michael Vlach, "Plantation Landscapes of the Antebellum South," in *Before Freedom Came: African-American Life in the Antebellum South*, ed. Edward D. C. Campbell Jr., and Kym S. Rice (Charlottesville: University Press of Virginia, 1991), 21–50; Blassingame, *Slave Community*, 254; Rawick, *The American Slave*, vol. 16 (Maryland narratives), 61.

20. Rivers, *Slavery in Florida*, 132–33; Amon DeLaughter journal, Collection of Elizabeth Sims, Madison County, FL, 16, 60; Louis Goldsborough to Elizabeth Gamble Wirt, January 2, 1833, Louis Goldsborough to William Wirt, February 1834, and Louis Goldsborough to wife, August 31, 1855, Louis Goldsborough papers, Library of Congress; Joshua Hoyet Frier journal, Florida State Archives, Tallahassee, 35–36; Zephaniah Kingsley, *A Treatise on the Patriarchal or Cooperative System of Society as It Exists in Some Governments, and Colonies in America, and in the United State under the Name of Slavery with Its Necessity and Advantages* (Freeport, NY: Books for Libraries, 1971), 14; Arch Fredric Blakey, Ann Smith Lainhart, and Winston Bryant Stephens Jr., eds., *Rose Cottage Chronicles: Civil War Letters of the Bryant-Stephens Families of North Florida* (Gainesville: University Press of Florida, 1998), 233–34; Laura Randall journal, entry of November 22, 1827, Wirt Papers; Rawick, *The*

American Slave, vol. 16 (Maryland narratives), 6, 37, vol. 17 (Florida narratives), 259, 350, 355; Blight, *Frederick Douglass*, 32.

21. Rawick, *The American Slave*, vol. 17 (Florida narratives), 34, 47, 59, 66, 77, 97, 102, 120, 126, 133, 158, 165, 186, 195, 207, 213, 226, 234, 259, 303, and 329–30, vol. 16 (Maryland narratives), 6, 52, vol. 16 (Ohio narratives), 87; Elizabeth Wirt to Laura W. Randall, November 13, 1827, and Thomas Randall to William Wirt, March 20, April 7, 17, 1833, Wirt Papers; John Lewis Will, February 6, 1855, file no. 1275, Duval County, FL, probate records; Rabun Scarborough to Sister, Oct. 7, 1861, 15, Rabun Scarborough Letters, Strozier Library, Florida State University, Tallahassee; Michael G. Schene, "Robert and John Grattan Gamble: Middle Florida Entrepreneurs," *Florida Historical Quarterly* 54 (July 1975): 61–73; Daniel L. Schafer, *Anna Madgigine Jai Kingsley: African Princess, Florida Slave, Planation Owner* (Gainesville: University Press of Florida, 2018), 20; Kathryn T. Abbey, "Documents Relating to El Destino and Chemonie Plantations, Middle Florida, 1828–1868, Part 1," *Florida Historical Quarterly* 7 (January 1929),179–213; Kathryn T. Abbey, "Documents Relating to El Destino and Chemonie Plantations, Middle Florida, 1828–1868, Part 2," *Florida Historical Quarterly* 7 (April 1929), 291–329; Kathryn T. Abbey, "Documents Relating to El Destino and Chemonie Plantations, Middle Florida, 1828–1868, Part 3," *Florida Historical Quarterly* 8 (July 1929), 3–46; Kathryn T. Abbey, "Documents Relating to El Destino and Chemonie Plantations, Middle Florida, 1828, 1868, Part 4," *Florida Historical Quarterly* 8 (October 1929), 79–111; Ulrich B. Phillips and James A. Glunt, eds., *Florida Plantation Records from the Papers of George Noble Jones* (St. Louis: Missouri Historical Society, 1927), 62–63; Stephen Harvell interview, 2, box 7, folder 3, Florida Negro Papers, University of South Florida Library Special Collections, Tampa; Kingsley B. Gibbs journal, entry of December 25, 1841, Florida State University, Strozier Library Special Collections; Rivers, "Troublesome Property," 104–27; Smith, *Slavery in Antebellum Florida*, 80.

22. Sheppard interview; Rawick, *The American Slave*, vol. 17 (Florida narratives), 32–38, 58, 250, 338, 356–57, vol. 16 (Kentucky narratives), 25, vol. 16 (Maryland narratives), 6, 53, vol. 16 (Ohio narratives), 87; David H. Wiggins Diary, entry of April 17, 1842, Florida State Archives; *St. Augustine (FL) Record*, October 21, 1934; Theresa A. Singleton, "Archaeology of Slave Life," in Campbell and Rice, *Before Freedom Came*, 172; Rivers, *Slavery in Florida*, 130–31; Charles Sackett Sydnor, *Slavery in Mississippi* (New York: D. Appleton Century, 1933; repr. Gloucester, MA: Peter Smith, 1965), 34; Phillip Morgan, "The Ownership of Property by Slaves in Mid-nineteenth Century Low Country," *Journal of Southern History*, 49 (August 1983): 399–420; Phillip D. Morgan, *Slave Counterpoint: Black Culture in the Eighteenth-Century Chesapeake and Lowcountry* (Chapel Hill: University of North Carolina Press, 1998); Phillip Morgan, "Work and Culture: The Task System and the World of Lowcountry Blacks, 1700–1800," *William and Mary Quarterly* 39 (October 1982): 563–99; Jeff Forret, "Slaves, Poor Whites, and the Underground Economy of the Rural Carolinas," *Journal of Southern History* 70 (November 2004): 783–824; Blakey, Lainhart, and Stephens, *Rose Cottage Chronicles*, 226; Harvell interview; Rivers, "Troublesome Property," 115; Sarah Brown Bryant interview, box 7, folder 3, Florida Negro Papers; *Tampa (FL) Daily Times*, July 27, 1923; Leland Hawes, "One-Time Slave Sheds Light on Life in Tampa," *Tampa (FL) Sunday Tribune*, March 19, 1989; Martin,

Florida during the Territorial Days, 113; *Floridian* (Tallahassee), June 27, 1835; Peter J. Parish, *Slavery: History and Historians* (New York: HarperCollins, 1989), 66; Richard Follett, Eric Foner, and Walter Johnson, *Slavery's Ghost: The Problem of Freedom in the Age of Emancipation* (Baltimore: Johns Hopkins University Press, 2011), 8–30.

23. John Daffin to Col. Parkhill, August 1, 1854, Parkhill Papers; Rawick, *The American Slave*, vol. 17 (Florida narratives), 59, 181, 330, and 339; Amon DeLaughter journal, 13, 72; Ossian B. Hart to Catharine S. Hart, June 5, 1863, Dena E. Snodgrass Collection, P. K. Yonge Library of Florida History, University of Florida, Gainesville; William W. Brown, *A Narrative of My Own Life (a Fugitive Slave)* (Boston: Antislavery Society, 1847), 126–28; Smith, *Slavery in Antebellum Florida*, 80–82; John B. Boles, *Black Southerners, 1619–1869* (Lexington: University of Kentucky Press, 1963), 867; Charles Joyner, "The World of the Plantation Slaves," in Campbell and Rice, *Before Freedom Came*, 55–56, 70; Debra Gray White, "Female Slaves in the Plantation South," in *Before Freedom Came*, ed. Edward D. C. Campbell Jr., and Kym S. Rice (Charlottesville: University Press of Virginia, 1991), 108–10; Blakey, Lainhart, and Stephens, *Rose Cottage Chronicles*, 240; Shane White and Graham White, *Stylin: African American Expressive Culture from Its Beginnings to the Zoot Suit* (Ithaca, NY: Cornell University Press, 1998), 5–37; Rabun Scarborough to Sister, February 13, 1862, Rabun Scarborough Letters, 24; Blight, *Frederick Douglass*, 23; "John Eaton," *Magnolia (FL) Advertiser*, February 27, 1830; "Just Received," *Magnolia (FL) Advertiser*, February 27, 1830; "Jesse Ferguson, Commission Merchant," *Pensacola Floridian*, March 4, 1822;

24. Rawick, *The American Slave*, vol. 16 (Maryland narratives), 26–27, vol. 3, part 3 (South Carolina narratives), 43, and vol. 4, part 2 (Texas narratives), 241.

25. Sheppard interview; Rivers, *Slavery in Florida*, 120–21; James Oakes, *Slavery and Freedom: An Interpretation of the Old South* (New York: Vintage Books), 141; Blight, *Frederick Douglass*, 23; Baptist, *Creating an Old South*, 212.

26. Sheppard interview; Rivers, "Slavery in Microcosm," 236–37; Eugene D. Genovese, *The World the Slaveholders Made: Two Essays in Interpretation* (New York: Vintage Books, 1990), 1–19; Groene, *Ante-bellum Tallahassee*, 93–117; see also Larry E. Hudson, *To Have and to Hold: Slave Work and Family Life in Antebellum South Carolina* (Athens: University of Georgia Press, 1997); Joyner, "The World of the Plantation Slaves," 73–81; Herman R. Lantz, "Family and Kin as Revealed in the Narratives of Ex-Slaves," *Social Science Quarterly* 60 (March 1980): 667–75; Rawick, *The American Slave*, vol. 17 (Florida narratives), 35, 214, 244, and 353; Paisley, *The Red Hills of Florida*, 169; Tera Hunter, *To 'Joy My Freedom: Southern Black Women's Lives and Labors After the Civil War* (Cambridge, MA: Harvard University Press, 1998), 40.

27. Sheppard interview.

28. Oakes, *Slavery and Freedom*, 142; Sheppard interview. On plantation overseers, particularly see Tristan Stubbs, *Masters of Violence: The Plantation Overseers of Eighteenth-Century Virginia, South Carolina, and Georgia* (Columbia: University of South Carolina Press, 2018), 1–45; Scarborough, *The Overseer*; Van Deburg, *Slave Drivers*, 3–30.

29. Wiethoff, "Enslaved Africans' Rivalry," 429–55.

30. Sheppard interview; estate inventory, James Page probate estate, case file 879, Leon County Courthouse, Tallahassee; Phillips and Glunt, *Florida Plantation Records*,

97; Louis Goldsborough to Elizabeth W. Goldsborough, September 22, 1836, Goldsborough Papers.

31. Rivers, *Slavery in Florida*, 23–25; Denham, *"A Rogue's Paradise,"* 120–40; see also Scarborough, *The Overseer*, 3–19; Blassingame, *Slave Community*, 163; Peter Kolchin, *American Slavery: 1619–1877* (New York: Hill and Wang, 1993), 103; Parish, *Slavery*, 32, Van Deburg, *Slave Drivers*, 3–30; Paisley, *Red Hills of Florida*, 169; Benjamin Drew, *The Refugee, or The Narratives of Fugitive Slavers in Canada, 1856* (New York: Johnson Reprint, 1968), 19, 166.

32. Sheppard interview.

33. Rawick, *The American Slave*, vol. 17 (Florida narratives), 353.

34. Sheppard interview; Rawick, *The American Slave*, vol. 17 (Florida narratives), 353; Pine Hill Plantation Papers, 12, 64, 72, Florida State University, Strozier Library Special Collections; Rivers, *Slavery in Florida*, 23–25; Denham, *"A Rogue's Paradise,"* 120–40; see also Scarborough, *The Overseer*, 5–6; Blassingame, *Slave Community*, 163; Kolchin, *American Slavery*, 103; Parish, *Slavery*, 32; Van Deburg, *Slave Drivers*, 3–30; Richard Saunders deposition, case 1214-A, 168–701, Leon County Court House, Tallahassee; William Warren Rogers and Erica R. Clark, *The Croom Family and the Goodwood Plantation: Land, Litigation, and Southern Lives* (Athens: University of Georgia Press, 2016), 121; Phillips and Glunt, *Florida Plantation Records*, 110 and 562–68; Leslie H. Owens, *This Species of Property: Slave Life and Culture in the Old South* (New York: Oxford Press, 1976), 5; Mary Q. McRory and Edith C. Barrows, *History of Jefferson County, Florida* (Monticello, FL: Kiwanis Club, 1935), 87; Helen M. Edwards Memoirs, n.p., Florida State University, Strozier Library Special Collections; Paisley, *Red Hills of Florida*, 169–83; Amon DeLaughter journal, passim; Smith, *Slavery in Antebellum Florida*, 20–21; Jerrell Shofner, *Jackson County, Florida: A History* (Marianna: Jackson County Heritage Association, 1985), 40; Lynn Willoughby, "Apalachicola Aweigh: Shipping and Seamen at Florida's Premier Cotton Port," *Florida Historical Quarterly* 69 (October 1990): 178–94; Willoughby, *Fair to Middlin': The Antebellum Cotton Trade of the Apalachicola/Chattahoochee River Valley* (Tuscaloosa: University of Alabama Press, 1993), 19–31; Harry P. Owen, "Apalachicola: The Beginning," *Florida Historical Quarterly* 48 (July 1969): 1–25; Ellen Call Long, *Florida Breezes; or, Florida, New and Old* (Gainesville: University Press of Florida, 1962), 35; Baptist, *Half Has Never Been Told*, 133; Philip Morgan, "Task and Gang Systems: The Organization of Labor on New World Plantations," in *Work and Labor in Early America*, edited by Stephen Innes (Chapel Hill: University of North Carolina Press, 1998), 189–220; Morgan, "Work and Culture," 563–99; Darlene Clark Hine, William C. Hine, and Stanley Harrold, *The African-American Odyssey* (Upper Saddle River, NJ: Prentice Hall, 2000), 129–30; Charles Ball, *Slavery in the United States: A Narrative of the Life and Adventures of Charles Ball, a Black Man, Who Lived Forty Years in Maryland, South Carolina and Georgia, as a Slave, under Various Masters, and Was One Year in the Navy with Commodore Barney, during the Late War, Containing an Account of the Manners and Treatment of Slaves, with Observations upon the State of Morals amongst the Cotton Planters, and the Perils and Sufferings of a Fugitive Slave, Who Twice Escaped from the Cotton Country* (New York: John S. Taylor, 1837), 213; Henry Bibb, *Narrative of the Life and Adventures of Henry Bibb, an American Slave, Written by Himself* (New York: published by the author, 1850; Mnemosyne, 1969), 116–17.

35. Louis Goldsborough to Elizabeth W. Goldsborough, August 13, 1836, no. 434, Louis Goldsborough Papers; Scarborough, *The Overseer*, xi; Michael Wayne, *Death of an Overseer: Reopening a Murder Investigation from the Plantation South* (New York: Oxford University Press, 2001), 9–10 and 88–91; "An Overseer Wanted," *Pensacola (FL) Gazette*, February 3, 1838.

Chapter 4 • Challenges, Calamities, and the Ministry

1. See Stephanie E. Smallwood, *Saltwater Slavery: A Middle Passage from Africa to American Diaspora* (Cambridge, MA: Harvard University Press, 2008), 190; Jack Sheppard interview with James Page, January 21–22, 1880, Bethel Missionary Baptist Church Library, Tallahassee, FL; "Snow in Florida," *Savannah Georgian*, March 6, 1829; Damian Alan Pargas, *Slavery and Forced Migration in the Antebellum South* (New York: Cambridge University Press, 2015), 4.

2. Sven Beckert, *Empire of Cotton* (New York: Vintage, 2015); Pargas, *Slavery and Forced Migration*, 4; Paul Ortiz, *An African American and Latinx History of the United States* (Boston: Beacon Press, 2018), 43; Anthony E. Dixon, *Florida's Negro War Black Seminoles and the Second Seminole War: 1835–1842* (Tallahassee: AHRA, 2014), 21–138; Stephanie D. Moussalli, "Florida Constitution: The Statehood, Banking & Slavery Controversies," *Florida Historical Quarter* 74 (Spring 1996): 423; Thomas Randall to Elizbeth Wirt, September 20, 1834, William Wirt Papers, Maryland Historical Society, Baltimore; Leon County, FL, deeds and mortgage records, Book E, 33, Leon County Courthouse, Tallahassee. On the Second Seminole War and blacks' participation in it, see Larry Eugene Rivers, *Rebels and Runaways: Slave Resistance in 19th Century Florida* (Urbana: University of Illinois Press, 2012), 131–45; Larry Eugene Rivers, *Slavery in Florida: Territorial Days to Emancipation* (Gainesville: University Press of Florida, 2000), 201–209; Canter Brown Jr., "The Florida Crisis of 1826–27 and the Second Seminole War," *Florida Historical Quarterly* 73 (April 1995): 419–42; C. S. Monaco, *The Second Seminole War and the Limits of American Aggression* (Baltimore: Johns Hopkins University Press, 2018), 8 and 26–44; Kenneth W. Porter, *The Black Seminoles: History of a Freedom-Seeking People*, rev. and ed. Alcione M. Amos and Thomas P. Senter (Gainesville: University Press of Florida, 1996), 111–23; Kenneth W. Porter, "The Early Life of Luis Pacheco Nee Fatio," *Negro History Bulletin* 7 (December 1943): 52, 54, 62, and 64; Kenneth W. Porter, "Farewell to John Horse," *Phylon* 8 (1947): 265–73; Kenneth W. Porter, "Florida Slaves and Free Negroes in the Seminole War, 1835–1842," *Journal of Negro History* 28 (April 1943): 390–421; Kenneth W. Porter, "John Caesar, Seminole Negro Partisan," *Journal of Negro History* 31 (April 1946): 362–72; Kenneth W. Porter, "The Negro Abraham," *Florida Historical Quarterly* 25 (July 1946): 1–43; Kenneth W. Porter, "Negro Guides and Interpreters in the Early States of the Seminole War, Dec. 28, 1835–Mar. 6, 1837," *Journal of Negro History* 35 (April 1950): 174–82; Kenneth W. Porter, "Negroes and the Seminole War, 1835–1842," *Journal of Southern History* 30 (November 1964): 427–50; Kenneth W. Porter, "Relations between Negroes and Indians within the Present Limits of the United States," *Journal of Negro History* 27 (January 1932): 287–367; Kenneth W. Porter, "Seminole Flight from Fort Marion," *Florida Historical Quarterly* 22 (January 1994): 113–33; "Indian Attacks," *Floridian* (Tallahassee), February 15, 1834; "A Runaway," *Florida Herald* (St. Augustine), September 6, 1832; "Public Meeting,"

Floridian (Tallahassee), June 8, 1839; "$100 Reward," *Key West (FL) Enquirer*, April 11, 1835, and January 17, 1836; "Union Bank of Florida," *Floridian* (Tallahassee), September 10, 1841; "Union Bank of Florida," *Star of Florida* (Tallahassee), December 22, 1841;"The Union Bank of Florida," *St. Augustine (FL) News*, May 21, 1842; "Rivals," *News* (St. Augustine), July 2, 1842; "Micanopy," *Florida Herald* (St. Augustine), July 2, 1836; Clarence E. Carter, *American State Papers: Military Affairs* (Washington, DC: Government Printing Office, 1956–62), 4:453, 22:763.

3. Shepperd interview.

4. On medical practices on Tuscawilla plantation and in antebellum Florida and throughout the South, see Thomas Randall to William Wirt, April 13, October 14, 1828, Elizabeth Wirt to Laura Randall, October 12, 1837, Louis Goldsborough to William Wirt, February 1, 1834, Ellen McCormick to Elizabeth Wirt, April 15, 1842, and Louisa A. Wirt to Elizabeth Wirt, July 14, 1844, Wirt Papers; Amon DeLaughter journal, 48, 71, 75, 95–96, and 110; Arch Fredric Blakey, Ann Smith Lainhart, and Winston Bryant Stephens Jr., eds., *Rose Cottage Chronicles: Civil War Letters of the Bryant-Stephens Families of North Florida* (Gainesville: University Press of Florida, 1998), 75, 119, 150–51, 156, 197–98, and 225; Ulrich B. Phillips and James A. Glunt, eds., *Florida Plantation Records from the Papers of George Noble Jones* (St. Louis: Missouri Historical Society, 1927), 79 and 95–96; Kingsley B. Gibbs journal, entries of September 1, 1841, June 19, 1842, and April 30, 1843, Florida State University, Strozier Library Special Collections, Tallahassee; Charles W. Bannerman diaries, entries of October 1, 1846, September 11, 23, 27, and October 9, 1847, Florida State Archives, Tallahassee; Ashby E. Hammond, *The Medical Profession in Nineteenth Century Florida: A Biographical Register* (Gainesville: George A. Smathers Libraries, 1996), 400, 445–46, 502–3, and 691–92; William Dusinberre, *Them Dark Days: Slavery in the American Rice Swamps* (New York: Oxford University Press, 1996), 84, 121; Richard H. Steckel, "Slave Mortality: An Analysis of Evidence from Plantation Records," *Social Science History* 3 (October 1979): 86–114; Richard H. Steckel, "Slave Marriage and the Family," *Journal of Family History* 5 (Winter 1980): 406–21; Eugene D. Genovese, *The World the Slaveholders Made: Two Essays in Interpretation* (New York: Vintage Books, 1990), 62; Charles Joyner, "The World of the Plantation Slaves," in *Before Freedom Came*, ed. Edward D. C. Campbell Jr. and Kym S. Rice (Charlottesville: University Press of Virginia, 1991), 58–59; Deborah Gray White, "Female Slaves in the Plantation South," in Campbell and Rice, *Before Freedom Came*, 112; William K. Scarborough, *The Overseer: Plantation Management in the Old South* (Baton Rouge: Louisiana State University, 1966), 67–68; Thomas F. Pettigrew, *A Profile of the Negro American* (Princeton, NJ: Van Nostrand, 1964), 34–47.

5. Scarborough, *The Overseer*, 55–58; John Parkhill to My dear Washington, August 3, 1852, John Parkhill Papers, Southern Historical Collection, University of North Carolina, Chapel Hill; Edward Baptist, *Creating an Old South: Middle Florida's Plantation Frontier before the Civil War* (Chapel Hill: University of North Carolina Press, 2000), 188, 334; "Two Hundred and Fifty Dollars Reward," *Tallahassee Floridian*, May 6 and 15, 1839.

6. Jerrell Shofner, *History of Jefferson County, Florida* (Tallahassee: Sentry Press, 1976), 86 and 104–6; Thomas Randall to William Wirt, October 11, 1830, Wirt Papers; Casablanca plantation ledger, 1842, James Patton Anderson Papers, P. Y. Yonge

Library of Florida History, University of Florida, Gainesville; *Acts of the Legislative Council of the Territory of Florida, Passed at Their Ninth Session, Commencing January Third, and Ending February Thirteenth, 1831* (Tallahassee: Gibson and Smith, 1832), 52–53; Clarence E. Carter, *Territorial Papers, XXII, Florida Territory* (Washington, DC: Government Printing Office, 1956–62), 997.

7. John Gamble diary, 68, Jefferson County Historical Society, Monticello, FL; Clifton Paisley, *The Red Hills of Florida, 1528–1865* (Tuscaloosa: University of Alabama Press, 1989), 97 and 103–4; Louis Goldsborough to Elizabeth W. Goldsborough, August 28, 1836, Louis Goldsborough Papers, Library of Congress; *Floridian* (Tallahassee), Saturday, December 28, 1839, 2; "Indian Hostilities!," *Jacksonville (FL) Courier,* December 17, 24, 1835; George Rawick, ed., *The American Slave: A Composite Autobiography,* vol. 17 (Florida narratives) (Westport: CT: Greenwood Press, 1972), 10–21. For an interesting depiction of the Second Seminole War as described by black participant Sampson Forrester, see "Seminole Indians' Grim Prophet Issued Torture Death Warrants for White and Negro Prisoners," *Tampa (FL) Sunday Tribune,* January 2, 1955; see also Larry Eugene Rivers and Canter Brown Jr., "'The Indispensable Man': John Horse and Florida's Second Seminole War," *Journal of the Georgia Association of Historians* 18 (1997): 1–23; Paul Ortiz, *Emancipation Betrayed: The Hidden History of Black Organizing and White Violence in Florida from Reconstruction to the Bloody Election of 1920* (Berkley: University of California Press, 2005), xxii; Dixon, *Florida's Negro War,* 7; Rivers, *Rebels and Runaways,* 131–145; Ray Granade, "Slave Unrest in Florida," *Florida Historical Quarterly* 55 (July 1976): 18–36; "Indian Warriors," *Floridian* (Pensacola), September 22, 1821; "Runaway Negroes," *East Florida Herald* (St. Augustine), October 16, 1824; "The Indian Removals," *Florida Herald* (St. Augustine), April 1, 1835; "Public Notice," *Jacksonville (FL) Courier,* December 10, 1835; "Our Indian Affairs," *Florida Herald* (St. Augustine), June 1, 1837; "To the Public!," *East Florida Herald* (St. Augustine), April 11, 1826; "Public Notice," *Jacksonville (FL) Courier,* December 24, 1835; "$100 Reward," *Key West (FL) Enquirer,* February 7, 1835; "Head Quarters," *Jacksonville (FL) Courier,* December 12, 1835; "The Courier," *Jacksonville (FL) Courier,* February 11, 1836; "Public Notice," *Jacksonville (FL) Courier,* December 17, 1836; Louis Goldsborough to wife Elizabeth W. Goldsborough, August 28, 1836 (No. # 437–438), Wirt Papers; "Indians," *Floridian* (Tallahassee), February 20, 1836; "Laws of the Territorial Council," *Floridian* (Tallahassee), February 18, 1837; "Indians," *Floridian* (Tallahassee), November 16, 1839; "Indian Attacks," *Floridian* (Tallahassee), May 7, 1826, and December 28, 1839; "The Seminoles," *Floridian* (Tallahassee), December 2, 1835; "Runaway Negro," *Floridian* (Tallahassee), June 12, 1841; William J. Sloan to Dear Captain, June 16, 1853, John C. Casey Papers, Thomas Gilcrease Museum, Tulsa, OK; "Cedar Keys, Fla.," *Key West (FL) Key of the West,* November 3, 1882; "Public Notice," *Jacksonville (FL) Courier,* December 10, 1835; "Florida Volunteers," *Ocala Argus,* March 26, 1848; "$75 Reward," *Ancient City* (St. Augustine, FL), March 16, 1850; DeLaughter journal, April 26, 1858, 79; "Mr. Thomas Footman," *East Floridian* (Fernandina), March 15, 1860; Rawick, *The American Slave,* vol. 17 (Florida narratives), 7–9; Stanley W. Campbell, *The Slave Catchers: Enforcement of the Fugitive Slave Law, 1850–1860* (Chapel Hill: University of North Carolina Press, 1970), 110–47; Beckert, *Empire of Cotton,* 107–8.

8. Shofner, *Jefferson County*, 86, 105; Carter, *Territorial Papers*, vols. 22–26, *Florida*, 25:190; Canter Brown Jr., "Race Relations in Territorial, 1821–1845," *Florida Historical Quarterly* 73 (January 1995): 287–307; "Runaway Captured," *Jacksonville (FL) Courier*, May 17, 1835; "Indians," *Floridian* (Tallahassee), November 16, 1839; *Floridian* (Tallahassee), December 28 1839, 2; Sheppard interview; Rivers, *Rebels and Runaways*, 55–58, 83, 164; James W. Covington, *The Seminoles of Florida* (Gainesville: University Press of Florida, 1993), 3–27; "Proclamation: By Robert Raymond Reid, Governor of Florida," *St. Joseph (FL) Times*, September 26, 1840; "The Seminoles," *Jacksonville (FL) Courier*, December 24, 1835; "The Courier," *Jacksonville (FL) Courier*, January 7, 1836; "Carter," *Gazette* (Pensacola, FL), June 26, 1824.

9. John Parkhill entry, Leon County, FL, tax books, 1838–1839 (microfilm), Florida State Library, Tallahassee; Julia F. Hering, "Plantation Economy in Leon County, 1830–1890," *Florida Historical Quarterly* 33 (July 1954): 32–47; Shofner, *Jefferson County*, 108–15; Baptist, *Creating an Old South*, 111–15; *Fifth Census or Enumeration of the Inhabitants of the United States as Corrected at the Department of State, 1830* (Washington, DC: Duff Green, 1832), 157; Leon County, FL, deed and mortgage records, Book D, 2–7; Leon County Courthouse, Tallahassee.

10. Sheppard interview; "James Page," *Floridian* (Tallahassee), December 12, 1835, 3; Michael Gannon, *Florida: A Short History* (Gainesville: University Press of Florida, 2003), 32; "District of East Florida-Superior Court," *News* (St. Augustine), May 21, 1842; "The Union Bank of Florida," *Florida Herald and Southern Democrat* (St. Augustine), December 24, 1840.

11. Michael G. Schene, "Robert and John Grattan Gamble: Middle Florida Entrepreneurs," *Florida Historical Quarterly* 54 (July 1975): 61–73; Michael Denham, *Florida Founder William P. DuVal: Frontier Bon Vivant* (Columbia: University of South Carolina Press, 2015), 268; William P. DuVal to John Parkhill, July 23, 1838, 1838–1839, box 1, John Parkhill Papers; "The Electors of the Middle District of Florida," *Sentinel* (FL), May 21, 1841; "The Union Bank of Florida," *Floridian* (Tallahassee), February 15, 1835, April 11, 1840, May 22, 1841, September 10, 1841, and December 18, 1841; "Anecdote," *Floridian* (Tallahassee), April 25, 1840; "The Committee Banks," *Floridian* (Tallahassee), March 7, 1840; "Banks: The Union Bank of Florida," *St. Augustine Florida Herald and Southern Democrat*, December 24, 1840; "Aging Columns Mark Site of Former Chaires Mansion," *News-Democrat* (Tallahassee), October 19, 1947.

12. Leon County, FL, deed and mortgage records, Book F, 385; John Parkhill entry, 1840 federal census, Leon County, FL, 23; "Union Bank Formed," *Tallahassee Floridian*, February 15, 1835; "Stockholders of the Union Bank," *Tallahassee State of Florida*, December 22, 1841; John Parkhill entries, 1829, 1839, 1843, and 1844, Leon County, FL, tax rolls; Sheppard interview.

13. Sheppard interview; Mary Louise Ellis and William W. Rogers, *Favored Land: Tallahassee* (Norfolk, VA: Donning, 1988), 48–50; "Sickness and Deaths in Tallahassee," *Star of Florida* (Tallahassee), August 25, 1841; Bertram Groene, *Ante-bellum Tallahassee* (Tallahassee: Florida Heritage Foundation, 1981), 53–54; John Gamble diary, 68, Jefferson County Historical Society, Monticello, Florida.

14. Orville Vernon Burton, *In My Father's House Are Many Mansions: Family and Community in Edgefield, South Carolina* (Chapel Hill: University of North Carolina Press, 1985), 27–29.

15. Rivers, *Slavery in Florida*, 117; Rawick, *The American Slave*, vol. 17 (Florida narratives), 35, 37–50, 80, 165–66, and 214–15; Zephaniah Kingsley, *A Treatise on the Patriarchal or Cooperative System of Society as It Exists in Some Governments, and Colonies in America, and in the United State under the Name of Slavery with Its Necessity and Advantages* (Freeport, NY: Books for Libraries, 1971), 14; Robert Hall, "Black and White Christians in Florida, 1822–1861," in *Masters and Slaves in the House of the Lord*, ed. John Boles (Lexington: University Press of Kentucky, 1988), 81; Mary Kemp Davis, *Nat Turner before the Bar of Judgment: Fictional Treatments of the Southampton Slave Insurrection* (Baton Rouge: Louisiana State University, 1999), 4–10, 43, 60–76, and 130–73; Robert Hall, "Religious Symbolism of the Iron Pot: The Plausibility of a Congo-Angola Origin," *Western Journal of Black Studies* 13 (Fall 1989): 125–29; "Sickness and Death in Tallahassee," *Star of Florida* (Tallahassee), August 25, 1841; Albert J. Raboteau, interviewed by Maya Berkley, Center for Interfaith Relations, June 27, 2008; Albert J. Raboteau, *Slave Religion: The "Invisible Institution" in the Antebellum South* (New York: Oxford University Press, 1978), 212; George Patterson McKinney Sr. and Richard I. McKinney Jr., *History of the Black Baptists of Florida: 1850–1935* (Miami: Florida Memorial College Press, 1987), 17, 20, 23, 24, 28, 29, 3, 39, 40, 42, 50, 54, and 117.

16. Sheppard interview.

17. Sheppard interview; Peter Kolchin, *American Slavery: 1619–1877* (New York: Hill and Wang, 1993), 105; David Dennard, "Religion in the Quarters: A Study of Slave Preachers in the Antebellum South, 1800–1860" (PhD diss., Northwestern University, 1983), 39–42; "James Page," *Florida Sentinel* (Tallahassee), February 15, 1853; Alfred Farrell interview with former bondman Titus T. Bynes of South Carolina, September 25, 1936, Titusville, FL, Works Progress Administration Federal Writers' Project, *Slave Narratives*, 52–53, Bethel Baptist Church Library, Tallahassee, Florida.

18. Dennard, "Religion in the Quarters," 16 and 30; Rawick, *The American Slave*, vol. 17 (Florida narratives), 250–53; see also Henry Clay Bruce, *The New Man: Twenty-Nine Years a Slave, Twenty-Nine Years a Free Man* (York, PA: Anstadt and Sons, 1895; repr., Lincoln: University of Nebraska Press, 1997), 72; Norman R. Yetman, *Life under the "Peculiar Institution": Selections from the Slave Narratives* (New York: Holt, Rinehart and Winston, 1970), 335; Raboteau, *Slave Religion*, 232; Stephen H. Webb, "Introducing Black Harry Hoosier: The History Behind Indiana's Namesake," *Indiana Magazine of History* 98 (March 2002): 30–41; Mason Crum, *The Negro in the Methodist Church* (New York: Methodist Church, 1951), 23, 3–19; W. P. Harrison, *The Gospel among the Slaves* (Nashville, TN: Publishing House of the M. E. Church, South, 1893), 3–19; Charles V. Hamilton, *The Black Preacher in America* (New York: William Morrow, 1972), 68; William Edward Burghart DuBois, *The Negro Church* (Atlanta: Atlanta University Press, 1903), 5; Joshua A. Licorish, *Harry Hosier: African Pioneer Preacher* (Philadelphia: Afro-American Associations, 1967), 1; William White, *The African Preacher* (Philadelphia: Presbyterian Board of Publications, 1849), 35–61; John A. Oates, *The Story of Fayetteville* (Charlotte, NC: Dowd Press, 1950), 695–701; Kolchin, *American Slavery*, 144; Henry Bibb, *Narrative of the Life and Adventures of Henry Bibb, an American Slave, Written by Himself* (New York: published by the author, 1850; Mnemosyne, 1969), 20–23 and 119–130; Rawick, *The American Slave*, vol., 17 (Florida narratives), 156–64; "Revivals," *St. Augustine (FL) News*, July 2, 1842; "Thirty Dollars Reward," *Republican* (Jacksonville, FL), September 25, 1851.

19. Chanta M. Haywood, *Prophesying Daughters: Black Women Preachers and the Word, 1823–1913* (Columbia: University of Missouri Press, 2016), 98–101; David J. Coles, "The Florida Diaries of Daniel E. Wiggins, 1836–1841," *Florida Historical Quarterly* 73 (April 1995): 489–90; Robert Elder, *The Sacred Mirror: Evangelicalism, Honor and Identity in the Deep South, 1790–1860* (Chapel Hill: University of North Carolina Press, 2016), 139; Paul Harvey, *Bounds of Their Habitation: Race and Religion in American History* (London: Rowman & Littlefield, 2017), 3–5.

20. Haywood, *Prophesying Daughters*, 98–98; Coles, "Florida Diaries of Daniel H. Wiggins," 489–90; Elder, *Sacred Mirror*, 139; Harvey, *Bounds of Their Habitation*, 3–5, Britt Rusert, *Fugitive Science: Empiricism and Freedom in Early African American Culture* (New York: New York University Press, 2017), 137–41.

21. Sheppard interview; Stephen Ward Angell, *Bishop Henry McNeal Turner and African-American Religion in the South* (Knoxville: University of Tennessee Press, 1992), 10–11; Haywood, *Prophesying Daughters*, 40–41; Yolanda Pierce, *Hell without Fire: Slavery, Christianity, and the Antebellum Spiritual Narrative* (Gainesville: University Press of Florida, 2005), 14–36.

22. Elder, *Sacred Mirror*, 139; Sandy Dwayne Martin, *For God and Race: The Religious and Political Leadership of AMEZ Bishop James Walker Hood* (Columbia: University of South Carolina Press, 1999), 28; Burton *In My Father's House Are Many Mansions*, 22.

23. Haywood, *Prophesying Daughters*, 78–79; Ortiz, *Emancipation Betrayed*, 1–2; Howard Thurman, *Jesus and the Disinherited* (Boston: Beacon Press, 1996), 30–31; Howard Thurman, *The Luminous Darkness: A Personal Interpretation of the Anatomy of Segregation and the Ground of Hope* (New York: Harper and Row, 1965); Richmond, IN: Friends United Press 1999), x; Howard Thurman, *With Head and Heart: The Autobiography of Howard Thurman* (New York: Harcourt Brace, 1979), 20–21.

24. Rivers, *Slavery in Florida*, 107; Joyner, "World of the Plantation Slaves," 73–81; Ira Berlin, "Slaves' Changing World," in *A History of the African American People: The History, Traditions and Culture of African Americans*, ed. James Oliver Horton and Lois E. Horton (Detroit, MI: Wayne State University Press, 1997), 57–59; Larry Eugene Rivers, "Madison County, Florida—1830 to 1860: A Case Study in Land, Labor, and Prosperity," *Journal of Negro History* 78 (Fall 1993): 238; Larry Eugene Rivers, "Slavery and the Political Economy of Gadsden County, Florida: 1823–1861," *Florida Historical Quarterly* 70 (July 1991): 8; Edward Baptist, *The Half Has Never Been Told: Slavery and the Making of American Capitalism* (New York: Basic Books, 2014), 200–201.

25. Raboteau, *Slave Religion*, 4–42 and 211–88; W. E. B. Du Bois, *The Suppression of the African Slave-Trade to the United States of America, 1638–1870* (New York: Dover, 1970), 168–193.

26. Rivers, *Slavery in Florida*, 107; Joyner, "World of the Plantation Slaves," 73–81; Berlin, "Slaves' Changing World," 57–59; Rivers, "Madison County, Florida" 238; Rivers, "Gadsden County, Florida," 8; Douglas Foster et al., *The Encyclopedia of the Stone-Campbell Movement* (Grand Rapids, MI: William B. Eerdmans, 2012), 1–39; Baptist, *Half Has Never Been Told*, 200–201; Frances H. Minor, ed., *Federal Writers' Project American Guide, Bulletin Supplementary Instructions No 9 #E* (Miami, FL: US Government Printing Office, 1937), 1–7.

27. Susan Bradford Eppes, *The Negro of the Old South: A Bit of Period History* (Chicago: Joseph G. Branch, 1925), 175; see also Susan Bradford Eppes, *Through Some*

Eventful Years (Macon, GA: J. W. Burke, 1926), 175; Eric Foner, *Give Me Liberty: An American History* (New York: W. W. Norton, 2017), 328.

28. Rivers, *Slavery in Florida*, 116–117; Rawick, *The American Slave*, vol. 17 (Florida narratives), 245; Phillips and Glunt, *Florida Plantation Records*, 31; Larry Eugene Rivers, "Baptist Minister James Page: Alternatives for African American Leadership in Post–Civil War Florida," in *Florida's Heritage of Diversity: Essays in Honor of Samuel Proctor*, ed. Mark I. Greenberg, William Warren Rogers, and Canter Brown Jr. (Tallahassee, FL: Sentry Press, 1997), 47; Work Projects Administration Federal Writer's Project, *Slave Narratives* (Jacksonville, FL, 1937), 234–41, 280; Edward Earl Joiner, *A History of Florida Baptists* (Jacksonville: Convention Press, 1972), 17; Pigeon Creek Baptist Church minutes, entry of July 20, 1822, Florida State Library, Tallahassee; Gary W. McDonough, ed., *The Florida Negro: A Federal Writers' Project Legacy* (Jackson: University Press of Mississippi, 1993), 28–29.

29. Spencer Grew, Lonnie G. Bunch III, and Clement A. Price, eds., *Memories of the Enslaved: Voices from the Slave Narratives, Anna Scott, Florida Religious Services, Slavery and American Religion* (New York: Praegar, 2015), 9; Rivers, "Baptist Minister James Page," 47; Joiner, *A History of Florida Baptists*, 17; Ruby Terrill Lomax, "Negro Baptizing," and Lewis Baldwin, "Festivity and Celebration in Black Methodist Tradition, 1813–1981," in *How Sweet the Sound: The Spirit of African American History*, ed. Nancy-Elizabeth Fitch (New York: Harcourt Brace, 2000), 386–90 and 391–98; Rawick, *The American Slave*, vol. 17 (Florida narratives), 280.

30. Sheppard interview; John Parkhill, 1826–1827, 1:23–52, John Parkhill Papers; Dennard, "Religion in the Quarters," 78; Leon County, FL, deed and mortgage records, Book E, 44; Joiner, *A History of Florida Baptists*, 30–31.

31. Raboteau, "The Secret Religion of Slaves," 2; Rawick, *The American Slave*, vol. 17 (Florida narratives), 35, 166, 215.

32. Rivers, *Slavery in Florida*, 120; Rawick, *The American Slave*, vol. 17 (Florida narratives), 214.

33. "Savannah Ga. Baptist," *Afro-American* (Baltimore), October 16, 1895; Baptist, *Half Has Never Been Told*, 210–13; John Campbell Butler, *Historical Record of Macon and Central Georgia* (Macon, GA: J. W. Burke, 1879), 64; Canter Brown Jr., *Ossian Bingley Hart, Florida's Loyalist Reconstruction Governor* (Baton Rouge: Louisiana State University Press, 1997), 187.

34. Sheppard interview; Rivers, *Slavery in Florida*, 114, 123, 229–50; Charles S. Long, *History of the A.M.E. Church in Florida* (Philadelphia: A.M.E. Book Concern, 1937), 55–57; Rawick, *The American Slave*, vol. 17 (Florida narratives), 35, 245; Oliver O. Howard to Lizzie Howard, July 22, 1857, Oliver O. Howard Papers, Bowdoin College Library, Brunswick, ME; see also Raboteau, *Slave Religion*, 305–18 and 163–70; Kingsley, *A Treatise*, 13–15; Edward A. Pearson, ed., *Designs against Charleston: The Trial Record of Denmark Vesey Slave Conspiracy 1822* (Chapel Hill: University of North Carolina Press, 1999), 1–164; David Robertson, *Denmark Vesey* (New York: Alfred A. Knopf, 1999), 1–10 and 41–56; Douglas R. Egerton, *He Shall Go out Free: The Lives of Denmark Vesey* (Madison, WI: Madison House, 1999), 154–74; Joshua D. Rothman, *Flush Times and Fever Dreams: A Story of Capitalism and Slavery in the Age of Jackson* (Athens: University of Georgia Press, 2012), 248–50.

35. "Carrying Slaves Away," *Florida Sentinel* (Tallahassee), April 14, 1830; "Fifty Dollars Reward—Negro," *Floridian* (Tallahassee), February 14, 1835; "Fifty Dollars Reward," *Floridian* (Tallahassee), February 28, 1835; "Negroes Still At-Large," *News* (St. Augustine, FL), January 20, 1844; "Public Opinion at the North upon the Slavery Question," *Commercial Advertiser* (Apalachicola, FL), February 8, 1844; "Insurrection of Dominica," *Star of Florida* (Tallahassee), July 19, 1844.

36. "Harboring Runaways," *East Florida Herald* (St. Augustine), October 30, 1824; "To The Honorable John Spencer, Mayor," *East Floridian* (St. Augustine), August 14, 1843; "A True Bill," *News* (St. Augustine, FL), August 12, 1843, October 7, 1843, and November 25, 1843; "Slaves Escape," *Tallahassee Floridian*, February 20, 1858; "Foreigner Arrested," *Jacksonville (FL) Courier*, August 3, 1835; "Public Meeting," *Jacksonville (FL) Courier*, September 2, 1835; "Public Meeting," *Jacksonville (FL) Courier*, September 3, 1835; "Effects of the Fanatics," *Jacksonville (FL) Courier*, October 8, 1835; "The Slavery Question," *Jacksonville (FL) Courier*, September 3, 1835; "Abolitionists in the Area," *Jacksonville (FL) Courier*, August 20, 1835; "Slave Uprising Hysteria," *Jacksonville (FL) Courier*, September 17 and October 8, 1835; "Committed to Jail," *Florida Herald* (St. Augustine), September 10, 1835; "African Negroes," *Floridian* (Tallahassee), May 20, 1837; "Insurrection of Dominica," *Star of Florida* (Tallahassee), July 19, 1844; "Fugitive," *Pensacola (FL) Gazette*, July 29, 1828; "$25 Reward," *Gazette* (Pensacola, FL), October 14, 1828; "Came To," *Gazette and Florida Advertiser* (Pensacola), November 7, 1828; "Runaway—Titus—$200 Reward," *Pensacola (FL) Gazette*, May 6, 1837; *Florida Sentinel* (Tallahassee), June 3, 1855; Shofner, *Jefferson County*, 137–39; David F. Allmendinger Jr., *Nat Turner and the Rising in Southampton County* (Baltimore: Johns Hopkins University Press, 2014), 1–8 and 96–98; Ira Berlin, *The Long Emancipation: The Demise of Slavery in the United States* (Cambridge, MA: Harvard University Press, 2015), 27–28; William D. Mosely diary, 40, Strozier Library, Florida State University, Tallahassee; Rivers, *Rebels and Runaways*, 55–57; Jonathan Walker, *Trial and Imprisonment of Jonathan Walker at Pensacola, Florida for Aiding Slaves to Escape from Bondage* (Boston: Anti-Slavery Office, 1845; repr., Gainesville: University Press of Florida, 1974), 8–14, 32–45, 72–73, 82–85, and 108–10; "Jonathan Walker Trial, " *Pensacola (FL) Gazette*, June 29, 1844; "Effects of the Fanatics," *Jacksonville (FL) Courier*, October 8, 1835; James M. Denham, *"A Rogue's Paradise": Crime and Punishment in Antebellum Florida, 1821–1861* (Tuscaloosa: University of Alabama Press, 1997), 97; *Boston Liberator*, March 28, 1845, 50; Donorena Harris, "Abolitionist Sentiment in Florida, 1821–1860" (master's thesis, Florida State University, 1989), 14; "Fugitive Slaves, *Apalachicola (FL) Commercial Advertiser*, February 18, 1849; "Abolition of Slavery," *St Joseph (FL) Times*, April 7, 1840; "The Difference between a Free Negro and a Fugitive Slave, *Ancient City* (St. Augustine), October 18, 1851; "Underground Railroad," *Florida News* (Fernandina), May 31, 1858; "Revolution in Hayti," *Florida News* (Fernandina), January 27, 1859; "Arrival of Several Fugitive Slaves in Canada," *Florida News* (Fernandina), May 19, 1859; Granade, "Slave Unrest in Florida," 18–36; Scott Christianson, *Freeing Charles: The Struggle to Free a Slave on the Eve of the Civil War* (Urbana: University of Illinois Press, 2010), 1–6, 40, 82–96, and 120–45; Stanley Harrold, *The Rise of Aggressive Abolitionism: Addresses to the Slaves* (Lexington:

University Press of Kentucky, 2004), 97–116; J. Brent Morris, *Oberlin, Hotbed of Abolitionism: College, Community, and the Fight for Freedom and Equality in Antebellum America* (Chapel Hill: University of North Carolina Press, 2014), 81–107; Paul Ortiz, *An African American and Latinx History of the United States* (Boston: Beacon Press, 2018), 43; "The Slave Case at Carlisle, Pa.—Sentence of the Rioters," *Newport (FL) Gazette*, October 6, 1847, "Black Sailors Are Restricted from Coming Ashore," *Commercial Advertiser* (Apalachicola, FL), January 4 and 25, 1849; "$350 Dollars Reward," *Florida Herald and Southern Democrat* (St. Augustine), August 7, 1843.

37. Raboteau, *Slave Religion*, 163–64; Eugene D. Genovese, *Roll, Jordan, Roll: The World the Slaves Made* (New York: Pantheon Books, 1974), 592–97.

38. Sheppard interview; Rawick, *The American Slave*, vol. 17 (Florida narratives), 10–21, 62–63, 335–41; Sally Hadden, *Slave Patrols: Law and Violence in Virginia and the Carolinas* (Cambridge, MA: Harvard University Press, 2001), 71–104 and 137–166; Ortiz, *An African American and Latinx History*, 26; Stanley Harrold, *Border War: Fighting over Slavery before the Civil War* (Chapel Hill: University of North Carolina Press, 2010), 1–69; Vincent Harding, *There Is a River: The Black Struggle for Freedom in America* (New York: Mariner Books, 1993), 21–49.

Chapter 5 • *Forging Family Ties*

1. Jack Sheppard interview with James Page, January 21–22, 1880, Bethel Missionary Baptist Church Library, Tallahassee, FL; Larry Eugene Rivers, "Slavery in Microcosm: Leon County, Florida, 1824–1860," *Journal of Negro History* 66 (Fall 1981): 236–37.

2. Sheppard interview.

3. Sheppard interview; Dylan C. Penningroth, *The Claims of Kinfolk: African American Property and Community in the Nineteenth-Century South* (Chapel Hill: University of North Carolina Press, 2003), 79–109; Brenda Stevenson, *Life in Black and White: Family and Community in the Slave South* (New York: Oxford University Press, 1996), 226; Wilma King, *Stolen Childhood: Slave Youth in Nineteenth-Century American* (Bloomington: Indiana University Press, 1995), 64; see also Bibb's concern about the religiosity of his future wife Malinda in Henry Bibb, *Narrative of the Life and Adventures of Henry Bibb, Written by Himself* (New York: published by the author, 1850; Mnemosyne, 1969), 36–37.

4. Sheppard interview, Charles Sackett Sydnor, *Slavery in Mississippi* (New York: D. Appleton Century, 1933; repr. Gloucester, MA: Peter Smith, 1965), 63–64, 316; George Rawick, ed., *The American Slave: A Composite Autobiography*, vol. 16 (Maryland narratives) (Westport: CT: Greenwood Press, 1972), 66; Steven E. Brown, "Sexuality in the Slave Community," *Phylon* 42 (Spring 1981): 3.

5. Sheppard interview; James M. McPherson, *Battle Cry of Freedom: The Civil War Era* (New York: Oxford University Press, 1988), 31; James Oakes, *Slavery and Freedom: An Interpretation of the Old South* (New York: Vintage Books), 147.

6. Sheppard interview; Reginald Washington, "Sealing the Sacred Bonds of Holy Matrimony: Freedmen's Bureau Marriage Records," *Prologue Magazine* 37 (Spring 2005), 1–3; George Rawick, ed., *The American Slave: A Composite Autobiography*, vol. 17 (Florida narratives), 35, 327, and 331; King, *Stolen Childhood*, 63; Theodore Rosengarten, *Tombee: Portrait of a Cotton Planter* (New York: Morrow, 1986), 1–9.

7. Mary A. Livermore, *The Story of My Life, or the Sunshine and Shadow of Seventy Years* (Hartford, CT: A. D. Worthington), 355–57.

8. Hubert Fox, ed., *Francis Tuckett, A Journey in the United States in the Years 1829 and 1830* (Plymouth, UK: St Nicholas Books, 1976), 56–57.

9. Sheppard interview; John W. Blassingame, *The Slave Community: Plantation Life in the Antebellum South* (New York: Oxford University Press, 1979), 35–40; Tyler D. Parry, "Married in Slavery Times: Jumping the Broom in Atlantic Perspective," *Journal of Southern History* 81 (May 2015): 273–312; Rawick, *The American Slave*, vol. 16 (Maryland narratives), 7, vol. 16 (Virginia narratives), 15, vol. 17 (Florida narratives), 35, 331; Brenda Stevenson, *Life in Black and White: Family and Community in the Slave South* (New York: Oxford University Press, 1996), 228–29.

10. Joan Cashin, *Family Venture: Men and Women on the Southern Frontier* (Baltimore: Johns Hopkins University Press, 1991), 4, 15–29; Marli F. Weiner, *Mistresses and Slaves: Plantation Women in South Carolina, 1830–80* (Urbana: University of Illinois Press, 1997), 121–25; Jane Turner Censer, *North Carolina Planters and Their Children* (Baton Rouge: Louisiana State University, 1984), 141–48; James Page to Miss Harriet Parkhill, July, 15, 1859, James Page to Miss H. R. Parkhill, March 18, 1867, James Page to Miss Harriet My Dear Young Mistress, November 15, 1867, James Page to Dear Miss Harriet, June 13, 1870, and James Page to Miss Harriet, April 13, 1875, John Parkhill Papers, Southern Historical Collection, University of North Carolina, Chapel Hill.

11. Deborah Gray White, "Female Slaves in the Plantation South," in *Before Freedom Came*, ed. Edward D. C. Campbell Jr., and Kym S. Riche (Charlottesville: University Press of Virginia, 1991), 120; Daina Berry, *"Swing the Sickle for the Harvest Is Ripe": Gender and Slavery in Antebellum Georgia* (Urbana: University of Illinois Press, 2010), 133.

12. Sheppard interview; Earnestine Jenkins and Darlene Clark Hine, eds., *A Question of Manhood*, vol. 1, *A Reader in U.S. Black Men's History and Masculinity* (Bloomington: Indiana University Press, 2001), 10–34; Janna Jabour, *Scarlett's Sisters: Young Women in the Old South* (Chapel Hill: University of North Carolina Press, 2007), 11.

13. Sheppard interview; James Page to Harriet Parkhill, June 13, 1870, April 13, 1875, John Parkhill Papers; Rawick, *The American Slave*, vol. 17 (Florida narratives), 47–51; Weiner, *Mistresses and Slaves*, 113, 182–85; Leslie Schwalm, *A Hard Fight for We: Women's Transition from Slavery to Freedom in South Carolina* (Urbana: University of Illinois Press, 1997), 34–37; Stephanie McCurry, *Masters of Small Worlds: Yeoman Households, Gender Relations, and the Political Culture of the Antebellum South Carolina Low Country* (New York: Oxford University Press, 1997), 72–85; Sydney Nathans, *To Free a Family: The Journey of Mary Walker* (Cambridge, MA: Harvard University Press, 2012), 23–49.

14. *The American Almanac and Repository of Useful Knowledge, for the Year 1838* (Boston: Charles Bowen, 1839), 109; Chanta M. Haywood, *Prophesying Daughters: Black Women Preachers and the Word, 1823–1913* (Columbia: University of Missouri Press, 2016), 46, 53–54, 61; 1 Cor. 14:34–35; James Oliver Horton, *Free People of Color: Inside the African American Community* (Washington, DC: Smithsonian Institution Press, 1993), 102–3.

15. Sheppard interview; Stephanie M. H. Camp, *Closer to Freedom: Enslaved Women and Everyday Resistance in the Plantation South* (Chapel Hill: University of North Carolina Press, 2004), 46–47; Larry Eugene Rivers, *Slavery in Florida: Territorial Days to Emancipation* (Gainesville: University Press of Florida, 2000), 87–88, 151–58; James M. Denham, *"A Rogue's Paradise": Crime and Punishment in Antebellum Florida, 1821–1861* (Tuscaloosa: University of Alabama Press, 1997); Bertram Groene, *Ante-bellum Tallahassee* (Tallahassee: Florida Heritage Foundation, 1981), 105.

16. Sheppard interview; Emily West, *Chains of Love: Slave Couples in Antebellum South Carolina* (Urbana: University of Illinois Press, 2004), 30.

17. Sheppard interview.

18. Sheppard interview; James Page to Dear Miss Harriet, June 13, 1870, John Parkhill Papers.

19. Sheppard interview; Jeff Forret, "'Deaf & Dumb, Blind, Insane or Idiotic': The Census, Slaves, and Disability in the Late Antebellum South," *Journal of Southern History* 82 (August 2016): 503–48; Marli F. Weiner and Mazie Hough, *Sex, Sickness, and Slavery: Illness in the Antebellum South* (Urbana: University of Illinois Press, 2012), 3, 8–12, and 28–29; Edward Baptist, *The Half Has Never Been Told: Slavery and the Making of American Capitalism* (New York: Basic Books, 2014), 314; Gretchen Long, *Doctoring Freedom: The Politics of African American Medical Care in Slavery and Emancipation* (Chapel Hill: University of North Carolina Press, 2012), 45–59; Rawick, *The American Slave*, vol. 16 (Maryland narratives), 30 and 52; Drew G. Faust, *James Henry Hammond and the Old South: A Design for Mastery* (Baton Rouge: Louisiana State University Press, 1982), 72–73.

20. Sheppard interview.

21. Baptist, *Half Has Never Been Told*, 281; Sheppard interview; Vernon Valentine Palmer, *Through the Codes Darkly: Slave Law and Civil Law in Louisiana* (Clark: Lawbook Exchange, 2012), 3–19; David Blight, *Frederick Douglass: Prophet of Freedom* (New York: Simon and Schuster, 2018), 687; "Laws of the Territory," *Floridian* (Tallahassee), June 27, 1835; David S. Doddington, *Contesting Slave Masculinity in the American South* (New York: Cambridge University Press, 2019), 30–50.

22. Baptist, *Half Has Never Been Told*, 235; White, "Female Slaves in the Plantation South," 113; Walter Johnson, *River of Dark Dreams: Slavery and Empire in the Cotton Kingdom* (Cambridge, MA: Harvard University, 2013), 170; Carolyn Newton Curry, *Suffer and Grow Strong: The Life of Ella Gertrude Clanton Thomas, 1834–1907* (Macon, GA: Mercer University Press, 2014), 1–3 and 67; Faust, *James Henry Hammond and the Old South*, 85–86; McCurry, *Masters of Small Worlds*, 72.

23. Kent Anderson Leslie, *Woman of Color, Daughter of Privilege: Amanda America Dickson, 1849–1893* (Athens: University of Georgia Press, 1995), 1–14; Gregory D. Smithers, *Slave Breeding: Sex Violence, and Memory in African American History* (Gainesville: University Press of Florida, 2012), 10 and 20–38; H. G. Jones and David Southern, *Miss Mary's Money: Fortune and Misfortune in a North Carolina Plantation Family, 1760–1924* (Jefferson, NC: McFarland, 2015), 4–27; Peter J. Parish, *Slavery: History and Historians* (New York: HarperCollins, 1989), 87; Faust, "Slavery in the American Experience," 8; White, "Female Slaves in the Plantation South," 113; Peter Wood, *Black Majority: Negroes in Colonial South Carolina from 1670 through the Stono*

Rebellion (New York: Alfred A. Knopf, 1974), 98, 139–41; Benjamin Drew, ed., *A North-Side View of Slavery: The Refugee; or The Narratives of Fugitive Slaves in Canada* (Boston: John P. Jewett, 1856, 1st repr., New York: Johnson Reprint, 1969), 1–16 and 82–87; see also slave narratives at National Humanities Center, 2007, nationalhuman itiescenter.org/pds/; Documenting the American South, docsouth.unc.edu/index.html; Walter Johnson, *Soul by Soul: Inside the Antebellum Slave Market* (Cambridge, MA: Harvard University Press, 1999), 115; Melton A. McLaurin, *Celia: A Slave* (New York: Avon, 1999), 1–39; Charles Joyner, "The World of the Plantation Slaves," in *Before Freedom Came*, ed. Edward D. C. Campbell Jr. and Kym S. Rice (Charlottesville: University Press of Virginia, 1991), 63–64; Ella Gertrude Clanton Thomas journal, 7:71, Manuscript Department, Robert R. Perkins Library, Duke University, Durham, NC; see also Curry, *Suffer and Grow Strong*, 5; Phillip D. Morgan, "Interracial Sex in the Chesapeake and the British Atlantic World: 1700–1820," in *Sally Hemings and Thomas Jefferson, Memory, and Civil Culture*, ed. Peter Onuf (Charlottesville: University of Virginia Press, 1999), 75–76; Rawick, *The American Slave*, vol. 17 (Florida narratives), 34, 51–55, and 77; Nell Irvin Painter, *Southern History across the Color Line* (Chapel Hill: University of North Carolina Press, 2002), 42–92.

24. Painter, *Southern History Across the Color Line*, 25, 28–32; Deborah Gray White, *Ar'n't I a Woman? Female Slaves in the Plantation South* (New York: W. W. Norton, 1985), 10–72; Drew Gilpin Faust, *Mothers of Invention: Women of the Slave-holding South in the American Civil War* (Chapel Hill: University of North Carolina Press, 1996), 73, 126–27, and 200; Harriet Jacobs, *Incidents in the Life of a Slave Girl, Written by Herself* (Boston: priv. pub., 1861), 3–39; Calvin Schermerhorn, *Money over Mastery, Family over Freedom: Slavery in the Antebellum Upper South* (Baltimore: Johns Hopkins University, Press, 2011), 110–11; Curry, *Suffer and Grow Strong*, 65–67; Jabour, *Scarlett's Sisters*, 91–92 and 140; W. L. Bost, interviewed by Marjorie Jones, September 17, 1937, and Sarah Rhodes interviewed by Mary K. Roberts, January 17, 1936, 139–46, Bethel Baptist Church Library, Tallahassee, FL; Sheppard interview; Haywood, *Prophesying Daughters*, 7; Achille Murat, *America and the Americans*, trans. Henry J. Bradfield (Buffalo, NY: G. H. Derby, 1851), 3–19; Achille Murat, *A Moral and Political Sketch of the United States of North America* (London: Effingham Wilson, 1833), 10–30; Zephaniah Kingsley, *A Treatise on the Patriarchal or Cooperative System of Society as It Exists in Some Governments, and Colonies in America, and in the United State under the Name of Slavery with Its Necessity and Advantages* (Freeport, NY: Books for Libraries, 1971), 14–15; Amon DeLaughter journal, entry of December 24, 1855, collection of Elizabeth Sims, Madison County, FL; Drew G. Faust, "Culture, Conflict, and Community: The Meaning of Power on an Antebellum Plantation," *Journal of Social History* 14 (Fall 1980): 83–97; Faust, *James Henry Hammond and the Old South*, 6–88; Faust, "Slavery in the American Experience," 1–19; Eugene D. Genovese, *Roll, Jordan, Roll: The World the Slaves Made* (New York: Pantheon Books, 1974), 417–18; Catherine Clinton, *The Plantation Mistress: Woman's World in the Old South* (New York: Pantheon, 1984), 204.

25. Shepperd interview; Thomas A. Foster, *Rethinking Rufus: Sexual Violations of Enslaved Men* (Athens: University of Georgia Press, 2019), 1–10 and 31–48.

26. Shepperd interview; Baptist, *Half Has Never Been Told*, 238; Annette Gordon-Reed, *Thomas Jefferson and Sally Hemings: An American Controversy* (Charlottesville:

University of Virginia Press, 1998), 4–5 and 224–35; Robin Sager, *Marital Cruelty in Antebellum America* (Baton Rouge: Louisiana State University Press, 2016), 1–108; Morgan, "Interracial Sex in the Chesapeake and the British Atlantic World," 52–84; Joshua D. Rothman, "James Callender and Social Knowledge of Interracial Sex in Antebellum Virginia," in *Sally Hemings and Thomas Jefferson: History, Memory, and Civil Culture*, ed. Jan Ellen Lewis and Peter S. Onuf (Charlottesville: University Press of Virginia, 1999), 87–113; Henry Wiencek, *Master of the Mountain: Thomas Jefferson and His Slaves* (New York: Farrar, Straus and Giroux, 2012), 7–17, 152–53, 169, 187–207, and 275.

27. "The Parkhills," Florida Plantations Past, More Plantations 3, accessed April 19, 2019, http://www.dejaelaine.com/miscplantations1.html; *Fifth Census; or Enumeration of the United States (1830): A Schedule of the Whole Number of Persons within the Several Districts of the United States* (Washington, DC: Duff Green, 1832), 156–49; *Sixth Census or Enumeration of the Inhabitants of the United States as Corrected at the Department of State in 1840* (Washington, DC: Rives and Blair, 1841), 454–58; "Union Bank of Florida," *Star of Florida* (Tallahassee), December 22, 1841.

28. Ann L. Murphey to Larry Eugene Rivers, March 1, 1997, collection of the author; Harriet Randolph Parkhill, "Elder James Page: 1805–1883," in *History of the Black Baptists of Florida, 1850–1985*, by George Patterson McKinney Sr. and Richard I. McKinney Jr. (Miami: Florida Memorial College Press, 1987), 357.

29. Harriet Randolph Parkhill, "Sketch of John Parkhill, 1915," folder 14, John Parkhill Papers; Thomas Allen Glenn, *Some Colonial Mansion and Those Who Lived in Them* (Philadelphia: Henry T. Coates, 1898), 1:457; Randolph Whitfield and John Chipman, *The Florida Randolphs 1829–1978* (Atlanta: Randolph Whitfield, 1987), 11, 62. As one scholar noted, Thomas Jefferson and Sally Hemings's children were named after favored family members and their son, Eston, was named after Jefferson's favorite cousin, John Eston Randolph; see Annette Gordon-Reed, "'Take Care of Me When Dead': Jefferson Legacies," *Journal of the Early Republic* 40 (Spring 2020): 10. Gordon-Reed, *Thomas Jefferson and Sally Hemmings*, 199; Clifton Paisley, *The Red Hills of Florida, 1528–1865* (Tuscaloosa: University of Alabama Press, 1989), 88.

30. "Ruined Cities in Florida," *Florida Mirror* (Fernandina), December 4, 1880; Groene, *Ante-bellum Tallahassee*, 54–55, 121, 133, and 165. Some relations believed that John Parkhill purchased the Bel Air estate as a gift for his third wife, Lucy B. Randolph Parkhill; see, for example, Ann L. Murphey to Larry Eugene Rivers, March 1, 1997, collection of the author.

Chapter 6 • Intensifying Pastoral Duties and Leadership Responsibilities

1. Jack Sheppard interview with James Page, January 21–22, 1880, Bethel Missionary Baptist Church Library, Tallahassee, FL; Yolanda Pierce, *Hell without Fires: Slavery, Christianity, and the Antebellum Spiritual Narrative* (Gainesville: University Press of Florida, 2005), 1–12; James Oakes, *Slavery and Freedom: An Interpretation of the Old South* (New York: Vintage Books), 150; Norman R. Yetman, *Life under the "Peculiar Institution": Selections from the Slave Narratives* (New York: Holt, Rinehart and Winston, 1970), 95; Spencer Grew, Lonnie G. Bunch III, and Clement A. Price, eds., *Memories of the Enslaved: Voices from the Slave Narratives,*

Anna Scott, Florida Religious Services, Slavery and American Religion (New York: Praegar, 2015), 9. The words "dazzled many eyes" is generally used to express excitement among people or an audience; they have been used by numerous writers, among them John Armstrong Crozier. *The Life of the Rev. Henry Montgomery* (Clearwater, FL: Arkose Press, 2015), 589; and James M. McPherson, *Battle Cry of Freedom: The Civil War Era* (New York: Oxford University Press, 1988), 63.

2. Jack Sheppard, "Brief Reflections of Father James Page," May 18, 1905, Bethel Missionary Baptist Church, Tallahassee, FL; Sheppard interview.

3. Sheppard interview; Samuel Dixie Jr. interview, August 4, 2019, Tallahassee, FL; Larry Eugene Rivers, *Slavery in Florida: Territorial Days to Emancipation* (Gainesville: University Press of Florida, 2000), 122; see also Ulrich B. Phillips and James A. Glunt, eds., *Florida Plantation Records from the Papers of George Noble Jones* (St. Louis: Missouri Historical Society, 1927), 31, 108, and 118–19.

4. R. J. Blackett, *The Captive's Quest for Freedom: Fugitive Slaves, the 1850 Fugitive Slave Law, and the Politics of Slavery* (New York: Cambridge University Press, 2018), 1–62; Chanta M. Haywood, *Prophesying Daughters: Black Women Preachers and the Word, 1823–1913* (Columbia: University of Missouri Press, 2016), 22–23; Larry Eugene Rivers, *Rebels and Runaways: Slave Resistance in 19th Century Florida* (Urbana: University of Illinois Press, 2012), 52–56, 96, 122–23, 133, and 142; Frederick Douglass, *Narrative of the Life of Frederick Douglass, An American Slave* (Cambridge, MA: Belknap/Harvard University Press, 1969), 338–47; Stephen Ward Angell, *Bishop Henry McNeal Turner and African-American Religion in the South* (Knoxville: University of Tennessee Press, 1992), 16; Sarah E. Cornell, "Citizens of Nowhere: Fugitive Slaves and Free African Americans in Mexico, 1833–1857," *Journal of American History* 100 (September 2013): 351–374.

5. George Rawick, ed., *The American Slave: A Composite Autobiography*, vol. 17 (Florida narratives) (Westport, CT: Greenwood Press, 1972), 244–45.

6. Sheppard interview; Antonio Rafael de la Cova, *Colonel Henry Theodore Titus: Antebellum Soldier of Fortune and Florida Pioneer* (Columbia: University of South Carolina Press, 2016), 3–39; "Non-resident Slaves," *Commercial Advertiser* (Apalachicola, FL), March 11, 1844;

7. Sheppard interview, Rivers, *Slavery in Florida*, 106–24.

8. Sheppard interview; Rawick, *The American Slave*, vol. 17 (Florida narratives), 62–63; Sally Hadden, *Slave Patrols: Law and Violence in Virginia and the Carolinas* (Cambridge, MA: Harvard University Press, 2001), 71–104 and 137–66; Milton C. Gardner Jr., *History of First Baptist Church: 1849 to 1894* (Thomasville, GA: First Baptist Church, 1999), 3–4; Benjamin Drew, ed., *A North-Side View of Slavery: The Refugee; or The Narratives of Fugitive Slaves in Canada* (Boston: John P. Jewett, 1856, 1st repr., New York: Johnson Reprint, 1969), 351.

9. Angell, *Bishop Henry McNeal Turner*, 253; Shephard interview.

10. Sheppard interview; Rawick, *The American Slave*, vol. 17 (Florida narratives), 35, 54–55, 97–98, 222, and 252.

11. Peter Kolchin, *American Slavery: 1619–1877* (New York: Hill and Wang, 1993), 148; Sheppard interview; Daniel W. Stowell, *Rebuilding Zion: The Religious Reconstruction of the South, 1863–1877* (New York: Oxford University Press, 1998), 6–7; John B. Boles, *Black Southerners, 1619–1869* (Lexington: University of Kentucky Press,

1963), 140–81. For a slave who was taught the rituals of the Catholic Church, see slave narrative of Charles Coles, in Rawick, *The American Slave*, vol. 17 (Florida narratives), 4–5; Bertram Groene, *Ante-bellum Tallahassee* (Tallahassee: Florida Heritage Foundation, 1981), 123–25; Ellen Call Long, "Essay on the History of Florida" (microfilm), 32, Richard Keith Call Collection, P. K. Yong Library of Florida History, University of Florida, Gainesville, FL, reel 140-B.

12. Rawick, *The American Slave*, vol. 17 (Florida narratives), 213 and 353; Edward Baptist, *The Half Has Never Been Told: Slavery and the Making of American Capitalism* (New York: Basic Books, 2014), 149; Art Rosenbaum and Margo Rosenbaum, *Shout Because You're Free: The African American Ring Shout Tradition in Coastal Georgia* (Athens: University of Georgia Press, 1998), 1–13; Nathan Hatch, *Democratizing American Christianity* (New Haven, CT: Yale University Press, 1989), 102–13; Walter Pitts, *Old Ship of Zion: The Afro-Baptist Ritual in the African Diaspora* (New York: Oxford University Press, 1996), 3–38; David Robertson, *Denmark Vesey* (New York: Alfred A. Knopf, 1999), 1–10 and 41–56; William S. Pollitzer, *The Gullah People and Their African Heritage* (Athens: University of Georgia Press, 1999), 1–45.

13. Zephaniah Kingsley, *A Treatise on the Patriarchal or Cooperative System of Society as It Exists in Some Governments, and Colonies in America, and in the United State under the Name of Slavery with Its Necessity and Advantages* (Freeport, NY: Books for Libraries, 1971), 13; Susan Bradford Eppes, *The Negro of the Old South: A Bit of Period History* (Chicago: Joseph G. Branch, 1925), 175; Rawick, *The American Slave*, vol. 17 (Florida narratives), 184–88.

14. Sheppard interview; Angell, *Bishop Henry McNeal Turner*, 253–74.

15. Sheppard interview; Rawick, *The American* Slave, vol. 17 (Florida narratives), 35, 245, and 353; Pitts, *Old Ship of Zion*, 59.

16. Sheppard interview; Alonzo Johnson and Paul Jersild, eds., *"Ain't Gonna Lay My 'Ligion Down": African American Religion in the South* (Columbia: University of South Carolina Press, 1996), 60–63.

17. Sheppard interview. Among the many excellent works on the historical evolution of eschatology, see Paul O'Callaghan, *Christ Our Hope: An Introduction to Eschatology* (Washington, DC: Catholic University of American Press, 2011); Jeffrey D. Bingham and Glenn R. Kreider, eds., *Eschatology: Biblical, Historical, and Practical Approaches* (Grand Rapids, MI: Kregel Academic, 2016).

18. David Dennard, "Religion in the Quarters: A Study of Slave Preachers in the Antebellum South, 1800–1860" (PhD diss., Northwestern University, 1983), 90; Benjamin E. Mays and Joseph W. Nicholson, *The Negro's Church* (New York: Institute of Social and Religious Research, 1933), 59; Shane White and Graham White, *The Sounds of Slavery: Discovering African American History through Songs, Sermons, and Speech* (Boston: Beacon Press, 2005), 120–44; Rawick, *The American Slave*, vol. 17 (Florida narratives), 146–54; Wayne Croft, *The Motif of Hope in African American Preaching during Slavery and the Post–Civil War Era: There's a Bright Side Somewhere* (Lanham, MD: Lexington Books, 2017), 24.

19. John Hope Franklin, "The Great Confrontations: The South and the Problem of Change," *Journal of Southern History* 38 (February 1972): 10; Robert L. Hall, "'Yonder Come Day': Religious Dimensions of the Transition from Slavery to Freedom in Florida," *Florida Historical Quarterly* 65 (April 1987): 411–32; Orville

Vernon Burton, *In My Father's House Are Many Mansions: Family and Community in Edgefield, South Carolina* (Chapel Hill: University of North Carolina Press, 1985), 52–85; Dennard, "Religion in the Quarters," 12 and 86; Rawick, *The American* Slave, vol. 17 (Florida narratives), 35, 97–98, and 252; Larry Eugene Rivers, "A Troublesome Property: Master-Slave Relations in Florida, 1821–1865," in *The African American Heritage of Florida*, ed. David R. Colburn and Jane L. Landers (Gainesville: University Press of Florida, 1995), 107; Rawick, *The American Slave*, vol. 17 (Florida narratives), 54–55, 86–92, and 222; John G. Crowley, *Primitive Baptists of the Wiregrass South:1815 to the Present* (Gainesville: University Press of Florida, 1998), 89–90.

20. Clifton Paisley, *The Red Hills of Florida, 1528–1865* (Tuscaloosa: University of Alabama Press, 1989), 73; Dennard, "Religion in the Quarters," 86; Rawick, *The American Slave*, vol. 17 (Florida narratives), 35, 97–98, and 252; Rivers, "Troublesome Property," 107; Cooper C. Kirk, "A History of the Southern Presbyterian Church in Florida, 1821–1891" (PhD diss., Florida State University, 1966), 226–27; "Church Duty to the Colored Race," *Christian Index* (Penfield, GA), February 2, 1854.

21. Angell, *Bishop Henry McNeal Turner*, 253–74; Rawick, *The American Slave*, vol. 17 (Florida narratives), 171–77.

22. Sheppard interview; Rawick, *The American Slave,* vol. 17 (Florida narratives), 86–92.

23. Rivers, *Slavery in Florida*, 122; Phillips and Glunt, eds., *Florida Plantation Records*, 31, 108, and 118–19.

24. Rivers, *Slavery in Florida*, 130; Rawick, *The American Slave*, vol. 17 (Florida narratives), 33, 250, 338, and 356–57; Kingsley B. Gibbs journal, entry of December 25, 1841, 24, Florida State University Strozier Library Special Collections, Tallahassee, FL; Kingsley, *Treatise*, 12; Ira Berlin, "Slaves' Changing World," in *A History of the African American People: The History, Traditions and Culture of African Americans*, ed. James Oliver Horton and Lois E. Horton (Detroit, MI: Wayne State University Press, 1997), 53; Phillips and Glunt, *Florida Plantation Records*, 48; Boles, *Black Southerners*, 89.

25. Rivers, *Slavery in Florida*, 121–22; Dennard, "Religion in the Quarters," 88; Larry Eugene Rivers, "Baptist Minister James Page: Alternatives for African American Leadership in Post-Civil War Florida," in *Florida's Heritage of Diversity: Essays in Honor of Samuel Proctor*, ed. Mark I. Greenberg, William Warren Rogers, and Canter Brown Jr. (Tallahassee, FL: Sentry Press, 1997), 47; Henry Clay Bruce, *The New Man: Twenty-Nine Years a Slave, Twenty-Nine Years a Free Man* (York, PA: Anstadt and Sons, 1895; repr., Lincoln: University of Nebraska Press, 1997), 189; Rawick, *The American Slave*, vol. 17 (Florida narratives), 54.

26. Dennard, "Religion in the Quarters," 51, 72–128; Sheppard interview.

27. Rawick, *The American Slave*, vol. 17 (Florida narratives), 97–98, 165–166, and 352–53; Boles, *Black Southerners*, 157; Amon DeLaughter journal, entry of October 15, 1854, collection of Elizabeth Sims, Madison County, FL; Nancy Bullock Woolridge, "Slave Preacher—Portrait of a Leader," *Journal of Negro Education* 14 (Winter 1945): 28–37; interview of Albert Raboteau by Maya Berkley, June 27, 2008, Center for Interfaith Relations, Louisville, KY; Albert J. Raboteau, *Slave Religion: The "Invisible Institution" in the Antebellum South* (New York: Oxford University Press, 1978), 309–10 and 313.

28. Rawick, *The American Slave*, vol. 17 (Florida narratives), 35; Boles, *Black Southerners*, 157–58; Angell, *Bishop Henry McNeal Turner*, 258.

29. Angell, *Bishop Henry McNeal Turner*, 19; Eugene D. Genovese, *Roll, Jordan, Roll: The World the Slaves Made* (New York: Pantheon Books, 1974), 266; Baptist, *Half Has Never Been Told*, 210.

30. Rawick, *The American Slave*, vol. 17 (Florida narratives), 165; Sheppard interview; Rawick, *The American Slave*, vol. 17 (Florida narratives), 234–40. For the report of the *Wakulla Times*, see *Sentinel* (Tallahassee, FL), February 15, 1853; William E. Montgomery, *Under Their Own Vine and Fig Tree: The African-American Church in the South, 1865–1900* (Baton Rouge: Louisiana State University Press, 1993), 271.

31. John Gamble diary, entry of January 26, 1847, Jefferson County Historical Society, Monticello, FL; Phillips and Glunt, *Florida Plantation Records*, 34–36, 92–93, 128, 140, and 373; Rivers, *Slavery in Florida*, 119–20; "Death of 'Dolly,'" *Republican* (Jacksonville, FL), June 5, 1851; "Death of 'Dolly,'" *Constitutionalist* (Augusta, GA), June 19, 1851; Phillip D. Morgan, *Slave Counterpoint: Black Culture in the Eighteenth-Century Chesapeake and Lowcountry* (Chapel Hill: University of North Carolina Press, 1998), 42.

32. Sheppard interview.

33. Sheppard interview; David Blight, *Frederick Douglass: Prophet of Freedom* (New York: Simon and Schuster, 2018), 87–101; Rivers, *Rebels and Runaways*, 77–89.

34. John Hope Franklin and Loren Schweninger, *Runaway Slaves: Rebels on the Plantation, 1790–1860* (New York: Oxford University Press, 1999), 19, 118–19, and 215; Keith P. Griffler, *Front Line of Freedom: African Americans and the Forging of the Underground Railroad in the Ohio Valley* (Lexington: University Press of Kentucky, 2004), 1–11; Matthew J. Clavin, *Aiming for Pensacola: Fugitive Slaves on the Atlantic and Southern Frontiers* (Cambridge, MA: Harvard University Press, 2015), 93–146; Eric Foner, *Gateway to Freedom: The Hidden History of the Underground Railroad* (New York: W. W. Norton, 2015), 91–118 and 151–89; Paul Ortiz, *An African American and Latinx History of the United States* (Boston: Beacon Press, 2018), 60–61; "Runaways," *Floridian and Advocate* (Tallahassee), July 18, 1834; "Runaway," *Florida Herald* (St. Augustine), June 7, 1831; "Runaway," *Jacksonville Florida News*, October 10, 1857; "$20 Reward," *Tallahassee Floridian*, June 1, 1833; "Notice," *Apalachicolian* (FL), December 26, 1840; "$50 Reward," *Floridian* (Tallahassee), May 31, 1839; "$20 Reward," *Floridian* (Tallahassee), April 18, 1846; "Rewards," *Pensacola (FL) Gazette*, October 14, 1828; "Runaway," *Pensacola (FL) Gazette*, February 24, 1838; Groene, *Ante-bellum Tallahassee*, 110–11; "For President Zachary Taylor," *Commercial Advertiser* (Apalachicola, FL), February 28, 1847; "$200 Reward," *Gazette* (Pensacola, FL), May 6, 1837; Rivers, *Rebels and Runaways*, 1–106; Eric Armstrong Dunbar, *Never Caught: The Washingtons' Relentless Pursuit of Their Runaway Slave, Ona Judge* (New York: INK/Atria, 2017), 161–66; Foner, *Gateway to Freedom*, 35–63; R. J. M. Blackett, *Making Freedom: The Underground Railroad and the Politics of Slavery* (Chapel Hill: University of North Carolina Press, 2013), 25–37.

35. Sheppard interview.

36. Angell, *Bishop Henry McNeal Turner*, 261; Blight, *Frederick Douglass*, xv; Hatch, *Democratizing American Christianity*, 220–26; "Colored Churches," *Christian Index* (Penfield, GA), March 10, 1853; "Tallahassee, Florida," *Christian Index* (Penfield, GA),

March 6, 1846; Manisha Sinha, *The Slave's Cause: A History of Abolition* (New Haven, CT: Yale University Press, 2017), 27–35.

37. Burton, *In My Father's House Are Many Mansions*, 75–79; "The Editor of the N. Y. Courier," *Commercial Advertiser* (Apalachicola, FL), October 14, 1844.

38. Sheppard interview. "The Impressment of Negroes," *Cedar Key (FL) Telegraph*, February 15, 1860; "Office and English and Sun of Florida," *Gainesville (FL) Cotton States*, November 26, 1864; Wilma King, *Stolen Childhood: Slave Youth in Nineteenth-Century American* (Bloomington: Indiana University Press, 1995), 43–65.

Chapter 7 • Stepping toward Civil War

1. Jack Sheppard interview with James Page, January 21–22, 1880, Bethel Missionary Baptist Church Library, Tallahassee, FL; James Oakes, Michael E. McGerr, and Jan Lewis, *Of the People: To 1877* (New York: Oxford University Press, 2017), 389; Peter Kolchin, *American Slavery: 1619–1877* (New York: Hill and Wang, 1993), 179; John Parkhill entry, 1854 Leon County, FL, tax roll (microfilm), Florida State Archives, Tallahassee.

2. Leon County, FL, will records, Book A, 3–9, Leon County Courthouse, Tallahassee (hereafter, John Parkhill last will and testament); see, for example, Marie Jenkins Schwartz, *Ties That Bound: Founding First Ladies and Slaves* (Chicago: University of Chicago Press, 2017), 1–2 .

3. "Obituary," *Floridian and Journal* (Tallahassee), October 20 and November 3, 1855; "Obituary," *Floridian* (Tallahassee), November 3, 1855; Sheppard interview; Alice Carter, "What Happened to Slaves When Their Owners Died," accessed April 21, 2019 @www2.vcdh.virginia.edu; John Parkhill last will and testament; Donald Ivey, *The Life and Times of George Washington Parkhill (A.D. 1822–1862): A Chronological Biography* (St. Petersburg, FL: Pinellas County Historical Museum, 1996), 38; "Flood-Nicholson-Copland-Parkhill-Mays Line," "Genealogy of Elizabeth Parkhill Mays of Monticello Florida," and "Cols. John and S. Parkhill," November 4, 1855, Florida State Library, Tallahassee; Virginia Parkhill to John Parkhill, January 9, 1838, John Parkhill Papers, Southern Historical Collection, University of North Carolina, Chapel Hill; Loren Schweninger, *Families in Crisis in the Old South: Divorce, Slavery, and the Law* (Chapel Hill: University of North Carolina Press, 2012), 99 and 154; Jane Turner Censer, *North Carolina Planters and Their North Carolina Planters and Their Children* (Baton Rouge: Louisiana State University Press, 1984); "Sale of Slaves," *Florida Sentinel* (Tallahassee) April 15, 1841; Robert McColley, review of *In Old Virginia: Slavery, Farming, and Society in the Journal of John Walker*, by Claudia L. Bushman, *American Historical Review* 108 (April 2003): 516–17; "Negro, Slavery—the Whys and the Wherefores," *Florida News* (Fernandina), April 24, 1858; Walter Johnson, *Soul by Soul: Inside the Antebellum Slave Market* (Cambridge, MA: Harvard University Press, 1999), 25–27.

4. Kolchin, *American Slavery*, 162; "$30 Reward!," *Apalachicola (FL) Gazette*, October 2, 1839, and December 21, 1839; "Valuable Negro Boy for Sale at Auction," *Commercial Advertiser* (Apalachicola) October 30, 1847; "U.S. Marshal's Sale," *Key West (FL) Enquirer*, June 13, 1835; "Master's Sale," *Tallahassee Floridian and Journal*, January 15 and 29, 1859; records of the probate court, Marion County, Florida, petition of Frances C. Blitch, July 17, 1860, Probate Packets, Series L172, reel 10,

Florida State Archives; "Estate Sale," *Lake City Columbian*, August 8, 1863; "Sheriff's Sale," *Florida Herald* (St. Augustine), February 9, 1847; "Administratrix Sale," *Florida News* (Fernandina), April 7, 1849; "Sheriffs Sale," *Magnolia Advertiser* (Tallahassee, FL), February 23 and March 2, 1830; "Executor's Sale," *Florida News* (Fernandina), January 20, 1858; Benjamin Drew, ed., *A North-Side View of Slavery: The Refugee; or The Narratives of Fugitive Slaves in Canada* (Boston: John P. Jewett, 1856, 1st repr., New York: Johnson Reprint, 1969), 274.

5. Jerrell H. Shofner, *Daniel Ladd: Merchant Prince of Florida* (Gainesville: University of Florida Press, 1978), 109–113; George Patterson McKinney Sr. and Richard I. McKinney Jr., *History of the Black Baptists of Florida: 1850–1935* (Miami: Florida Memorial College Press, 1987), 19; "James Page," Florida Baptist Historical Society, https://floridabaptisthistory.org, accessed January 27, 2019; Enoch Hutchinson, ed., *The Baptist Memorial, and Monthly Record, Devoted to the History, Biography, Literature and Statistics of the Denomination*, vol. 10 (New York: Z. P. Hatch, 1851), 310; J. Lansing Burrows, ed., *American Baptist Register for 1852* (Philadelphia: American Baptist Publican Society, 1853), 48–49; Sven Beckert, *Empire of Cotton* (New York: Vintage, 2015), 221.

6. "James Page"; McKinney and McKinney, *History of the Black Baptists of Florida*, 19–21; Shofner, *Daniel Ladd*, 112; John Parkhill to Robert Parkhill, September 27, 1851, John Parkhill Papers; "Distinguished Arrival," *Sentinel* (Tallahassee, FL), February 15, 1853.

7. Sheppard interview.

8. "Terrible Storm," *Floridian and Journal* (Tallahassee), August 30, 1851; John Parkhill to Robert Parkhill, September 27, 1851, John Parkhill Papers; "Distinguished Arrival," *Sentinel* (Tallahassee, FL), February 15, 1853.

9. John Parkhill last will and testament; Ivey, *George Washington Parkhill*, 11; Censer, *North Carolina Planters and Their Children*, 140.

10. John Parkhill last will and testament; Ivey, *George Washington Parkhill*, 11.

11. David Dennard, "Religion in the Quarters: A Study of Slave Preachers in the Antebellum South, 1800–1860" (PhD diss., Northwestern University, 1983), 63–65; John Parkhill last will and testament.

12. Thelma Bates, "The Legal Status of the Negro in Florida," *Florida Historical Society* 7 (January 1928): 159–81; Joseph Klebaner, "American Manumission Laws and the Responsibility for Supporting Slaves," *Virginia Magazine of History and Biography* 6 (October 1955): 445–46; An Act to Prevent the Manumission of Slaves, in Certain Cases, in This Territory, *Acts of the Florida Legislative Council of the Territory of Florida: Passed at Their Eighth Session, 1829*, November 21, 1829 (Tallahassee: Printed at the Floridian & Advocate Office, 1829), 134–35, Florida State Archives, Tallahassee.

13. Andrew Levy, *The First Emancipator: The Forgotten Story of Robert Carter, the Founding Father Who Freed His Slaves* (New York: Random House, 2015), 27–29 and 181–83; Marfe Ferguson Delano, *George Washington, His Slaves, and His Revolutionary Transformation* (Washington, DC: National Geographic Books, 2013), 49–54; Schwartz, *Ties That Bound*, 238–39; John McCullough, *John Adams* (New York: Simon & Schuster, 2001), 649.

14. E. Gordon Bigelow, *Frontier Eden* (Tallahassee: Florida Press, 1966), 37–38; last will and testament of Zephaniah Kingsley (transcript), box 1, Zephaniah Kinsley

collection, P. K. Yonge Library of Florida History, University of Florida Libraries, Gainesville. On Zephaniah Kingsley, see Daniel L. Schafer, *Zephaniah Kingsley Jr. and the Atlantic World: Slave Trader, Plantation Owner, Emancipator* (Gainesville: University Press of Florida, 2013). On Anna Madgigine Jai Kingsley, see Daniel L. Schafer, *Anna Madgigine Jai Kingsley: African Princess, Florida Slave, Plantation Owner* (Gainesville: University Press of Florida, 2018).

15. Larry Eugene Rivers, "A Troublesome Property: Master-Slave Relations in Florida, 1821–1865," in *The African American Heritage of Florida*, ed. David R. Colburn and Jane L. Landers (Gainesville: University Press of Florida, 1995), 104–27; George Rawick, ed., *The American Slave: A Composite Autobiography*, vol. 17 (Florida narratives) (Westport: CT: Greenwood Press, 1972), 214 and 244–45; Gary Mormino, ed., "Florida Slave Narratives," *Florida Historical Quarterly* 66 (April 1988): 411–12; Dennard, "Religion in the Quarters," 57–62.

16. Rawick, *The American Slave*, vol. 17 (Florida narratives), 33, 250, 338, and 356–57; "A Church Constituted at Belair," *Christian Index* (Macon, GA), February 27, 1861; John B. Boles, *Black Southerners 1619–1869* (Lexington: University of Kentucky Press, 1963), 39; Sheppard interview; Phillip D. Morgan, *Slave Counterpoint: Black Culture in the Eighteenth-Century Chesapeake and Lowcountry* (Chapel Hill: University of North Carolina Press, 1998), 23–139; Ira Berlin, "Slaves' Changing World," in *A History of the African American People: The History, Traditions and Culture of African Americans*, ed. James Oliver Horton and Lois E. Horton (Detroit, MI: Wayne State University Press, 1997), 53; entry of December 25, 1841, Kingsley B. Gibbs journal, Florida State University, Strozier Library Special Collections, Tallahassee; Zephaniah Kingsley, *A Treatise on the Patriarchal or Cooperative System of Society as It Exists in Some Governments, and Colonies in America, and in the United State under the Name of Slavery with Its Necessity and Advantages* (Freeport, NY: Books for Libraries, 1971), 12; Ulrich B. Phillips and James A. Glunt, eds., *Florida Plantation Records from the Papers of George Noble Jones* (St. Louis: Missouri Historical Society, 1927), 48.

17. James G. Graham to John Parkhill, March 27, 1838, John Parkhill Papers; Ivey, *George Washington Parkhill*, 2, 35.

18. Ivey, *George Washington Parkhill*, 2–3; Sheppard interview; http://www.davemanuel.com/inflation-calculator.php?theyear=1856&amountmoney=35000.

19. Inventories and appraisals, Book C. 1853–1872, 58–59, Leon County, Florida Courthouse, probate records.

20. See *Seventh Census of the United States, 1850, Florida* (Washington, DC: Government Printing Office, 1853), 390–400; *Statistical View of the United States: Embracing its Territory, Population—White, Free Colored, and Slave, Moral and Social Condition, Industry, Property, and Revenue; The Detailed Statistics of Cities, Towns, and Counties Being a Compendium of the Seventh Census* (Washington DC: Government Printing Office, 1853), 82–83; Ivey, *George Washington Parkhill*, 9–10.

21. Genevieve Parkhill Lykes, *Gift of Heritage* (Tampa, FL: priv. pub., 1969), 5; Sheppard interview; James Page to H. R. Parkhill, August 22, 1859, John Parkhill Papers; G. W. Parkhill entry, 1860 Leon County, FL, tax rolls (microfilm), Florida State Archives.

22. "Church Duty to the Colored Race," *Christian Index* (Penfield, GA), February 2, 1854; Doak Campbell, *First Baptist of Tallahassee* (Tallahassee: Florida State University, n.d.), 4; Edward Baptist, *The Half Has Never Been Told: Slavery and*

the Making of American Capitalism (New York: Basic Books, 2014), 210; Sheppard interview.

23. "Important If True," *Floridian and Journal* (Tallahassee), December 6, 1856; "Negro Insurrections," *New York Tribune*, December 17, 1856; Sheppard interview; "The Kansas Report," *Ocala Florida Home Companion*, February 2 and March 16, 1858.

24. Donorena Harris, "Abolitionist Sentiment, in Florida, 1821–1860" (master's thesis, Florida State University, 1989), 14; Larry Eugene Rivers, *Slavery in Florida: Territorial Days to Emancipation* (Gainesville: University Press of Florida, 2000), 184, 220, and 224–25; Ray Granade, "Slave Unrest in Florida," *Florida Historical Quarterly* 55 (July 1976): 8–36; Ivey, *George Washington Parkhill*, 11; W. Caleb McDaniel, *The Problem of Democracy in the Age of Slavery: Garrisonian Abolitionists and Transatlantic Reform* (Baton Rouge: Louisiana State University Press, 2013), 45–85; Ethan J. Kytle, *Romantic Reformers and the Antislavery Struggle in the Civil War Era* (New York: Cambridge University Press, 2014), 35–79.

25. Lykes, *Gift of Heritage*, 5; Ivey, *George Washington Parkhill*, 11; "An Uncolored Account of a Colored Duel," *Tallahassee (FL) Star*, March 13, 1839; "Proclamation by Robert Raymond Reid, Governor of Florida," *News* (St. Johns, FL), April 12, 1840; "$20 Reward," *Floridian and Journal* (Tallahassee), December 20, 1851; "$30 Reward for Runaways George and Adam," *Floridian and Journal* (Tallahassee), January 29, 1853; To My Darling Wife from Eben J. Loomis, July 3, 1866, folder 4 of 4, Wilder-Loomis Family Papers, University of Florida, P. K. Yonge Library, Gainesville, FL; Sarah Rhodes, interviewed by Mary K. Roberts, New Smyrna, FL, Federal Writers' Project, January 17, 1936; "George the Runaway," *Tallahassee (FL) Floridian and Journal*, January 22, 1851, December 30, 1851, January 22, 1853, and January 29, 1853; "The Stabbing at Wolest," *West Florida Times* (Pensacola), March 17, 1857; "Jeffry Bolding, a Slave, 'Is Gone, but Not Forgotten,'" *Sarasota (FL) Herald-Tribune*, February 16, 1976.

26. Sheppard interview; Ellen Call Long, *Florida Breezes; or, Florida, New and Old* (Jacksonville: Ashmead Bros., 1882; repr., with an introduction and index by Margaret Louise Chapman, Gainesville: University Press of Florida, 1962), 181; Rawick, *The American Slave*, vol. 17 (Florida narratives), 213 and 353; Rivers, *Slavery in Florida*, 118–19.

27. Ivey, *George Washington Parkhill*, 11; G. W. Parkhill entry, *Population of the United States in 1860: Compiled from the Original Returns of The Eighth Census* (slave schedule) (Washington, DC: US Government Printing Office, 1864), 52–55; http://www.davemanuel.com/inflation-calculator.php?the year=1860&amountmoney=$169000.

28. Ivey, *George Washington Parkhill*, 11–15; John E. Johns, *Florida during the Civil War* (Gainesville: University Press of Florida, 1963), 11–15; *Florida Secession Convention, Proceedings of the Convention of the People of Florida at Called Sessions, Begun and Held at the Capitol in Tallahassee, on Tuesday, February 26th, and Thursday, April 18th, 1861* (Tallahassee: Office of the Floridian and Journal, 1861), 3, 3–8, 13–14; Paul Ortiz, *An African American and Latinx History of the United States* (Boston: Beacon Press, 2018), 62; Leonard Todd, *Carolina Clay: The Life and Legend of the Slave Potter Dave* (New York: W. W. Norton, 2018), 144–45.

29. Ivey, George Washington Parkhill, 11; Johns, *Florida during the Civil War*, 11–15; Constitution or Form of Government for the People of Florida: Ordinance of Secession, 7; Ortiz, *An African American and Latinx History*, 62.

30. Sheppard interview; William Cathcart, ed., *The Baptist Encyclopedia: Dictionary of the Doctrines, Ordinances, Usages, Confessions of Faith, Suffering, Labors, and Successes, and the General History of the Baptist Denomination in All Lands, with Numerous Biographical Sketches of Distinguished American and Foreign Baptists, and a Supplement* (Philadelphia: Louis H. Everts, 1881), 2:878.

31. Sheppard interview; "A Letter from Florida," *Christian Index* (Macon, GA), December 8, 1858; on particular churches and congregations, see WPA Church Records at Florida Memory, Florida State Archives, Tallahassee, Florida.

32. *Proceedings of the Eighteenth Annual Session of the Florida Baptist Association, Liberty Church* (Grooverville, Brooks County, GA, October 19, 1860), 7.

Chapter 8 • The Civil War Years

1. James M. McPherson, *Battle Cry of Freedom: The Civil War Era* (New York: Oxford University Press, 1988), 182–85; William Cunningham Gray, *Life of Abraham Lincoln for the Young Man and the Sabbath School* (Cincinnati: A. B. Closson Jr., 1868), 148–49.

2. Mary Louise Ellis and William W. Rogers, *Favored Land: Tallahassee* (Norfolk, VA: Donning, 1988), 56; Donald Ivey, *The Life and Times of George Washington Parkhill (A.D. 1822–1862): A Chronological Biography* (St. Petersburg, FL: Pinellas County Historical Museum, 1996), 11–16; John E. Johns, *Florida during the Civil War* (Gainesville: University Press of Florida, 1963), 1–21; Herbert J. Doherty, *Richard Keith Call: Southern Unionist* (Gainesville: University Press of Florida, 1901), 158; William Watson Davis, *The Civil War and Reconstruction in Florida* (New York: Columbia University Press, 1913; repr. ed. Gainesville: University of Florida Press, 1964), 91–213.

3. Ivey, *George Washington Parkhill*, 21; Genevieve Parkhill Lykes, *Gift of Heritage* (Tampa, FL: priv. pub., 1969), 6–7; Clifton Paisley, "Tallahassee through the Storebooks: War Clouds and War, 1860–1863," *Florida Historical Quarterly* 51 (July 1972): 48; Ivey interview with Catherine Mays, January 1996, Heritage Village-Pinellas County Historical Museum, Pinellas County, FL; Jack Sheppard, "Brief Reflections of Father James Page, May 18, 1905, Bethel Missionary Baptist Church, Tallahassee, FL; R. Boyd Murphree, "As the General Lay Dying: The Diary of a Confederate Officer's Florida Odyssey," *Florida Historical Quarterly* 86 (Winter 2008): 300–327; Clifton Paisley, *The Red Hills of Florida, 1528–1865* (Tuscaloosa: University of Alabama Press, 1989), 198–203; "Thomasville Guards," *Southern Enterprise* (Thomasville, GA), June 27, 1860; "Maj. Gen. Parkhill," *Southern Enterprise* (Thomasville, GA), June 19, 1861.

4. John Adams, *Warrior at Heart: Governor John Milton, King Cotton, Rebel Florida 1860–1865* (Altona, MB: Friesen Press, 2015), 230–33; Ivey, *George Washington Parkhill*, 23–24; George Parkhill to Lizzie Parkhill, October 28, 1861, George Washington Parkhill Papers, Special Collections Department of Robert Manning Strozier Library, Florida State University, Tallahassee, Florida; Paisley, *Red Hills of Florida*, 198; Murphree, "As the General Lay Dying," 300–327; Harriet Owsley, *Frank Lawrence Owsley: Historian of the Old South* (Nashville, TN: Vanderbilt University Press, 1990), 93–104.

5. R. Scarborough to My Sister[wife], September 16 and 20, 1861, October 7, 11, 15, 18, and 29, 1861, The Civil War Letters of Rabun Scarborough, Apalachicola, Florida, 1861–1862, Florida State Library, Tallahassee, FL; Winston Stephens to Octavia

Stephens, December 12, 1861, July 24, 1862, Bryant-Stephens Family Papers, P. K. Yonge Library, University of Florida, Gainesville, FL.

6. Jack Sheppard interview with James Page, January 21–22, 1880, Bethel Missionary Baptist Church Library, Tallahassee, FL; George Parkhill to Lizzie Parkhill, March 12, 20, 24, April 21, 26, May 4, 18, 26, 1862, George Washington Parkhill Papers; Ivey, *George Washington Parkhill*, 31; Lykes, *Gift of Heritage*, 7.

7. Sheppard interview; Ivey, *George Washington Parkhill*, 36; Lykes, *Gift of Heritage*, 9; John P. Ingle Jr., "Soldiering with the Second Florida Infantry Regiment," *Florida Historical Quarterly* 59 (January 1981): 336–37; Richard C. Parkhill to Lizzie Parkhill, June 28, 1862, George Washington Parkhill Papers; Ivey interview with Catherine Mays; E. B. Long and Barbara Long, *The Civil War Day by Day: An Almanac, 1861–1869* (Garden City, NY: Doubleday, 1971), 230–34; Clarence L. Mohr, *On the Threshold of Freedom: Masters and Slaves in Civil War Georgia* (Athens: University of Georgia Press, 1986), 286–91; McPherson, *Battle Cry of Freedom*, 395–401; Benjamin Drew, ed., *A North-Side View of Slavery: The Refugee; or The Narratives of Fugitive Slaves in Canada* (Boston: John P. Jewett, 1856, 1st repr., New York: Johnson Reprint, 1969), 249; George Rawick, ed., *The American Slave: A Composite Autobiography*, vol. 4, part 1 (Texas narratives) (Westport: CT: Greenwood Press, 1972), 50; Stephanie McCurry, *Women's War: Fighting and Surviving the American Civil War* (Cambridge, MA: Harvard University Press, 2019), 63–122.

8. Sheppard interview; Ivey, *George Washington Parkhill*, 36; Lykes, *Gift of Heritage*, 9; Long and Long, *Civil War Day by Day*, 230–34. On the Union blockade of Florida's coastline and state policies regarding production on farms and plantations, see Robert A. Taylor, *Rebel Storehouse: Florida in the Confederate Economy* (Tuscaloosa: University of Alabama Press, 1995), 3–12; see Governor of Florida to the Confederate Secretary of War, February 17, 1863, in Ira Berlin, Barbara J. Fields, Thavolia Glymph, Joseph Reidy, and Leslie S. Rowland, eds. *Freedom: A Documentary History of Emancipation, 1861–1867*, ser. 1 (New York: Cambridge University Press, 2007), 1:746–47.

9. Sheppard interview. For an excellent analysis of the term "self-emancipation," see David Williams, *I Freed Myself: African American Self-Emancipation in the Civil War Era* (New York: Cambridge University Press, 2014), 1–10, 55, and 57–58; see also Merton Dillon, *Slavery Attacked: Southern Slaves and Their Allies* (Baton Rouge: Louisiana State University Press, 1999), 243; David G. Smith, *On the Edge of Freedom: The Fugitive Slave Issue in South Central Pennsylvania, 1820–1870* (New York: Fordham University Press, 2013); Emily West, *Family or Freedom: People of Color in the Antebellum South* (Lexington: University Press of Kentucky, 2012); Erica L. Ball, *To Live an Antislavery Life: Personal Politics and the Antebellum Black Middle Class* (Athens: University of Georgia Press, 2012), 23–49; V. Jacque Voegeli, "A Rejected Alternative: Union Policy and the Relocation of Southern 'Contrabands' at the Dawn of Emancipation," *Journal of Southern History* 69 (November 2003), 765–90; Edward Baptist, *The Half Has Never Been Told: Slavery and the Making of American Capitalism* (New York: Basic Books, 2014), 402; Frederick Douglass, *Narrative of the Life of Frederick Douglass, An American Slave* (Cambridge, MA: Belknap/Harvard University Press, 1969), 4; Graham Russell Hodges, *David Ruggles: A Black Abolitionist and the Underground Railroad in New York City* (Chapel Hill: University of North Carolina Press, 2010), 4; Josephine Brown, *Biography of an American Bondman, by His Daughter* (Boston: R. F. Wallcut, 1856), 50; William H.

Boole, *Antidote to Rev. H. J. Van Dyke's Pro-Slavery Discourse* (New York: Edmund Jones, 1861), 8; David Williams and Teresa Crisp Williams, "'Yes, We All Shall Be Free': African Americans Make the Civil War a Struggle for Freedom," in *African Americans in the Nineteenth Century: People and Perspectives*, ed. Dixie Ray Haggard (Santa Barbara, CA: ABC-Clio, 2010), 84; Almon Underwood, *A Discourse on the Death of the Late Rev. C. T. Torrey, a Martyr to Human Rights* (Newark, NJ: Small and Ackerman, 1846), 9; Osborn P. Anderson, *A Voice from Harper's Ferry* (Boston: self-published, 1861), 21; Berlin et al., *Freedom*, 103–56; "From Pensacola," *Augusta Daily* (GA), April 2 and 5, 1862; Rawick, ed., *The American Slave*, vol. 16 (Virginia narratives), 42.

10. Phillip Foner, ed., *Life and Writings of Frederick Douglass* (New York: International, 1975), 3:317–18; David Blight, *Frederick Douglass: Prophet of Freedom* (New York: Simon and Schuster, 2018), 385.

11. Williams, *I Freed Myself*, 55, 57–58; Larry Eugene Rivers, *Rebels and Runaways: Slave Resistance in 19th Century Florida* (Urbana: University of Illinois Press, 2012), 156; "Our Condition," *Florida Sentinel* (Tallahassee), May 6, 1862; Larry Eugene Rivers, "Madison County, Florida—1830 to 1860: A Case Study in Land, Labor, and Prosperity," *Journal of Negro History* 78 (Fall 1993): 241; Rawick, *The American Slave*, vol. 17 (Florida narratives), 247; Amon DeLaughter journal (transcript), entries of October 1, 1859, November 5, May 26, September 10, and October 6, 1860, collection of Elizabeth Sims, Madison County, FL, photocopy in possession of the author; *The Acts and Resolutions of the General Assembly of Florida at Its Eleventh Session, Begun and Held at the Capitol, in the City of Tallahassee, on Monday, November 18, 1861* (Tallahassee: Dyke and Carlisle, 1862), 38–43; Martha Hodes, *White Women, Black Men: Illicit Sex in the 19th Century South* (New Haven, CT: Yale University Press, 1997), 140.

12. Sheppard interview; "Runaways," *Columbian* (Lake City, FL), March 15, 1865, 2; W. E. B. DuBois, *Black Reconstruction: An Essay toward a History of the Part Which Black Folk Played in the Attempt to Reconstruct Democracy in America, 1860–1880* (New York: Meridian Books, 1965), 55–83. See also Matthew J. Clavin, *Aiming for Pensacola: Fugitive Slaves on the Atlantic and Southern Frontiers* (Cambridge, MA: Harvard University Press, 2015), 93–177; Bob Luke and John David Smith, *Soldiering for Freedom: How the Union Army Recruited, Trained, and Deployed the U.S. Colored Troops* (Baltimore: Johns Hopkins University Press, 2014), 16; Charlton W. Tebeau and William Marina, *A History of Florida* (Miami, FL: University of Miami Press, 1999), 181; Paul Ortiz, *An African American and Latinx History of the United States* (Boston: Beacon Press, 2018), 68; Richard Follett, Eric Foner, and Walter Johnson, *The Problem of Freedom in the Age of Emancipation: Slavery's Ghost* (Baltimore: Johns Hopkins University Press, 2011), 1–7.

13. McPherson, *Battle Cry of Freedom*, 290–94 and 484–90; Sheppard interview.

14. Williams, *I Freed Myself*, 56–58 "Negro Soldiers Engaged," *Philadelphia Inquirer*, May 26, 1864; "The Negro Troops," *New York Times*, February 21, 1863; "Negro Soldiers—the Question Settled and Its Consequences," *New York Times*, June 11, 1863; Edmund Kirke, *Among the Pines; or, South in Secession Time* (New York: J. R. Gilmore, 1862), 90–91; Paisley, *Red Hills of Florida*, 169–209; Larry Eugene Rivers, *Slavery in Florida: Territorial Days to Emancipation* (Gainesville: University Press of Florida, 2000), 229–50; Rivers, *Rebels and Runaways*, 146–59; Elizabeth Regosin, *Freedom's Promise: Ex-Slave Families and Citizenship in the Age of Emancipation*

(Charlottesville: University Press of Virginia, 2002), 3–4; Baptist, *Half Has Never Been Told*, 400; Bob Luke and John David Smith, *Soldiering for Freedom: How the Union Army Recruited, Trained, and Deployed the U.S. Colored Troops* (Baltimore: Johns Hopkins University Press, 2014), 4, 14, 18, 37, 45, and 82–85; "Negroes as Soldiers," *Peninsula* (Jacksonville, FL), April 7, 1864; "Runaways," *Columbian* (Lake City, FL), March 15, 1865; Rawick, *The American Slave*, vol. 16 (Virginia narratives), 21–22; For interesting studies of the willingness of free blacks and slaves to join the Union military to help defeat the Confederacy, see, for example, Johari Jabir, *Conjuring Freedom: Music and Masculinity in the Civil War's "Gospel Army"* (Columbus: Ohio State University Press, 2017), 3–17; Douglas R. Egerton, *Thunder at the Gates: The Black Civil War Regiments That Redeemed America* (New York: Basic Books, 2016), 45–69; David J. Smith, *Lincoln and the U.S. Colored Troops* (Carbondale: Southern Illinois University Press, 2013), 10–19; John Ashworth, *The Republic in Crisis, 1848–1861* (New York: Cambridge University Press, 2012); Eric Foner, *The Fiery Trial: Abraham Lincoln and American Slavery* (New York: W. W. Norton, 2015); Gary W. Gallagher, *Causes Won, Lost, and Forgotten: How Hollywood and Popular Art Shape What We Know about the Civil War* (Chapel Hill: University of North Carolina Press, 2008); George M. Fredrickson, *Big Enough to Be Inconsistent: Abraham Lincoln Confronts Slavery and Race* (Cambridge, MA: Harvard University Press, 2008); Drew Gilpin Faust, *This Republic of Suffering: Death and the American Civil War* (New York: Vintage, 2008); Noralee Frankel, *Freedom's Women: Black Women and Families in the Civil War Era Mississippi* (Bloomington: Indiana University Press, 1999); William Nulty, *Confederate Florida: The Road to Olustee* (Tuscaloosa: University of Alabama Press, 1990); Benjamin Quarles, *The Negro in the Civil War* (New York: Da Capo Press, 1988); Steven Hahn, *Political Worlds of Slavery and Freedom* (New York: Da Capo Press, 1988), 55–115; Chandra Manning, *Troubled Refuge: Struggles for Refuge in the Civil War* (New York: Alfred A. Knopf, 2016), 39–71.

15. David J. Coles, *The Battle of Olustee and the Olustee Battlefield Site: A Brief History* (Gainesville: Olustee Battlefield Citizen Support Organization, 1992), 1–23; Luke and Smith, *Soldiering for Freedom*, 14, 92–95; Rivers, *Slavery in Florida*, 151–52; John David Smith, ed., *Black Soldiers in Blue: African American Troops in the Civil War Era* (Chapel Hill: University of North Carolina Press, 2002), 8–29; Frankie H. Fennell, "Blacks in Jacksonville, 1840–1865" (master's thesis, Florida State University, 1978), 77–100; David J. Coles, "'They Fought like Devils': Black Troops in Florida during the Civil War," in *Florida's Heritage of Diversity: Essays in Honor of Samuel*, ed. Mark I. Greenberg, William Warren Rogers, and Canter Brown Jr. (Tallahassee: Sentry Press, 1997), 38–39; Harvey Argyle, *As I Saw* (San Francisco: Home, 1902), 1–7; *A Voice from Rebel Prisons: Giving an Account of Some of the Horrors of Stockades at Andersonville, Milan, and Other Prisons, by a Returned Prisoner of War* (Boston: George C. Rand and Avery, 1865), 4; William Penniman reminiscences, January 28, 1862, to May 10, 1865, Southern Historical Collection, University of North Carolina, Chapel Hill; "Letters from Confederate Soldiers, 1861–1865" (transcript), Georgia Department of Archives and History, Atlanta, 481.

16. David J. Coles, "'Far from Fields of Glory'" (PhD diss., Florida State University, 1996), 315–64; Steven M. Stowe, ed., *A Southern Practice: The Diary and Autobiography of Charles A. Hentz M.D.* (Charlottesville: University Press of Virginia, 2000),

603–604; "News by Rebel Sources: Battle Near Newport, Florida," *Florida Union* (Jacksonville), March 11, 1865; "The Yankees Routed," *Daily Constitutionalist* (Augusta, GA), March 19, 1865; "Florida," *New York Herald*, March 22, 1865.

17. Stowe, *Southern Practice*, 603–510; "The Recent Advance on Tallahassee," *Daily Constitutionalist* (Augusta, GA), March 28, 1865.

18. "Last Note on Natural Bridge Controversy," *Tallahassee (FL) Democrat*, November 7, 1918; "The Recent Advance on Tallahassee," *Daily Constitutionalist* (Augusta, GA), March 28, 1865.

19. David J. Coles, "Unpretending Service: The James L. Davis, the Tahoma, and the East Gulf Blockading Squadron," *Florida Historical Quarterly* 71 (July 1992): 41–62; Taylor, *Rebel Storehouse*, 44–65; Tracey Revels, *Florida's Civil War: Terrible Sacrifices* (Macon, GA: Mercer University Press, 2016), 95–100, 139, 154, and 161.

20. Susan Bradford Eppes, *Through Some Eventful Years* (Macon, GA: J. W. Burke, 1926), 207–8; "The Impressment of Negroes," *Cedar Key (FL) Telegraph*, February 15, 1860; "Office and English and Suv of Florida," *Gainesville (FL) Cotton States*, November 26, 1864; "Hire of Negroes, Teams, Wagons and Drivers," *Gainesville (FL) Cotton States*, March 19, 1864; "Negro Volunteers," *Peninsula* (Fernandina), September 24, 1864; "$25 Reward," *Jacksonville (FL) Southern Rights*, October 4, 1862; Official Records of the Union and Confederate Navies in the War of the Rebellion, series 1, vol. 1, report of Lt. Howell, U.S.N., off Sea Horse Key, February 1862, Naval War of the Rebellion file (Washington, DC: Government Printing Office, 1894–1922), 134–136, Cornell University Library, Ithaca, New York; "An Agency to Assist Fugitive Slaves to Return to Their Masters," *East Floridian* (Fernandina), March 15, 1860; "Success of General Banks with the Negroes," *Peninsula* (Jacksonville, FL), April 14, 1864; "Confederate Employment of Negro Troops," *Quincy (FL) Semi-weekly Dispatch*, March 15, 1865; "By Telegraph," *Lake City (FL) Columbian*, August 12, 1863; "Negroes as Soldiers," *Jacksonville (FL) Peninsula*, April 7, 1864; Drew Glipin Faust, in *Before Freedom Came*, ed. Edward D. C. Campbell Jr. and Kym S. Rice (Charlottesville: University Press of Virginia, 1991), 18.

21. Lykes, *Gift of Heritage*, 8–10.

22. "Ordination," *Christian Index* (Macon, GA), April 4, 1860; William Cathcart, ed., *The Baptist Encyclopedia: Dictionary of the Doctrines, Ordinances, Usages, Confessions of Faith, Suffering, Labors, and Successes, and the General History of the Baptist Denomination in All Lands, with Numerous Biographical Sketches of Distinguished American and Foreign Baptists, and a Supplement* (Philadelphia: Louis H. Everts, 1881), 2:207.

23. Sheppard interview. On particular churches and congregations, see WPA Church Records at Florida Memory, Florida State Archives, Tallahassee; "Confederation Employment of Negro Troops," *Quincy (FL) Semi-weekly Dispatch*, March 15, 1865.

24. "Death of Aged Minister," *Jacksonville (FL) Evening Metropolis*, January 15, 1912; "Rev. James Page," *Christian Index* (Atlanta, GA), May 24, 1883; "Rev. Jas. Page," *Weekly Floridian* (Tallahassee), March 20, 1883; "Letter from Florida—1865," "Memorial Services for Rev. James Page," *Banner-Lacon* (Ocala, FL), June 23, 1883; *Colored American Magazine* 13 (August 1907): 118; Canter Brown Jr., *Florida's Black Public Officials, 1867–1924* (Tuscaloosa: University of Alabama Press, 1998), 117.

25. Sheppard interview; Rawick, *The American Slave*, vol. 17 (Florida narratives), 80–81, 178, 214, 245–46, 254, 351, and 359–60; Thomas Wentworth Higginson, *Army Life in a Black Regiment* (Boston: Fields, Osgood, 1870; repr. ed., Boston: Beacon Press, 1962), 23; Janet Neary, *Fugitive Testimony: On the Visual Logic of Slave Narratives* (New York: Fordham University Press, 2016), 164–73; Helen M. Edwards memoirs, printed and bound, n.d., 1–5, Special Collections Department, Robert M. Strozier Library, Florida State University, Tallahassee; Paisley, *Red Hills of Florida*, 169; Sergio A. Lussana, *My Brother Slaves: Friendship, Masculinity, and Resistance in the Antebellum South* (Lexington: University Press of Kentucky, 2016), 23–39.

26. Rivers, *Slavery in Florida*, 239; Rawick, *The American Slave*, vol. 17 (Florida narratives), 98 and 178; Kenneth M. Stampp, *The Peculiar Institution: Slavery in the Ante-bellum South* (New York: Alfred A. Knopf, 1956; repr., New York: Vintage Books, 1964), 30; Joshua Hoyet Frier journal, 13, Florida State Archives, Tallahassee; Tracey Revels, "Grander in Her Daughters: Florida's Women during the Civil War," *Florida Historical Quarterly* 77 (Winter 1999): 275; Gary W. McDonough ed., *Florida Negro: A Federal Writers' Project Legacy* (Jackson: University Press of Mississippi, 1993), 61; Brian E. Michaels, *The River Flows North: A History of Putnam County, Florida* (Palatka, FL: Taylor, 1986), 99; Gerald Schwartz, ed., *Woman Doctor's Civil War: Esther Hill Hawk's Diary* (Columbia: University of South Carolina Press, 1984), 77 and 82; Edwin L. Williams Jr., "Negro Slavery in Florida, Part 1," *Florida Historical Quarterly* 28 (October 1949): 93–103; Edwin L. Williams, "Negro Slavery in Florida, Part 2," *Florida Historical Quarterly* 28 (January 1950): 187–90; P. K. Rose, "Black Dispatches: Black American Contributions to the Union Intelligence during the Civil War," Central Intelligence Agency, March 16, 2007, Langley, McLean, Virginia; Ortiz, *An African American and Latinx History*, 68; Blight, *Frederick Douglass*, 435; John Eaton, *Grant, Lincoln, and the Freedmen: Reminiscences of the Civil War* (New York: Longman's Green, 1907), 173–75; Rawick, *The American Slave*, vol 16 (Ohio narratives), 59; "From Pensacola," *Augusta (GA) Daily Chronicle and Sentinel*, February 15, 1861; *Albany (GA) Patriot*, March 14, 1861; "From Pensacola," *Augusta (GA), Daily Chronicle and Sentinel*, April 2 and 5, 1862.

27. John Leonidas Rosser, *A History of Florida Baptists* (Nashville, TN: Broadman Press, 1949), 48; "Florida Baptist Convention," *Charleston (SC) Mercury*, November 17, 1863; "Meetings of Associations," *Christian Index* (Macon, GA), October 21, 1864; Harriet Randolph Parkhill, "Elder James Page: 1805–1883," in *History of the Black Baptists of Florida, 1850–1985*, by George Patterson McKinney Sr. and Richard I. McKinney Jr. (Miami: Florida Memorial College Press, 1987), 357.

28. John C. Ley, *Fifty-Two Years in Florida* (Nashville: TN: Publishing House of the M.E. Church, South, 1899), 90; Donald S. Hepburn, "Florida Baptists Support the Confederate Cause," *Journal of Florida Baptist Heritage* 16 (2014): 44–57; Penny Baumgardner, "Florida Baptists Strong in Faith and Hope," *Journal of Florida Baptist Heritage* 16 (2014): 58–69.

29. *Proceedings of the Eighteenth Annual Session of the Florida Baptist Association, Held with Liberty Church, Commencing on Friday, October 19, 1860* (Grooverville, Brooks County, GA, October 19, 1860), 7; "The Florida Baptist Association," *Christian Index* (Macon, GA), September 18, 1863; "Meetings of Associations," *Christian Index* (Macon, GA), October 21, 1864.

30. Lykes, *Gift of Heritage*, 9.

31. Johns, *Florida during the Civil War*, 208–209; "Florida Correspondence," *Christian Recorder* (Philadelphia), July 8, 1865.

Chapter 9 • Emancipation and Congressional Reconstruction

1. Gary Loderhose, *Way Down Upon the Suwannee River: Sketches of Florida during the Civil War* (San Jose, CA: Author's Choice Press, 2000), 151; Edwin T. Williams journal, entry of April 9, 1865, the Historical Foundation of the Presbyterian and Reformed Churches, Montreat, NC; Steven M. Stowe, ed., *A Southern Practice: The Diary and Autobiography of Charles A. Hentz M.D.* (Charlottesville: University Press of Virginia, 2000), 611; Daniel R. Weinfeld, *The Jackson County War: Reconstruction and Resistance in Post–Civil War Florida* (Tuscaloosa: University of Alabama Press, 2012), 3–5.

2. James M. McPherson, *Battle Cry of Freedom: The Civil War Era* (New York: Oxford University Press, 1988), 745–52; John E. Johns, *Florida during the Civil War* (Gainesville: University Press of Florida, 1963), 205–211; Jack Sheppard interview with James Page, January 21–22, 1880, Bethel Missionary Baptist Church Library, Tallahassee, FL; David Blight, *Frederick Douglass: Prophet of Freedom* (New York: Simon and Schuster, 2018), 299; Darlene Clark Hine, William C. Hine, and Stanley Harrold, *The African-American Odyssey* (Upper Saddle River, NJ: Prentice Hall, 2000), 148, 185–91; Ezra Greenspan, *William Wells Brown: An African American Life* (New York: W. W. Norton, 2014), 1–135.

3. Edwin T. Williams journal, entry of April 9, 1865; John S. Wilson, *"The Dead of the Synod of Georgia": Necrology or Memorials of Deceased Ministers Who Have Died during the First Twenty Years after Its Organization* (Atlanta: Franklin, 1869), 375–77.

4. "Florida Correspondence," *Christian Recorder* (Philadelphia), July 8, 1865; "Letter from 3d U.S.C.T.," *Christian Recorder* (Philadelphia), August 12, 1865; W. E. B. DuBois, *Black Reconstruction: An Essay toward a History of the Part Which Black Folk Played in the Attempt to Reconstruct Democracy in America, 1860–1880* (New York: Meridian Books, 1965), 139 and 670. For other stellar studies of white planters and elites' efforts to control the labor of the newly freed men and women, please see, Paul Ortiz, *Emancipation Betrayed: The Hidden History of Black Organizing and White Violence in Florida from Reconstruction to the Bloody Election of 1920* (Berkley: University of California Press, 2005), 14; Steven Hahn, *A Nation under Our Feet: Black Political Struggles in the Rural South from Slavery to the Great Migration* (Cambridge, MA: Belknap / Harvard University Press, 2005); John C. Rodrigue, *Reconstruction in the Cane Fields: From Slavery to Wage Labor in Louisiana's Sugar Parishes, 1862–1920* (Baton Rouge: Louisiana State University Press, 2001); Tera Hunter, *To 'Joy My Freedom: Southern Black Women's Lives and Labors After the Civil War* (Cambridge, MA: Harvard University Press, 1998); Leslie Schwalm, *A Hard Fight for We: Women's Transition from Slavery to Freedom in South Carolina* (Urbana: University of Illinois Press, 1997); Eric Foner, *Reconstruction: America's Unfinished Revolution, 1863–1877* (New York: Harper and Row, 1988); Leon F. Litwack, *Been in the Storm So Long: The Aftermath of Slavery* (New York: Vintage, 1980); John H. Franklin, *Reconstruction after the Civil War* (Chicago: University of Chicago Press, 1961), 3–35.

5. Sheppard interview; George Rawick, ed., *The American Slave: A Composite Autobiography*, vol. 17 (Florida narratives) (Westport: CT: Greenwood Press, 1972),

214, 245–46, 254, and 359–60; Larry Eugene Rivers, *Slavery in Florida: Territorial Days to Emancipation* (Gainesville: University Press of Florida, 2000), 215.

6. Sheppard interview; Rivers, *Slavery in Florida*, 215; Ulrich B. Phillips and James A. Glunt, eds., *Florida Plantation Records from the Papers of George Noble Jones* (St. Louis: Missouri Historical Society, 1927), 71–72 and 88–91; Charles Joyner, "The World of the Plantation Slaves," in *Before Freedom Came*, ed. Edward D. C. Campbell Jr. and Kym S. Rice (Charlottesville: University Press of Virginia, 1991), 90–91; Kathryn T. Abbey, comp., "Documents Relating to El Destino and Chemonie Plantations, Middle Florida, 1828–1868," Part 4, *Florida Historical Quarterly* 7 (January 1929): 80; Susan Bradford Eppes, *The Negro of the Old South: A Bit of Period History* (Chicago: Joseph G. Branch, 1925), 116–17; Kathryn L. Morgan, "Caddy Buffers: Legends of a Middle-Class Negro Family in Philadelphia," *Keystone Folklore Quarterly* 9 (Summer 1996): 75; Litwack, *Been in the Storm So Long*, 187.

7. Rawick, *The American Slave*, vol. 17 (Florida narratives), 169, vol. 3, part 3 (South Carolina narratives), 234; Carole Emberton, *Beyond Redemption: Race, Violence, and the American South after the Civil War* (Chicago: Chicago Press, 2013), 136–205; Rene Hayden Anthony E. Kaye, Kate Masur, Steven F. Miller, Susan E. O'Donovan, Leslie S. Rowland, and Stephen A. West, eds., *Freedom: A Documentary History of Emancipation, 1861–1867* (Chapel Hill: University of North Carolina Press, 2013), 35–49; Jim Downs, *Sick from Freedom: African American Illness and Suffering during the Civil War and Reconstruction* (New York: Oxford University Press, 2012), 65–94; Kidada E. Williams, *They Left Great Marks on Me: African American Testimonies of Racial Violence from Emancipation to World War I* (New York: New York University Press, 2012), 1–68; William Link, *Atlanta, Cradle of the New South: Race and Remembering in the Civil War's Aftermath* (Chapel Hill: University of North Carolina Press, 2013), 12–53; Wilbert J. Jenkins, *Climbing Up to Glory: A Short History of African Americans during the Civil War and Reconstruction* (Wilmington, DE: SR Books, 2002), 211–31; Elizabeth Regosin, *Freedom's Promise: Ex-Slave Families and Citizenship in the Age of Emancipation* (Charlottesville: University Press of Virginia, 2002), 3–22; J. Douglass Smith, *Managing White Supremacy: Race, Politics, and Citizenship in Jim Crow Virginia* (Chapel Hill: University of North Carolina Press, 2002), 9–39; Henry A. Wallace, *Democracy Reborn: Selected from Public Papers and Edited with an Introduction and Notes by Russell Lord* (New York: Da Capo Press, 1973), 52–59; "Land and Labor," *Christian Recorder* (Philadelphia), May 31, 1877.

8. See, for example, Ortiz, *Emancipation Betrayed*, 9, 14; Emberton, *Beyond Redemption*, 136–205; Hayden et al., *Freedom*, 35–49.

9. Sheppard interview. See also Helen M. Edwards memoirs, Florida State University, Strozier Library Special Collections, Tallahassee; Clay Ouzts, "Landlords and Tenants: Sharecropping and the Cotton Culture in Leon County, Florida 1865–1885," *Florida Historical Quarterly* 75 (Summer 1996): 1–23; Rawick, *The American Slave*, vol. 17 (Florida narratives), 74–78 and 279–85; Mark A. Lause, *Free Labor: The Civil War and the Making of an American Working Class* (Urbana: University of Illinois Press, 2015), 17–45; G. Ward Hubbs, *Searching for Freedom after the Civil War: Klansman, Carpetbagger, Scalawag, and Freedman* (Tuscaloosa: University of Alabama Press, 2015), 10–49.

10. Sheppard interview.

11. Sheppard interview; Murray D. Laurie, "Union Academy: A Freedmen's Bureau School in Gainesville, Florida," *Florida Historical Quarterly* 65 (October 1986): 163–74.

12. Joe Richardson, *The Negro in the Reconstruction of Florida, 1865–1877* (Tallahassee: Florida State University Press, 1965), 1–36; Harriet Randolph Parkhill, "Elder James Page: 1805–1883," in *History of the Black Baptists of Florida, 1850–1985*, by George Patterson McKinney Sr. and Richard I. McKinney Jr. (Miami: Florida Memorial College Press, 1987); "Letter from Florida—1865," *Colored American Magazine* 13 (August 1907): 118.

13. Canter Brown Jr., "'Where Are Now the Hopes I Cherished?': The Life and Times of Robert Meacham," *Florida Historical Quarterly* 69 (July 1990): 3–13; "Letter from Florida—1865," 118; Richardson, *Negro in the Reconstruction of Florida*, 84, 94–95, 107, 153, 164–65, 189, 192, and 213; Canter Brown Jr., *Florida's Black Public Officials, 1867–1924* (Tuscaloosa: University of Alabama Press, 1998), 5–13, 32–33, 18, 20–21, 27, 30–31, 34–35, 40–41, 55–59, 59, and 109–10; Larry Eugene Rivers and Canter Brown Jr., *Laborers in the Vineyard of the Lord* (Gainesville, University Press of Florida, 2001), 14–16, 30–31, 36–37, 39–41, 45–48, 50–52, 54–60, 69–71, 73–76, 78, 82–83, 85–87, 89, 97–98, 101, 103, 106–7, 109, 111, 120, 144, 146, 154, 164, and 197; George M. Barbour, *Florida for Tourists, Invalids, and Settlers* (New York: Appleton, 1883), 234–240; "Education," *Florida Dispatch* (Tallahassee), July 11, 1877; "From Tallahassee," *Daily News and Herald* (Savannah, GA), May 28, 1867.

14. "Letter from Florida—1865," 118; Gorham Greely to George Whipple, September 10, 1865, American Missionary Association Collection, Amistad Research Center, Tulane University, New Orleans, LA; "Address," *Weekly Floridian* (Tallahassee), December 24, 1878; "St. James Celebrates History," *Capitol Outlook* (Tallahassee, FL), June 10–16, 2004.

15. Sheppard interview; Rivers and Brown, *Laborers in the Vineyard of the Lord*, 30–81; Richardson, *Negro in the Reconstruction of Florida*, 83–96; Larry Eugene Rivers, "Baptist Minister James Page: Alternatives for African American Leadership in Post–Civil War Florida," in *Florida's Heritage of Diversity: Essays in Honor of Samuel Proctor*, ed. Mark I. Greenberg, William Warren Rogers, and Canter Brown Jr. (Tallahassee, FL: Sentry Press, 1997), 47–49; Brown, *Florida's Black Public Officials*, 1–28; Ortiz, *Emancipation Betrayed*, 20; "Public Meeting at the Church of Rev. Mr. Pearce," *Sentinel* (Tallahassee, FL), December 17, 1868; "Laws of the State of Florida, Passed at the Second Legislature," *Sentinel* (Tallahassee, FL), February 27, 1869; "The AME Conference," *Christian Recorder* (Philadelphia), January 22, 1870; Richard Follett, Eric Foner, and Walter Johnson, *The Problem of Freedom in the Age of Emancipation: Slavery's Ghost* (Baltimore: Johns Hopkins University Press, 2001), 8–30.

16. Foner, *Reconstruction*, 7, 176–227.

17. "From Florida," *New York Tribune*, September 5, 1865; Paul Ortiz, *An African American and Latinx History of the United States* (Boston: Beacon Press, 2018), 57–58; "Fourth of July in Tallahassee," *Florida Union* (Jacksonville), July 11, 1868.

18. William Watson Davis, *The Civil War and Reconstruction in Florida* (New York: Columbia University Press, 1913; repr. ed. Gainesville: University of Florida Press, 1964), 357–60; Jerrell H. Shofner, *Nor Is It Over Yet: Florida in the Era of Reconstruction, 1863–1877* (Gainesville: University Press of Florida, 1974), 36–39; John Wallace,

Carpetbag Rule in Florida: The Inside Workings of Civil Government in Florida after the Close of the Civil War (Jacksonville, FL: Da Cost, 1888; repr. CreateSpace, 2012), 5–9; Ortiz, *Emancipation Betrayed*, 27; United States Congress, *Testimony Taken by the Joint Select Committee to Inquire into the Condition of Affairs in the Late Insurrectionary States: Miscellaneous and Florida* (Washington, DC: Government Printing Office, 1872), 168.

19. "From Florida," *New York Tribune*, September 5, 1865; Wallace, *Carpetbag Rule in Florida*, 11–16; "The Florida Convention—Gov. Marvin's Message," *Cleveland (OH) Leader*, November 10, 1865.

20. Frederick Douglass, *Life and Times of Frederick Douglass* (Mineloa, NY: Dover, 2003), 387–89; Blight, *Frederick Douglass*, 487; John H. Franklin and Alfred A. Moss Jr., *From Slavery to Freedom: A History of African American* (New York: Alfred A. Knopf, 1988), 208.

21. Wallace, *Carpetbag Rule in Florida*, 17–36; Sheppard interview; Richardson, *Negro in the Reconstruction of Florida*, 42–52; Brown, *Florida's Black Public Officials*, 3; Howard Meyer, *The Amendment That Refused to Die: Equality and Justice Deferred; The History of the Fourteenth Amendment* (New York: Madison Books, 200), 61–68; Foner, *Reconstruction*, 261–63; Ted Tunnell, *Crucible of Reconstruction: War, Radicalism and Race in Louisiana, 1862–1877* (Baton Rouge: Louisiana State University Press, 1984), 103–7.

22. Sheppard interview; J. B. Collins to T. W. Osborn, February 8, 1866, records of the Bureau of Refugees, Freedmen, and Abandoned Lands, Record Group 105, National Archives, Washington, DC; Otis Oliver Howard, *Autobiography of Oliver Otis Howard, Major General, United States Army*, 2 vols. (New York: Baker and Taylor Company, 1908), 2:206–28; Canter Brown Jr., *Ossian Bingley Hart, Florida's Loyalist Reconstruction Governor* (Baton Rouge: Louisiana State University Press, 1997), 70, 95–96, 167–68, and 243; Robert Harrison, "Welfare and Employment Policies of the Freedmen's Bureau in the District of Columbia," *Journal of Southern History* 72 (February 2006): 75–110; Weinfeld, *The Jackson County War*, 9–10, 13, 32–35, 45–48, and 55. For the plight of blacks concerning health care during the Civil War and Reconstruction, please see Jim Downs, *Sick From Freedom: African-American Illness and Suffering during the Civil War and Reconstruction* (New York: Oxford University Press, 2012), 6–76; Margaret Humphreys, *Intensely Human: The Health of the Black Soldier in the American Civil War* (Baltimore: Johns Hopkins University Press, 2008), 23–77; Gretchen Long, *Doctoring Freedom: The Politics of African American Medical Care in Slavery and Emancipation* (Chapel Hill: University of North Carolina Press, 2012), 35–49.

23. James M. McPherson, afterword to *The Freedmen's Bureau and Reconstruction: Reconsiderations*, ed. Paul A. Cimbala and Randall M. Miller (New York: Fordham University Press, 1999), 344–45; Sheppard interview; Alva T. Stone, "Diary of a Freedmen's Bureau Agent: Alfred B. Grunwell in Jefferson County, Florida," *Florida Historical Quarterly* 96 (Summer 2017): 37. Among the many fine works available on the Bureau of Refugees, Freedmen, and Abandoned Lands, see also George Bentley, *A History of the Freedmen's Bureau* (Philadelphia: University of Pennsylvania Press, 1955); and Claude F. Oubre, *Forty Acres and a Mule: The Freedmen's Bureau and Black Land Ownership* (Baton Rouge: Louisiana State University Press, 2012); Blight, *Frederick Douglass*, 479; Paul H. Bergeron, ed., *The Papers of Andrew Johnson* (Knox-

ville: University of Tennessee Press, 1993), 10:313–14 and 318–20, Hans L. Trefousse, *Andrew Johnson: A Biography* (New York: W. W. Norton, 1989), 245–59.

24. Wallace, *Carpetbag Rule in Florida*, 42.

25. Sheppard interview; Wallace, *Carpetbag Rule in Florida*, 42; Richardson, *Negro in the Reconstruction of Florida*, 141–42; Peter Rachleff, *Black Labor in Richmond, 1865–1890* (Urbana: University of Illinois Press, 1989), 3–35.

26. James Page to Harriet Parkhill February 17, 1866, John Parkhill Papers, Southern Historical Collection, University of North Carolina, Chapel Hill; John W. Alvord, "Schools Taught by Freedmen," *Freedman's Journal* 1 (February 1866): 2–3. White instructors came to Florida after the Civil War to teach the newly freed men and women; see, for example, Eben Jenks Loomis to my darling wife from Eben Jenks Loomis, Jacksonville, April 28, 1866, Wilder-Loomis Family Papers, 1866–1888, folder 3, P. K. Yonge Library, University of Florida, Gainesville; "Schools Taught by Freedmen," *Freedman's Journal* (New York), February (n.d.), 1866; "Teachers Monthly School Report for November, 1868, Name of School—Baptist Church School, Teacher, James Page," and "Teachers Monthly School Report for May, 1868, Baptist Church School, Teacher, James Page" (microfilm), in Freedmen's Bureau Papers, roll 15, P. K. Yonge Library.

27. Page to Harriet Parkhill, January 9, February 17, March 28, 1866, John Parkhill Papers; Sheppard interview; Joe M. Richardson, "Joseph L. Wiley: A Black Florida Education," *Florida Historical Quarterly* 71 (April 1993): 458–72.

28. Shofner, *Nor Is It Over Yet*, 53; Leon County marriage records, Book X, 193, 200–201, Leon County Courthouse, Tallahassee, FL; Sheppard interview.

29. Sheppard interview; Leon County marriage records, Book X, 210; "Big Growth Shown in Baptist History," *Tallahassee (FL) Democrat*, November 6, 1949; Rawick, *The American Slave*, vol. 17 (Florida narratives), 72.

30. Sheppard interview; "Laying the Corner Stone," *Semi-weekly Floridian* (Tallahassee), February 20, 1866; "The AME Conference," *Christian Recorder* (Philadelphia), January 22, 1870; Ortiz *Emancipation Betrayed*, 20; see also Rivers and Brown, *Laborers in the Vineyard of the Lord*, 5–49; "Religious Wants of the Colored People," *Religious Herald* (Richmond, VA), July 1866.

31. Foner, *Reconstruction*, 228–80; Shofner, *Nor Is It Over Yet*, 102–3, 157–62; Blight, *Frederick Douglass*, 487; Douglass, *Life and Times*; Benjamin Quarles, *Frederick Douglass* (Washington, DC: Associated, 1948), 232–34.

32. Richardson, *Negro in the Reconstruction of Florida*, 97–101; George R. Bentley, "The Political Activity of the Freedmen's Bureau in Florida," *Florida Historical Quarterly* 28 (July 1949): 29.

33. Sheppard interview; Richardson, *Negro in the Reconstruction of Florida*, 19–24; Shofner, *Nor Is It Over Yet*, 123–26; Wallace, *Carpetbag Rule in Florida*, 40–42.

34. Leon County deed records, Book A, 12–15; Leon County Courthouse, Tallahassee, FL; Sheppard interview; Steven Hahn, comp., *Freedom: A Documentary History of Emancipation, 1861–1867*, ser. 3 (Chapel Hill: University of North Carolina Press, 2008), 1:418.

35. James Page to Harriet Parkhill, March 18, 1867, John Parkhill Papers.

36. Foner, *Reconstruction*, 271–91; Brown, *Ossian Bingley Hart*, 195–96; Ossian B. Hart to J. F. Meline, June 22, 1867, Incoming Correspondence of the Third Military

District, 1867–1868, Bureau of Civil Affairs, entry 5782, box 2, Record Group 393, National Archives, Washington, DC.

37. Brown, *Ossian Bingley Hart*, 188–89; "Grand Mass Meeting of the Colored Citizens of Jacksonville," *Florida Union* (Jacksonville), June 1, 1867.

38. "The Hart Convention—of Whom Composed and What It Did," *St. Augustine (FL) Examiner*, July 27, 1867; Hart to Meline, June 26, 1867, Incoming Correspondence of the Third Military District, 1867–1868; "Union Republican Convention," *Florida Union* (Jacksonville), July 20, 1867; "Proceedings of the Republican State Convention," *Sentinel* (Tallahassee, FL), July 15, 1867; "The Republican State Convention—Enthusiasm of the Delegates—Separate Organization of the Blacks Reprobated—Conservatism," *New York Tribune*, July 27, 1867.

39. Dorothy Dodd, "Bishop Pearce and the Reconstruction of Leon County," *Apalachee* (Fall 1946): 5–12; Wallace, *Carpetbag Rule in Florida*, 41–46; Richardson, *Negro in the Reconstruction of Florida*, 141–45; Brown, *Ossian Bingley Hart*, 201–2; Brown, "Robert Meacham," 7; "The 'Mule Team' Ticket," *St. Augustine (FL) Examiner*, February 22, 1868.

40. Shofner, *Nor Is It Over* Yet, 163–77; "Letter from Florida," *Daily News and Herald* (Savannah, GA), December 11, 1867; James C. Clark, "John Wallace and the Writing of Reconstruction History," *Florida Historical Quarterly* 67 (April 1989): 409–27; Sheppard interview; James Page to Harriet Parkhill, November 10, 1868, John Parkhill Papers; Ortiz, *An African American and Latinx History*, 59; "Election Frauds, So-Called," *Florida Union* (Jacksonville), July 16, 1868; "Grand Mass Meeting of the Colored Citizens," *Florida Union* (Jacksonville), June 1, 1867;

41. Ouzts, "Landlords and Tenants," 3; Clifton Paisley, "Tallahassee through the Storebooks: War Clouds and War, 1860–1863," *Florida Historical Quarterly* 51 (July 1972): 49; Wallace, *Carpetbag Rule in Florida*, 41–46, 86–88; Richardson, *Negro in the Reconstruction of Florida*, 327–33; Canter Brown Jr., "Carpetbagger Intrigues, Black Leadership, and a Southern Loyalist Triumph: Florida's Gubernatorial Election of 1872," *Florida Historical Quarterly* 72 (January 1994): 275–83; Brown, "Robert Meacham," 3–4. For an interesting study of black women's push for full citizenship rights during and after slavery, see Sharon Romeo, *Gender and the Jubilee: Black Freedom and the Reconstruction of Citizenship in Civil War Missouri* (Athens: University of Georgia Press, 2016), 3–39; Hudson L. David Jr., *The Fourteenth Amendment: Equal Protection under the Law* (New York: Enslow, 2002), 25–40; Meyer, *The Amendment That Refused to Die*, 61–63.

42. Wallace, *Carpetbag Rule in Florida*, 350–58, 362, 382–85, and 393–94; *Journal of the Proceedings of the Constitutional Convention, 1868* (Tallahassee, FL: Edward M. Cheney, 1868), 17.

43. Dodd, "Bishop Pearce and the Reconstruction of Leon County," 5–12; Davis, *Reconstruction*, 467; Bentley, *History of the Freedmen's Bureau*, 185–91; Samuel Sullivan Cox, *Three Decades of Federal Legislation 1855–1885* (Tecumseh, MI: A. W. Mills, 1885), 517–18; Robert Cassanello, "The Right to Vote and the Long Nineteenth Century in Florida," *Florida Historical Quarterly* 95 (Fall 2016): 194–220; Garrett Epps, *Democracy Reborn: The Fourteenth Amendment and the Fight for Equal Rights in Post–Civil War America* (New York: Holt Paperbacks, 2007), 78, 122–66, 185, and 253; Martha S. Jones, *Birthright Citizens: A History of Race and Rights in Antebellum*

America (New York: Cambridge University Press, 2018), 146–53; Kurt T. Lash, *The Fourteenth Amendment and the Privileges and Immunities of American Citizenship* (New York: Cambridge University Press, 2015), 1–8; David, *The Fourteenth Amendment*, 25–40; Meyer, *The Amendment That Refused to Die*, 61–63; Sheppard interview, Ortiz, *Emancipation Betrayed*, 11; Richard Nelson Current, *Those Terrible Carpetbaggers: A Reinterpretation* (New York: Oxford University Press, 1988), 85; Link, *Atlanta, Cradle of the New South*, 1–5; C. Vann Woodward, *Origins of the New South* (Baton Rouge: Louisiana State University Press, 1951), ix; Paul Gaston, *The New South Creed: A Study in Southern Mythmaking* (New York: Vintage, 1970), 7–9.

Chapter 10 • *Radical Reconstruction and Its Aftermath*

1. Canter Brown Jr., *Florida's Black Public Officials, 1867–1924* (Tuscaloosa: University of Alabama Press, 1998), 3–16.

2. "Election Frauds—So-Called," *Weekly Floridian* (Tallahassee), July 7, 1868; "Religious and Educational," *Weekly Floridian* (Tallahassee), April 9, 1872.

3. Jack Sheppard interview with James Page, January 21–22, 1880, Bethel Missionary Baptist Church Library, Tallahassee, FL.

4. Evelyn Brooks Higginbotham, *Righteous Discontent: The Women's Movement in the Black Baptist Church, 1880–1920* (Cambridge, MA: Harvard University Press, 1993), 14 and 15–18; Glenda Elizabeth Gilmore, *Gender and Jim Crow: Women and the Politics of White Supremacy in North Carolina, 1896–1920* (Chapel Hill: University of North Carolina Press, 1996), 210 and 212–24; Tera Hunter, *To 'Joy My Freedom: Southern Black Women's Lives and Labors After the Civil War* (Cambridge, MA: Harvard University Press, 1998), 68–82; Samuel Dixie Jr. interview, August 4, 2019, Tallahassee, FL; Elsa Barkley Brown, "To Catch the Vision of Freedom: Reconstructing Southern Black Women's Political History, 1865–1880," in *African American Women and the Vote, 1837–1965*, ed. Ann D. Gordon (Amherst: University of Massachusetts Press, 1997), 66–99.

5. Sheppard interview; *Journal of the Senate, for the First Session, Fifteenth Legislature, of the State of Florida* (Tallahassee: Office of the Tallahassee Sentinel, 1868), 13; James Page appointment to Leon County Commission, Records of Commissions Issued, Record Group 156, series 259, vol. 28, Florida State Archives, Tallahassee.

6. "A Very Pretty Fight as It Stands," *Weekly Floridian* (Tallahassee), October 27, 1868; "Leon County Commissioners," *Florida Union* (Jacksonville), November 18, 1868.

7. "The Colored Baptist Church," *Tallahassee (FL) Sentinel*, January 30, 1869; "The New Baptist Church," *Tallahassee (FL) Sentinel*, April 24, 1869; Sheppard interview; Dixie interview.

8. Sheppard interview; Leon County, FL, deed records, Book P, 41, County Courthouse, Tallahassee, FL; "105th Anniversary," *Tallahassee (FL) Democrat*, October 25, 1975; Richard L. McKinney, "American Baptist and Black Education in Florida," *American Baptist Quarterly* 11 (December 1992): 309; Robert L. Hall, "Tallahassee Black Churches, 1865–1885," *Florida Historical Quarterly* (October 1979): 191; "Florida Affairs," *Savannah Morning News*, January 23, 1873.

9. George Patterson McKinney Sr. and Richard I. McKinney Jr., *History of the Black Baptists of Florida: 1850–1935* (Miami: Florida Memorial College Press, 1987),

36–37; "Baptist Association of Florida," *Alabama State Journal* (Montgomery), October 23, 1869.

10. Altermese Smith Bentley, *History of the First South Florida Missionary Baptist Association 1868–1988* (Chuluota, FL: Mickler House, 1998), 10–17; McKinney, "American Baptist and Black Education in Florida," 309; McKinney and McKinney, *History of the Black Baptists of Florida*, 38–40.

11. "Baptist Association of Florida," *Alabama State Journal* (Montgomery), October 23, 1869; "Letter from Tallahassee," *Christian Recorder* (Philadelphia), November 14, 1868; Paul Ortiz, *Emancipation Betrayed: The Hidden History of Black Organizing and White Violence in Florida from Reconstruction to the Bloody Election of 1920* (Berkley: University of California Press, 2005), 22–23; "Colored Baptists and Education," *Christian Index* (Atlanta, GA), June 6, 1878; "The Church at Tallahassee," *Christian Index and Southwestern Baptist* (Atlanta, GA), June 13, 1878; "Letter from Florida," *Baptist* (Memphis, TN), March 28, 1878.

12. "General State Election," *Tallahassee (FL) Sentinel*, January 14, 1871; Sheppard interview; Joe Richardson, *The Negro in the Reconstruction of Florida, 1865–1877* (Tallahassee: Florida State University Press, 1965), 8; Lee H. Warner, *Free Men in an Age of Servitude: Three Generations of a Black Family* (Lexington: University Press of Kentucky, 1992), 99–101; Robert Cassanello, "The Right to Vote and the Long Nineteenth Century in Florida," *Florida Historical Quarterly* 95 (Fall 2016): 194–220; "Leon Local Tickets—What Conservatives Ought to Do," *Weekly Floridian* (Tallahassee), November 1, 1870; "Colored Baptists and Education," *Christian Index and South-Western Baptist* (Atlanta), June 6, 1878.

13. "Leon Radicals in Trouble," *Weekly Floridian* (Tallahassee), July 12, 1870; "Radical Mass Meeting," *Weekly Floridian* (Tallahassee), September 13, 1870; "Leon Local Tickets—What Conservatives Ought to Do"; "Republican County Convention," *Sentinel* (Tallahassee, FL), July 16, 1870; "Republican Meeting," *Sentinel* (Tallahassee, FL), August 13, 1870; "Republican Convention," *Sentinel* (Tallahassee, FL), September 24, 1870; "Republican Mass Meeting in Tallahassee," *Sentinel* (Tallahassee, FL), November 11, 1870; "Election Day," *Sentinel* (Tallahassee, FL), November 12, 1870;

14. "Florida Items," *Savannah (GA) Morning News*, November 19, 1870.

15. "General State Election," *Tallahassee (FL) Sentinel*, January 14, 1871; "Returns for the General State Election," *Tallahassee (FL) Sentinel*, January 14, 1871; "County Commissioners," *Weekly Floridian* (Tallahassee), November 11, 1870; Ortiz, *Emancipation Betrayed*, 11; Richard Nelson Current, *Those Terrible Carpetbaggers: A Reinterpretation* (New York: Oxford University Press, 1988), 85; "The Union," *Weekly Floridian* (Tallahassee), December 17, 1873; "A Colored Movement," *Weekly Floridian* (Tallahassee), June 19, 1877; "Something about Florida," *Christian Index* (Atlanta), April 5, 1883; "Keep It before the Negroes," *Examiner* (St. Augustine, FL), July 27, 1867.

16. "The Tallahassee Excursionists," *Savannah (GA) Morning News*, July 6, 1871.

17. Ortiz, *Emancipation Betrayed*, 23–27; Ralph L. Peek, "Aftermath of Military Reconstruction, 1868–1869," *Florida Historical Quarterly* 43 (October 1963): 123–41; Ralph L. Peek, "Lawlessness in Florida 1868–1871," *Florida Historical Quarterly* 40 (October 1961): 184; "The Ku Klux Klan in Florida," *Christian Recorder*, November 27, 1873; Daniel R. Weinfeld, *The Jackson County War: Reconstruction and Resistance in Post–Civil War Florida* (Tuscaloosa: University of Alabama Press, 2012), xiii; Richard-

son, *The Negro in the Reconstruction of Florida*, 164–85; Jerrell H. Shofner, *Jackson County, Florida: A History* (Marianna: Jackson County Heritage Association, 1985), 280.

18. Sheppard interview; Genevieve Parkhill Lykes, *Gift of Heritage* (Tampa, FL: priv. pub., 1969), 10; "Republican Candidates for the Legislature," *Weekly Floridian* (Tallahassee), November 18, 1873.

19. Jack Sheppard, "Brief Reflections of Father James Page," May 18, 1905, Bethel Missionary Baptist Church, Tallahassee, FL.

20. Brown, *Florida's Black Public Officials*, 114; "Justice of the Peace," *Weekly Floridian* (Tallahassee), March 11, 1873; "Justice of the Peace, *Sentinel* (Tallahassee, FL), May 6, 1876; "Florida Affairs," *Savannah (GA) Morning News*, March 11, 1873, and January 20, 1877.

21. "Florida Affairs," *Savannah (GA) Morning News*, March 11, 1873; Canter Brown Jr., *Ossian Bingley Hart, Florida's Loyalist Reconstruction Governor* (Baton Rouge: Louisiana State University Press, 1997), 251–68, 275–76, and 294–96; *Acts & Resolutions Adopted by the Legislature of Florida, 1873* (Tallahassee: Charles E. Dyke, State Printer, 1874), 25–26; Sheppard interview.

22. "Skating for the Colored People," *Weekly Floridian* (Tallahassee), March 11, 1873; "Florida Affairs," *Savannah (GA) Morning News*, March 11, 1873; "The Tallahassee Florida says," *Daily Advertiser* (Savannah, GA), March 11, 1873; Reginald Ellis, *Between Washington and Du Bois: The Racial Politics of James Edward Sheppard* (Gainesville: University Press of Florida, 2017), 14–15 and 101–5l; David H. Jackson, *A Chief Lieutenant of the Tuskegee Machine: Charles Banks of Mississippi* (Gainesville: University Press of Florida, 2020), 3–38; Darius Young, *Robert R. Church Jr. and the African American Political Struggle* (Gainesville: University Press of Florida, 2019), 1, 15, 63, 87, 116, and 125; "Florida: Business, Civil Rights, and Politics," *People's Advocate* (Washington, DC), April 24, 1880.

23. "City and State Items," *Tallahassee (FL) Sentinel*, April 9, 1870; Sheppard interview.

24. Leon County, FL, deed records, Book P, 552, Leon County Courthouse, Tallahassee, FL; Paul A. Cimbala, *The Freedmen's Bureau: Reconstructing the American South after the Civil War* (Malabar, FL: Krieger, 2005), 3–10, 26–38, 52–61, and 77–90; Paul A. Cimbala, *Under the Guardianship of the Nation: The Freedmen's Bureau and the Reconstruction of Georgia, 1865–1870* (Athens: University of Georgia Press, 1997), 54; Paul A. Cimbala, "The Freedmen's Bureau, the Freedmen, and Sherman's Grant in Reconstruction Georgia, 1865–1867," *Journal of Southern History* 55 (November 1989): 597–632; E. A. Edwards to Dear Sir, October 19, 1871, roll 2, American Missionary Association Collection, Amistad Research Center, Tulane University, New Orleans, LA; "Tornado in Florida," *Daily Phoenix* (Columbia, SC), September 25, 1873; "Tallahassee, Fl," *Weekly Floridan* (Tallahassee), September 30, 1873;

25. James Page to Harriet R. Parkhill, Jacksonville, October 14, 1870, April 13, 1875, John Parkhill Papers; Sheppard interview.

26. Sheppard interview; *Minutes of the Second Annual Session of the Florida Bethlehem Association, Held with Mt. Moriah Baptist Church, Gainesville, Florida, October 6–8, 1870* (Gainesville: Florida Bethlehem Association, 1870), 1–5; "The Florida Convention and the Temperance Question," *Christian Index* (Atlanta), January 18, 1883; "Temperance in Florida," *Christian Index* (Atlanta), May 3, 1883;

"South Florida," *Christian Index* (Atlanta), January 25, 1883; "The Baptists of Florida," *Christian Index* (Atlanta), March 15, 1883.

27. "Florida," *Christian Index and Southwestern Baptist* (Atlanta), January 1, 1871; Sheppard interview; McKinney and McKinney, *History of Black Baptists in Florida*, 40–43; "Haters of Evil," *Christian Era* (Boston), September 11, 1873; "Morning Services," *Weekly Floridian* (Tallahassee), January 21, 1873.

28. McKinney and McKinney, *History of Black Baptists in Florida*, 47–49; "Religious and Educational," *Weekly Floridian* (Tallahassee), April 9, 1872; "Laying the Corner Stone," *Tallahassee (FL) Sentinel*, April 29, 1873; "Obituary," *Semi-weekly Floridian* (Tallahassee), August 16, 1866; "George Walker Is in Race for Circuit Judge," *Tallahassee (FL) Democrat*, September 30, 1931; Sheppard interview; "A Meeting of Ministers and Elders," *Sentinel* (Tallahassee, FL), January 1, 1841; "Rev. James Page," *Sentinel* (Tallahassee, FL), May 18, 1872; "Primitive Baptist Church Cornerstone Laid," *Sentinel* (Tallahassee, FL), March 13, 1873; "Colored Baptist Church at this place," *Sentinel* (Tallahassee, FL), March 6, 1875.

29. "Haters of Evil," *Christian Era* (Boston), September 11, 1873; McKinney and McKinney, *History of Black Baptists in Florida*, 41, 45–46.

30. Brown, *Ossian Bingley Hart*, 294; Brown, *Florida's Black Public Officials*, 28–31, 92; Learotha Williams Jr., "'A Wider Field of Usefulness': The Life and Times of Jonathan Clarkson Gibbs 1828–1874" (PhD diss., Florida State University, 2003), 3–43; Peter D. Klingman, *Josiah Walls, Florida's Black Congressman of Reconstruction* (Gainesville: University Press of Florida, 1976), 30–51.

31. Jerrell H. Shofner, *Nor Is It Over Yet: Florida in the Era of Reconstruction, 1863–1877* (Gainesville: University Press of Florida, 1974), 272–74; Sheppard interview. On the Freedmen's Bank, see Walter Fleming, *The Freedmen's Savings Bank: A Chapter in the Economic History of the Negro Race* (Chapel Hill: University of North Carolina Press, 2013), 19–40 and 50–51; David Blight, *Frederick Douglass: Prophet of Freedom* (New York: Simon and Schuster, 2018), 545–50.

32. James Page to Harriet R. Parkhill, April 13, 1875. Page may have earned some money for managing Tuscawilla during the 1870s since the plantation had produced, according to newspaper account, "a large quantity of cotton," which was insured for $3,000. "Fire at Tuscawilla," *Morning News* (Savannah, GA), 1872.

33. John Wallace, *Carpetbag Rule in Florida: The Inside Workings of Civil Government in Florida after the Close of the Civil War* (Jacksonville, FL: Da Cost, 1888; repr. CreateSpace, 2012), 343; Shofner, *Nor Is It Over Yet*, 288–313; Brown, *Florida's Black Public Officials*, 36–38; "Official Report of the Proceedings of the Republican State Convention," *Daily Florida Union* (Jacksonville), June 13, 1876; "Republican State Convention Held," *Weekly Floridian* (Tallahassee), August 15, 1876, 3; "State News," *Tallahassee (FL) Sentinel*, October 28, 1876; Sheppard interview. For a more positive view of Governor Stearns and his accomplishments, see Ann Bert Reuter, "The Reconstruction of Marcellus Lovejoy Stearns: Florida's Last Reconstruction Governor" (master's thesis, Harvard University, 2004); "From Greenville, Florida," *Christian Index* (Atlanta), June 14, 1883; "Something about Florida," Christian Index (Atlanta, GA), May 10, 1883; "Florida," *People's Advocate* (Washington, DC), March 11, 1882.

34. Shofner, *Nor Is It Over Yet*, 314–39; Brown, *Florida's Black Public Officials*, 39–54; "Proceedings of the Colored Convention," *Daily Sun and Press* (Jacksonville,

FL), July 8, 1877; "The Colored Convention," *Weekly Floridian* (Tallahassee), July 10 and 14, 1877; "Delegates in the State Colored Convention," *Sentinel* (Tallahassee, FL), May 13, 1876.

35. "Tallahassee, Florida," *Weekly Floridian* (Tallahassee), September 23, 1873; Minutes of the Leon County Board of Public Instruction, 1877–May 1883, 1–13, Office of the Clerk of the County Courthouse, Tallahassee, FL; Sheppard interview.

36. "The Church of Tallahassee," *Christian Index and Southwestern Baptist* (Atlanta), June 6, 1878; Sheppard interview; McKinney and McKinney, *History of Black Baptists in Florida*, 50–53; "City and States Items," *Sentinel* (Tallahassee, FL), March 6, 1875.

37. *Minutes of the Florida Baptist State Convention held at Live Oak, Florida, Thursday Morning, October 9, 1879* (Live Oak: Florida State Convention, 1880), 16; "Florida Baptist State Convention," *Sentinel* (Tallahassee, FL), December 3, 1870; "The Colored Missionary Baptist Convention in Georgia," *Christian Index* (Atlanta), June 3, 1886.

38. Minutes of the Leon County Board of Public Instruction, 1877–May 1883; Sheppard interview.

Epilogue

1. Jack Sheppard interview with James Page, January 21–22, 1880, Bethel Missionary Baptist Church Library, Tallahassee, FL

2. Jack Sheppard interview.

3. Douglass Blackmon, *Slavery by Another Name: The Re-enslavement of Black Americans from the Civil War to World War II* (New York: Doubleday, 2008), 4.

4. For excellent studies of the forced labor system that developed in the South after the Civil War, see Blackmon, *Slavery by Another Name*, 360–94; Matthew J. Mancini, *One Dies, Get Another: Convict Leasing in the American South, 1866–1928* (Columbia: University of South Carolina Press, 1996), 23 and 76. For other excellent studies concerning the convict-leasing system during and after Reconstruction, see Daniel Novak, *The Wheel of Servitude: Black Forced Labor after Slavery* (Lexington: University Press of Kentucky, 2014), 12–39; Alex Lichtenstein, *Twice the Work of Free Labor: The Political Economy of Convict Labor in the New South* (New York: Verso, 1996), 39–62; David M. Oshinsky, *Worse Than Slavery: Parchman Farm and the Ordeal of Jim Crow Justice* (Florence, MA: Free Press, 1997), 42–61; Sheppard interview.

5. *Proceedings of the Florida Baptist State Convention Held with the Baptist Church, Tallahassee, January 9–12, 1880*, 1–6; *Proceedings of the Bethlehem Baptist State Convention of Florida held at Damascus Church, Madison, Florida, February 5–7, 1880*, 1–7; Michele Mitchell, *Righteous Propagation: African Americans and the Politics of Racial Destiny after Reconstruction* (Chapel Hill: University of North Carolina Press, 2004), 3–15; Sheppard interview.

6. "Lecture by Pure-Blooded African," *Weekly Floridian* (Tallahassee), August 3, 1880. For more on Jacob C. Hazeley, see Kenneth Barnes, *Journey of Hope: The Back-to-Africa Movement in Arkansas in the Late 1800s* (Chapel Hill: University of North Carolina Press, 2004), 46–47; Edwin T. Williams journal, May 9, 1860, the Historical Foundation of the Presbyterian and Reformed Churches, Montreat, NC.

7. Lewis G. Jordan, *Negro Baptist History, U.S.A., 1750–1930* (Nashville: Sunday School Publishing Board, N.B.C., 1930), 100–102, 154, 160, 169, and 172.

8. "Uncle Tom Mason," *Weekly Floridian* (Tallahassee), January 18, 1881; Larry Eugene Rivers, "Baptist Minister James Page: Alternatives for African American Leadership in Post–Civil War Florida," in *Florida's Heritage of Diversity: Essays in Honor of Samuel Proctor*, ed. Mark I. Greenberg, William Warren Rogers, and Canter Brown Jr. (Tallahassee, FL: Sentry Press, 1997), 50; Larry Eugene Rivers, "Reconstruction in Leon County, Florida: 1865–1877," *Florida A&M University Research Bulletin* 30 (September 1988): 1–34.

9. Leon County, FL, deed records, Book BB, 270; "Legislative Directory," *Weekly Floridian* (Tallahassee), January 18, 1881.

10. "Colored," *Weekly Floridan* (Tallahassee), January 21, 1873; "The Rev. James Page," *Weekly Floridian* (Tallahassee), April 30, 1882; Sheppard interview.

11. "Rev. James Page," *Christian Index* (Atlanta), March 24, 1883.

12. "Rev. James Page," Christian Index (Atlanta), March 20, 1883.

13. "Rev. Jas Page," *Weekly Floridian* (Tallahassee), March 20, 1883; "Rev. James Page," *Christian Index* (Atlanta), March 24, 1883; Samuel Dixie Jr. interview, August 4, 2019, Tallahassee, FL; see also Canter Brown Jr., *Ossian Bingley Hart, Florida's Loyalist Reconstruction Governor* (Baton Rouge: Louisiana State University Press, 1997), 297–300, Jerrell H. Shofner, *Nor Is It Over Yet: Florida in the Era of Reconstruction, 1863–1877* (Gainesville: University Press of Florida, 1974), 27–39; John Wallace, *Carpetbag Rule in Florida: The Inside Workings of Civil Government in Florida after the Close of the Civil War* (Jacksonville: Da Cost, 1888; repr. CreateSpace, 2012), 38–45; Eric Foner, *Reconstruction: America's Unfinished Revolution, 1863–1877* (New York: Harper and Row, 1988), 35–36 and 198–216; Eric Foner, *Give Me Liberty: An American History* (New York: W. W. Norton, 2107), 434–73; Deborah Gray White, Mia Bay, and Waldo E. Martin Jr., *Freedom on My Mind: A History of African Americans with Documents* (New York: Bedford / St. Martin's Press, 2017), 299–329; Joe Richardson, *The Negro in the Reconstruction of Florida, 1865–1877* (Tallahassee: Florida State University Press, 1965), 141–45; Canter Brown Jr., "Carpetbagger Intrigues, Black Leadership, and a Southern Loyalist Triumph: Florida's Gubernatorial Election of 1872," *Florida Historical Quarterly* 72 (January 1994): 275–83; W. E. B. DuBois, *Black Reconstruction: An Essay toward a History of the Part Which Black Folk Played in the Attempt to Reconstruct Democracy in America, 1860–1880* (New York: Meridian Books, 1965), 35–39; Paul Ortiz, *An African American and Latinx History of the United States* (Boston: Beacon Press, 2018), 71–94; Frank J. Scaturro, *The Supreme Court's Retreat from Reconstruction: A Distortion of Constitutional Jurisprudence* (Westport, CT: Greenwood Press, 2000), 37–89.

14. "Memorial Services," *Ocala (FL) Banner-Lacon*, June 23, 1883; Canter Brown Jr. and Barbara Gray Brown, *Family Records of the African American Pioneers of Tampa and Hillsborough County* (Tampa: University of Tampa Press, 2003), 47–50; "The Republican Party and the Negro," *Weekly Floridian* (Tallahassee), May 2, 1882; "Rev. James Page," *Christian Index* (Atlanta), May 24, 1883;

15. Sheppard interview; Samuel Dixie Jr. interview; Sheppard, "Brief Reflections on Father Page," James Page Estate Inventory, March 1883. For the pain suffered by other slaves who were uprooted in either the inter- or intrastate slave trade, see for example, Charles Ball, *Slavery in the United States: A Narrative of the Life and Adventures of Charles Ball, a Black Man, Who Lived Forty Years in Maryland, South*

Carolina and Georgia, as a Slave, under Various Masters, and Was One Year in the Navy with Commodore Barney, during the Late War, Containing an Account of the Manners and Treatment of Slaves, with Observations upon the State of Morals amongst the Cotton Planters, and the Perils and Sufferings of a Fugitive Slave, Who Twice Escaped from the Cotton Country (New York: John S. Taylor, 1837), 213; Henry Bibb, *Narrative of the Life and Adventures of Henry Bibb, an American Slave, Written by Himself* (New York: published by the author, 1850; Mnemosyne, 1969), 116–17; Damian Alan Pargas, *Slavery and Forced Migration in the Antebellum South* (New York: Cambridge University Press, 2015), 1–50; "Smithfield Buys Meats Division of Tampa Firm," *Norfolk (VA) Daily Press*, September 25, 1996; Mike Vogel, "Family Feud," *Florida Trend* 44, no. 6 (September 1, 2001): 62; "Tampa Home of Lykes Family Member Sells for 9.5 Million," *Tampa Bay Times*, October 3–6, 2019.

16. Sheppard interview; quote frequently misattributed to George Orwell.

17. Sheppard interview, James Page to Harriet Parkhill, July 15, 1859, John Parkhill Papers, 1813–1891, Southern Historical Collection, University of North Carolina, Chapel Hill; Stephen Ward Angell, *Bishop Henry McNeal Turner and African-American Religion in the South* (Knoxville: University of Tennessee Press, 1992), 266–68; David H. Jackson, *A Chief Lieutenant of the Tuskegee Machine: Charles Banks of Mississippi* (Gainesville: University Press of Florida, 2008), 38–69; Reginald Ellis, *Between Washington and Du Bois: The Racial Politics of James Edward Sheppard* (Gainesville: University Press of Florida, 2017), 25–69; Lewis V. Baldwin, *The Voice of Conscience: The Church in the Mind of Martin Luther King, Jr.* (New York: Oxford University Press, 2010), 3–51.

18. Sheppard interview.

19. Sheppard interview; Rivers, "Baptist Minister James Page," 43–54; Larry Eugene Rivers, "A Troublesome Property: Master-Slave Relations in Florida, 1821–1865," in *The African American Heritage of Florida*, ed. David R. Colburn and Jane L. Landers (Gainesville: University Press of Florida, 1995), 106–8.

20. Sheppard interview.

21. Darlene Clark Hine, William C. Hine, and Stanley Harrold, *African Americans: A Concise History* (Upper Saddle River, NJ: Prentice Hall, 2000), 241–587.

22. Sheppard interview; Pargas, *Slavery and Forced Migration*, 1–50; Lucy Beverly Randolph Parkhill, "Brief History of John Parkhill and His Family, February 8, 1859 and October 17, 1866," folder 14, John Parkhill Papers; "Obituary," *Floridian and Journal* (Tallahassee), Saturday, October 20, 1855; "Obituary," *Floridian* (Tallahassee), November 3, 1855.

23. Sheppard interview; George Rawick, ed., *The American Slave: A Composite Autobiography*, vol. 17 (Florida narratives) (Westport: CT: Greenwood Press, 1972), 165 and 244–45.

www.ingramcontent.com/pod-product-compliance
Lightning Source LLC
Chambersburg PA
CBHW020348100426
42812CB00035B/3399/J